Airman Knowledge Testing Supplement for Instrument Rating

2017

U.S. Department of Transportation
FEDERAL AVIATION ADMINISTRATION
Flight Standards Service

Preface

This Airman Knowledge Testing Supplement is designed by the Federal Aviation Administration (FAA) Flight Standards Service. It is intended for use by Airman Knowledge Testing (AKT) Organization Designation Authorization (ODA) Holders and other entities approved and/or authorized to administer airman knowledge tests on behalf of the FAA in the following knowledge areas:

Instrument Rating—Airplane (IRA)
Instrument Rating—Rotorcraft/Helicopter (IRH)
Instrument Rating—Powered Lift (IPL)
Instrument Flight Instructor—Powered Lift (IPI)
Instrument Rating—Foreign Pilot (IFP)
Instrument Flight Instructor—Airplane (FII)
Instrument Flight Instructor—Rotorcraft/Helicopter - (FIH)
Instrument Flight Instructor—Airplane (added rating) (AIF)
Instrument Flight Instructor—Rotorcraft/Helicopter (added rating) (HIF)
Ground Instructor—Instrument (IGI)

FAA-CT-8080-3F supercedes FAA-CT-8080-3E, Computer Testing Supplement for Instrument Rating, dated 2005.

Comments regarding this supplement, or any AFS-630 publication, should be sent in email form to the following address:

AFS630comments@faa.gov

Contents

APPENDIX 1

GENERAL INFORMATION

ABBREVIATIONS

The following abbreviations/acronyms are those commonly used within this Directory. Other abbreviations/acronyms may be found in the Legend and are not duplicated below. The abbreviations presented are intended to represent grammatical variations of the basic form. (Example–"req" may mean "request", "requesting", "requested", or "requests").

Abbreviation	Description
A/G	air/ground
AAF	Army Air Field
AAS	Airport Advisory Service
AB	Airbase
abm	abeam
ABn	Aerodrome Beacon
abv	above
ACC	Air Combat Command Area Control Center
acft	aircraft
ACLS	Automatic Carrier Landing System
act	activity
ACWS	Aircraft Control and Warning Squadron
ADA	Advisory Area
ADCC	Air Defense Control Center
ADCUS	Advise Customs
addn	addition
ADF	Automatic Direction Finder
adj	adjacent
admin	administration
ADR	Advisory Route
advs	advise
advsy	advisory
AEIS	Aeronautical Enroute Information Service
AER	approach end rwy
AFA	Army Flight Activity
AFB	Air Force Base
afct	affect
AFFF	Aqueous Film Forming Foam
AFHP	Air Force Heliport
AFIS	Aerodrome Flight Information Service
afld	airfield
AFOD	Army Flight Operations Detachment
AFR	Air Force Regulation
AFRC	Armed Forces Reserve Center/Air Force Reserve Command
AFRS	American Forces Radio Stations
AFS	Air Force Station
AFSS	Automated Flight Service Station
AFTN	Aeronautical Fixed Telecommunication Network
AG	Agriculture
A–G, A–GEAR	Arresting Gear
agcy	Agency
AGL	above ground level
AHP	Army heliport
AID	Airport Information Desk
AIS	Aeronautical Information Services
AL	Approach and Landing Chart
ALF	Auxiliary Landing Field
ALS	Approach Light System
ALSF–1	High Intensity ALS Category I configuration with sequenced Flashers (code)
ALSF–2	High Intensity ALS Category II configuration with sequenced Flashers (code)
alt	altitude
altn	alternate

Abbreviation	Description
AM	Amplitude Modulation, midnight til noon
AMC	Air Mobility Command
amdt	amendment
AMSL	Above Mean Sea Level
ANGS	Air National Guard Station
ant	antenna
AOE	Airport/Aerodrome of Entry
AP	Area Planning
APAPI	Abbreviated Precision Approach Path Indicator
apch	approach
apn	apron
APP	Approach Control
Apr	April
aprx	approximate
APU	Auxiliary Power Unit
apv, apvl	approve, approval
ARB	Air Reserve Base
ARCAL (CANADA)	Aircraft Radio Control of Aerodrome Lighting
ARFF	Aircraft Rescue and Fire Fighting
ARINC	Aeronautical Radio Inc
arng	arrange
arpt	airport
arr	arrive
ARS	Air Reserve Station
ARSA	Airport Radar Service Area
ARSR	Air Route Surveillance Radar
ARTCC	Air Route Traffic Control Center
AS	Air Station
ASAP	as soon as possible
ASDA	Accelerate–Stop Distance Available
ASDE	Airport Surface Detection
ASDE–X	Airport Surface Detection Equipment–Model X
asgn	assign
ASL	Above Sea Level
ASOS	Automated Surface Observing System
ASR	Airport Surveillance Radar
ASSC	Airport Surface Surveillance Capability
ASU	Aircraft Starting Unit
ATA	Actual Time of Arrival
ATC	Air Traffic Control
ATCC	Air Traffic Control Center
ATCT	Airport Traffic Control Tower
ATD	Actual Time of Departure Along Track Distance
ATIS	Automatic Terminal Information Service
ATS	Air Traffic Service
attn	attention
Aug	August
auth	authority
auto	automatic
AUW	All Up Weight (gross weight)
aux	auxiliary
AVASI	abbreviated VASI
avbl	available
AvGas	Aviation gasoline
avn	aviation
AvOil	aviation oil

LEGEND 1.—Abbreviations.

GENERAL INFORMATION

Abbreviation	Description
AWOS	Automatic Weather Observing System
AWSS	Automated Weather Sensor System
awt	await
awy	airway
az	azimuth
BA	braking action
BASH	Bird Aircraft Strike Hazard
BC	back course
bcn	beacon
bcst	broadcast
bdry	boundary
bldg	building
blkd	blocked
blo, blw	below
BOQ	Bachelor Officers Quarters
brg	bearing
btn	between
bus	business
byd	beyond
C	Commercial Circuit (Telephone)
CAC	Centralized Approach Control
cap	capacity
cat	category
CAT	Clear Air Turbulence
CCW or cntclkws	counterclockwise
ceil	ceiling
CERAP	Center Radar Approach Control
CG	Coast Guard
CGAF	Coast Guard Air Facility
CGAS	Coast Guard Air Station
CH, chan	channel
CHAPI	Chase Helicopter Approach Path Indicator
chg	change
cht	chart
cir	circle, circling
CIV, civ	Civil, civil, civilian
ck	check
CL	Centerline Lighting System
cl	class
clnc	clearance
clsd	closed
CNATRA	Chief of Naval Air Training
cnl	cancel
cntr	center
cntrln	centerline
Co	Company, County
CO	Commanding Officer
com	communication
comd	command
Comdr	Commander
coml	commercial
compul	compulsory
comsn	commission
conc	concrete
cond	condition
const	construction
cont	continue
CONUS	Continental United States
convl	conventional
coord	coordinate
copter	helicopter
corr	correct
CPDLC	Controller Pilot Data Link Communication

Abbreviation	Description
crdr	corridor
cros	cross
CRP	Compulsory Reporting Point
crs	course
CS	call sign
CSTMS	Customs
CTA	Control Area
CTAF	Common Traffic Advisory Frequency
ctc	contact
ctl	control
CTLZ	Control Zone
CVFR	Controlled Visual Flight Rules Areas
CW	Clockwise, Continuous Wave, Carrier Wave
dalgt	daylight
D–ATIS	Digital Automatic Terminal Information Service
daylt	daylight
db	decibel
DCL	Departure Clearance
Dec	December
decom	decommission
deg	degree
del	delivery
dep	depart
DEP	Departure Control
destn	destination
det	detachment
DF	Direction Finder
DH	Decision Height
DIAP	DoD Instrument Approach Procedure
direc	directional
disem	disseminate
displ	displace
dist	district, distance
div	division
DL	Direct Line to FSS
dlt	delete
dly	daily
DME	Distance Measuring Equipment (UHF standard, TACAN compatible)
DNVT	Digital Non–Secure Voice Telephone
DoD	Department of Defense
drct	direct
DSN	Defense Switching Network (Telephone)
DSN	Defense Switching Network
dsplcd	displaced
DT	Daylight Savings Time
dur	during
durn	duration
DV	Distinguished Visitor
E	East
ea	each
EAT	Expected Approach Time
ECN	Enroute Change Notice
EFAS	Enroute Flight Advisory Service
eff	effective, effect
E–HA	Enroute High Altitude
E–LA	Enroute Low Altitude
elev	elevation
ELT	Emergency Locator Transmitter
EMAS	Engineered Material Arresting System
emerg	emergency
eng	engine

Legend 1A.—Abbreviations.

6 GENERAL INFORMATION

Abbreviation	Description
EOR	End of Runway
eqpt	equipment
ERDA	Energy Research and Development Administration
E–S	Enroute Supplement
est	estimate
estab	establish
ETA	Estimated Time of Arrival
ETD	Estimated Time of Departure
ETE	Estimated Time Enroute
ETS	European Telephone System
EUR	European (ICAO Region)
ev	every
evac	evacuate
exc	except
excld	exclude
exer	exercise
exm	exempt
exp	expect
extd	extend
extn	extension
extv	extensive
F/W	Fixed Wing
FAA	Federal Aviation Administration
fac	facility
FAWS	Flight Advisory Weather Service
fax	facsimile
FBO	Fixed Base Operator
FCC	Flight Control Center
FCG	Foreign Clearance Guide
FCLP	field carrier landing practice
fcst	forecast
Feb	February
FIC	Flight Information Center
FIH	Flight Information Handbook
FIR	Flight Information Region
FIS	Flight Information Service
FL	flight level
fld	field
flg	flashing
FLIP	Flight Information Publication
flt	flight
flw	follow
FM	Fan Marker, Frequency Modulation
FOC	Flight Operations Center
FOD	Foreign Object Damage
fone	telephone
FPL	Flight Plan
fpm	feet per minute
fr	from
freq	frequency, frequent
Fri	Friday
frng	firing
FSC	Flight Service Center
FSS	Flight Service Station
ft	foot
ftr	fighter
GA	Glide Angle
gal	gallon
GAT	General Air Traffic (Europe–Asia)
GCA	Ground Control Approach
GCO	Ground Communication Outlet
gldr	glider
GND	Ground Control
gnd	ground

Abbreviation	Description
govt	government
GP	Glide Path
Gp	Group
GPI	Ground Point of Intercept
grad	gradient
grd	guard
GS	glide slope
GWT	gross weight
H	Enroute High Altitude Chart (followed by identification)
H+	Hours or hours plus...minutes past the hour
H24	continuous operation
HAA	Height Above Airport/Aerodrome
HAL	Height Above Landing Area
HAR	Height Above Runway
HAT	Height Above Touchdown
haz	hazard
hdg	heading
HDTA	High Density Traffic Airport/Aerodrome
HF	High Frequency (3000 to 30,000 KHz)
hgr	hangar
hgt	height
hi	high
HIRL	High Intensity Runway Lights
HIWAS	Hazardous Inflight Weather Advisory Service
HO	Service available to meet operational requirements
hol	holiday
HOLF	Helicopter Outlying Field
hosp	hospital
HQ	Headquarters
hr	hour
HS	Service available during hours of scheduled operations
hsg	housing
hvy	heavy
HW	Heavy Weight
hwy	highway
HX	station having no specific working hours
Hz	Hertz (cycles per second)
I	Island
IAP	Instrument Approach Procedure
IAS	Indicated Air Speed
IAW	in accordance with
ICAO	International Civil Aviation Organization
ident	identification
IFF	Identification, Friend or Foe
IFR	Instrument Flight Rules
IFR–S	FLIP IFR Supplement
IFSS	International Flight Service Station
ILS	Instrument Landing System
IM	Inner Marker
IMC	Instrument Meteorological Conditions
IMG	Immigration
immed	immediate
inbd	inbound
Inc	Incorporated
incl	include
incr	increase
indef	indefinite
info	information
inop	inoperative
inst	instrument

LEGEND 1B.—Abbreviations.

GENERAL INFORMATION

Abbreviation	Description
instl	install
instr	instruction
int	intersection
intcntl	intercontinental
intcp	intercept
intl	international
intmt	intermittent
ints	intense, intensity
invof	in the vicinity of
irreg	Irregularly
Jan	January
JASU	Jet Aircraft Starting Unit
JATO	Jet Assisted Take–Off
JOAP	Joint Oil Analysis Program
JOSAC	Joint Operational Support Airlift Center
JRB	Joint Reserve Base
Jul	July
Jun	June
K or Kt	Knots
kHz	kilohertz
KIAS	Knots Indicated Airspeed
KLIZ	Korea Limited Identification Zone
km	Kilometer
kw	kilowatt
L	Compass locator (Component of ILS system) under 25 Watts, 15 NM, Enroute Low Altitude Chart (followed by identification)
L	Local Time
LAA	Local Airport Advisory
LAHSO	Land and Hold–Short Operations
L–AOE	Limited Airport of Entry
LAWRS	Limited Aviation Weather Reporting Station
lb, lbs	pound (weight)
LC	local call
lcl	local
LCP	French Peripheral Classification Line
lctd	located
lctn	location
lctr	locator
LCVASI	Low Cost Visual Approach Slope Indicator
lczr	localizer
LD	long distance
LDA	Landing Distance Available
ldg	landing
LDIN	Lead–in Lights
LDOCF	Long Distance Operations Control Facility
len	length
lgt, lgtd, lgts	light, lighted, lights
LIRL	Low Intensity Runway Lights
LLWAS	Low–Level Wind Shear Alert System
LLZ	Localizer (Instrument Approach Procedures Identification only)
LMM	Compass locator at Middle Marker ILS
lo	low
LoALT or LA	Low Altitude
LOC	Localizer
LOM	Compass locator at Outer Marker ILS
LR	Long Range, Lead Radial
LRA	Landing Rights Airport
LRRS	Long Range RADAR Station
LSB	lower side band
ltd	limited
M	meters, magnetic (after a bearing), Military Circuit (Telephone)
MACC	Military Area Control Center
mag	magnetic
maint	maintain, maintenance
maj	major
MALS	Medium Intensity Approach Lighting System
MALSF	MALS with Sequenced Flashers
MALSR	MALS with Runway Alignment Indicator Lights
Mar	March
MARA	Military Activity Restricted Area
MATO	Military Air Traffic Operations
MATZ	Military Aerodrome Traffic Zone
max	maximum
mb	millibars
MCAC	Military Common Area Control
MCAF	Marine Corps Air Facility
MCALF	Marine Corps Auxiliary Landing Field
MCAS	Marine Corps Air Station
MCB	Marine Corps Base
MCC	Military Climb Corridor
MCOLF	Marine Corps Outlying Field
MDA	Minimum Descent Altitude
MEA	Minimum Enroute Altitude
med	medium
MEHT	Minimum Eye Height over Threshold
mem	memorial
MET	Meteorological, Meteorology
METAR	Aviation Routine Weather Report (in international MET figure code)
METRO	Pilot–to–Metro voice cell
MF	Medium Frequency (300 to 3000 KHz), Mandatory Frequency (Canada)
MFA	Minimum Flight Altitude
mgmt	Management
mgr	manager
MHz	Megahertz
mi	mile
MID/ASIA	Middle East/Asia (ICAO Region)
MIJI	Meaconing, Intrusion, Jamming, and Interference
Mil, mil	military
min	minimum, minute
MIRL	Medium Intensity Runway Lights
misl	missile
mkr	marker (beacon)
MM	Middle Marker of ILS
mnt	monitor
MOA	Military Operations Area
MOCA	Minimum Obstruction Clearance Altitude
mod	modify
MOG	Maximum (aircraft) on the Ground
Mon	Monday
MP	Maintenance Period
MR	Medium Range
MRA	Minimum Reception Altitude
mrk	mark, marker
MSAW	minimum safe altitude warning
msg	message
MSL	Mean Sea Level
msn	Mission

LEGEND 1C.—Abbreviations.

8

GENERAL INFORMATION

Abbreviation	Description
mt	mount, mountain
MTAF	Mandatory Traffic Advisory Frequency
MTCA	Military Terminal Control Area
mthly	monthly
MUAC	Military Upper Area Control
muni	municipal
MWARA	Major World Air Route Area
N	North
N/A	not applicable
NA	not authorized (For Instrument Approach Procedure take–off and alternate MINIMA only)
NAAS	Naval Auxiliary Air Station
NADC	Naval Air Development Center
NADEP	Naval Air Depot
NAEC	Naval Air Engineering Center
NAES	Naval Air Engineering Station
NAF	Naval Air Facility
NALCO	Naval Air Logistics Control Office
NALF	Naval Auxiliary Landing Field
NALO	Navy Air Logistics Office
NAS	Naval Air Station
NAT	North Atlantic (ICAO Region)
natl	national
nav	navigation
navaid	navigation aid
NAVMTO	Navy Material Transportation Office
NAWC	Naval Air Warfare Center
NAWS	Naval Air Weapons Station
NCRP	Non–Compulsory Reporting Point
NDB	Non–Directional Radio Beacon
NE	Northeast
nec	necessary
NEW	Net Explosives Weight
ngt	night
NM	nautical miles
nml	normal
NMR	nautical mile radius
No or Nr	number
NOLF	Naval Outlying Field
NORDO	Lost communications or no radio installed/available in aircraft
NOTAM	Notice to Airmen
Nov	November
npi	non precision instrument
Nr or No	number
NS	Naval Station
NS ABTMT	Noise Abatement
NSA	Naval Support Activity
NSF	Naval Support Facility
NSTD, nstd	nonstandard
ntc	notice
NVD	Night Vision Devices
NVG	Night Vision Goggles
NW	Northwest
NWC	Naval Weapons Center
O/A	On or about
O/S	out of service
O/R	On Request
OAT	Operational Air Traffic
obsn	observation
obst	obstruction
OCA	Oceanic Control Area
ocnl	occasional
Oct	October

Abbreviation	Description
ODALS	Omnidirectional Approach Lighting System
ODO	Operations Duty Officer
offl	official
OIC	Officer In Charge
OLF	Outlying Field
OLS	Optical Landing System
OM	Outer Marker, ILS
opr	operate, operator, operational
OPS, ops	operations
orig	original
OROCA	Off Route Obstruction Clearance Altitude
ORTCA	Off Route Terrain Clearance Altitude
OT	other times
OTS	out of service
outbd	outbound
ovft	overflight
ovrn	overrun
OX	oxygen
P/L	plain language
PAC	Pacific (ICAO Region)
PAEW	personnel and equipment working
PALS	Precision Approach and Landing System (NAVY)
PAPI	Precision Approach Path Indicator
PAR	Precision Approach Radar
para	paragraph
parl	parallel
pat	pattern
PAX	Passenger
PCL	pilot controlled lighting
pent	penetrate
perm	permanent
perms	permission
pers	personnel
PFC	Porous Friction Courses
PJE	Parachuting Activities/Exercises
p–line	power line
PM	Post meridian, noon til midnight
PMRF	Pacific Missile Range Facility
PMSV	Pilot–to–Metro Service
PN	prior notice
POB	persons on board
POL	Petrol, Oils and Lubricants
posn	position
PPR	prior permission required
prcht	parachute
pref	prefer
prev	previous
prim	primary
prk	park
PRM	Precision Runway Monitor
pro	procedure
proh	prohibited
pt	point
PTD	Pilot to Dispatcher
pub	publication
publ	publish
PVASI	Pulsating Visual Approach Slope Indicator
pvt	private
pwr	power
QFE	Altimeter Setting above station

Legend 1D.—Abbreviations.

GENERAL INFORMATION

Abbreviation	Description
QNE	Altimeter Setting of 29.92 inches which provides height above standard datum plane
QNH	Altimeter Setting which provides height above mean sea level
qtrs	quarters
quad	quadrant
R/T	Radiotelephony
R/W	Rotary/Wing
RACON	Radar Beacon
rad	radius, radial
RAIL	Runway Alignment Indicator Lights
RAMCC	Regional Air Movement Control Center
R–AOE	Regular Airport of Entry
RAPCON	Radar Approach Control (USAF)
RATCF	Radar Air Traffic Control Facility (Navy)
RCAG	Remote Center Air to Ground Facility
RCAGL	Remote Center Air to Ground Facility Long Range
RCL	runway centerline
RCLS	Runway Centerline Light System
RCO	Remote Communications Outlet
rcpt	reception
RCR	Runway Condition Reading
rcv	receive
rcvr	receiver
rdo	radio
reconst	reconstruct
reful	refueling
reg	regulation, regular
REIL	Runway End Identifier Lights
rel	reliable
relctd	relocated
REP	Reporting Point
req	request
RETIL	Rapid Exit Taxiway Indicator Light
Rgn	Region
Rgnl	Regional
rgt	right
rgt tfc	right traffic
rlgd	realigned
RLLS	Runway Lead-in Light System
rmk	remark
rng	range, radio range
RNP	Required Navigation Performance
RON	Remain Overnight
Rot Lt or Bcn	Rotating Light or Beacon
RPI	Runway Point of Intercept
rpt	report
rqr	require
RR	Railroad
RRP	Runway Reference Point
RSC	Runway Surface Condition
RSDU	Radar Storm Detection Unit
RSE	Runway Starter Extension/Starter Strip
RSRS	Reduced Same Runway Separation
rstd	restricted
rte	route
ruf	rough
RVR	Runway Visual Range
RVSM	Reduced Vertical Separation Minima
rwy	runway
S	South
S/D	Seadrome
SALS	Short Approach Lighting System
SAR	Search and Rescue
Sat	Saturday
SAVASI	Simplified Abbreviated Visual Approach Slope Indicator
SAWRS	Supplement Aviation Weather Reporting Station
sby	standby
Sched	scheduled services
sctr	sector
SDF	Simplified Directional Facility
SE	Southeast
sec	second, section
secd	secondary
SELCAL	Selective Calling System
SELF	Strategic Expeditionary Landing Field
SEng	Single Engine
Sep	September
SFA	Single Frequency Approach
sfc	surface
SFL	Sequence Flashing Lights
SFRA	Special Flight Rules Area
SID	Standard Instrument Departure
SIDA	Secure Identification Display Area
SIF	Selective Identification Feature
sked	schedule
SM	statute miles
SOAP	Spectrometric Oil Analysis Program
SOF	Supervisor of Flying
SPB	Seaplane Base
SR	sunrise
SRE	Surveillance Radar Element of GCA (Instrument Approach Procedures Identification only)
SS	sunset
SSALS/R	Simplified Short Approach Lighting System/with RAIL
SSB	Single Sideband
SSR	Secondary Surveillance Radar
STA	Straight-in Approach
std	standard
stn	station
stor	storage
str–in	Straight–in
stu	student
subj	subject
sum	summer
Sun	Sunday
sur	surround
survl	survival, surveillance
suspd	suspended
svc	service
svcg	servicing
SW	Southwest
sys	system
TA	Transition Altitude
TAC	Tactical Air Command
TAF	Aerodrome (terminal or alternate) forecast in abbreviated form
TALCE	Tanker Aircraft Control Element
TCA	Terminal Control Area
TCH	Threshold Crossing Height
TCTA	Transcontinental Control Area
TD	Touchdown
TDWR	Terminal Doppler Weather Radar
TDZ	Touchdown Zone
TDZL	Touchdown Zone Lights

LEGEND 1E.—Abbreviations.

10 GENERAL INFORMATION

Abbreviation	Description
tfc	traffic
thld	threshold
thou	thousand
thru	through
Thu	Thursday
til	until
tkf, tkof	take–off
TLv	Transition Level
tmpry	temporary
TODA	Take–Off Distance Available
TORA	Take–Off Run Available
TP	Tire Pressure
TPA	Traffic Pattern Altitude
TRACON	Terminal Radar Approach Control (FAA)
tran	transient
trans	transmit
trml	terminal
trng	training
trns	transition
TRSA	Terminal Radar Service Area
Tue	Tuesday
TV	Television
TWEB	Transcribed Weather Broadcast
twr	tower
twy	taxiway
UACC	Upper Area Control Center (used outside US)
UAS	Unmanned Aerial Systems
UC	Under Construction
UCN	Urgent Change Notice
UDA	Upper Advisory Area
UDF	Ultra High Frequency Direction Finder
UFN	until further notice
UHF	Ultra High Frequency (300 to 3000 MHz)
UIR	Upper Flight Information Region
unauthd	unauthorized
unavbl	unavailable
unctl	uncontrolled
unk	unknown
unlgtd	unlighted
unltd	unlimited
unmrk	unmarked
unmto	unmonitored
unrel	unreliable
unrstd	unrestricted
unsatfy	unsatisfactory
unsked	unscheduled
unsvc	unserviceable
unuse, unusbl	unusable
USA	United States Army
USAF	United States Air Force
USB	Upper Side Band
USCG	United States Coast Guard
USMC	United States Marine Corps
USN	United States Navy
UTA	Upper Control Area
UTC	Coordinated Universal Time
V	Defense Switching Network (telephone, formerly AUTOVON)
V/STOL	Vertical and Short Take–off and Landing aircraft
VAL	Visiting Aircraft Line
var	variation (magnetic variation)
VASI	Visual Approach Slope Indicator
vcnty	vicinity
VDF	Very High Frequency Direction Finder
veh	vehicle
vert	vertical
VFR	Visual Flight Rules
VFR–S	FLIP VFR Supplement
VHF	Very High Frequency (30 to 300 MHz)
VIP	Very Important Person
vis	visibility
VMC	Visual Meteorological Conditions
VOIP	Voice Over Internet Protocol
VOLMET	Meteorological Information for Aircraft in Flight
VOT	VOR Receiver Testing Facility
W	Warning Area (followed by identification), Watts, West, White
WCH	Wheel Crossing Height
Wed	Wednesday
Wg	Wing
WIE	with immediate effect
win	winter
WIP	work in progress
WSO	Weather Service Office
WSFO	Weather Service Forecast Office
wk	week
wkd	weekday
wkly	weekly
wng	warning
wo	without
WSP	Weather System Processor
wt	weight
wx	weather
yd	yard
yr	year
Z	Greenwich Mean Time (time groups only)

LEGEND 1F.—Abbreviations.

12

AIRPORT/FACILITY DIRECTORY LEGEND

SAMPLE

(1) **CITY NAME**

AIRPORT NAME (2) (ALTERNATE NAME) (3) (LTS)(KLTS) (4) CIV/MIL (5) 3 N (6) UTC–6(–5DT) (7) N34°41.93′ W99°20.20′ (8) **JACKSONVILLE COPTER H–4G, L–19C IAP, DIAP, AD** (9)

(11) 200 (12) B (13) TPA—1000(800) (14) AOE LRA (15) Class IV, ARFF Index A (16) NOTAM FILE ORL (17) Not insp.

(18) **RWY 18–36:** H12004X200 (ASPH–CONC–GRVD)
S–90, D–160, 2D–300 PCN 80 R/B/W/T HIRL CL
RWY 18: RLLS. MALSF. TDZL. REIL. PAPI(P2R)—GA 3.0° TCH 36′. RVR–TMR. Thld dsplcd 300′. Trees. Rgt tfc. 0.3% up.
RWY 36: ALSF1. 0.4% down.
RWY 09–27: H6000X150 (ASPH) MIRL
RWY 173–353: H3515X150 (ASPH–PFC) AUW PCN 59 F/A/W/T

(19) **LAND AND HOLD–SHORT OPERATIONS**

LDG RWY	HOLD–SHORT POINT	AVBL LDG DIST
RWY 18	09–27	6500
RWY 36	09–27	5400

(20) **RUNWAY DECLARED DISTANCE INFORMATION**
RWY 18: TORA–12004 TODA–12004 ASDA–11704 LDA–11504
RWY 36: TORA–12004 TODA–12004 ASDA–12004 LDA–11704

(21) **ARRESTING GEAR/SYSTEM**
RWY 18 HOOK E5 (65′ OVRN) BAK–14 BAK–12B (1650′)
BAK–14 BAK–12B (1087′) HOOK E5 (74′ OVRN) **RWY 36**

(22) **SERVICE:** S4 **FUEL** 100LL, JET A **OX** 1, 3 **LGT** ACTIVATE MALSR Rwy 29, REIL Rwy 11, VASI Rwy 11, HIRL Rwy 11–29, PAPI Rwy 17 and Rwy 35, MIRL Rwy 17–35—CTAF. **MILITARY— A–GEAR** E–5 connected on dep end, disconnected on apch end.
JASU 3(AM32A–60) 2(A/M32A–86) **FUEL** J8(Mil)(NC–100, A)
FLUID W SP PRESAIR LOX **OIL** O–128 **MAINT** S1 Mon–Fri 1000–2200Z‡
TRAN ALERT Avbl 1300–0200Z‡ svc limited weekends.

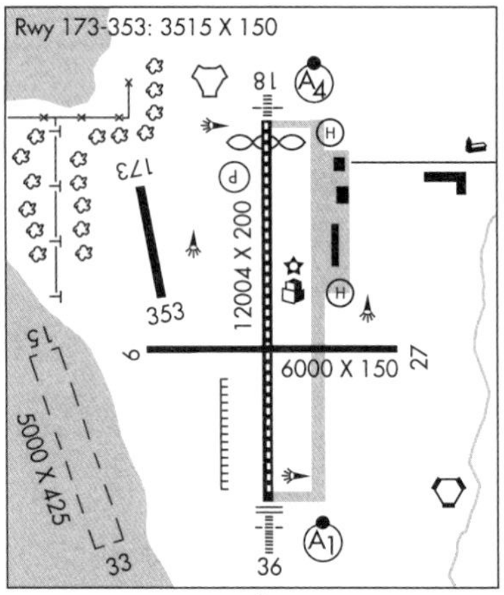

(23) **AIRPORT REMARKS:** Special Air Traffic Rules—Part 93, see Regulatory Notices. Attended 1200–0300Z‡. Parachute Jumping. Deer invof arpt. Heavy jumbo jet training surface to 9000′. Twy A clsd indef. Flight Notification Service (ADCUS) avbl.

(24) **MILITARY REMARKS: ANG** PPR/Official Business Only. Base OPS DSN 638–4390, C503–335–4222. Ctc Base OPS 15 minutes prior to ldg and after dep. Limited tran parking.

(25) **AIRPORT MANAGER:** (580) 481–5739

(26) **WEATHER DATA SOURCES: AWOS–1** 120.3 (202) 426–8000. LAWRS.

(27) **COMMUNICATIONS: SFA CTAF** 122.8 **UNICOM** 122.95 **ATIS** 127.25 273.5 (202) 426–8003 **PTD** 372.2
NAME FSS (ORL) on arpt. 123.65 122.65 122.2
NAME RCO 112.2T 112.1R (NAME RADIO)
®**NAME APP/DEP CON** 128.35 257.725 (1200–0400Z‡)
TOWER 119.65 255.6 (1200–0400Z‡) **GND CON** 121.7 **GCO** 135.075 (ORLANDO CLNC) **CLNC DEL** 125.55
CPDLC D–HZWXR, D–TAXI, DCL (LOGON KMEM)
NAME COMD POST (GERONIMO) 311.0 321.4 6761 **PMSV METRO** 239.8 **NAME OPS** 257.5

(28) **AIRSPACE: CLASS B** See VFR Terminal Area Chart.

(29) **VOR TEST FACILITY (VOT):** 116.7

(30) **RADIO AIDS TO NAVIGATION:** NOTAM FILE ORL. VHF/DF ctc FSS.
(H) VORTAC 112.2 MCO Chan 59 N28°32.55′ W81°20.12′ at fld. 1110/8E.
(H) TACAN Chan 29 CBU (109.2) N28°32.65′ W81°21.12′ at fld. 1115/8E.
HERNY NDB (LOM) 221 OR N28°37.40′ W81°21.05′ 177° 5.4 NM to fld.
ILS/DME 108.5 I–ORL Chan 22 Rwy 18. Class IIE. LOM HERNY NDB.
ASR/PAR (1200–0400Z‡)

(31) **COMM/NAV/WEATHER REMARKS:** Emerg frequency 121.5 not avbl at twr.

• •

HELIPAD H1: H100X75 (ASPH)
HELIPAD H2: H60X60 (ASPH) (1)
HELIPORT REMARKS: Helipad H1 lctd on general aviation side and H2 lctd on air carrier side of arpt.

• •

187 TPA 1000(813)
WATERWAY 15–33: 5000X425 (WATER)
SEAPLANE REMARKS: Birds roosting and feeding areas along river banks. Seaplanes operating adjacent to SW side of arpt not visible from twr and are required to ctc twr.

All bearings and radials are magnetic unless otherwise specified. All mileages are nautical unless otherwise noted.
All times are Coordinated Universal Time (UTC) except as noted. All elevations are in feet above/below Mean Sea Level (MSL) unless otherwise noted.
The horizontal reference datum of this publication is North American Datum of 1983 (NAD83), which for charting purposes is considered equivalent to World Geodetic System 1984 (WGS 84).

LEGEND 2.—Airport/Facility Directory.

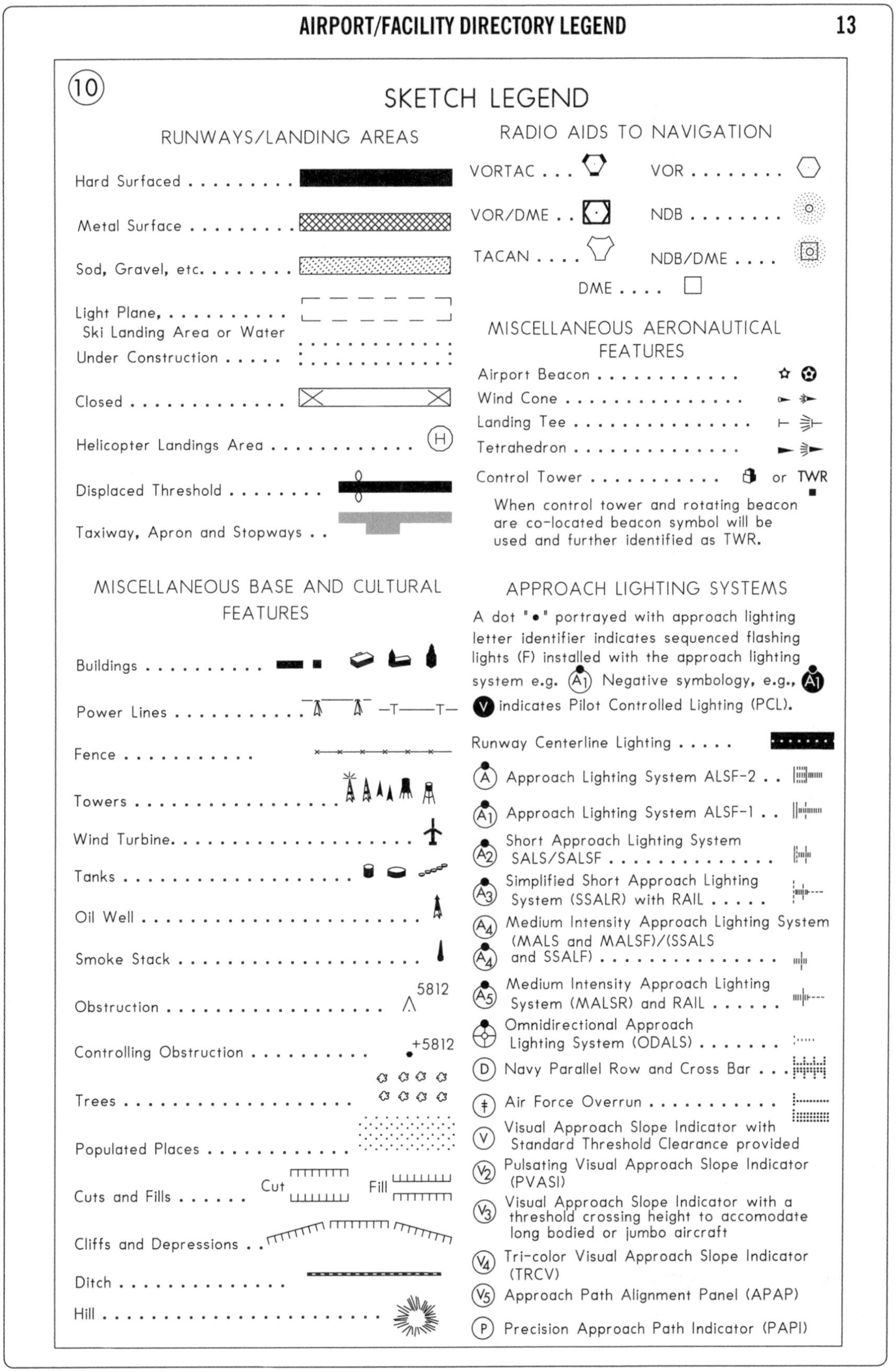

AIRPORT/FACILITY DIRECTORY LEGEND 13

(10)

SKETCH LEGEND

RUNWAYS/LANDING AREAS

Hard Surfaced . . . .

Metal Surface . . . .

Sod, Gravel, etc. . . . .

Light Plane, ...
Ski Landing Area or Water

Under Construction . . . . .

Closed . . . .

Helicopter Landings Area . . . . (H)

Displaced Threshold . . . .

Taxiway, Apron and Stopways . .

RADIO AIDS TO NAVIGATION

VORTAC . . . VOR . . . .

VOR/DME . . NDB . . . .

TACAN . . . . NDB/DME . . . .

DME . . . .

MISCELLANEOUS AERONAUTICAL FEATURES

Airport Beacon . . . .

Wind Cone . . . .

Landing Tee . . . .

Tetrahedron . . . .

Control Tower . . . . or TWR

When control tower and rotating beacon are co-located beacon symbol will be used and further identified as TWR.

MISCELLANEOUS BASE AND CULTURAL FEATURES

Buildings . . . .

Power Lines . . . . –T——T–

Fence . . . .

Towers . . . .

Wind Turbine. . . . .

Tanks . . . .

Oil Well . . . .

Smoke Stack . . . .

Obstruction 5812

Controlling Obstruction . . . . +5812

Trees . . . .

Populated Places . . . .

Cuts and Fills . . . . . . Cut Fill

Cliffs and Depressions . .

Ditch . . . .

Hill . . . .

APPROACH LIGHTING SYSTEMS

A dot "•" portrayed with approach lighting letter identifier indicates sequenced flashing lights (F) installed with the approach lighting system e.g. (A1) Negative symbology, e.g., (A1) (V) indicates Pilot Controlled Lighting (PCL).

Runway Centerline Lighting . . . . .

(A) Approach Lighting System ALSF-2 . .

(A1) Approach Lighting System ALSF-1 . .

(A2) Short Approach Lighting System SALS/SALSF . . . .

(A3) Simplified Short Approach Lighting System (SSALR) with RAIL . . . . .

(A4) Medium Intensity Approach Lighting System (MALS and MALSF)/(SSALS and SSALF) . . . .

(A5) Medium Intensity Approach Lighting System (MALSR) and RAIL . . . . . .

Omnidirectional Approach Lighting System (ODALS) . . . .

(D) Navy Parallel Row and Cross Bar . . .

Air Force Overrun . . . .

(V) Visual Approach Slope Indicator with Standard Threshold Clearance provided

(V2) Pulsating Visual Approach Slope Indicator (PVASI)

(V3) Visual Approach Slope Indicator with a threshold crossing height to accomodate long bodied or jumbo aircraft

(V4) Tri-color Visual Approach Slope Indicator (TRCV)

(V5) Approach Path Alignment Panel (APAP)

(P) Precision Approach Path Indicator (PAPI)

LEGEND 3.—Airport/Facility Directory.

AIRPORT/FACILITY DIRECTORY LEGEND

LEGEND

This directory is a listing of data on record with the FAA on public–use airports, military airports and selected private–use airports specifically requested by the Department of Defense (DoD) for which a DoD Instrument Approach Procedure has been published in the U.S. Terminal Procedures Publication. Additionally this listing contains data for associated terminal control facilities, air route traffic control centers, and radio aids to navigation within the conterminous United States, Puerto Rico and the Virgin Islands. Civil airports and joint Civil/Military airports which are open to the public are listed alphabetically by state, associated city and airport name and cross–referenced by airport name. Military airports and private–use (limited civil access) joint Military/Civil airports are listed alphabetically by state and official airport name and cross–referenced by associated city name. Navaids, flight service stations and remote communication outlets that are associated with an airport, but with a different name, are listed alphabetically under their own name, as well as under the airport with which they are associated.

The listing of an airport as open to the public in this directory merely indicates the airport operator's willingness to accommodate transient aircraft, and does not represent that the airport conforms with any Federal or local standards, or that it has been approved for use on the part of the general public. Military airports, private–use airports, and private–use (limited civil access) joint Military/Civil airports are open to civil pilots only in an emergency or with prior permission. See Special Notice Section, Civil Use of Military Fields.

The information on obstructions is taken from reports submitted to the FAA. Obstruction data has not been verified in all cases. Pilots are cautioned that objects not indicated in this tabulation (or on the airports sketches and/or charts) may exist which can create a hazard to flight operation. Detailed specifics concerning services and facilities tabulated within this directory are contained in the Aeronautical Information Manual, Basic Flight Information and ATC Procedures.

The legend items that follow explain in detail the contents of this Directory and are keyed to the circled numbers on the sample on the preceding pages.

① CITY/AIRPORT NAME

Civil and joint Civil/Military airports which are open to the public are listed alphabetically by state and associated city. Where the city name is different from the airport name the city name will appear on the line above the airport name. Airports with the same associated city name will be listed alphabetically by airport name and will be separated by a dashed rule line. A solid rule line will separate all others. FAA approved helipads and seaplane landing areas associated with a land airport will be separated by a dotted line. Military airports and private–use (limited civil access) joint Military/Civil airports are listed alphabetically by state and official airport name.

② ALTERNATE NAME

Alternate names, if any, will be shown in parentheses.

③ LOCATION IDENTIFIER

The location identifier is a three or four character FAA code followed by a four–character ICAO code, when assigned, to airports. If two different military codes are assigned, both codes will be shown with the primary operating agency's code listed first. These identifiers are used by ATC in lieu of the airport name in flight plans, flight strips and other written records and computer operations. Zeros will appear with a slash to differentiate them from the letter "O".

④ OPERATING AGENCY

Airports within this directory are classified into two categories, Military/Federal Government and Civil airports open to the general public, plus selected private–use airports. The operating agency is shown for military, private–use and joint use airports. The operating agency is shown by an abbreviation as listed below. When an organization is a tenant, the abbreviation is enclosed in parenthesis. No classification indicates the airport is open to the general public with no military tenant.

A	US Army	MC	Marine Corps
AFRC	Air Force Reserve Command	MIL/CIV	Joint Use Military/Civil Limited Civil Access
AF	US Air Force	N	Navy
ANG	Air National Guard	NAF	Naval Air Facility
AR	US Army Reserve	NAS	Naval Air Station
ARNG	US Army National Guard	NASA	National Air and Space Administration
CG	US Coast Guard	P	US Civil Airport Wherein Permit Covers Use by Transient Military Aircraft
CIV/MIL	Joint Use Civil/Military Open to the Public		
DND	Department of National Defense Canada	PVT	Private Use Only (Closed to the Public)

⑤ AIRPORT LOCATION

Airport location is expressed as distance and direction from the center of the associated city in nautical miles and cardinal points, e.g., 4 NE.

⑥ TIME CONVERSION

Hours of operation of all facilities are expressed in Coordinated Universal Time (UTC) and shown as "Z" time. The directory indicates the number of hours to be subtracted from UTC to obtain local standard time and local daylight saving time UTC–5(–4DT). The symbol ‡ indicates that during periods of Daylight Saving Time (DST) effective hours will be one hour earlier than shown. In those areas where daylight saving time is not observed the (–4DT) and ‡ will not be shown. Daylight saving time is in effect from 0200 local time the second Sunday in March to 0200 local time the first Sunday in November. Canada and all U.S. Conterminous States observe daylight saving time except Arizona and Puerto Rico, and the Virgin Islands. If the state observes daylight saving time and the operating times are other than daylight saving times, the operating hours will include the dates, times and no ‡ symbol will be shown, i.e., April 15–Aug 31 0630–1700Z, Sep 1–Apr 14 0600–1700Z.

LEGEND 4.—Airport/Facility Directory.

AIRPORT/FACILITY DIRECTORY LEGEND

⑦ GEOGRAPHIC POSITION OF AIRPORT—AIRPORT REFERENCE POINT (ARP)

Positions are shown as hemisphere, degrees, minutes and hundredths of a minute and represent the approximate geometric center of all usable runway surfaces.

⑧ CHARTS

Charts refer to the Sectional Chart and Low and High Altitude Enroute Chart and panel on which the airport or facility is located. Helicopter Chart locations will be indicated as COPTER. IFR Gulf of Mexico West and IFR Gulf of Mexico Central will be depicted as GOMW and GOMC.

⑨ INSTRUMENT APPROACH PROCEDURES, AIRPORT DIAGRAMS

IAP indicates an airport for which a prescribed (Public Use) FAA Instrument Approach Procedure has been published. DIAP indicates an airport for which a prescribed DoD Instrument Approach Procedure has been published in the U.S. Terminal Procedures. See the Special Notice Section of this directory, Civil Use of Military Fields and the Aeronautical Information Manual 5–4–5 Instrument Approach Procedure Charts for additional information. AD indicates an airport for which an airport diagram has been published. Airport diagrams are located in the back of each Chart Supplement volume alphabetically by associated city and airport name.

⑩ AIRPORT SKETCH

The airport sketch, when provided, depicts the airport and related topographical information as seen from the air and should be used in conjunction with the text. It is intended as a guide for pilots in VFR conditions. Symbology that is not self–explanatory will be reflected in the sketch legend. The airport sketch will be oriented with True North at the top. Airport sketches will be added incrementally.

⑪ ELEVATION

The highest point of an airport's usable runways measured in feet from mean sea level. When elevation is sea level it will be indicated as "00". When elevation is below sea level a minus "–" sign will precede the figure.

⑫ ROTATING LIGHT BEACON

B indicates rotating beacon is available. Rotating beacons operate sunset to sunrise unless otherwise indicated in the AIRPORT REMARKS or MILITARY REMARKS segment of the airport entry.

⑬ TRAFFIC PATTERN ALTITUDE

Traffic Pattern Altitude (TPA)—The first figure shown is TPA above mean sea level. The second figure in parentheses is TPA above airport elevation. Multiple TPA shall be shown as "TPA—See Remarks" and detailed information shall be shown in the Airport or Military Remarks Section. Traffic pattern data for USAF bases, USN facilities, and U.S. Army airports (including those on which ACC or U.S. Army is a tenant) that deviate from standard pattern altitudes shall be shown in Military Remarks.

⑭ AIRPORT OF ENTRY, LANDING RIGHTS, AND CUSTOMS USER FEE AIRPORTS

U.S. CUSTOMS USER FEE AIRPORT—Private Aircraft operators are frequently required to pay the costs associated with customs processing.

AOE—Airport of Entry. A customs Airport of Entry where permission from U.S. Customs is not required to land. However, at least one hour advance notice of arrival is required.

LRA—Landing Rights Airport. Application for permission to land must be submitted in advance to U.S. Customs. At least one hour advance notice of arrival is required.

NOTE: Advance notice of arrival at both an AOE and LRA airport may be included in the flight plan when filed in Canada or Mexico. Where Flight Notification Service (ADCUS) is available the airport remark will indicate this service. This notice will also be treated as an application for permission to land in the case of an LRA. Although advance notice of arrival may be relayed to Customs through Mexico, Canada, and U.S. Communications facilities by flight plan, the aircraft operator is solely responsible for ensuring that Customs receives the notification. (See Customs, Immigration and Naturalization, Public Health and Agriculture Department requirements in the International Flight Information Manual for further details.)

U.S. CUSTOMS AIR AND SEA PORTS, INSPECTORS AND AGENTS

Northeast Sector (New England and Atlantic States—ME to MD)	407–975–1740
Southeast Sector (Atlantic States—DC, WV, VA to FL)	407–975–1780
Central Sector (Interior of the US, including Gulf states—MS, AL, LA)	407–975–1760
Southwest East Sector (OK and eastern TX)	407–975–1840
Southwest West Sector (Western TX, NM and AZ)	407–975–1820
Pacific Sector (WA, OR, CA, HI and AK)	407–975–1800

⑮ CERTIFICATED AIRPORT (14 CFR PART 139)

Airports serving Department of Transportation certified carriers and certified under 14 CFR part 139 are indicated by the Class and the ARFF Index; e.g. Class I, ARFF Index A, which relates to the availability of crash, fire, rescue equipment. Class I airports can have an ARFF Index A through E, depending on the aircraft length and scheduled departures. Class II, III, and IV will always carry an Index A.

AIRPORT CLASSIFICATIONS

Type of Air Carrier Operation	Class I	Class II	Class III	Class IV
Scheduled Air Carrier Aircraft with 31 or more passenger seats	X			
Unscheduled Air Carrier Aircraft with 31 or more passengers seats	X	X		X
Scheduled Air Carrier Aircraft with 10 to 30 passenger seats	X	X	X	

LEGEND 5.—Airport/Facility Directory.

16

AIRPORT/FACILITY DIRECTORY LEGEND

INDICES AND AIRCRAFT RESCUE AND FIRE FIGHTING EQUIPMENT REQUIREMENTS

Airport Index	Required No. Vehicles	Aircraft Length	Scheduled Departures	Agent + Water for Foam
A	1	<90′	≥1	500#DC or HALON 1211 or 450#DC + 100 gal H_2O
B	1 or 2	≥90′, <126′	≥5	Index A + 1500 gal H_2O
		≥126′, <159′	<5	
C	2 or 3	≥126′, <159′	≥5	Index A + 3000 gal H_2O
		≥159′, <200′	<5	
D	3	≥159′, <200′		Index A + 4000 gal H_2O
		>200′	<5	
E	3	≥200′	≥5	Index A + 6000 gal H_2O

> Greater Than; < Less Than; ≥ Equal or Greater Than; ≤ Equal or Less Than; H_2O–Water; DC–Dry Chemical.

NOTE: The listing of ARFF index does not necessarily assure coverage for non–air carrier operations or at other than prescribed times for air carrier. ARFF Index Ltd.—indicates ARFF coverage may or may not be available, for information contact airport manager prior to flight.

(16) NOTAM SERVICE

All public use landing areas are provided NOTAM service. A NOTAM FILE identifier is shown for individual landing areas, e.g., "NOTAM FILE BNA". See the AIM, Basic Flight Information and ATC Procedures for a detailed description of NOTAMs. Current NOTAMs are available from flight service stations at 1–800–WX–BRIEF (992–7433) or online through the FAA PilotWeb at https://pilotweb.nas.faa.gov. Military NOTAMs are available using the Defense Internet NOTAM Service (DINS) at https://www.notams.faa.gov. Pilots flying to or from airports not available through the FAA PilotWeb or DINS can obtain assistance from Flight Service.

(17) FAA INSPECTION

All airports not inspected by FAA will be identified by the note: Not insp. This indicates that the airport information has been provided by the owner or operator of the field.

(18) RUNWAY DATA

Runway information is shown on two lines. That information common to the entire runway is shown on the first line while information concerning the runway ends is shown on the second or following line. Runway direction, surface, length, width, weight bearing capacity, lighting, and slope, when available are shown for each runway. Multiple runways are shown with the longest runway first. Direction, length, width, and lighting are shown for sea–lanes. The full dimensions of helipads are shown, e.g., 50X150. Runway data that requires clarification will be placed in the remarks section.

RUNWAY DESIGNATION

Runways are normally numbered in relation to their magnetic orientation rounded off to the nearest 10 degrees. Parallel runways can be designated L (left)/R (right)/C (center). Runways may be designated as Ultralight or assault strips. Assault strips are shown by magnetic bearing.

RUNWAY DIMENSIONS

Runway length and width are shown in feet. Length shown is runway end to end including displaced thresholds, but excluding those areas designed as overruns.

RUNWAY SURFACE AND SURFACE TREATMENT

Runway lengths prefixed by the letter "H" indicate that the runways are hard surfaced (concrete, asphalt, or part asphalt–concrete). If the runway length is not prefixed, the surface is sod, clay, etc. The runway surface composition is indicated in parentheses after runway length as follows:

(AFSC)—Aggregate friction seal coat
(AM2)—Temporary metal planks coated with nonskid material
(ASPH)—Asphalt
(CONC)—Concrete
(DIRT)—Dirt
(GRVD)—Grooved
(GRVL)—Gravel, or cinders
(MATS)—Pierced steel planking, landing mats, membranes
(PEM)—Part concrete, part asphalt
(PFC)—Porous friction courses
(PSP)—Pierced steel plank
(RFSC)—Rubberized friction seal coat
(SAND)—Sand
(TURF)—Turf
(TRTD)—Treated
(WC)—Wire combed

LEGEND 6.—Airport/Facility Directory.

AIRPORT/FACILITY DIRECTORY LEGEND 17

RUNWAY WEIGHT BEARING CAPACITY

Runway strength data shown in this publication is derived from available information and is a realistic estimate of capability at an average level of activity. It is not intended as a maximum allowable weight or as an operating limitation. Many airport pavements are capable of supporting limited operations with gross weights in excess of the published figures. Permissible operating weights, insofar as runway strengths are concerned, are a matter of agreement between the owner and user. When desiring to operate into any airport at weights in excess of those published in the publication, users should contact the airport management for permission. Runway strength figures are shown in thousand of pounds, with the last three figures being omitted. Add 000 to figure following S, D, 2S, 2T, AUW, SWL, etc., for gross weight capacity. A blank space following the letter designator is used to indicate the runway can sustain aircraft with this type landing gear, although definite runway weight bearing capacity figures are not available, e.g., S, D. Applicable codes for typical gear configurations with S=Single, D=Dual, T=Triple and Q=Quadruple:

CURRENT	NEW	NEW DESCRIPTION
S	S	Single wheel type landing gear (DC3), (C47), (F15), etc.
D	D	Dual wheel type landing gear (BE1900), (B737), (A319), etc.
T	D	Dual wheel type landing gear (P3, C9).
ST	2S	Two single wheels in tandem type landing gear (C130).
TRT	2T	Two triple wheels in tandem type landing gear (C17), etc.
DT	2D	Two dual wheels in tandem type landing gear (B707), etc.
TT	2D	Two dual wheels in tandem type landing gear (B757, KC135).
SBTT	2D/D1	Two dual wheels in tandem/dual wheel body gear type landing gear (KC10).
None	2D/2D1	Two dual wheels in tandem/two dual wheels in tandem body gear type landing gear (A340–600).
DDT	2D/2D2	Two dual wheels in tandem/two dual wheels in double tandem body gear type landing gear (B747, E4).
TTT	3D	Three dual wheels in tandem type landing gear (B777), etc.
TT	D2	Dual wheel gear two struts per side main gear type landing gear (B52).
TDT	C5	Complex dual wheel and quadruple wheel combination landing gear (C5).

AUW—All up weight. Maximum weight bearing capacity for any aircraft irrespective of landing gear configuration.

SWL—Single Wheel Loading. (This includes information submitted in terms of Equivalent Single Wheel Loading (ESWL) and Single Isolated Wheel Loading).

PSI—Pounds per square inch. PSI is the actual figure expressing maximum pounds per square inch runway will support, e.g., (SWL 000/PSI 535).

Omission of weight bearing capacity indicates information unknown.

The ACN/PCN System is the ICAO standard method of reporting pavement strength for pavements with bearing strengths greater than 12,500 pounds. The Pavement Classification Number (PCN) is established by an engineering assessment of the runway. The PCN is for use in conjunction with an Aircraft Classification Number (ACN). Consult the Aircraft Flight Manual, Flight Information Handbook, or other appropriate source for ACN tables or charts. Currently, ACN data may not be available for all aircraft. If an ACN table or chart is available, the ACN can be calculated by taking into account the aircraft weight, the pavement type, and the subgrade category. For runways that have been evaluated under the ACN/PCN system, the PCN will be shown as a five–part code (e.g. PCN 80 R/B/W/T). Details of the coded format are as follows:

NOTE: Prior permission from the airport controlling authority is required when the ACN of the aircraft exceeds the published PCN or aircraft tire pressure exceeds the published limits.

(1) The PCN NUMBER—The reported PCN indicates that an aircraft with an ACN equal or less than the reported PCN can operate on the pavement subject to any limitation on the tire pressure.

(2) The type of pavement:
R — Rigid
F — Flexible

(3) The pavement subgrade category:
A — High
B — Medium
C — Low
D — Ultra–low

(4) The maximum tire pressure authorized for the pavement:
W — Unlimited, no pressure limit
X — High, limited to 254 psi (1.75 MPa)
Y — Medium, limited to 181 psi (1.25MPa)
Z — Low, limited to 73 psi (0.50 MPa)

(5) Pavement evaluation method:
T — Technical evaluation
U — By experience of aircraft using the pavement

RUNWAY LIGHTING

Lights are in operation sunset to sunrise. Lighting available by prior arrangement only or operating part of the night and/or pilot controlled lighting with specific operating hours are indicated under airport or military remarks. At USN/USMC facilities lights are available only during airport hours of operation. Since obstructions are usually lighted, obstruction lighting is not included in this code. Unlighted obstructions on or surrounding an airport will be noted in airport or military remarks. Runway lights nonstandard (NSTD) are systems for which the light fixtures are not FAA approved L–800 series: color, intensity, or spacing does not meet FAA standards. Nonstandard runway lights, VASI, or any other system not listed below will be shown in airport remarks or military

LEGEND 7.—Airport/Facility Directory.

service. Temporary, emergency or limited runway edge lighting such as flares, smudge pots, lanterns or portable runway lights will also be shown in airport remarks or military service. Types of lighting are shown with the runway or runway end they serve.

NSTD—Light system fails to meet FAA standards.
LIRL—Low Intensity Runway Lights.
MIRL—Medium Intensity Runway Lights.
HIRL—High Intensity Runway Lights.
RAIL—Runway Alignment Indicator Lights.
REIL—Runway End Identifier Lights.
CL—Centerline Lights.
TDZL—Touchdown Zone Lights.
ODALS—Omni Directional Approach Lighting System.
AF OVRN—Air Force Overrun 1000′ Standard Approach Lighting System.
MALS—Medium Intensity Approach Lighting System.
MALSF—Medium Intensity Approach Lighting System with Sequenced Flashing Lights.
MALSR—Medium Intensity Approach Lighting System with Runway Alignment Indicator Lights.
RLLS—Runway Lead–in Light System
SALS—Short Approach Lighting System.
SALSF—Short Approach Lighting System with Sequenced Flashing Lights.
SSALS—Simplified Short Approach Lighting System.
SSALF—Simplified Short Approach Lighting System with Sequenced Flashing Lights.
SSALR—Simplified Short Approach Lighting System with Runway Alignment Indicator Lights.
ALSAF—High Intensity Approach Lighting System with Sequenced Flashing Lights.
ALSF1—High Intensity Approach Lighting System with Sequenced Flashing Lights, Category I, Configuration.
ALSF2—High Intensity Approach Lighting System with Sequenced Flashing Lights, Category II, Configuration.
SF—Sequenced Flashing Lights.
OLS—Optical Landing System.
WAVE–OFF.

NOTE: Civil ALSF2 may be operated as SSALR during favorable weather conditions. When runway edge lights are positioned more than 10 feet from the edge of the usable runway surface a remark will be added in the "Remarks" portion of the airport entry. This is applicable to Air Force, Air National Guard and Air Force Reserve Bases, and those joint use airfields on which they are tenants.

VISUAL GLIDESLOPE INDICATORS

APAP—A system of panels, which may or may not be lighted, used for alignment of approach path.

PNIL	APAP on left side of runway	PNIR	APAP on right side of runway

PAPI—Precision Approach Path Indicator

P2L	2–identical light units placed on left side of runway	P4L	4–identical light units placed on left side of runway
P2R	2–identical light units placed on right side of runway	P4R	4–identical light units placed on right side of runway

PVASI—Pulsating/steady burning visual approach slope indicator, normally a single light unit projecting two colors.

PSIL	PVASI on left side of runway	PSIR	PVASI on right side of runway

SAVASI—Simplified Abbreviated Visual Approach Slope Indicator

S2L	2–box SAVASI on left side of runway	S2R	2–box SAVASI on right side of runway

TRCV—Tri–color visual approach slope indicator, normally a single light unit projecting three colors.

TRIL	TRCV on left side of runway	TRIR	TRCV on right side of runway

VASI—Visual Approach Slope Indicator

V2L	2–box VASI on left side of runway	V6L	6–box VASI on left side of runway
V2R	2–box VASI on right side of runway	V6R	6–box VASI on right side of runway
V4L	4–box VASI on left side of runway	V12	12–box VASI on both sides of runway
V4R	4–box VASI on right side of runway	V16	16–box VASI on both sides of runway

NOTE: Approach slope angle and threshold crossing height will be shown when available; i.e., –GA 3.5° TCH 37′.

PILOT CONTROL OF AIRPORT LIGHTING

Key Mike	Function
7 times within 5 seconds	Highest intensity available
5 times within 5 seconds	Medium or lower intensity (Lower REIL or REIL–Off)
3 times within 5 seconds	Lowest intensity available (Lower REIL or REIL–Off)

Available systems will be indicated in the Service section, e.g., **LGT** ACTIVATE HIRL Rwy 07–25, MALSR Rwy 07, and VASI Rwy 07—122.8.

Where the airport is not served by an instrument approach procedure and/or has an independent type system of different specification installed by the airport sponsor, descriptions of the type lights, method of control, and operating frequency will be explained in clear text. See AIM, "Basic Flight Information and ATC Procedures," for detailed description of pilot control of airport lighting.

RUNWAY SLOPE

When available, runway slope data will be provided. Runway slope will be shown only when it is 0.3 percent or greater. On runways less than 8000 feet, the direction of the slope up will be indicated, e.g., 0.3% up NW. On runways 8000 feet or greater, the slope will be shown (up or down) on the runway end line, e.g., RWY 13: 0.3% up., RWY 31: Pole. Rgt tfc. 0.4% down.

LEGEND 8.—Airport/Facility Directory.

AIRPORT/FACILITY DIRECTORY LEGEND

RUNWAY END DATA

Information pertaining to the runway approach end such as approach lights, touchdown zone lights, runway end identification lights, visual glideslope indicators, displaced thresholds, controlling obstruction, and right hand traffic pattern, will be shown on the specific runway end. "Rgt tfc"—Right traffic indicates right turns should be made on landing and takeoff for specified runway end. Runway Visual Range shall be shown as "RVR" appended with "T" for touchdown, "M" for midpoint, and "R" for rollout; e.g., RVR-TMR.

⑲ LAND AND HOLD–SHORT OPERATIONS (LAHSO)

LAHSO is an acronym for "Land and Hold–Short Operations" These operations include landing and holding short of an intersection runway, an intersecting taxiway, or other predetermined points on the runway other than a runway or taxiway. Measured distance represents the available landing distance on the landing runway, in feet.

Specific questions regarding these distances should be referred to the air traffic manager of the facility concerned. The Aeronautical Information Manual contains specific details on hold–short operations and markings.

⑳ RUNWAY DECLARED DISTANCE INFORMATION

TORA—Take–off Run Available. The length of runway declared available and suitable for the ground run of an aeroplane take–off.
TODA—Take–off Distance Available. The length of the take–off run available plus the length of the clearway, if provided.
ASDA—Accelerate–Stop Distance Available. The length of the take–off run available plus the length of the stopway, if provided.
LDA—Landing Distance Available. The length of runway which is declared available and suitable for the ground run of an aeroplane landing.

㉑ ARRESTING GEAR/SYSTEMS

Arresting gear is shown as it is located on the runway. The a–gear distance from the end of the appropriate runway (or into the overrun) is indicated in parentheses. A–Gear which has a bi–direction capability and can be utilized for emergency approach end engagement is indicated by a (B). Up to 15 minutes advance notice may be required for rigging A–Gear for approach and engagement. Airport listing may show availability of other than US Systems. This information is provided for emergency requirements only. Refer to current aircraft operating manuals for specific engagement weight and speed criteria based on aircraft structural restrictions and arresting system limitations.

Following is a list of current systems referenced in this publication identified by both Air Force and Navy terminology:

BI–DIRECTIONAL CABLE (B)

TYPE	DESCRIPTION
BAK–9	Rotary friction brake.
BAK–12A	Standard BAK–12 with 950 foot run out, 1–inch cable and 40,000 pound weight setting. Rotary friction brake.
BAK–12B	Extended BAK–12 with 1200 foot run, 1¼ inch Cable and 50,000 pounds weight setting. Rotary friction brake.
E28	Rotary Hydraulic (Water Brake).
M21	Rotary Hydraulic (Water Brake) Mobile.

The following device is used in conjunction with some aircraft arresting systems:

BAK–14	A device that raises a hook cable out of a slot in the runway surface and is remotely positioned for engagement by the tower on request. (In addition to personnel reaction time, the system requires up to five seconds to fully raise the cable.)
H	A device that raises a hook cable out of a slot in the runway surface and is remotely positioned for engagement by the tower on request. (In addition to personnel reaction time, the system requires up to one and one–half seconds to fully raise the cable.)

UNI–DIRECTIONAL CABLE

TYPE	DESCRIPTION
MB60	Textile brake—an emergency one–time use, modular braking system employing the tearing of specially woven textile straps to absorb the kinetic energy.
E5/E5–1/E5–3	Chain Type. At USN/USMC stations E–5 A–GEAR systems are rated, e.g., E–5 RATING–13R–1100 HW (DRY), 31L/R–1200 STD (WET). This rating is a function of the A–GEAR chain weight and length and is used to determine the maximum aircraft engaging speed. A dry rating applies to a stabilized surface (dry or wet) while a wet rating takes into account the amount (if any) of wet overrun that is not capable of withstanding the aircraft weight. These ratings are published under Service/Military/A-Gear in the entry.

FOREIGN CABLE

TYPE	DESCRIPTION	US EQUIVALENT
44B–3H	Rotary Hydraulic (Water Brake)	
CHAG	Chain	E–5

UNI–DIRECTIONAL BARRIER

TYPE	DESCRIPTION
MA–1A	Web barrier between stanchions attached to a chain energy absorber.
BAK–15	Web barrier between stanchions attached to an energy absorber (water squeezer, rotary friction, chain). Designed for wing engagement.

NOTE: Landing short of the runway threshold on a runway with a BAK–15 in the underrun is a significant hazard. The barrier in the down position still protrudes several inches above the underrun. Aircraft contact with the barrier short of the runway threshold can cause damage to the barrier and substantial damage to the aircraft.

OTHER

TYPE	DESCRIPTION
EMAS	Engineered Material Arresting System, located beyond the departure end of the runway, consisting of high energy absorbing materials which will crush under the weight of an aircraft.

LEGEND 9.—Airport/Facility Directory.

㉒ SERVICE

SERVICING—CIVIL

S1:	Minor airframe repairs.	S5:	Major airframe repairs.
S2:	Minor airframe and minor powerplant repairs.	S6:	Minor airframe and major powerplant repairs.
S3:	Major airframe and minor powerplant repairs.	S7:	Major powerplant repairs.
S4:	Major airframe and major powerplant repairs.	S8:	Minor powerplant repairs.

FUEL—CIVIL

CODE	FUEL
80	Grade 80 gasoline (Red)
100	Grade 100 gasoline (Green)
100LL	100LL gasoline (low lead) (Blue)
115	Grade 115 gasoline (115/145 military specification) (Purple)
A	Jet A, Kerosene, without FS–II*, FP** minus 40° C.
A+	Jet A, Kerosene, with FS–II*, FP** minus 40°C.
A++	Jet A, Kerosene, with FS–II*, CI/LI#, SDA##, FP** minus 40°C.
A++100	Jet A, Kerosene, with FS–II*, CI/LI#, SDA##, FP** minus 40°C, with +100 fuel additive that improves thermal stability characteristics of kerosene jet fuels.
A1	Jet A–1, Kerosene, without FS–II*, FP** minus 47°C.

CODE	FUEL
A1+	Jet A–1, Kerosene with FS–II*, FP** minus 47° C.
B	Jet B, Wide–cut, turbine fuel without FS–II*, FP** minus 50° C.
B+	Jet B, Wide–cut, turbine fuel with FS–II*, FP** minus 50° C
J4 (JP4)	(JP–4 military specification) FP** minus 58° C.
J5 (JP5)	(JP–5 military specification) Kerosene with FS–II, FP** minus 46°C.
J8 (JP8)	(JP–8 military specification) Jet A–1, Kerosene with FS–II*, CI/LI#, SDA##, FP** minus 47°C.
J8+100	(JP–8 military specification) Jet A–1, Kerosene with FS–II*, CI/LI#, SDA##,FP** minus 47°C, with +100 fuel additive that improves thermal stability characteristics of kerosene jet fuels.
J	(Jet Fuel Type Unknown)
MOGAS	Automobile gasoline which is to be used as aircraft fuel.

*(Fuel System Icing Inhibitor) **(Freeze Point) # (Corrosion Inhibitors/Lubricity Improvers) ## (Static Dissipator Additive)

NOTE: Certain automobile gasoline may be used in specific aircraft engines if a FAA supplemental type certificate has been obtained. Automobile gasoline, which is to be used in aircraft engines, will be identified as "MOGAS", however, the grade/type and other octane rating will not be published.

Data shown on fuel availability represents the most recent information the publisher has been able to acquire. Because of a variety of factors, the fuel listed may not always be obtainable by transient civil pilots. Confirmation of availability of fuel should be made directly with fuel suppliers at locations where refueling is planned.

OXYGEN—CIVIL

OX 1	High Pressure	OX 3	High Pressure—Replacement Bottles
OX 2	Low Pressure	OX 4	Low Pressure—Replacement Bottles

SERVICE—MILITARY

Specific military services available at the airport are listed under this general heading. Remarks applicable to any military service are shown in the individual service listing.

JET AIRCRAFT STARTING UNITS (JASU)—MILITARY

The numeral preceding the type of unit indicates the number of units available. The absence of the numeral indicates ten or more units available. If the number of units is unknown, the number one will be shown. Absence of JASU designation indicates non–availability.

The following is a list of current JASU systems referenced in this publication:

USAF JASU (For variations in technical data, refer to T.O. 35–1–7.)

ELECTRICAL STARTING UNITS:

A/M32A–86	AC: 115/200v, 3 phase, 90 kva, 0.8 pf, 4 wire DC: 28v, 1500 amp, 72 kw (with TR pack)
MC–1A	AC: 115/208v, 400 cycle, 3 phase, 37.5 kva, 0.8 pf, 108 amp, 4 wire DC: 28v, 500 amp, 14 kw
MD–3	AC: 115/208v, 400 cycle, 3 phase, 60 kva, 0.75 pf, 4 wire DC: 28v, 1500 amp, 45 kw, split bus
MD–3A	AC: 115/208v, 400 cycle, 3 phase, 60 kva, 0.75 pf, 4 wire DC: 28v, 1500 amp, 45 kw, split bus
MD–3M	AC: 115/208v, 400 cycle, 3 phase, 60 kva, 0.75 pf, 4 wire DC: 28v, 500 amp, 15 kw
MD–4	AC: 120/208v, 400 cycle, 3 phase, 62.5 kva, 0.8 pf, 175 amp, "WYE" neutral ground, 4 wire, 120v, 400 cycle, 3 phase, 62.5 kva, 0.8 pf, 303 amp, "DELTA" 3 wire, 120v, 400 cycle, 1 phase, 62.5 kva, 0.8 pf, 520 amp, 2 wire

LEGEND 10.—Airport/Facility Directory.

AIRPORT/FACILITY DIRECTORY LEGEND

AIR STARTING UNITS

AM32-95	150 +/- 5 lb/min (2055 +/- 68 cfm) at 51 +/- 2 psia
AM32A-95	150 +/- 5 lb/min @ 49 +/- 2 psia (35 +/- 2 psig)
LASS	150 +/- 5 lb/min @ 49 +/- 2 psia
MA-1A	82 lb/min (1123 cfm) at 130° air inlet temp, 45 psia (min) air outlet press
MC-1	15 cfm, 3500 psia
MC-1A	15 cfm, 3500 psia
MC-2A	15 cfm, 200 psia
MC-11	8,000 cu in cap, 4000 psig, 15 cfm

COMBINED AIR AND ELECTRICAL STARTING UNITS:

AGPU	AC: 115/200v, 400 cycle, 3 phase, 30 kw gen DC: 28v, 700 amp AIR: 60 lb/min @ 40 psig @ sea level
AM32A-60*	AIR: 120 +/- 4 lb/min (1644 +/- 55 cfm) at 49 +/- 2 psia AC: 120/208v, 400 cycle, 3 phase, 75 kva, 0.75 pf, 4 wire, 120v, 1 phase, 25 kva DC: 28v, 500 amp, 15 kw
AM32A-60A	AIR: 150 +/- 5 lb/min (2055 +/- 68 cfm at 51 +/- psia AC: 120/208v, 400 cycle, 3 phase, 75 kva, 0.75 pf, 4 wire DC: 28v, 200 amp, 5.6 kw
AM32A-60B*	AIR: 130 lb/min, 50 psia AC: 120/208v, 400 cycle, 3 phase, 75 kva, 0.75 pf, 4 wire DC: 28v, 200 amp, 5.6 kw

*NOTE: During combined air and electrical loads, the pneumatic circuitry takes preference and will limit the amount of electrical power available.

USN JASU

ELECTRICAL STARTING UNITS:

NC-8A/A1	DC: 500 amp constant, 750 amp intermittent, 28v; AC: 60 kva @ .8 pf, 115/200v, 3 phase, 400 Hz.
NC-10A/A1/B/C	DC: 750 amp constant, 1000 amp intermittent, 28v; AC: 90 kva, 115/200v, 3 phase, 400 Hz.

AIR STARTING UNITS:

GTC-85/GTE-85	120 lbs/min @ 45 psi.
MSU-200NAV/A/U47A-5	204 lbs/min @ 56 psia.
WELLS AIR START SYSTEM	180 lbs/min @ 75 psi or 120 lbs/min @ 45 psi. Simultaneous multiple start capability.

COMBINED AIR AND ELECTRICAL STARTING UNITS:

NCPP-105/RCPT	180 lbs/min @ 75 psi or 120 lbs/min @ 45 psi. 700 amp, 28v DC. 120/208v, 400 Hz AC, 30 kva.

ARMY JASU

59B2-1B	28v, 7.5 kw, 280 amp.

OTHER JASU

ELECTRICAL STARTING UNITS (DND):

CE12	AC 115/200v, 140 kva, 400 Hz, 3 phase
CE13	AC 115/200v, 60 kva, 400 Hz, 3 phase
CE14	AC/DC 115/200v, 140 kva, 400 Hz, 3 phase, 28vDC, 1500 amp
CE15	DC 22-35v, 500 amp continuous 1100 amp intermittent
CE16	DC 22-35v, 500 amp continuous 1100 amp intermittent soft start

AIR STARTING UNITS (DND):

CA2	ASA 45.5 psig, 116.4 lb/min

COMBINED AIR AND ELECTRICAL STARTING UNITS (DND)

CEA1	AC 120/208v, 60 kva, 400 Hz, 3 phase DC 28v, 75 amp AIR 112.5 lb/min, 47 psig

ELECTRICAL STARTING UNITS (OTHER)

C-26	28v 45kw 115-200v 15kw 380-800 Hz 1 phase 2 wire
C-26-B, C-26-C	28v 45kw: Split Bus: 115-200v 15kw 380-800 Hz 1 phase 2 wire
E3	DC 28v/10kw

AIR STARTING UNITS (OTHER):

A4	40 psi/2 lb/sec (LPAS Mk12, Mk12L, Mk12A, Mk1, Mk2B)
MA-1	150 Air HP, 115 lb/min 50 psia
MA-2	250 Air HP, 150 lb/min 75 psia

CARTRIDGE:

MXU-4A	USAF

Legend 11.—Airport/Facility Directory.

AIRPORT/FACILITY DIRECTORY LEGEND

FUEL—MILITARY

Fuel available through US Military Base supply, DESC Into–Plane Contracts and/or reciprocal agreement is listed first and is followed by (Mil). At commercial airports where Into–Plane contracts are in place, the name of the refueling agent is shown. Military fuel should be used first if it is available. When military fuel cannot be obtained but Into–Plane contract fuel is available, Government aircraft must refuel with the contract fuel and applicable refueling agent to avoid any breach in contract terms and conditions. Fuel not available through the above is shown preceded by NC (no contract). When fuel is obtained from NC sources, local purchase procedures must be followed. The US Military Aircraft Identaplates DD Form 1896 (Jet Fuel), DD Form 1897 (Avgas) and AF Form 1245 (Avgas) are used at military installations only. The US Government Aviation Into–Plane Reimbursement (AIR) Card (currently issued by AVCARD) is the instrument to be used to obtain fuel under a DESC Into–Plane Contract and for NC purchases if the refueling agent at the commercial airport accepts the AVCARD. A current list of contract fuel locations is available online at https://cis.energy.dla.mil/ip_cis/. See legend item 14 for fuel code and description.

SUPPORTING FLUIDS AND SYSTEMS—MILITARY

CODE	
ADI	Anti–Detonation Injection Fluid—Reciprocating Engine Aircraft.
W	Water Thrust Augmentation—Jet Aircraft.
WAI	Water–Alcohol Injection Type, Thrust Augmentation—Jet Aircraft.
SP	Single Point Refueling.
PRESAIR	Air Compressors rated 3,000 PSI or more.
De–Ice	Anti–icing/De–icing/Defrosting Fluid (MIL–A–8243).

OXYGEN:

LPOX	Low pressure oxygen servicing.
HPOX	High pressure oxygen servicing.
LHOX	Low and high pressure oxygen servicing.
LOX	Liquid oxygen servicing.
OXRB	Oxygen replacement bottles. (Maintained primarily at Naval stations for use in acft where oxygen can be replenished only by replacement of cylinders.)
OX	Indicates oxygen servicing when type of servicing is unknown.

NOTE: Combinations of above items is used to indicate complete oxygen servicing available;

LHOXRB	Low and high pressure oxygen servicing and replacement bottles;
LPOXRB	Low pressure oxygen replacement bottles only, etc.

NOTE: Aircraft will be serviced with oxygen procured under military specifications only. Aircraft will not be serviced with medical oxygen.

NITROGEN:

LPNIT — Low pressure nitrogen servicing.
HPNIT — High pressure nitrogen servicing.
LHNIT — Low and high pressure nitrogen servicing.

OIL—MILITARY

US AVIATION OILS (MIL SPECS):

CODE	GRADE, TYPE
O–113	1065, Reciprocating Engine Oil (MIL–L–6082)
O–117	1100, Reciprocating Engine Oil (MIL–L–6082)
O–117+	1100, O–117 plus cyclohexanone (MIL–L–6082)
O–123	1065, (Dispersant), Reciprocating Engine Oil (MIL–L–22851 Type III)
O–128	1100, (Dispersant), Reciprocating Engine Oil (MIL–L–22851 Type II)
O–132	1005, Jet Engine Oil (MIL–L–6081)
O–133	1010, Jet Engine Oil (MIL–L–6081)
O–147	None, MIL–L–6085A Lubricating Oil, Instrument, Synthetic
O–148	None, MIL–L–7808 (Synthetic Base) Turbine Engine Oil
O–149	None, Aircraft Turbine Engine Synthetic, 7.5c St
O–155	None, MIL–L–6086C, Aircraft, Medium Grade
O–156	None, MIL–L–23699 (Synthetic Base), Turboprop and Turboshaft Engines
JOAP/SOAP	Joint Oil Analysis Program. JOAP support is furnished during normal duty hours, other times on request. (JOAP and SOAP programs provide essentially the same service, JOAP is now the standard joint service supported program.)

TRANSIENT ALERT (TRAN ALERT)—MILITARY

Tran Alert service is considered to include all services required for normal aircraft turn–around, e.g., servicing (fuel, oil, oxygen, etc.), debriefing to determine requirements for maintenance, minor maintenance, inspection and parking assistance of transient aircraft. Drag chute repack, specialized maintenance, or extensive repairs will be provided within the capabilities and priorities of the base. Delays can be anticipated after normal duty hours/holidays/weekends regardless of the hours of transient maintenance operation. Pilots should not expect aircraft to be serviced for TURN–AROUNDS during time periods when servicing or maintenance manpower is not available. In the case of airports not operated exclusively by US military, the servicing indicated by the remarks will not always be available for US military aircraft. When transient alert services are not shown, facilities are unknown. NO PRIORITY BASIS—means that transient alert services will be provided only after all the requirements for mission/tactical assigned aircraft have been accomplished.

LEGEND 12.—Airport/Facility Directory.

AIRPORT/FACILITY DIRECTORY LEGEND 23

㉓ AIRPORT REMARKS

The Attendance Schedule is the months, days and hours the airport is actually attended. Airport attendance does not mean watchman duties or telephone accessibility, but rather an attendant or operator on duty to provide at least minimum services (e.g., repairs, fuel, transportation).

Airport Remarks have been grouped in order of applicability. Airport remarks are limited to those items of information that are determined essential for operational use, i.e., conditions of a permanent or indefinite nature and conditions that will remain in effect for more than 30 days concerning aeronautical facilities, services, maintenance available, procedures or hazards, knowledge of which is essential for safe and efficient operation of aircraft. Information concerning permanent closing of a runway or taxiway will not be shown. A note "See Special Notices" shall be applied within this remarks section when a special notice applicable to the entry is contained in the Special Notices section of this publication.

Parachute Jumping indicates parachute jumping areas associated with the airport. See Parachute Jumping Area section of this publication for additional Information.

Landing Fee indicates landing charges for private or non–revenue producing aircraft. In addition, fees may be charged for planes that remain over a couple of hours and buy no services, or at major airline terminals for all aircraft.

Note: Unless otherwise stated, remarks including runway ends refer to the runway's approach end.

㉔ MILITARY REMARKS

Joint Civil/Military airports contain both Airport Remarks and Military Remarks. Military Remarks published for these airports are applicable only to the military. Military and joint Military/Civil airports contain only Military Remarks. Remarks contained in this section may not be applicable to civil users. When both sets of remarks exist, the first set is applicable to the primary operator of the airport. Remarks applicable to a tenant on the airport are shown preceded by the tenant organization, i.e., (A) (AF) (N) (ANG), etc. Military airports operate 24 hours unless otherwise specified. Airport operating hours are listed first (airport operating hours will only be listed if they are different than the airport attended hours or if the attended hours are unavailable) followed by pertinent remarks in order of applicability. Remarks will include information on restrictions, hazards, traffic pattern, noise abatement, customs/agriculture/immigration, and miscellaneous information applicable to the Military.

Type of restrictions:

CLOSED: When designated closed, the airport is restricted from use by all aircraft unless stated otherwise. Any closure applying to specific type of aircraft or operation will be so stated. USN/USMC/USAF airports are considered closed during non–operating hours. Closed airports may be utilized during an emergency provided there is a safe landing area.

OFFICIAL BUSINESS ONLY: The airfield is closed to all transient military aircraft for obtaining routine services such as fueling, passenger drop off or pickup, practice approaches, parking, etc. The airfield may be used by aircrews and aircraft if official government business (including civilian) must be conducted on or near the airfield and prior permission is received from the airfield manager.

AF OFFICIAL BUSINESS ONLY OR NAVY OFFICIAL BUSINESS ONLY: Indicates that the restriction applies only to service indicated.

PRIOR PERMISSION REQUIRED (PPR): Airport is closed to transient aircraft unless approval for operation is obtained from the appropriate commander through Chief, Airfield Management or Airfield Operations Officer. Official Business or PPR does not preclude the use of US Military airports as an alternate for IFR flights. If a non–US military airport is used as a weather alternate and requires a PPR, the PPR must be requested and confirmed before the flight departs. The purpose of PPR is to control volume and flow of traffic rather than to prohibit it. Prior permission is required for all aircraft requiring transient alert service outside the published transient alert duty hours. All aircraft carrying hazardous materials must obtain prior permission as outlined in AFJI 11–204, AR 95–27, OPNAVINST 3710.7.

Note: OFFICIAL BUSINESS ONLY AND PPR restrictions are not applicable to Special Air Mission (SAM) or Special Air Resource (SPAR) aircraft providing person or persons on aboard are designated Code 6 or higher as explained in AFJMAN 11–213, AR 95–11, OPNAVINST 3722–8J. Official Business Only or PPR do not preclude the use of the airport as an alternate for IFR flights.

㉕ AIRPORT MANAGER

The phone number of the airport manager.

㉖ WEATHER DATA SOURCES

Weather data sources will be listed alphabetically followed by their assigned frequencies and/or telephone number and hours of operation.

ASOS—Automated Surface Observing System. Reports the same as an AWOS–3 plus precipitation identification and intensity, and freezing rain occurrence;

AWOS—Automated Weather Observing System

AWOS–A—reports altimeter setting (all other information is advisory only).

AWOS–AV—reports altimeter and visibility.

AWOS–1—reports altimeter setting, wind data and usually temperature, dew point and density altitude.

AWOS–2—reports the same as AWOS–1 plus visibility.

AWOS–3—reports the same as AWOS–1 plus visibility and cloud/ceiling data.

AWOS–3P reports the same as the AWOS–3 system, plus a precipitation identification sensor.

AWOS–3PT reports the same as the AWOS–3 system, plus precipitation identification sensor and a thunderstorm/lightning reporting capability.

LEGEND 13.—Airport/Facility Directory.

AIRPORT/FACILITY DIRECTORY LEGEND

AWOS–3T reports the same as AWOS–3 system and includes a thunderstorm/lightning reporting capability.

See AIM, Basic Flight Information and ATC Procedures for detailed description of Weather Data Sources.

AWOS–4—reports same as AWOS–3 system, plus precipitation occurrence, type and accumulation, freezing rain, thunderstorm and runway surface sensors.

HIWAS—See RADIO AIDS TO NAVIGATION

LAWRS—Limited Aviation Weather Reporting Station where observers report cloud height, weather, obstructions to vision, temperature and dewpoint (in most cases), surface wind, altimeter and pertinent remarks.

LLWAS—indicates a Low Level Wind Shear Alert System consisting of a center field and several field perimeter anemometers.

SAWRS—identifies airports that have a Supplemental Aviation Weather Reporting Station available to pilots for current weather information.

SWSL—Supplemental Weather Service Location providing current local weather information via radio and telephone.

TDWR—indicates airports that have Terminal Doppler Weather Radar.

WSP—indicates airports that have Weather System Processor.

When the automated weather source is broadcast over an associated airport NAVAID frequency (see NAVAID line), it shall be indicated by a bold ASOS, AWOS, or HIWAS followed by the frequency, identifier and phone number, if available.

(27) COMMUNICATIONS

Airport terminal control facilities and radio communications associated with the airport shall be shown. When the call sign is not the same as the airport name the call sign will be shown. Frequencies shall normally be shown in descending order with the primary frequency listed first. Frequencies will be listed, together with sectorization indicated by outbound radials, and hours of operation. Communications will be listed in sequence as follows:

Single Frequency Approach (SFA), Common Traffic Advisory Frequency (CTAF), Aeronautical Advisory Stations (UNICOM) or (AUNICOM), and Automatic Terminal Information Service (ATIS) along with their frequency is shown, where available, on the line following the heading "COMMUNICATIONS." When the CTAF and UNICOM frequencies are the same, the frequency will be shown as CTAF/UNICOM 122.8.

The FSS telephone nationwide is toll free 1–800–WX–BRIEF (1–800–992–7433). When the FSS is located on the field it will be indicated as "on arpt". Frequencies available at the FSS will follow in descending order. Remote Communications Outlet (RCO) providing service to the airport followed by the frequency and FSS RADIO name will be shown when available. FSS's provide information on airport conditions, radio aids and other facilities, and process flight plans. Airport Advisory Service (AAS) is provided on the CTAF by FSS's for select non–tower airports or airports where the tower is not in operation.

(See AIM, Para 4–1–9 Traffic Advisory Practices at Airports Without Operating Control Towers or AC 90–42C.)

Aviation weather briefing service is provided by FSS specialists. Flight and weather briefing services are also available by calling the telephone numbers listed.

Remote Communications Outlet (RCO)—An unmanned air/ground communications facility that is remotely controlled and provides UHF or VHF communications capability to extend the service range of an FSS.

Civil Communications Frequencies–Civil communications frequencies used in the FSS air/ground system are operated on 122.0, 122.2, 123.6; emergency 121.5; plus receive–only on 122.1.

a. 122.0 is assigned as the Enroute Flight Advisory Service frequency at selected FSS RADIO outlets.
b. 122.2 is assigned as a common enroute frequency.
c. 123.6 is assigned as the airport advisory frequency at select non–tower locations. At airports with a tower, FSS may provide airport advisories on the tower frequency when tower is closed.
d. 122.1 is the primary receive–only frequency at VOR's.
e. Some FSS's are assigned 50 kHz frequencies in the 122–126 MHz band (eg. 122.45). Pilots using the FSS A/G system should refer to this directory or appropriate charts to determine frequencies available at the FSS or remoted facility through which they wish to communicate.

Emergency frequency 121.5 and 243.0 are available at all Flight Service Stations, most Towers, Approach Control and RADAR facilities.

Frequencies published followed by the letter "T" or "R", indicate that the facility will only transmit or receive respectively on that frequency. All radio aids to navigation (NAVAID) frequencies are transmit only.

TERMINAL SERVICES

SFA—Single Frequency Approach.

CTAF—A program designed to get all vehicles and aircraft at airports without an operating control tower on a common frequency.

ATIS—A continuous broadcast of recorded non–control information in selected terminal areas.

D–ATIS—Digital ATIS provides ATIS information in text form outside the standard reception range of conventional ATIS via landline & data link communications and voice message within range of existing transmitters.

AUNICOM—Automated UNICOM is a computerized, command response system that provides automated weather, radio check capability and airport advisory information selected from an automated menu by microphone clicks.

UNICOM—A non–government air/ground radio communications facility which may provide airport information.

PTD—Pilot to Dispatcher.

APP CON—Approach Control. The symbol ® indicates radar approach control.

TOWER—Control tower.

GCA—Ground Control Approach System.

GND CON—Ground Control.

Legend 14.—Airport/Facility Directory.

AIRPORT/FACILITY DIRECTORY LEGEND

GCO—Ground Communication Outlet—An unstaffed, remotely controlled, ground/ground communications facility. Pilots at uncontrolled airports may contact ATC and FSS via VHF to a telephone connection to obtain an instrument clearance or close a VFR or IFR flight plan. They may also get an updated weather briefing prior to takeoff. Pilots will use four "key clicks" on the VHF radio to contact the appropriate ATC facility or six "key clicks" to contact the FSS. The GCO system is intended to be used only on the ground.

DEP CON—Departure Control. The symbol Ⓡ indicates radar departure control.

CLNC DEL—Clearance Delivery.

CPDLC—Controller Pilot Data Link Communication. FANS ATC data communication capability from the aircraft to the ATC Data Link system.

PRE TAXI CLNC—Pre taxi clearance.

VFR ADVSY SVC—VFR Advisory Service. Service provided by Non–Radar Approach Control.
Advisory Service for VFR aircraft (upon a workload basis) ctc APP CON.

COMD POST—Command Post followed by the operator call sign in parenthesis.

PMSV—Pilot–to–Metro Service call sign, frequency and hours of operation, when full service is other than continuous. PMSV installations at which weather observation service is available shall be indicated, following the frequency and/or hours of operation as "Wx obsn svc 1900–0000Z‡" or "other times" may be used when no specific time is given. PMSV facilities manned by forecasters are considered "Full Service". PMSV facilities manned by weather observers are listed as "Limited Service".

OPS—Operations followed by the operator call sign in parenthesis.

CON

RANGE

FLT FLW—Flight Following

MEDIVAC

NOTE: Communication frequencies followed by the letter "X" indicate frequency available on request.

㉘ AIRSPACE

Information concerning Class B, C, and part–time D and E surface area airspace shall be published with effective times, if available.

CLASS B—Radar Sequencing and Separation Service for all aircraft in CLASS B airspace.

CLASS C—Separation between IFR and VFR aircraft and sequencing of VFR arrivals to the primary airport.

TRSA—Radar Sequencing and Separation Service for participating VFR Aircraft within a Terminal Radar Service Area.

Class C, D, and E airspace described in this publication is that airspace usually consisting of a 5 NM radius core surface area that begins at the surface and extends upward to an altitude above the airport elevation (charted in MSL for Class C and Class D). Class E surface airspace normally extends from the surface up to but not including the overlying controlled airspace.

When part–time Class C or Class D airspace defaults to Class E, the core surface area becomes Class E. This will be formatted as:
AIRSPACE: CLASS C svc "times" ctc **APP CON** other times CLASS E:
or
AIRSPACE: CLASS D svc "times" other times CLASS E.

When a part–time Class C, Class D or Class E surface area defaults to Class G, the core surface area becomes Class G up to, but not including, the overlying controlled airspace. Normally, the overlying controlled airspace is Class E airspace beginning at either 700′ or 1200′ AGL and may be determined by consulting the relevant VFR Sectional or Terminal Area Charts. This will be formatted as:
AIRSPACE: CLASS C svc "times" ctc **APP CON** other times CLASS G, with CLASS E 700′ (or 1200′) AGL & abv:
or
AIRSPACE: CLASS D svc "times" other times CLASS G with CLASS E 700′ (or 1200′) AGL & abv:
or
AIRSPACE: CLASS E svc "times" other times CLASS G with CLASS E 700′ (or 1200′) AGL & abv.

NOTE: AIRSPACE SVC "TIMES" INCLUDE ALL ASSOCIATED ARRIVAL EXTENSIONS. Surface area arrival extensions for instrument approach procedures become part of the primary core surface area. These extensions may be either Class D or Class E airspace and are effective concurrent with the times of the primary core surface area. For example, when a part–time Class C, Class D or Class E surface area defaults to Class G, the associated arrival extensions will default to Class G at the same time. When a part–time Class C or Class D surface area defaults to Class E, the arrival extensions will remain in effect as Class E airspace.

NOTE: CLASS E AIRSPACE EXTENDING UPWARD FROM 700 FEET OR MORE ABOVE THE SURFACE, DESIGNATED IN CONJUNCTION WITH AN AIRPORT WITH AN APPROVED INSTRUMENT PROCEDURE.
Class E 700′ AGL (shown as magenta vignette on sectional charts) and 1200′ AGL (blue vignette) areas are designated when necessary to provide controlled airspace for transitioning to/from the terminal and enroute environments. Unless otherwise specified, these 700′/1200′ AGL Class E airspace areas remain in effect continuously, regardless of airport operating hours or surface area status. These transition areas should not be confused with surface areas or arrival extensions.

(See Chapter 3, AIRSPACE, in the Aeronautical Information Manual for further details)

LEGEND 15.—Airport/Facility Directory.

AIRPORT/FACILITY DIRECTORY LEGEND

(29) VOR TEST FACILITY (VOT)

The VOT transmits a signal which provided users a convenient means to determine the operational status and accuracy of an aircraft VOR receiver while on the ground. Ground based VOTs and the associated frequency shall be shown when available. VOTs are also shown with identifier, frequency and referenced remarks in the VOR Receiver Check section in the back of this publication.

(30) RADIO AIDS TO NAVIGATION

The Airport/Facility Directory section of the Chart Supplement lists, by facility name, all Radio Aids to Navigation that appear on FAA, Aeronautical Information Services Visual or IFR Aeronautical Charts and those upon which the FAA has approved an Instrument Approach Procedure, with exception of selected TACANs. All VOR, VORTAC, TACAN and ILS equipment in the National Airspace System has an automatic monitoring and shutdown feature in the event of malfunction. Unmonitored, as used in this publication, for any navigational aid, means that monitoring personnel cannot observe the malfunction or shutdown signal. The NAVAID NOTAM file identifier will be shown as "NOTAM FILE IAD" and will be listed on the Radio Aids to Navigation line. When two or more NAVAIDS are listed and the NOTAM file identifier is different from that shown on the Radio Aids to Navigation line, it will be shown with the NAVAID listing. NOTAM file identifiers for ILSs and its components (e.g., NDB (LOM) are the same as the associated airports and are not repeated. Automated Surface Observing System (ASOS), Automated Weather Observing System (AWOS), and Hazardous Inflight Weather Advisory Service (HIWAS) will be shown when this service is broadcast over selected NAVAIDs.

NAVAID information is tabulated as indicated in the following sample:

TACAN/DME Channel   Geographical Position   Site Elevation   Magnetic Variation

NAME (L) ABVORTAC 117.55 ABE Chan 122(Y) N40°43.60' W75°27.30' 180° 4.1 NM to fld. 1110/8E **AWOS. HIWAS.**

Class   Frequency   Identifier   Bearing and distance facility to center of airport   Automated Weather Observing System   Hazardous Inflight Weather Service

VOR unusable 020°–060° byd 26 NM blo 3,500'

Restriction within the normal altitude/range of the navigational aid (See primary alphabetical listing for restrictions on VORTAC and VOR/DME).

Note: Those DME channel numbers with a (Y) suffix require TACAN to be placed in the "Y" mode to receive distance information.

HIWAS—Hazardous Inflight Weather Advisory Service is a continuous broadcast of inflight weather advisories including summarized SIGMETs, convective SIGMETs, AIRMETs and urgent PIREPs. HIWAS is presently broadcast over selected VOR's throughout the U.S.

ASR/PAR—Indicates that Surveillance (ASR) or Precision (PAR) radar instrument approach minimums are published in the U.S. Terminal Procedures. Only part–time hours of operation will be shown.

LEGEND 16.—Airport/Facility Directory.

AIRPORT/FACILITY DIRECTORY LEGEND

RADIO CLASS DESIGNATIONS

VOR/DME/TACAN Standard Service Volume (SSV) Classifications

SSV Class	Altitudes	Distance (NM)
(T) Terminal	1000′ to 12,000′	25
(L) Low Altitude	1000′ to 18,000′	40
(H) High Altitude	1000′ to 14,500′	40
	14,500′ to 18,000′	100
	18,000′ to 45,000′	130
	45,000′ to 60,000′	100

NOTE: Additionally, (H) facilities provide (L) and (T) service volume and (L) facilities provide (T) service. Altitudes are with respect to the station's site elevation. Coverage is not available in a cone of airspace directly above the facility.

The term VOR is, operationally, a general term covering the VHF omnidirectional bearing type of facility without regard to the fact that the power, the frequency protected service volume, the equipment configuration, and operational requirements may vary between facilities at different locations.

AB	Automatic Weather Broadcast.
DF	Direction Finding Service.
DME	UHF standard (TACAN compatible) distance measuring equipment.
DME(Y)	UHF standard (TACAN compatible) distance measuring equipment that require TACAN to be placed in the "Y" mode to receive DME.
GS	Glide slope.
H	Non–directional radio beacon (homing), power 50 watts to less than 2,000 watts (50 NM at all altitudes).
HH	Non–directional radio beacon (homing), power 2,000 watts or more (75 NM at all altitudes).
H–SAB	Non–directional radio beacons providing automatic transcribed weather service.
ILS	Instrument Landing System (voice, where available, on localizer channel).
IM	Inner marker.
LDA	Localizer Directional Aid.
LMM	Compass locator station when installed at middle marker site (15 NM at all altitudes).
LOM	Compass locator station when installed at outer marker site (15 NM at all altitudes).
MH	Non–directional radio beacon (homing) power less than 50 watts (25 NM at all altitudes).
MM	Middle marker.
OM	Outer marker.
S	Simultaneous range homing signal and/or voice.
SABH	Non–directional radio beacon not authorized for IFR or ATC. Provides automatic weather broadcasts.
SDF	Simplified Direction Facility.
TACAN	UHF navigational facility–omnidirectional course and distance information.
VOR	VHF navigational facility–omnidirectional course only.
VOR/DME	Collocated VOR navigational facility and UHF standard distance measuring equipment.
VORTAC	Collocated VOR and TACAN navigational facilities.
W	Without voice on radio facility frequency.
Z	VHF station location marker at a LF radio facility.

LEGEND 17.—Airport/Facility Directory.

AIRPORT/FACILITY DIRECTORY LEGEND

ILS FACILITY PEFORMANCE CLASSIFICATION CODES

Codes define the ability of an ILS to support autoland operations. The two portions of the code represent Official Category and farthest point along a Category I, II, or III approach that the Localizer meets Category III structure tolerances.

Official Category: I, II, or III; the lowest minima on published or unpublished procedures supported by the ILS.

Farthest point of satisfactory Category III Localizer performance for Category I, II, or III approaches: A – 4 NM prior to runway threshold, B – 3500 ft prior to runway threshold, C – glide angle dependent but generally 750–1000 ft prior to threshold, T – runway threshold, D – 3000 ft after runway threshold, and E – 2000 ft prior to stop end of runway.

ILS information is tabulated as indicated in the following sample:

ILS/DME 108.5 I–ORL Chan 22 Rwy 18. Class IIE. LOM HERNY NDB.

ILS Facility Performance Classification Code (arrow pointing to "Class IIE")

FREQUENCY PAIRING TABLE

VHF FREQUENCY	TACAN CHANNEL	VHF FREQUENCY	TACAN CHANNEL	VHF FREQUENCY	TACAN CHANNEL	VHF FREQUENCY	TACAN CHANNEL
108.10	18X	108.55	22Y	111.05	47Y	114.85	95Y
108.30	20X	108.65	23Y	111.15	48Y	114.95	96Y
108.50	22X	108.75	24Y	111.25	49Y	115.05	97Y
108.70	24X	108.85	25Y	111.35	50Y	115.15	98Y
108.90	26X	108.95	26Y	111.45	51Y	115.25	99Y
109.10	28X	109.05	27Y	111.55	52Y	115.35	100Y
109.30	30X	109.15	28Y	111.65	53Y	115.45	101Y
109.50	32X	109.25	29Y	111.75	54Y	115.55	102Y
109.70	34X	109.35	30Y	111.85	55Y	115.65	103Y
109.90	36X	109.45	31Y	111.95	56Y	115.75	104Y
110.10	38X	109.55	32Y	113.35	80Y	115.85	105Y
110.30	40X	109.65	33Y	113.45	81Y	115.95	106Y
110.50	42X	109.75	34Y	113.55	82Y	116.05	107Y
110.70	44X	109.85	35Y	113.65	83Y	116.15	108Y
110.90	46X	109.95	36Y	113.75	84Y	116.25	109Y
111.10	48X	110.05	37Y	113.85	85Y	116.35	110Y
111.30	50X	110.15	38Y	113.95	86Y	116.45	111Y
111.50	52X	110.25	39Y	114.05	87Y	116.55	112Y
111.70	54X	110.35	40Y	114.15	88Y	116.65	113Y
111.90	56X	110.45	41Y	114.25	89Y	116.75	114Y
108.05	17Y	110.55	42Y	114.35	90Y	116.85	115Y
108.15	18Y	110.65	43Y	114.45	91Y	116.95	116Y
108.25	19Y	110.75	44Y	114.55	92Y	117.05	117Y
108.35	20Y	110.85	45Y	114.65	93Y	117.15	118Y
108.45	21Y	110.95	46Y	114.75	94Y	117.25	119Y

FREQUENCY PAIRING TABLE

The following is a list of paired VOR/ILS VHF frequencies with TACAN channels.

TACAN CHANNEL	VHF FREQUENCY	TACAN CHANNEL	VHF FREQUENCY	TACAN CHANNEL	VHF FREQUENCY	TACAN CHANNEL	VHF FREQUENCY
2X	134.5	25X	108.80	36X	109.90	47X	111.00
2Y	134.55	25Y	108.85	36Y	109.95	47Y	111.05
11X	135.4	26X	108.90	37X	110.00	48X	111.10
11Y	135.45	26Y	108.95	37Y	110.05	48Y	111.15
12X	135.5	27X	109.00	38X	110.10	49X	111.20
12Y	135.55	27Y	109.05	38Y	110.15	49Y	111.25
17X	108.00	28X	109.10	39X	110.20	50X	111.30
17Y	108.05	28Y	109.15	39Y	110.25	50Y	111.35
18X	108.10	29X	109.20	40X	110.30	51X	111.40
18Y	108.15	29Y	109.25	40Y	110.35	51Y	111.45
19X	108.20	30X	109.30	41X	110.40	52X	111.50
19Y	108.25	30Y	109.35	41Y	110.45	52Y	111.55
20X	108.30	31X	109.40	42X	110.50	53X	111.60
20Y	108.35	31Y	109.45	42Y	110.55	53Y	111.65
21X	108.40	32X	109.50	43X	110.60	54X	111.70
21Y	108.45	32Y	109.55	43Y	110.65	54Y	111.75
22X	108.50	33X	109.60	44X	110.70	55X	111.80
22Y	108.55	33Y	109.65	44Y	110.75	55Y	111.85
23X	108.60	34X	109.70	45X	110.80	56X	111.90
23Y	108.65	34Y	109.75	45Y	110.85	56Y	111.95
24X	108.70	35X	109.80	46X	110.90	57X	112.00
24Y	108.75	35Y	109.85	46Y	110.95	57Y	112.05

LEGEND 18.—Airport/Facility Directory.

AIRPORT/FACILITY DIRECTORY LEGEND

TACAN CHANNEL	VHF FREQUENCY	TACAN CHANNEL	VHF FREQUENCY	TACAN CHANNEL	VHF FREQUENCY	TACAN CHANNEL	VHF FREQUENCY
58X	112.10	77X	113.00	96X	114.90	115X	116.80
58Y	112.15	77Y	113.05	96Y	114.95	115Y	116.85
59X	112.20	78X	113.10	97X	115.00	116X	116.90
59Y	112.25	78Y	113.15	97Y	115.05	116Y	116.95
60X	133.30	79X	113.20	98X	115.10	117X	117.00
60Y	133.35	79Y	113.25	98Y	115.15	117Y	117.05
61X	133.40	80X	113.30	99X	115.20	118X	117.10
61Y	133.45	80Y	113.35	99Y	115.25	118Y	117.15
62X	133.50	81X	113.40	100X	115.30	119X	117.20
62Y	133.55	81Y	113.45	100Y	115.35	119Y	117.25
63X	133.60	82X	113.50	101X	115.40	120X	117.30
63Y	133.65	82Y	113.55	101Y	115.45	120Y	117.35
64X	133.70	83X	113.60	102X	115.50	121X	117.40
64Y	133.75	83Y	113.65	102Y	115.55	121Y	117.45
65X	133.80	84X	113.70	103X	115.60	122X	117.50
65Y	133.85	84Y	113.75	103Y	115.65	122Y	117.55
66X	133.90	85X	113.80	104X	115.70	123X	117.60
66Y	133.95	85Y	113.85	104Y	115.75	123Y	117.65
67X	134.00	86X	113.90	105X	115.80	124X	117.70
67Y	134.05	86Y	113.95	105Y	115.85	124Y	117.75
68X	134.10	87X	114.00	106X	115.90	125X	117.80
68Y	134.15	87Y	114.05	106Y	115.95	125Y	117.85
69X	134.20	88X	114.10	107X	116.00	126X	117.90
69Y	134.25	88Y	114.15	107Y	116.05	126Y	117.95
70X	112.30	89X	114.20	108X	116.10		
70Y	112.35	89Y	114.25	108Y	116.15		
71X	112.40	90X	114.30	109X	116.20		
71Y	112.45	90Y	114.35	109Y	116.25		
72X	112.50	91X	114.40	110X	116.30		
72Y	112.55	91Y	114.45	110Y	116.35		
73X	112.60	92X	114.50	111X	116.40		
73Y	112.65	92Y	114.55	111Y	116.45		
74X	112.70	93X	114.60	112X	116.50		
74Y	112.75	93Y	114.65	112Y	116.55		
75X	112.80	94X	114.70	113X	116.60		
75Y	112.85	94Y	114.75	113Y	116.65		
76X	112.90	95X	114.80	114X	116.70		
76Y	112.95	95Y	114.85	114Y	116.75		

(31) **COMM/NAV/WEATHER REMARKS:** These remarks consist of pertinent information affecting the current status of communications, NAVAIDs and weather.

LEGEND 19.—Airport/Facility Directory.

12320

TERMS/LANDING MINIMA DATA

IFR LANDING MINIMA

The United States Standard for Terminal Instrument Procedures (TERPS) is the approved criteria for formulating instrument approach procedures. Landing minima are established for six aircraft approach categories (ABCDE and COPTER). In the absence of COPTER MINIMA, helicopters may use the CAT A minimums of other procedures.

LANDING MINIMA FORMAT

In this example airport elevation is 1179, and runway touchdown zone elevation is 1152.

DA — Visibility (RVR 100's of feet) — Aircraft Approach Category — HAT/HATh

CATEGORY	A	B	C	D
S-ILS 27	1352/24 200 (200-½)			
S-LOC 27	1440/24 288 (300-½)			1440/50 288 (300-1)
CIRCLING	1540-1 361 (400-1)	1640-1 461 (500-1)	1640-1½ 461 (500-1½)	1740-2 561 (600-2)

Straight-in ILS to Runway 27

Straight-in with Glide Slope Inoperative or not used to Runway 27

MDA — HAA — Visibility in Statute Miles

All **weather** minimums in parentheses not applicable to Civil Pilots. Military Pilots refer to appropriate regulations.

COPTER MINIMA ONLY

CATEGORY	COPTER
H-176°	680-½ 363 (400-½)

Copter Approach Direction — Height of MDA/DA Above Landing Area (HAL)

No circling minimums are provided

RNAV (GPS) MINIMA EXAMPLE

CATEGORY	A	B	C	D
LPV DA	1540/24 258 (300-½)			
LNAV/VNAV DA	1600/24 318 (400-½)			1600/40 318 (400-¾)
LNAV MDA	1840/24 558 (600-½)		1840/50 558 (600-1)	1840/60 558 (600-1¼)
CIRCLING	1840-1 545 (600-1)		1840-1½ 545 (600-1½)	1860-2 565 (600-2)

NOTE: The W symbol indicates outages of the WAAS vertical guidance may occur daily at this location due to initial system limitations. WAAS NOTAMS for vertical outages are not provided for this approach. Use LNAV minima for flight planning at these locations, whether as a destination or alternate. For flight operations at these locations, when the WAAS avionics indicate that LNAV/VNAV or LPV service is available, then vertical guidance may be used to complete the approach using the displayed level of service. Should an outage occur during the procedure, reversion to LNAV minima may be required. As the WAAS coverage is expanded, the W will be removed.

RNAV minimums are dependent on navigation equipment capability, as stated in the applicable AFM, AFMS, or other FAA approved document. See AIM paragraph 5-4-5, AC 90-105 and AC 90-107 for detailed requirements for each line of minima.

AIRCRAFT APPROACH CATEGORIES

Aircraft approach category indicates a grouping of aircraft based on a speed of VREF, if specified, or if VREF not specified, 1.3 VSO at the maximum certificated landing weight. VREF, VSO, and the maximum certificated landing weight are those values as established for the aircraft by the certification authority of the country of registry. Helicopters are Category A aircraft. An aircraft shall fit in only one category. However, if it is necessary to operate at a speed in excess of the upper limit of the speed range for an aircraft's category, the minimums for the category for that speed shall be used. For example, an airplane which fits into Category B, but is circling to land at a speed of 145 knots, shall use the approach Category D minimums. As an additional example, a Category A airplane (or helicopter) which is operating at 130 knots on a straight-in approach shall use the approach Category C minimums. See following category limits:

MANEUVERING TABLE

Approach Category	A	B	C	D	E
Speed (Knots)	0-90	91-120	121-140	141-165	Abv 165

TERMS/LANDING MINIMA DATA

Legend 20.—Instrument Approach Procedures Explanation of Terms.

13122

TERMS/LANDING MINIMA DATA

CIRCLING APPROACH OBSTACLE PROTECTED AIRSPACE

The circling MDA provides vertical clearance from obstacles when conducting a circle-to-land maneuver within the obstacle protected area. Circling approach obstacle protected areas extend laterally and longitudinally from the centerlines and ends of all runways at an airport by the distances shown in the following tables. The areas are technically defined by the tangential connection of arcs drawn at the radius distance shown from each runway end.

STANDARD CIRCLING APPROACH MANEUVERING RADIUS

Circling approach protected areas developed prior to late 2012 used the radius distances shown in the following table, expressed in nautical miles (NM), dependent on aircraft approach category. The approaches using standard circling approach areas can be identified by the absence of the C symbol on the circling line of minima.

Circling MDA in feet MSL	Approach Category and Circling Radius (NM)				
	CAT A	CAT B	CAT C	CAT D	CAT E
All Altitudes	1.3	1.5	1.7	2.3	4.5

C EXPANDED CIRCLING APPROACH MANEUVERING AIRSPACE RADIUS

Circling approach protected areas developed after late 2012 use the radius distance shown in the following table, expressed in nautical miles (NM), dependent on aircraft approach category, and the altitude of the circling MDA, which accounts for true airspeed increase with altitude. The approaches using expanded circling approach areas can be identified by the presence of the C symbol on the circling line of minima.

Circling MDA in feet MSL	Approach Category and Circling Radius (NM)				
	CAT A	CAT B	CAT C	CAT D	CAT E
1000 or less	1.3	1.7	2.7	3.6	4.5
1001-3000	1.3	1.8	2.8	3.7	4.6
3001-5000	1.3	1.8	2.9	3.8	4.8
5001-7000	1.3	1.9	3.0	4.0	5.0
7001-9000	1.4	2.0	3.2	4.2	5.3
9001 and above	1.4	2.1	3.3	4.4	5.5

Comparable Values of RVR and Visibility

The following table shall be used for converting RVR to ground or flight visibility. For converting RVR values that fall between listed values, use the next higher RVR value; do not interpolate. For example, when converting 1800 RVR, use 2400 RVR with the resultant visibility of ½ mile.

RVR (feet)	Visibility (statute miles)	RVR (feet)	Visibility (statute miles)
1600	¼	4500	⅞
2400	½	5000	1
3200	⅝	6000	1¼
4000	¾		

RADAR MINIMA

	RWY	GS/TCH/RPI	CAT	DA/ MDA-VIS	HAT/ HATh/ HAA	CEIL-VIS	CAT	DA/ MDA-VIS	HAT/ HATh/ HAA	CEIL-VIS
PAR	10	2.5°/42/1000	ABCDE	**195**/16	100	(100-¼)				
	28	2.5°/48/1068	ABCDE	**187**/16	100	(100-¼)				
ASR	10		ABC	**560**/40	463	(500-¾)	DE	**560**/50	463	(500-1)
	28		AB	**600**/50	513	(600-1)	CDE	**600**/60	513	(600-1¼)
CIR	10		AB	**560**-1¼	463	(500-1¼)	CDE	**560**-1½	463	(500-1½)
	28		AB	**600**-1¼	503	(600-1¼)	CDE	**600**-1½	503	(600-1½)

Visibility (RVR 100's of feet)

Visibility in Statute Miles

All minimums in parentheses not applicable to Civil Pilots. Military Pilots refer to appropriate regulations.

Radar Minima:

1. Minima shown are the lowest permitted by established criteria. Pilots should consult applicable directives for their category of aircraft.
2. The circling MDA and weather minima to be used are those for the runway to which the final approach is flown- not the landing runway. In the above RADAR MINIMA example, a category C aircraft flying a radar approach to runway 10, circling to land on runway 28, must use an MDA of 560 feet with weather minima of 500-1½.

NOTE: Military RADAR MINIMA may be shown with communications symbology that indicates emergency frequency monitoring capability by the radar facility as follows:

(E) VHF and UHF emergency frequencies monitored
(V) VHF emergency frequency (121.5) monitored
(U) UHF emergency frequency (243.0) monitored

Additionally, unmonitored frequencies which are available on request from the controlling agency may be annotated with an "x".

A Alternate Minimums not standard. Civil users refer to tabulation. USA/USN/USAF pilots refer to appropriate regulations.

A NA Alternate minimums are Not Authorized due to unmonitored facility or absence of weather reporting service.

T Takeoff Minimums not standard and/or Departure Procedures are published. Refer to tabulation.

TERMS/LANDING MINIMA DATA

LEGEND 21.—Instrument Approach Procedures Explanation of Terms.

13290

GENERAL INFO

GENERAL INFORMATION

This publication is issued every 56 days and includes Standard Instrument Approach Procedures (SIAPS), Standard Instrument Departures (SIDs), Standard Terminal Arrivals (STARs), IFR Takeoff Minimums and (Obstacle) Departure Procedures (ODPs), IFR Alternate Minimums, and Radar Instrument Approach Minimums for use by civil and military aviation. The organization responsible for SIAPs, Radar Minimums, SIDs, STARs and graphic ODPs is identified in parentheses in the top margin of the procedure; e.g., (FAA), (FAA-O), (USA), (USAF), (USN). SIAPS with the (FAA) and (FAA-O) designation are regulated under 14 CFR, Part 97. SIAPs with the (FAA-O) designation have been developed under Other Transaction Agreement (OTA) by private providers and have been certified by the FAA. See 14 CFR, Part 91.175 (a) and the AIM for further details. 14 CFR, Part 91.175 (g) and the Special Notices section of the Airport/Facility Directory contains information on civil operations at military airports.

STANDARD TERMINAL ARRIVALS AND DEPARTURE PROCEDURES

The use of the associated codified STAR/DP and transition identifiers are requested of users when filing flight plans via teletype and are required for users filing flight plans via computer interface. It must be noted that when filing a STAR/DP with a transition, the first three coded characters of the STAR and the last three coded characters of the DP are replaced by the transition code. Examples: ACTON SIX ARRIVAL, file (AQN.AQN6); ACTON SIX ARRIVAL, EDNAS TRANSITION, file (EDNAS.AQN6). FREEHOLD THREE DEPARTURE, file (FREH3.RBV), FREEHOLD THREE DEPARTURE, ELWOOD CITY TRANSITION, file (FREH3.EWC).

RNAV DP and STAR. Effective March 15,2007, these procedures, formerly identified as Type-A and Type-B, will be designated as RNAV 1 in accordance with amended Advisory Circular (AC) and ICAO terminology.

Refer to AC 90-100A U.S. TERMINAL AND EN ROUTE AREA NAVIGATION (RNAV) OPERATIONS and the Aeronautical Information Manual for additional guidance regarding these procedures.

Standard RNAV 1 Procedure Chart Notes

NOTE: RNAV 1
NOTE: DME/DME/IRU or GPS required

Some procedures may require use of GPS and will be identified by a "GPS required" note.

RNAV 1 Procedure Characteristics and Operations

1. Require use of an RNAV system with DME/DME/IRU, and/or GPS inputs.
2. Require use of a CDI, flight director, and/or autopilot, in lateral navigation mode, for flight guidance while operating on RNAV paths (track, course, or direct leg). Other methods providing an equivalent level of performance may be acceptable.
3. RNAV paths may start as low as 500 feet above airport elevation.

GENERAL INFO
13290

LEGEND 22.—General Information.

ABBREVIATIONS

AAUP	Attention All Users Page
ADF	Automatic Direction Finder
AFIS	Automatic Flight Information Service
ALS	Approach Light System
ALSF	Approach Light System with Sequenced Flashing Lights
AP	Autopilot System
APCH	Approach
APP CON	Approach Control
ARR	Arrival
ASOS	Automated Surface Observing System
ASR/PAR	Published Radar Minimums at this Airport
ATIS	Automatic Terminal Information Service
AUNICOM	Automated UNICOM
AWOS	Automated Weather Observing System
AZ	Azimuth
BC	Back Course
BND	Bound
C	Circling
CAT	Category
CCW	Counter Clockwise
CDI	Course Deviation Indicator
Chan	Channel
CIR	Circling
CLNC DEL	Clearance Delivery
CNF	Computer Navigation Fix
CTAF	Common Traffic Advisory Frequency
CW	Clockwise
DA	Decision Altitude
DER	Departure End of Runway
DH	Decision Height
DME	Distance Measuring Equipment
DTHR	Displaced Threshold
ELEV	Elevation
EMAS	Engineered Material Arresting System
FAF	Final Approach Fix
FD	Flight Director System
FM	Fan Marker
FMS	Flight Management System
GCO	Ground Communications Outlet
GLS	Ground Based Augmentation System Landing System
GPI	Ground Point of Interception
GPS	Global Positioning System
GS	Glide Slope
HAA	Height above Airport
HAL	Height above Landing
HAT	Height above Touchdown
HATh	Height Above Threshold
HGS	Head-up Guidance System
HIRL	High Intensity Runway Lights
HUD	Head-up Display
IAF	Initial Approach Fix
ICAO	International Civil Aviation Organization
IF	Intermediate Fix
IM	Inner Marker
INT	Intersection
LAAS	Local Area Augmentation System
LDA	Localizer Type Directional Aid
Ldg	Landing
LIRL	Low Intensity Runway Lights
LNAV	Lateral Navigation
LOC	Localizer
LP	Localizer Performance
LPV	Localizer Performance with Vertical Guidance
LR	Lead Radial. Provides at least 2 NM (Copter 1 NM) of lead to assist in turning onto the intermediate/final course.
MAA	Maximum Authorized Altitude
MALS	Medium Intensity Approach Light System
MALSR	Medium Intensity Approach Light System with RAIL
MAP	Missed Approach Point
MDA	Minimum Descent Altitude
MIRL	Medium Intensity Runway Lights
MLS	Microwave Landing System
MM	Middle Marker
MRA	Minimum Reception Altitude
N/A	Not Applicable
NA	Not Authorized
NDB	Non-directional Radio Beacon
NFD	National Flight Database
NM	Nautical Mile
NoPT	No Procedure Turn Required (Procedure Turn shall not be executed without ATC clearance)
ODALS	Omnidirectional Approach Light System
ODP	Obstacle Departure Procedure
OM	Outer Marker
PRM	Precision Runway Monitor

LEGEND 23.—Abbreviations.

14149

GENERAL INFO

ABBREVIATIONS

R.. Radial
RA...................................... Radio Altimeter setting height
RAIL.................................... Runway Alignment Indicator Lights
RCLS................................... Runway Centerline Light System
REIL.................................... Runway End Identifier Lights
RF....................................... Radius-to-Fix
RLLS.................................... Runway Lead-in Light System
RNAV................................... Area Navigation
RNP..................................... Required Navigation Performance
RPI...................................... Runway Point of Intercept(ion)
RRL..................................... Runway Remaining Lights
Rwy..................................... Runway
RVR..................................... Runway Visual Range
S... Straight-in
SALS.................................... Short Approach Light System
SSALR.................................. Simplified Short Approach Light System with RAIL
SDF..................................... Simplified Directional Facility
SM...................................... Statute Mile
SOIA................................... Simultaneous Offset Instrument Approach
TAA.................................... Terminal Arrival Area
TAC.................................... TACAN
TCH.................................... Threshold Crossing Height (height in feet Above Ground level)
TDZ.................................... Touchdown Zone
TDZE.................................. Touchdown Zone Elevation
TDZ/CL............................... Touchdown Zone and Runway Centerline Lighting
TDZL.................................. Touchdown Zone Lights
THR.................................... Threshold
THRE.................................. Threshold Elevation
TODA.................................. Takeoff Distance Available
TORA.................................. Takeoff Run Available
TR...................................... Track
VASI................................... Visual Approach Slope Indicator
VCOA.................................. Visual Climb Over Airport
VDP.................................... Visual Descent Point
VGSI.................................. Visual Glide Slope Indicator
VNAV................................. Vertical Navigation
WAAS................................ Wide Area Augmentation System
WP/WPT............................ Waypoint (RNAV)

GENERAL INFO

14149

LEGEND 23A.—Abbreviations.

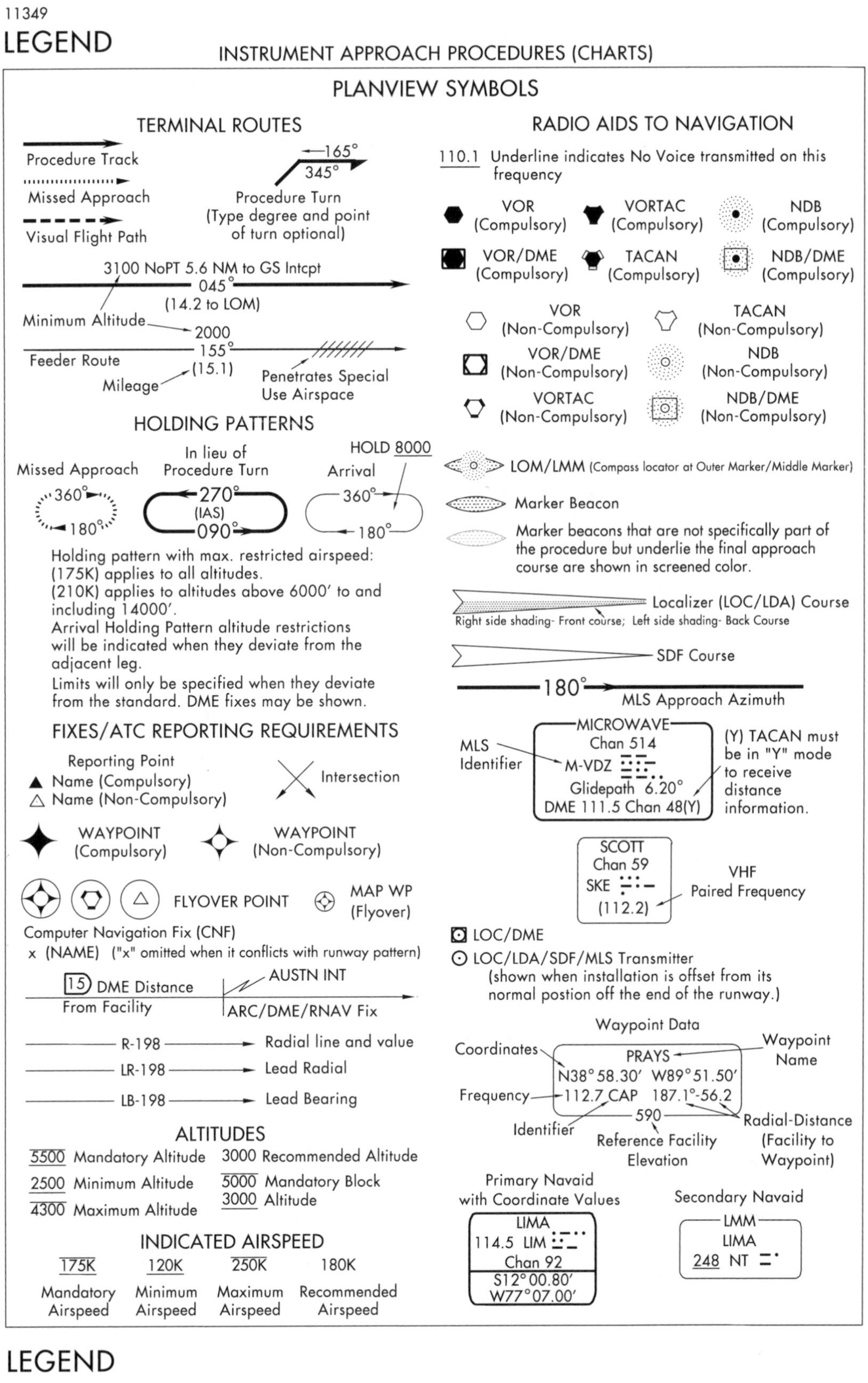

Legend 24.—Instrument Approach Procedures (Symbols).

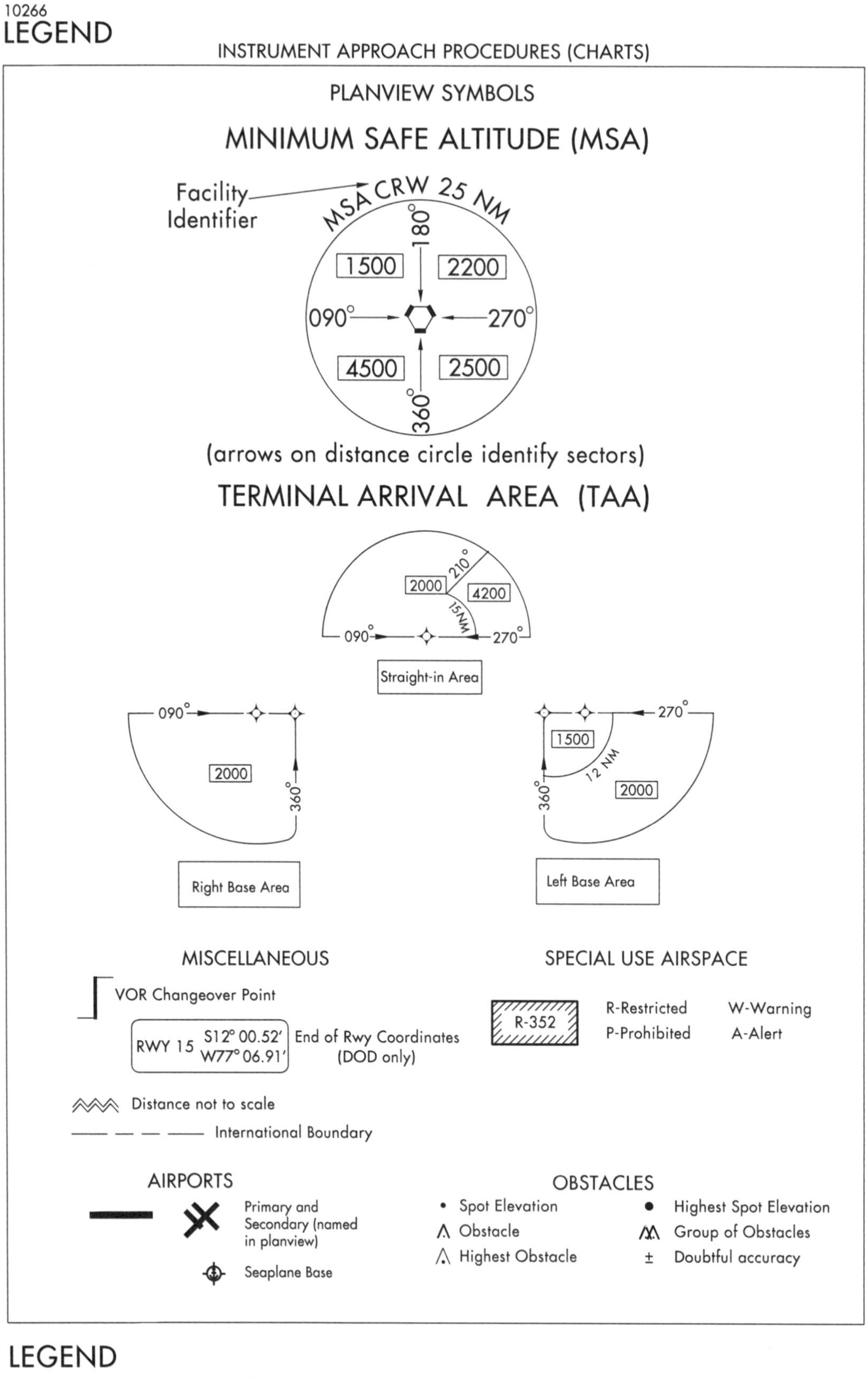

LEGEND 25.—Instrument Approach Procedures (Symbols).

13346
LEGEND

INSTRUMENT APPROACH PROCEDURES (CHARTS)

PROFILE VIEW

Two different methods are used for vertical guidance:

a. "GS" indicates an electronic glide slope or barometric vertical guidance is present. In the case of an Instrument Landing System (ILS) and Wide Area Augmentation System (WAAS) LPV approach procedures, an electronic signal provides vertical guidance. Barometric vertical guidance is provided for RNP and LNAV/VNAV instrument approach procedures. All ILS, LPV, RNP, and LNAV/VNAV will be in this format GS 3.00°/TCH 55, located in the lower left or right corner.

b. Other charts without electronic or barometric vertical guidance will be in this format ∠3.00°/TCH 55, indicating a non-precision vertical descent angle to assist in preventing controlled flight into terrain. On Civil (FAA) procedures, this information is placed above or below the procedure track following the fix it is based on.

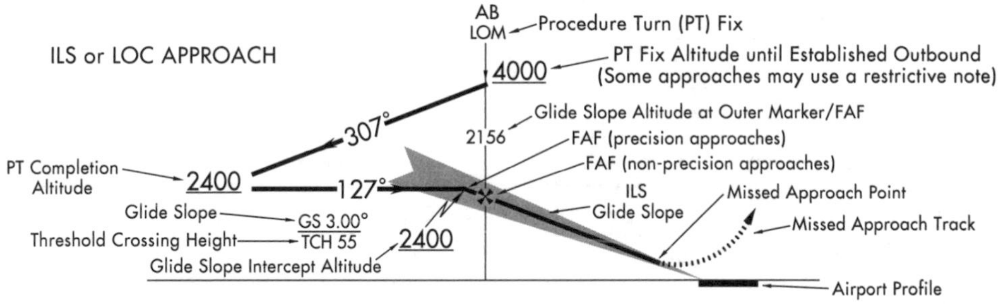

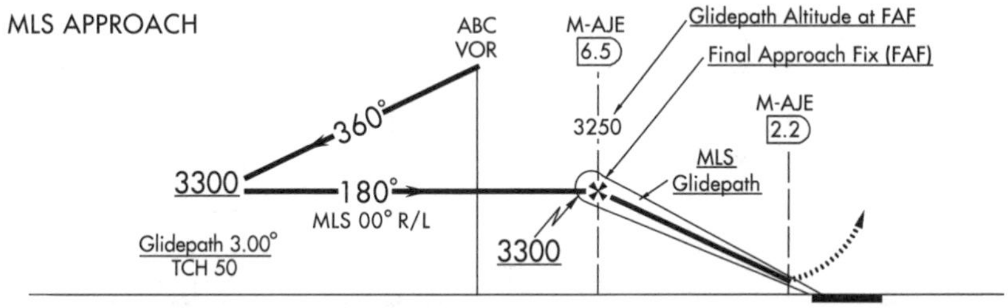

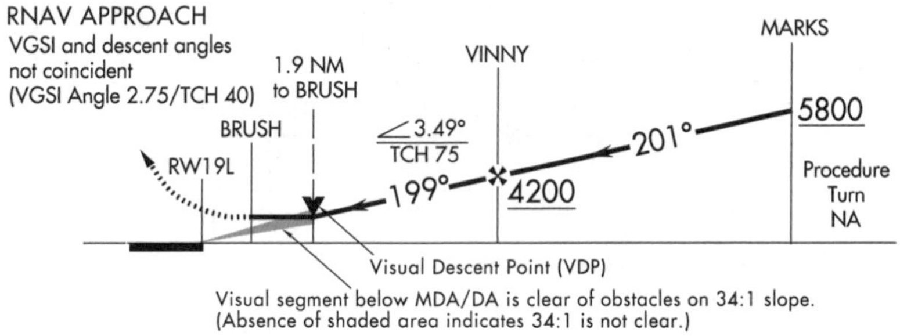

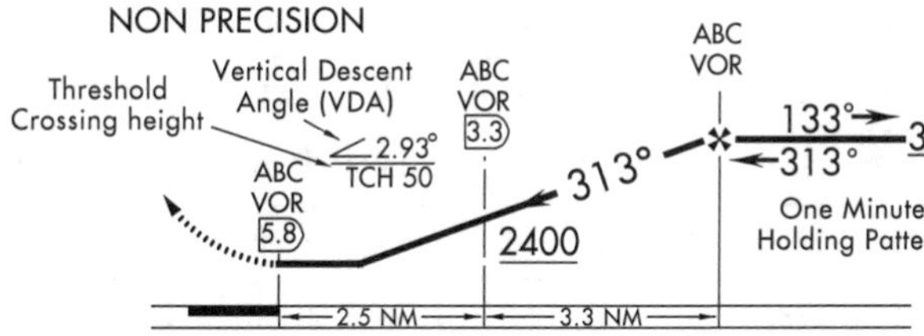

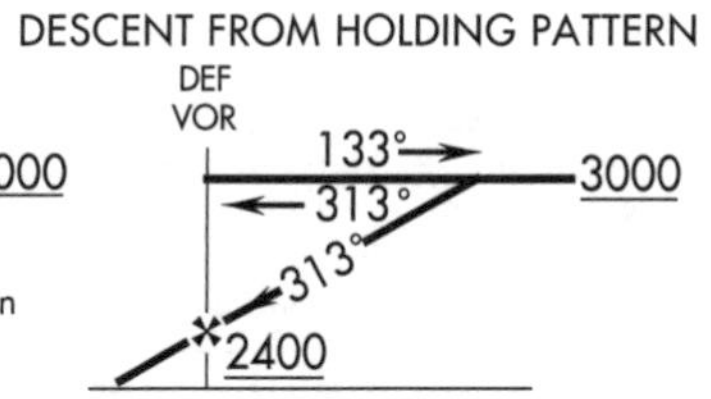

ALTITUDES

5500	Mandatory Altitude
2500	Minimum Altitude
4300	Maximum Altitude
3000	Recommended Altitude
5000 / 3000	Mandatory Block Altitude

PROFILE SYMBOLS

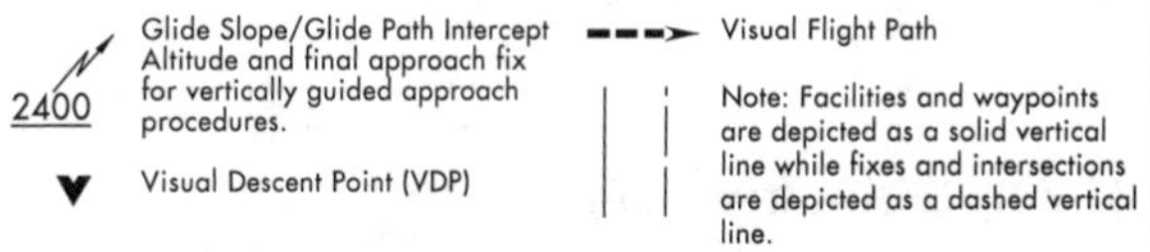

LEGEND
13346

LEGEND 26.—Instrument Approach Procedures (Profile).

CLIMB/DESCENT TABLE 10042

INSTRUMENT TAKEOFF OR APPROACH PROCEDURE CHARTS
RATE OF CLIMB/DESCENT TABLE

(ft. per min)

A rate of climb/descent table is provided for use in planning and executing climbs or descents under known or approximate ground speed conditions. It will be especially useful for approaches when the localizer only is used for course guidance. A best speed, power, altitude combination can be programmed which will result in a stable glide rate and altitude favorable for executing a landing if minimums exist upon breakout. Care should always be exercised so that minimum descent altitude and missed approach point are not exceeded.

CLIMB/ DESCENT ANGLE (degrees and tenths)	ft/NM	GROUND SPEED (knots)										
		60	90	120	150	180	210	240	270	300	330	360
2.0	210	210	320	425	530	635	743	850	955	1060	1165	1275
2.5	265	265	400	530	665	795	930	1060	1195	1325	1460	1590
VERTICAL PATH ANGLE 2.7	287	287	430	574	717	860	1003	1147	1290	1433	1576	1720
2.8	297	297	446	595	743	892	1041	1189	1338	1486	1635	1783
2.9	308	308	462	616	770	924	1078	1232	1386	1539	1693	1847
3.0	318	318	478	637	797	956	1115	1274	1433	1593	1752	1911
3.1	329	329	494	659	823	988	1152	1317	1481	1646	1810	1975
3.2	340	340	510	680	850	1020	1189	1359	1529	1699	1869	2039
3.3	350	350	526	701	876	1052	1227	1402	1577	1752	1927	2103
3.4	361	361	542	722	903	1083	1264	1444	1625	1805	1986	2166
3.5	370	370	555	745	930	1115	1300	1485	1670	1860	2045	2230
4.0	425	425	640	850	1065	1275	1490	1700	1915	2125	2340	2550
4.5	480	480	715	955	1195	1435	1675	1915	2150	2390	2630	2870
5.0	530	530	795	1065	1330	1595	1860	2125	2390	2660	2925	3190
5.5	585	585	880	1170	1465	1755	2050	2340	2635	2925	3220	3510
6.0	640	640	960	1275	1595	1915	2235	2555	2875	3195	3510	3830
6.5	690	690	1040	1385	1730	2075	2425	2770	3115	3460	3805	4155
7.0	745	745	1120	1490	1865	2240	2610	2985	3355	3730	4105	4475
7.5	800	800	1200	1600	2000	2400	2800	3200	3600	4000	4400	4800
8.0	855	855	1280	1710	2135	2560	2990	3415	3845	4270	4695	5125
8.5	910	910	1360	1815	2270	2725	3180	3630	4085	4540	4995	5450
9.0	960	960	1445	1925	2405	2885	3370	3850	4330	4810	5295	5775
9.5	1015	1015	1525	2035	2540	3050	3560	4065	4575	5085	5590	6100
10.0	1070	1070	1605	2145	2680	3215	3750	4285	4820	5355	5890	6430

CLIMB/DESCENT TABLE 10042

LEGEND 27.—Instrument Takeoff or Approach Procedure Charts, Rate-of-Climb/Descent Table.

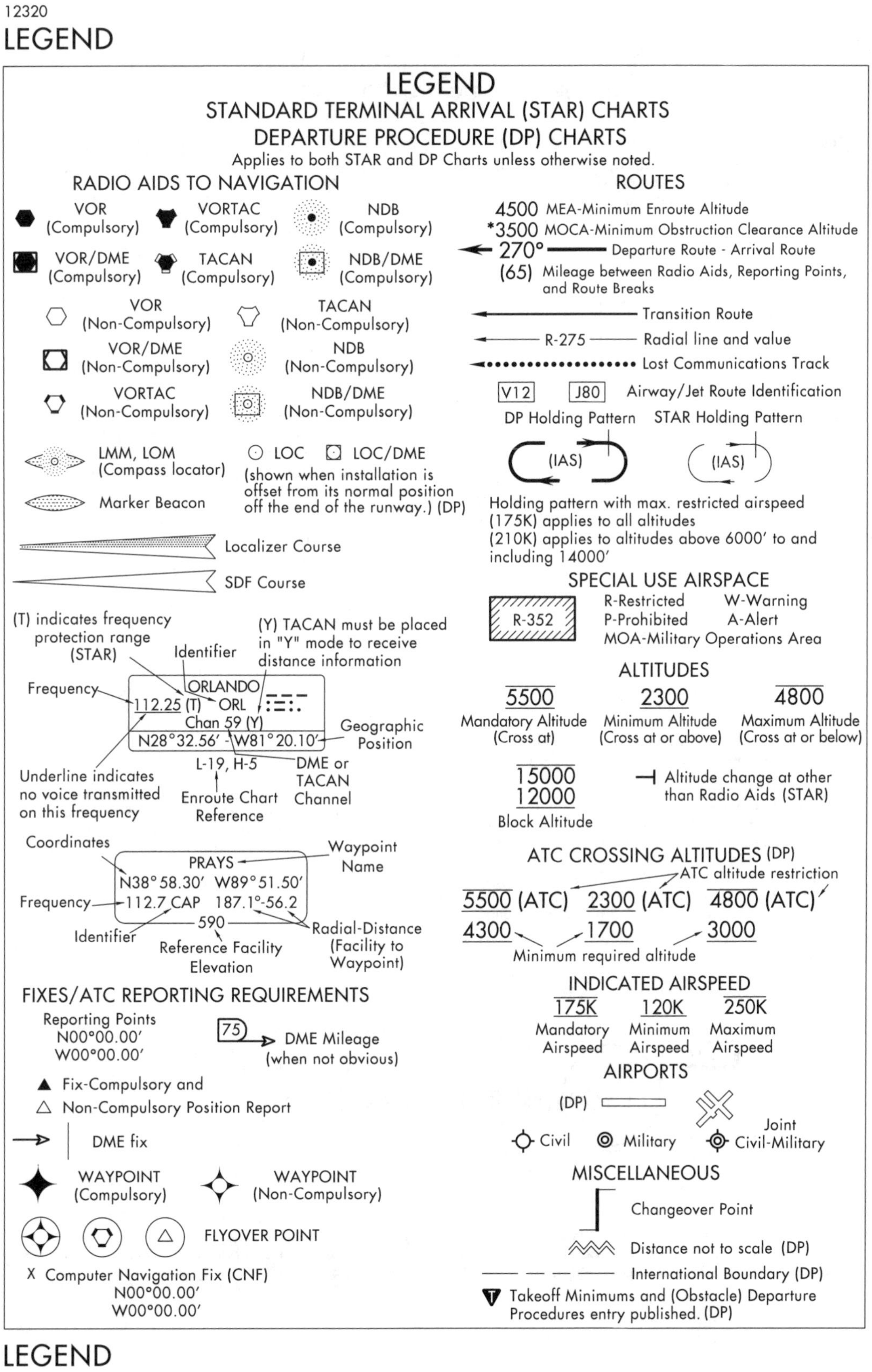

LEGEND 28.—Standard Arrival/Departure Charts.

13010

LEGEND

INSTRUMENT APPROACH PROCEDURES (CHARTS)

AIRPORT DIAGRAM/AIRPORT SKETCH

Runways

Hard Surface | Other Than Hard Surface | Stopways, Taxiways, Parking Areas, Water Runways | Displaced Threshold

Closed Runway | Closed Taxiway | Under Construction | Metal Surface

ARRESTING GEAR: Specific arresting gear systems; e.g., BAK12, MA-1A etc., shown on airport diagrams, not applicable to Civil Pilots. Military Pilots refer to appropriate DOD publications.

uni-directional | bi-directional | Jet Barrier

ARRESTING SYSTEM

REFERENCE FEATURES

Buildings..

24-Hour Self-Serve Fuel ##..

Tanks...

Obstructions..

Airport Beacon #..

Runway

Radar Reflectors..

Hot Spot..

Control Tower #...TWR

When Control Tower and Rotating Beacon are co-located, Beacon symbol will be used and further identified as TWR.

A fuel symbol is shown to indicate 24-hour self-serve fuel available, see appropriate A/FD, Alaska or Pacific Supplement for information.

Runway length depicted is the physical length of the runway (end-to-end, including displaced thresholds if any) but excluding areas designated as stopways.

A D symbol is shown to indicate runway declared distance information available, see appropriate A/FD, Alaska or Pacific Supplement for distance information.

Helicopter Alighting Areas

Negative Symbols used to identify Copter Procedures landing point.....................

Runway Threshold elevation............THRE 123

Runway TDZ elevation....................TDZE 123

0.3% DOWN

Runway Slope.................................0.8% UP

(shown when runway slope is greater than or equal to 0.3%)

NOTE:
Runway Slope measured to midpoint on runways 8000 feet or longer.

U.S. Navy Optical Landing System (OLS) "OLS" location is shown because of its height of approximately 7 feet and proximity to edge of runway may create an obstruction for some types of aircraft.

Approach light symbols are shown in the Flight Information Handbook.

Airport diagram scales are variable.

True/magnetic North orientation may vary from diagram to diagram

Coordinate values are shown in 1 or ½ minute increments. They are further broken down into 6 second ticks, within each 1 minute increments.

Positional accuracy within ±600 feet unless otherwise noted on the chart.

NOTE:
All new and revised airport diagrams are shown referenced to the World Geodetic System (WGS) (noted on appropriate diagram), and may not be compatible with local coordinates published in FLIP. (Foreign Only)

Runway Weight Bearing Capacity/or PCN Pavement Classification Number is shown as a codified expression.
Refer to the appropriate Supplement/Directory for applicable codes e.g.,
RWY 14-32 PCN 80 F/D/X/U S-75, D-185, 2S-175, 2D-325

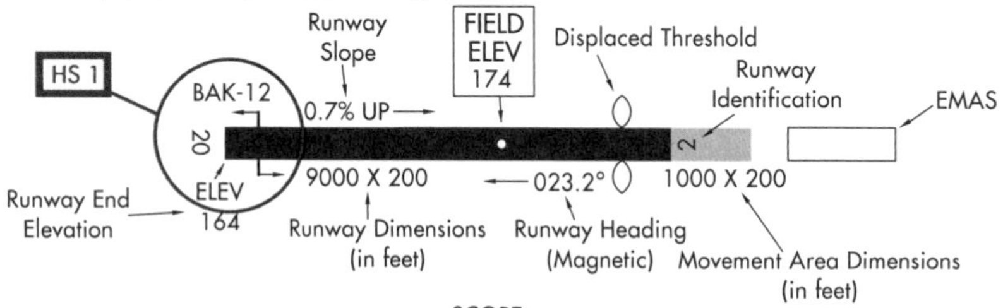

SCOPE

Airport diagrams are specifically designed to assist in the movement of ground traffic at locations with complex runway/taxiway configurations. Airport diagrams are not intended to be used for approach and landing or departure operations. For revisions to Airport Diagrams: Consult FAA Order 7910.4.

LEGEND

LEGEND 29.—Airport Diagram.

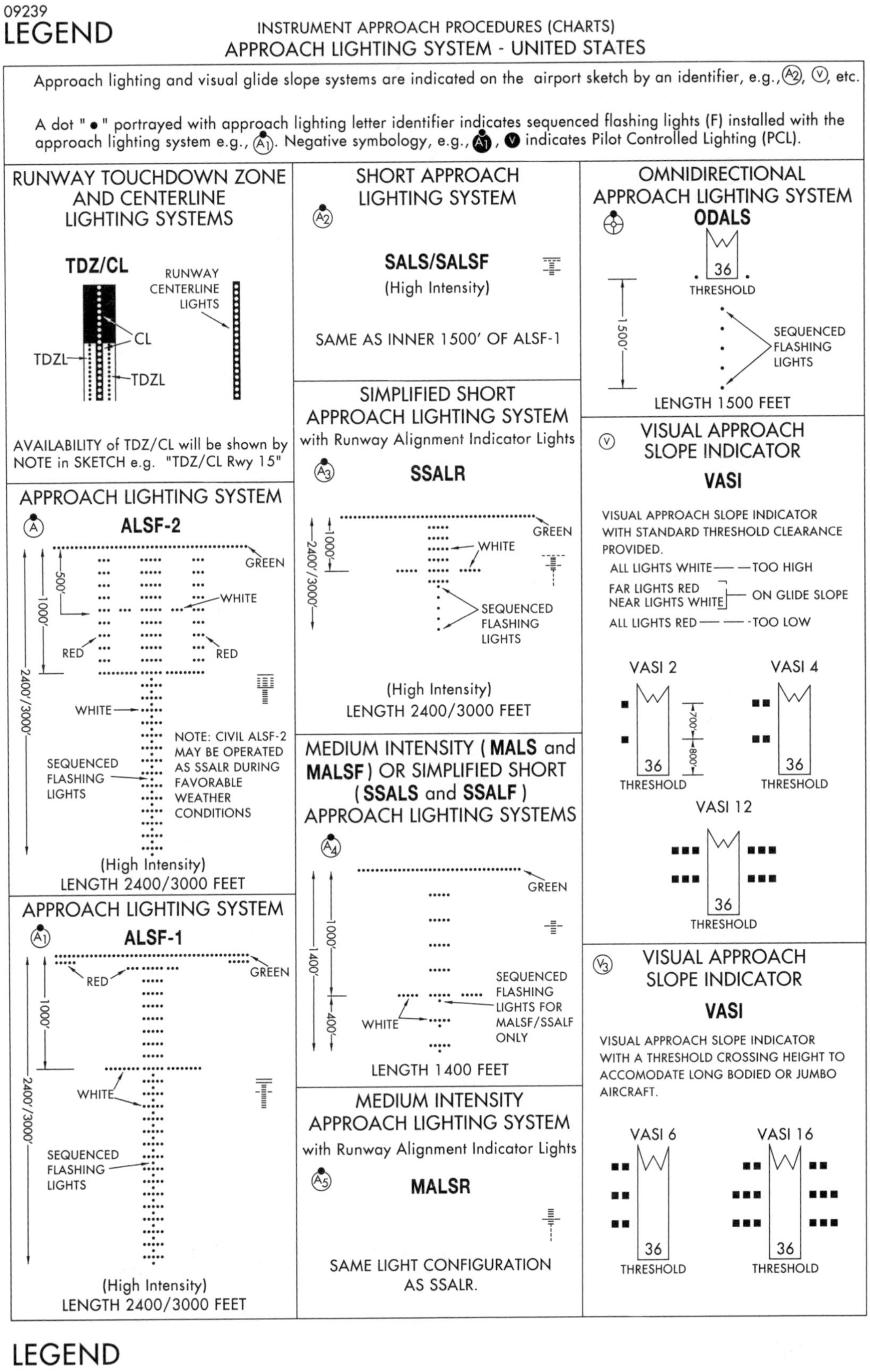

LEGEND 30.—Approach Lighting Systems.

04330

LEGEND

INSTRUMENT APPROACH PROCEDURES (CHARTS)
APPROACH LIGHTING SYSTEM - UNITED STATES

Approach lighting and visual glide slope systems are indicated on the airport sketch by an identifier, (A2), (V) etc.

A dot " • " portrayed with approach lighting letter identifier indicates sequenced flashing lights (F) installed with the approach lighting system e.g., (A1). Negative symbology, e.g., (A1), (V) indicates Pilot Controlled Lighting (PCL).

(P) PRECISION APPROACH PATH INDICATOR

PAPI

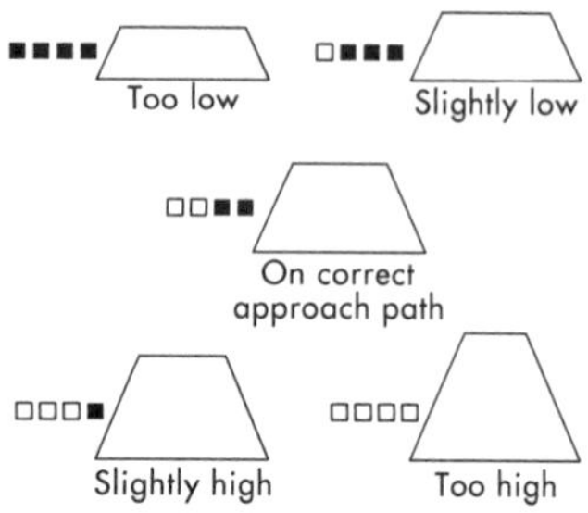

Legend: □ White ■ Red

(V1) "T"-VISUAL APPROACH SLOPE INDICATOR

"T"-VASI

"T" ON BOTH SIDES OF RWY
ALL LIGHTS VARIABLE WHITE.
CORRECT APPROACH SLOPE-ONLY CROSS BAR VISIBLE.
UPRIGHT "T"- FLY UP.
INVERTED "T"- FLY DOWN.
RED "T"- GROSS UNDERSHOOT.

(V2) PULSATING VISUAL APPROACH SLOPE INDICATOR

PVASI

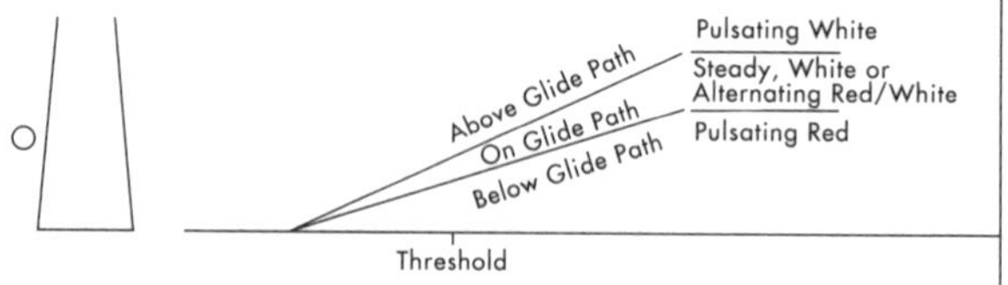

CAUTION: When viewing the pulsating visual approach slope indicators in the pulsating white or pulsating red sectors, it is possible to mistake this lighting aid for another aircraft or a ground vehicle. Pilots should exercise caution when using this type of system.

(V4) TRI-COLOR VISUAL APPROACH SLOPE INDICATOR

TRCV

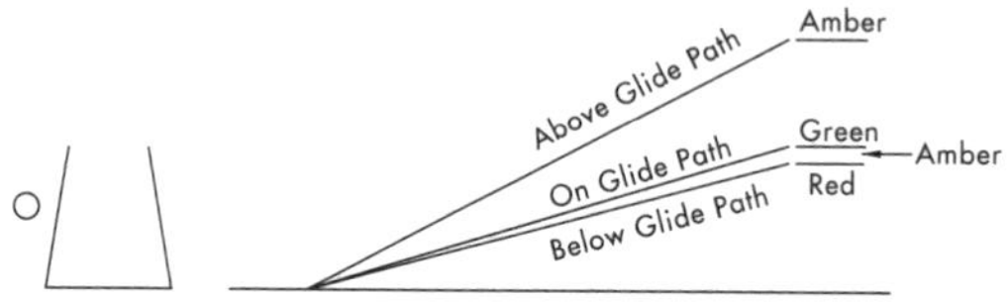

CAUTION: When the aircraft descends from green to red, the pilot may see a dark amber color during the transition from green to red.

(V5) ALIGNMENT OF ELEMENTS SYSTEMS

APAP

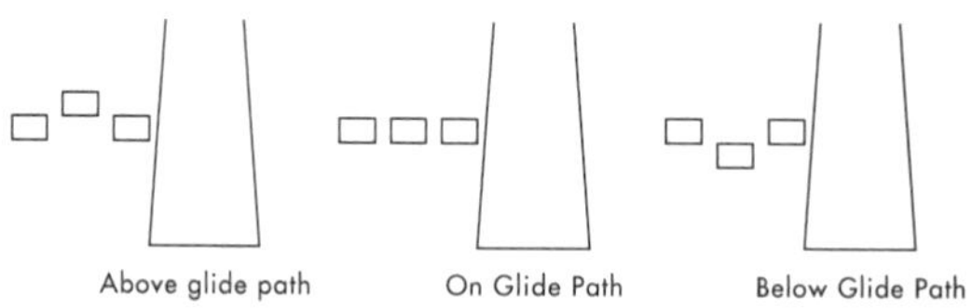

Painted panels which may be lighted at night.
To use the system the pilot positions the aircraft so the elements are in alignment.

LEGEND

LEGEND 31.—Approach Lighting System.

13122

INOP COMPONENTS

INOPERATIVE COMPONENTS OR VISUAL AIDS TABLE

Landing minimums published on instrument approach procedure charts are based upon full operation of all components and visual aids associated with the particular instrument approach chart being used. Higher minimums are required with inoperative components or visual aids as indicated below. If more than one component is inoperative, each minimum is raised to the highest minimum required by any single component that is inoperative. ILS glide slope inoperative minimums are published on the instrument approach charts as localizer minimums. This table may be amended by notes on the approach chart. Such notes apply only to the particular approach category(ies) as stated. See legend page for description of components indicated below.

(1) ILS, MLS, PAR and RNAV (LPV line of minima)

Inoperative Component or Aid	Approach Category	Increase Visibility
ALSF 1 & 2, MALSR, & SSALR	ABCD	¼ mile

(2) ILS with visibility minimum of 1,800 RVR

ALSF 1 & 2, MALSR, & SSALR	ABCD	To 4000 RVR
TDZL RCLS	ABCD	To 2400 RVR*
RVR	ABCD	To ½ mile

*1800 RVR authorized with the use of FD or AP or HUD to DA.

(3) VOR, VOR/DME, TACAN, LOC, LOC/DME, LDA, LDA/DME, SDF, SDF/DME, GPS, ASR and RNAV (LNAV/VNAV, LP, LNAV lines of minima)

Inoperative Visual Aid	Approach Category	Increase Visibility
ALSF 1 & 2, MALSR, & SSALR	ABCD	½ mile
SSALS,MALS, & ODALS	ABC	¼ mile

(4) NDB

ALSF 1 & 2, MALSR, & SSALR	C	½ mile
	ABD	¼ mile
MALS, SSALS, ODALS	ABC	¼ mile

INOP COMPONENTS

LEGEND 32.—Inoperative Components or Visual Aids Table.

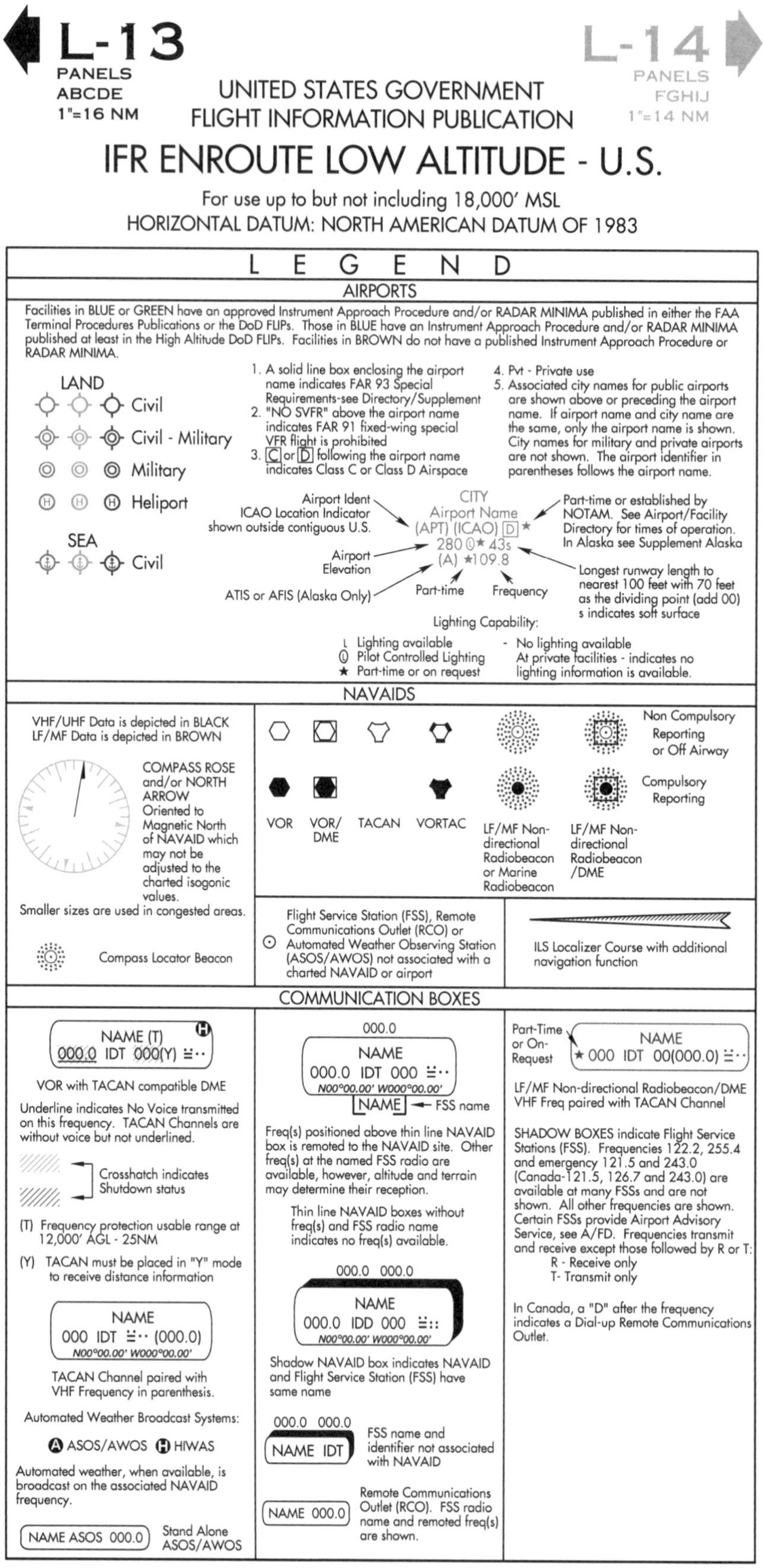

LEGEND 33.—IFR En Route Low Altitude (U.S.)

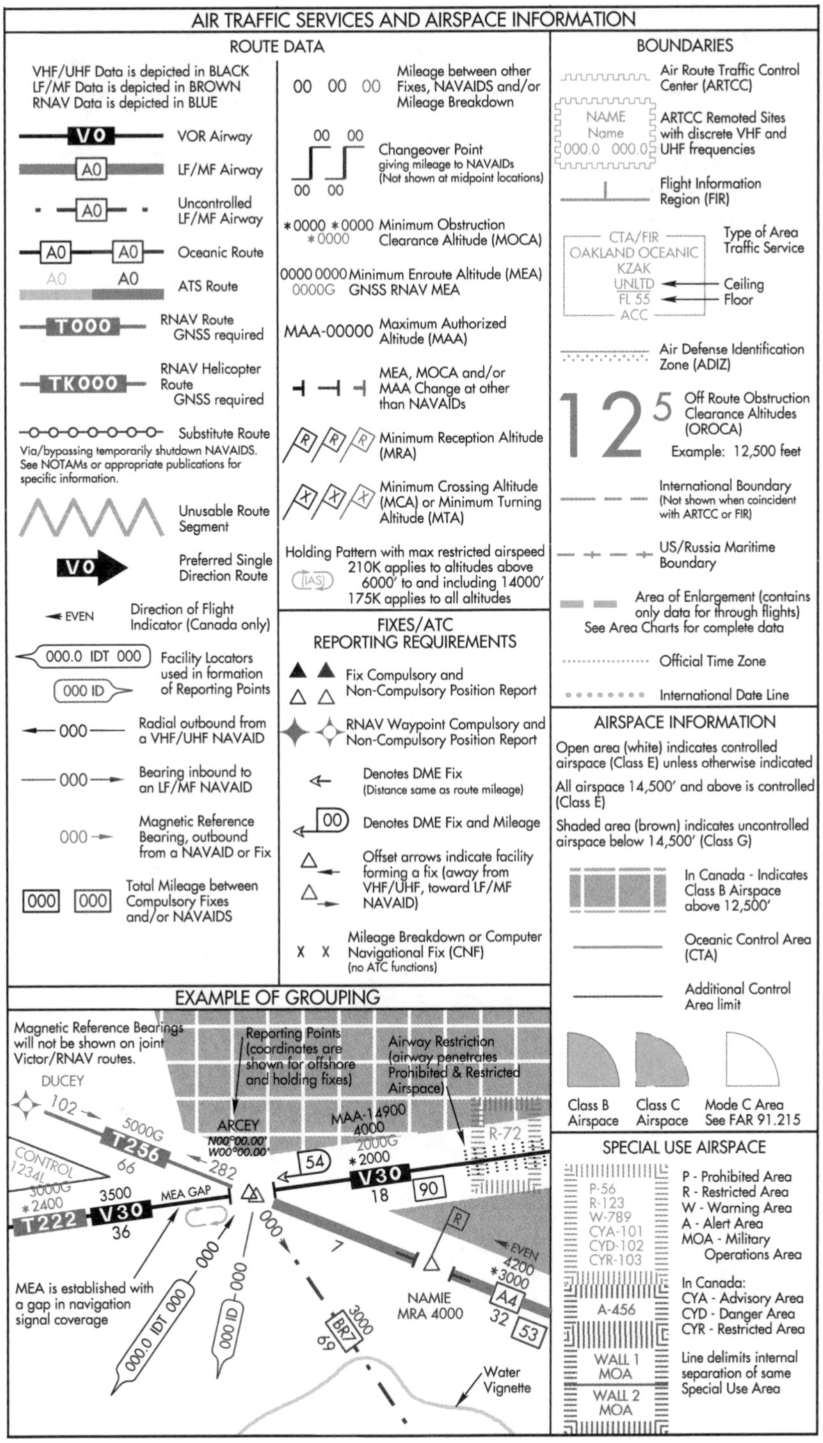

LEGEND 34.—IFR En Route Low Altitude (U.S.)

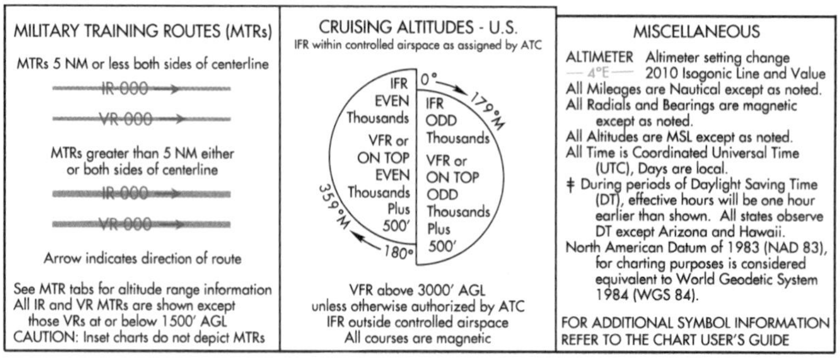

LEGEND 35.—IFR En Route Low Altitude (U.S.)

AIRCRAFT EQUIPMENT SUFFIXES	
SUFFIX	Aircraft Equipment Suffixes
	NO DME
/X	No transponder
/T	Transponder with no Mode C
/U	Transponder with Mode C
	DME
/D	No transponder
/B	Transponder with no Mode C
/A	Transponder with Mode C
	TACAN ONLY
/M	No transponder
/N	Transponder with no Mode C
/P	Transponder with Mode C
	AREA NAVIGATION (RNAV)
/Y	LORAN, VOR/DME, or INS with no transponder
/C	LORAN, VOR/DME, or INS, transponder with no Mode C
/I	LORAN, VOR/DME, or INS, transponder with Mode C
	ADVANCED RNAV WITH TRANSPONDER AND MODE C (if an aircraft is unable to operate with a transponder and/or Mode C, it will revert to the appropriate code listed above under Area Navigation.)
/E	Flight Management System (FMS) with en route, terminal, and approach capability. Equipment requirements are: (a) Dual FMS which meets the specifications of AC 25-15, Approval of Flight Management Systems in Transport Category Airplanes; AC 20-129, Airworthiness Approval of Vertical Navigation (VNAV) Systems for use in the U.S. NAS and Alaska; AC 20-130, Airworthiness Approval of Navigation or Flight Management Systems Integrating Multiple Navigation Sensors; or equivalent criteria as approved by Flight Standards. (b) A flight director and autopilot control system capable of following the lateral and vertical FMS flight path. (c) At least dual inertial reference units (IRU's). (d) A database containing the waypoints and speed/altitude constraints for the route and/or procedure to be flown that is automatically loaded into the FMS flight plan. (e) An electronic map. (U.S. and U.S. territories only unless otherwise authorized.)
/F	A single FMS with en route, terminal, and approach capability that meets the equipment requirements of /E, (a) through (d), above. (U.S. and U.S. territories only unless otherwise authorized.)
/G	Global Positioning System (GPS)/Global Navigation Satellite System (GNSS) equipped aircraft with en route and terminal capability.
/R	Required Navigational Performance (Denotes capability to operate in RNP designated airspace and routes)
/W	Reduced Vertical Separation Minima (RVSM)

LEGEND 36.—Aircraft Equipment Suffixes.

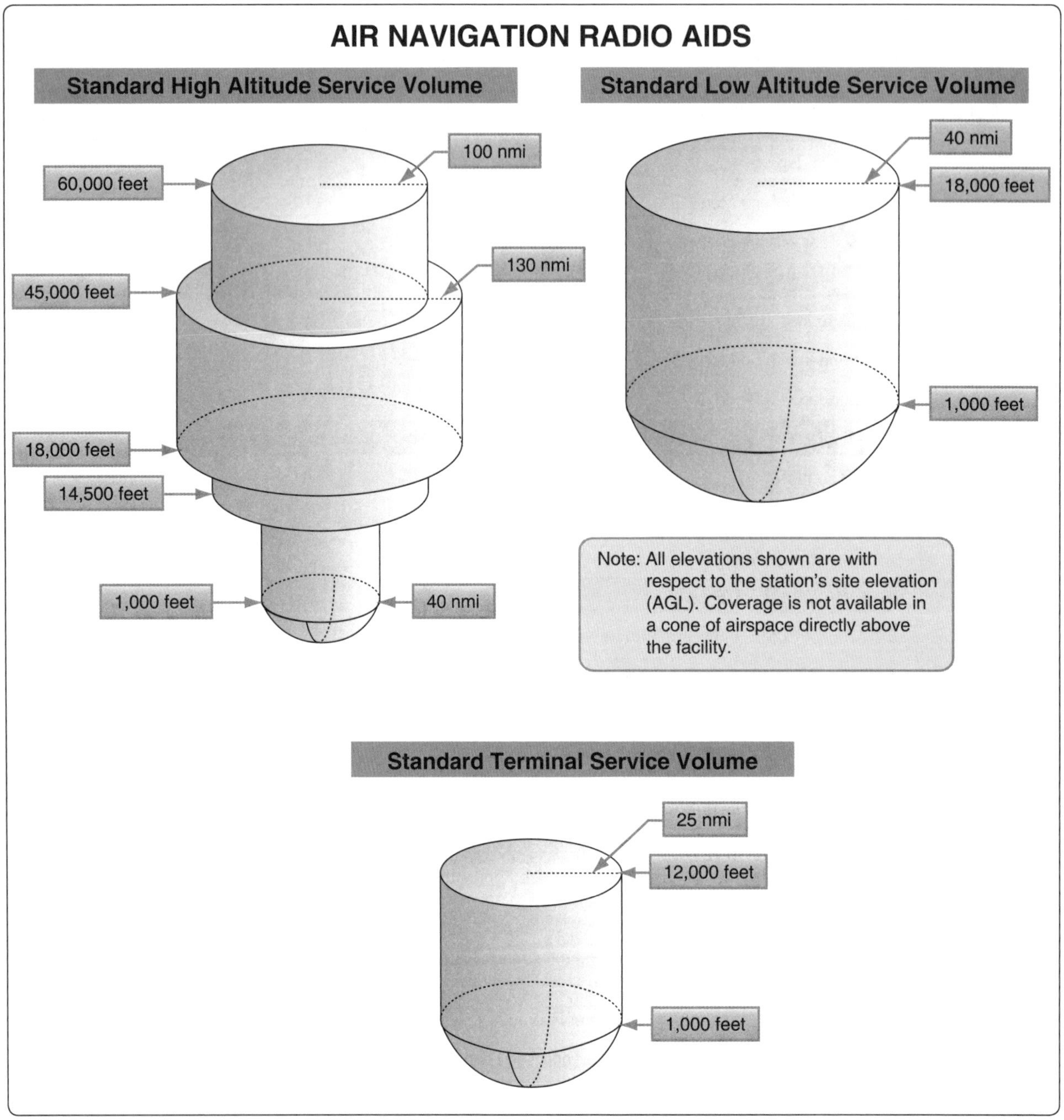

Legend 37.—Air Navigation Radio Aids.

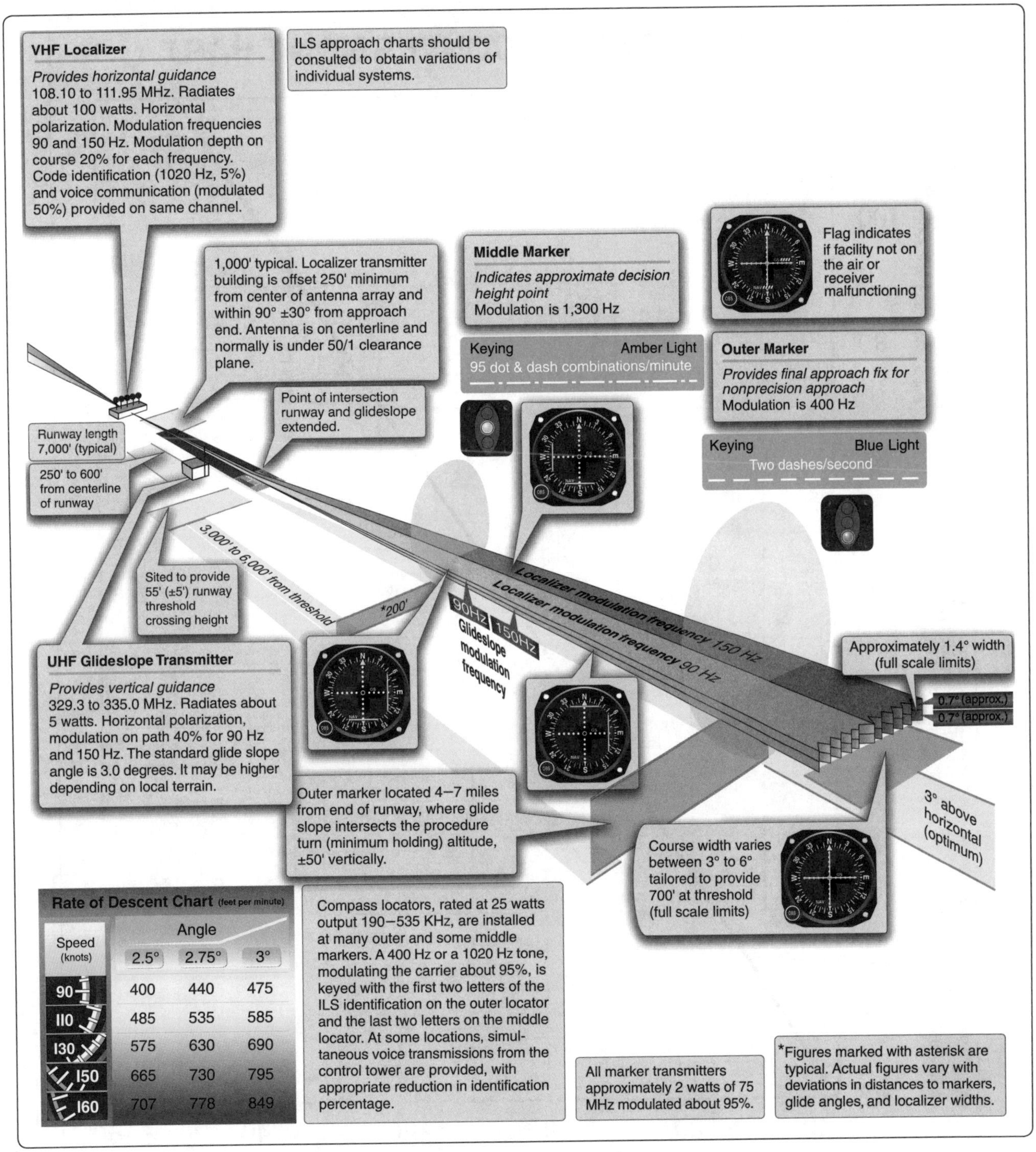

Rate of Descent Chart (feet per minute)

Speed (knots)	Angle 2.5°	2.75°	3°
90	400	440	475
110	485	535	585
130	575	630	690
150	665	730	795
160	707	778	849

LEGEND 38.—ILS Standard Characteristics and Terminology.

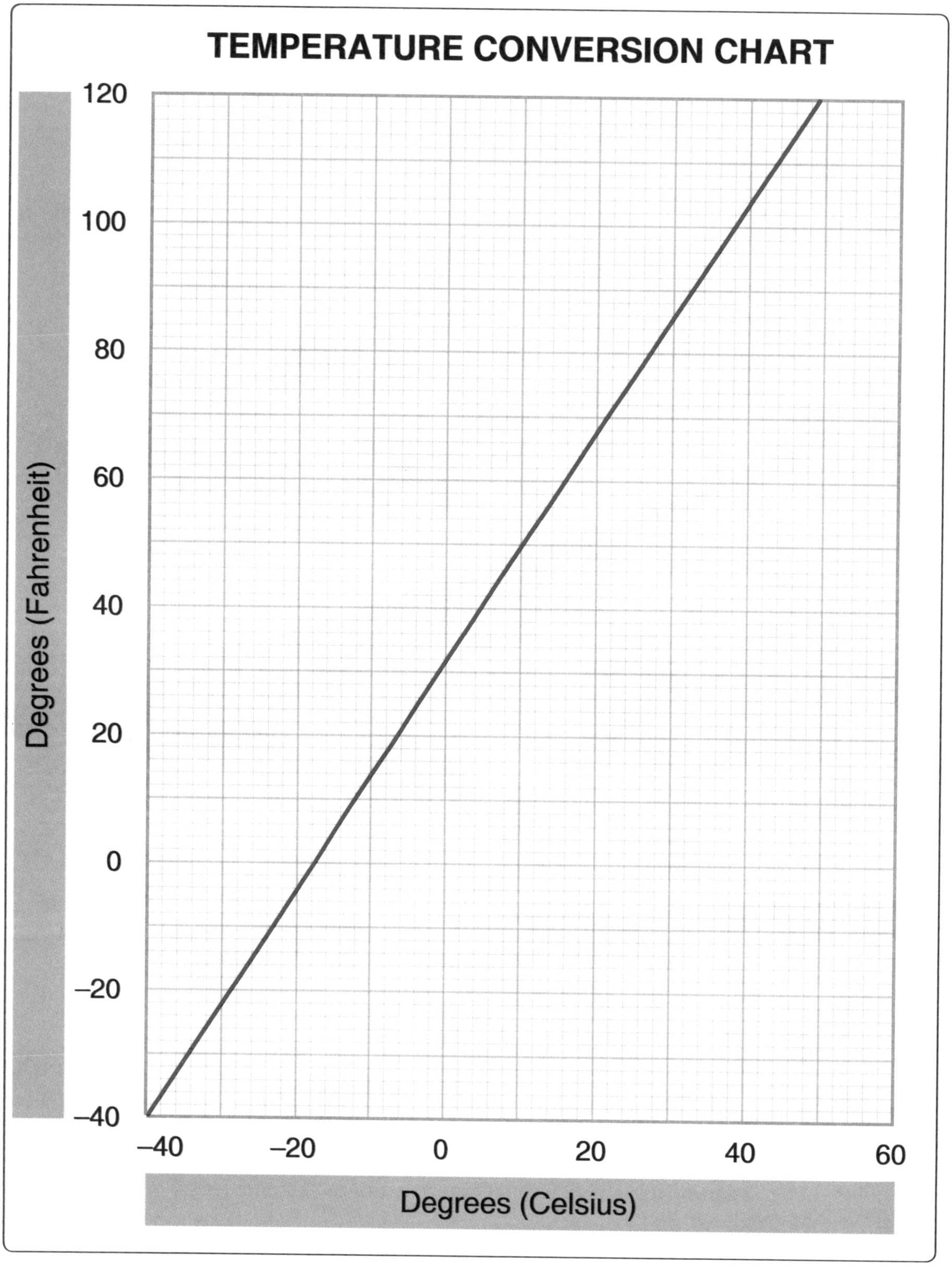

LEGEND 39.—Temperature Conversion Chart.

APPENDIX 2

VALID 1600Z FOR USE 0900-1500Z. TEMPS NEG ABV 24000

FT	3000	6000	9000	12000	18000	24000	30000	34000	39000
EMI	2807	2715-07	2728-10	2842-13	2867-21	2891-30	751041	771150	780855
ALB	0210	9900-07	2714-09	2728-12	2656-19	2777-28	781842	760150	269658
PSB		1509+04	2119+01	2233-04	2262-14	2368-26	781939	760850	780456
STL	2308	2613+02	2422-03	2431-08	2446-19	2461-30	760142	782650	760559

FIGURE 2.—Wind and Temperatures Aloft Forecast.

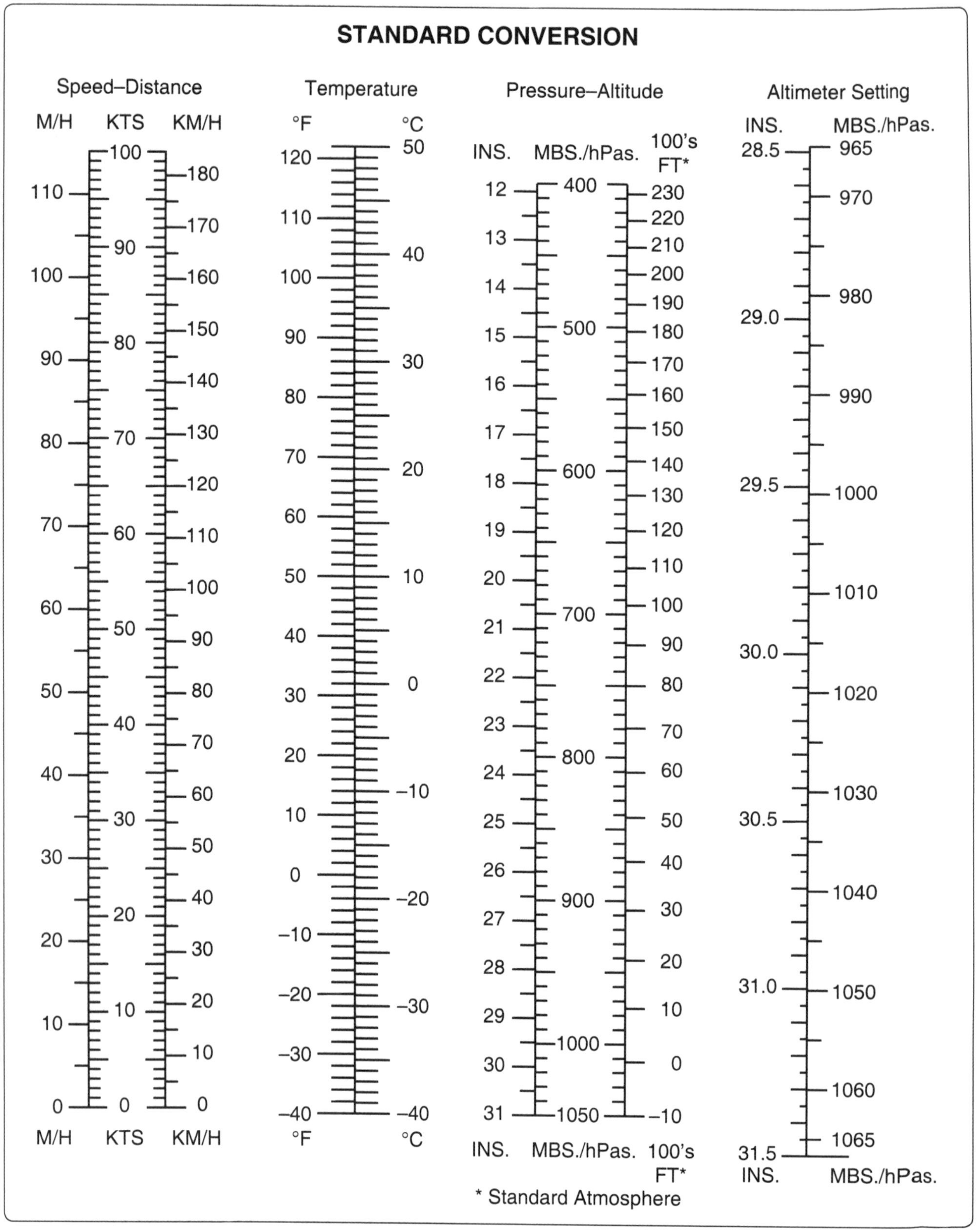

FIGURE 3.—Standard Conversion Chart.

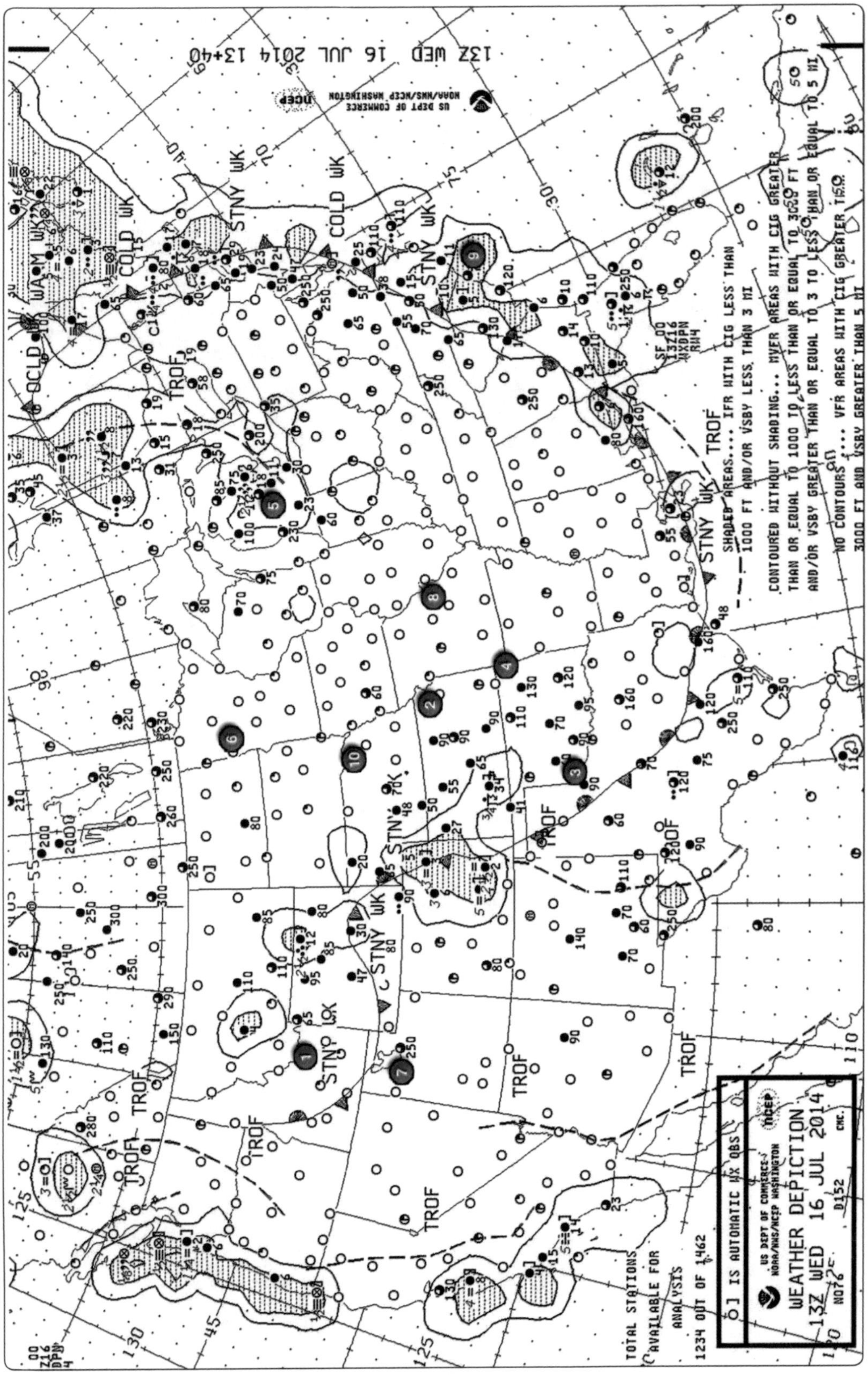

FIGURE 4.—Weather Depiction Chart.

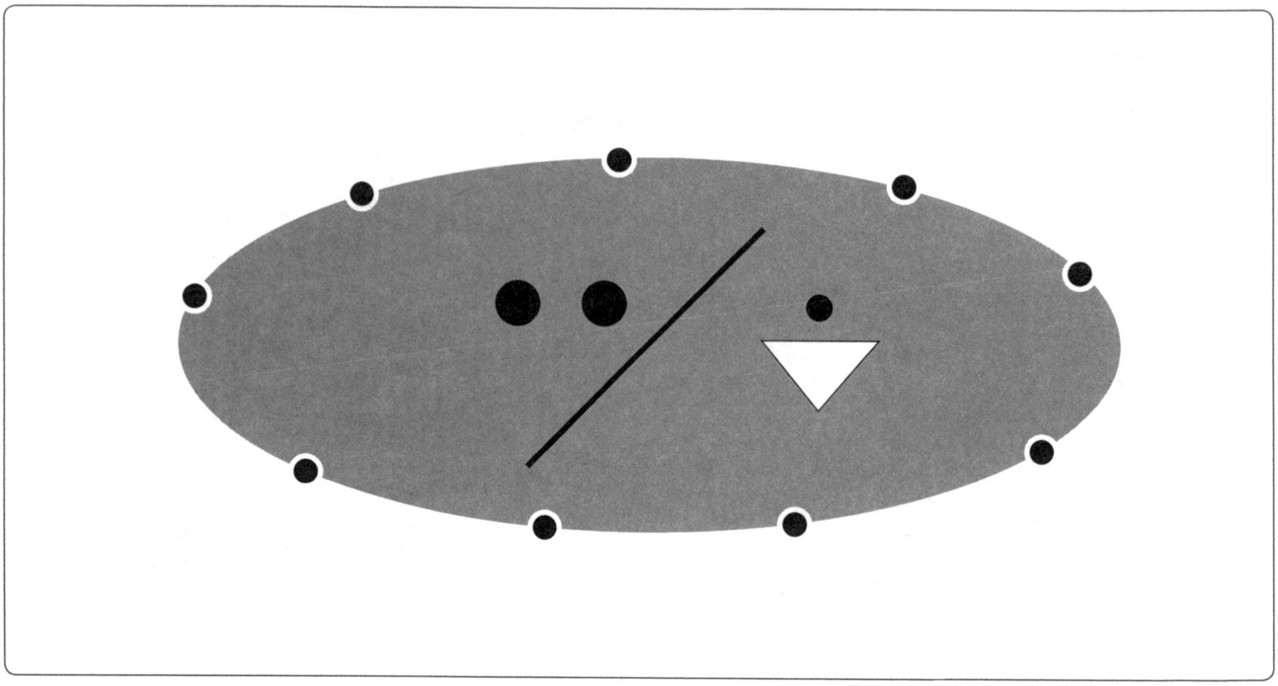

FIGURE 5.—Symbol Used on Low-Level Significant Weather Prognostic Chart.

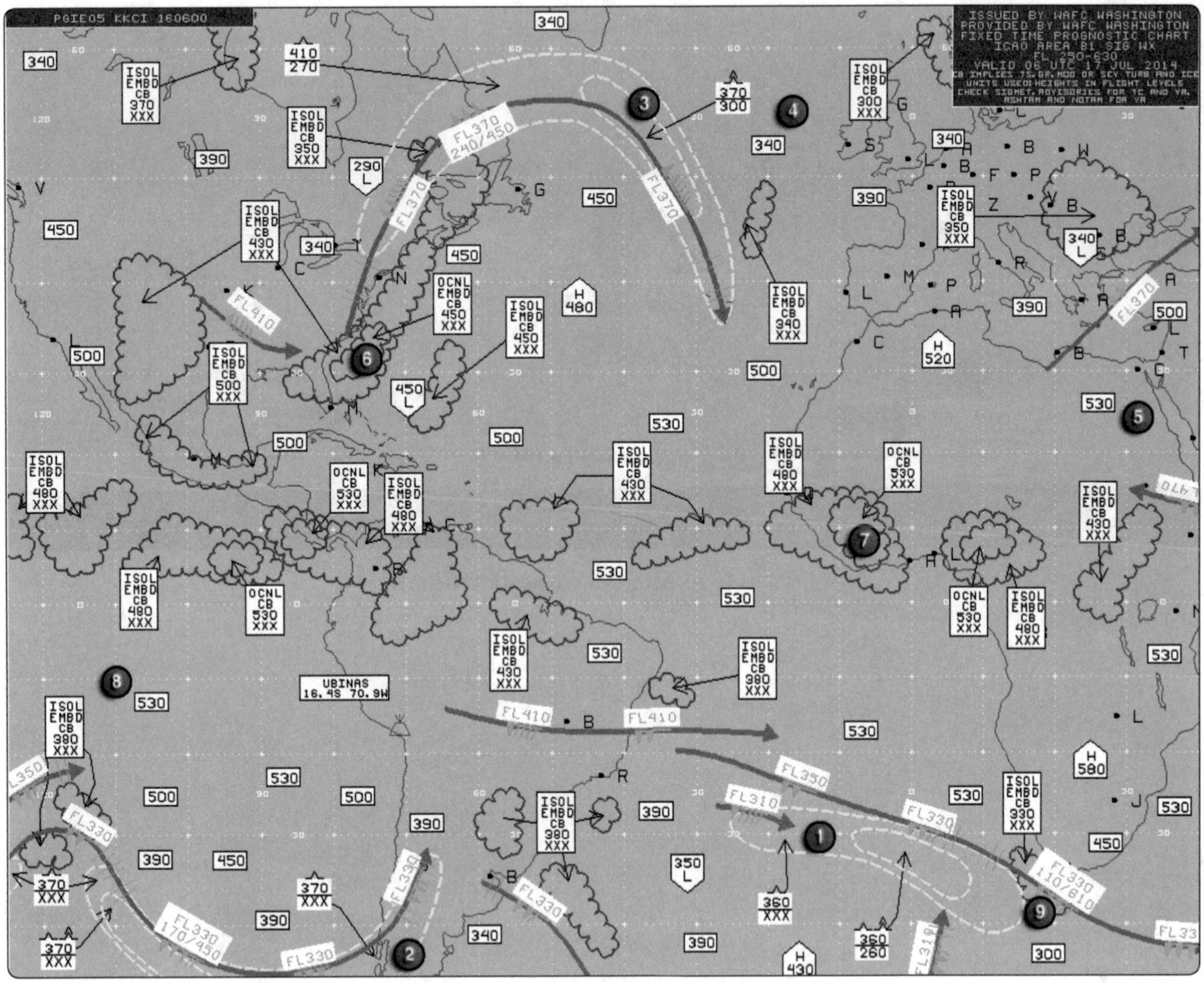

FIGURE 7.—High-Level Significant Weather Prognostic Chart.

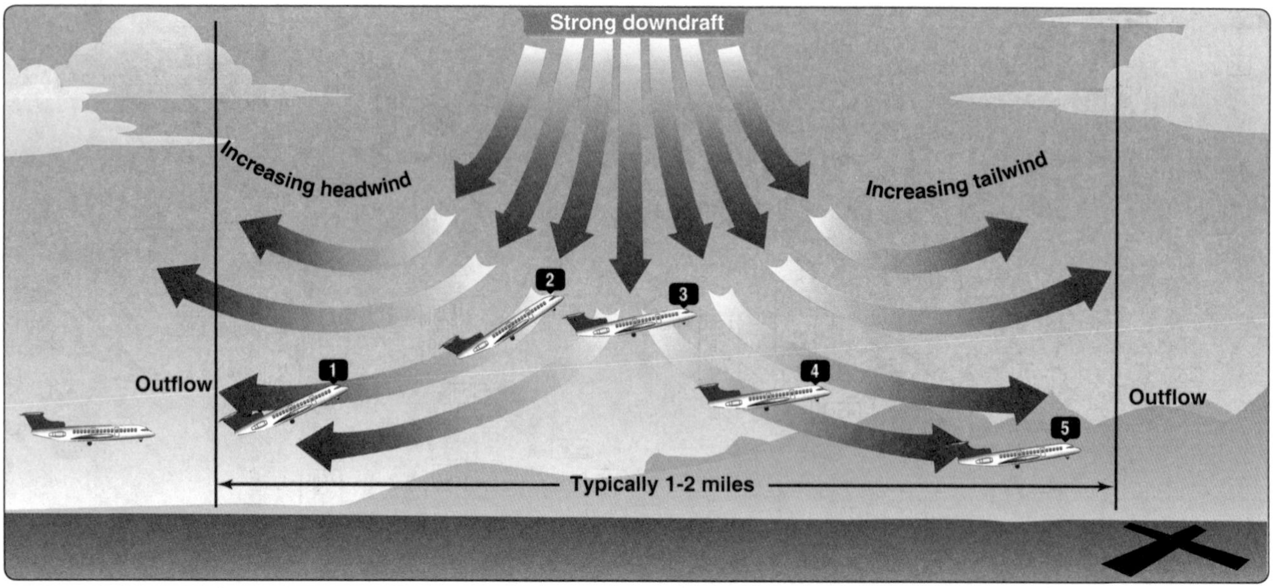

FIGURE 13.—Microburst Section Chart.

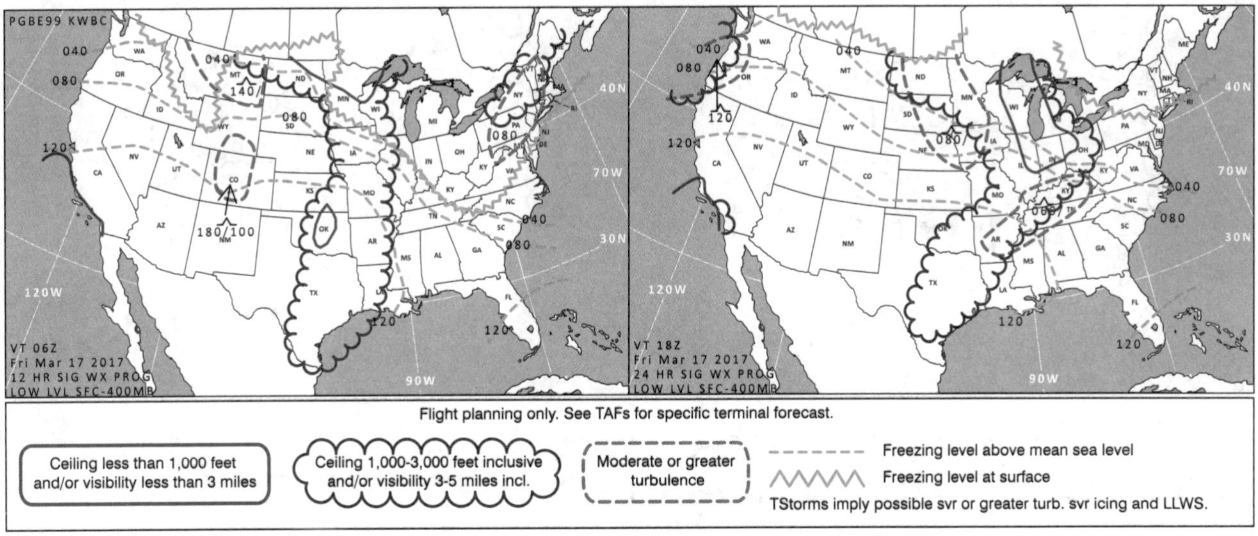

FIGURE 18.—U.S. Low-Level Significant Weather Prognostic Charts.

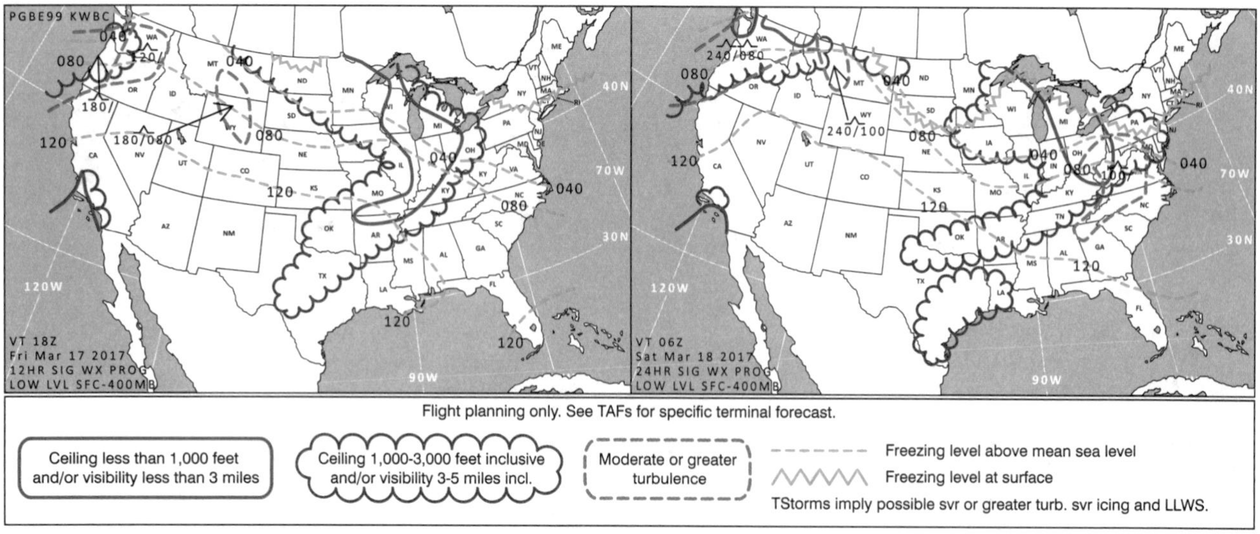

FIGURE 19.—U.S. Low-Level Significant Weather Prognostic Charts.

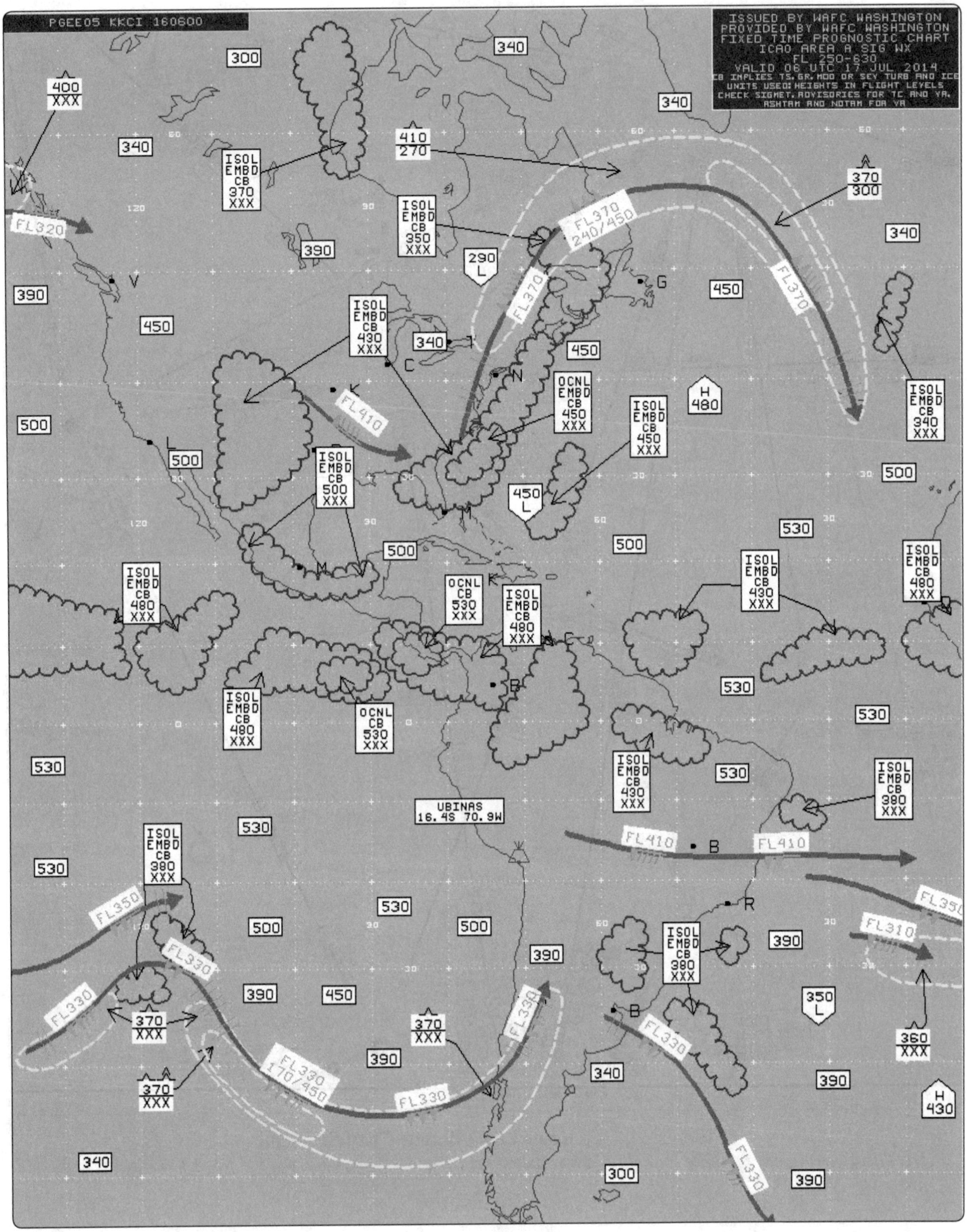

FIGURE 20.—High-Level Significant Weather Prognostic Chart.

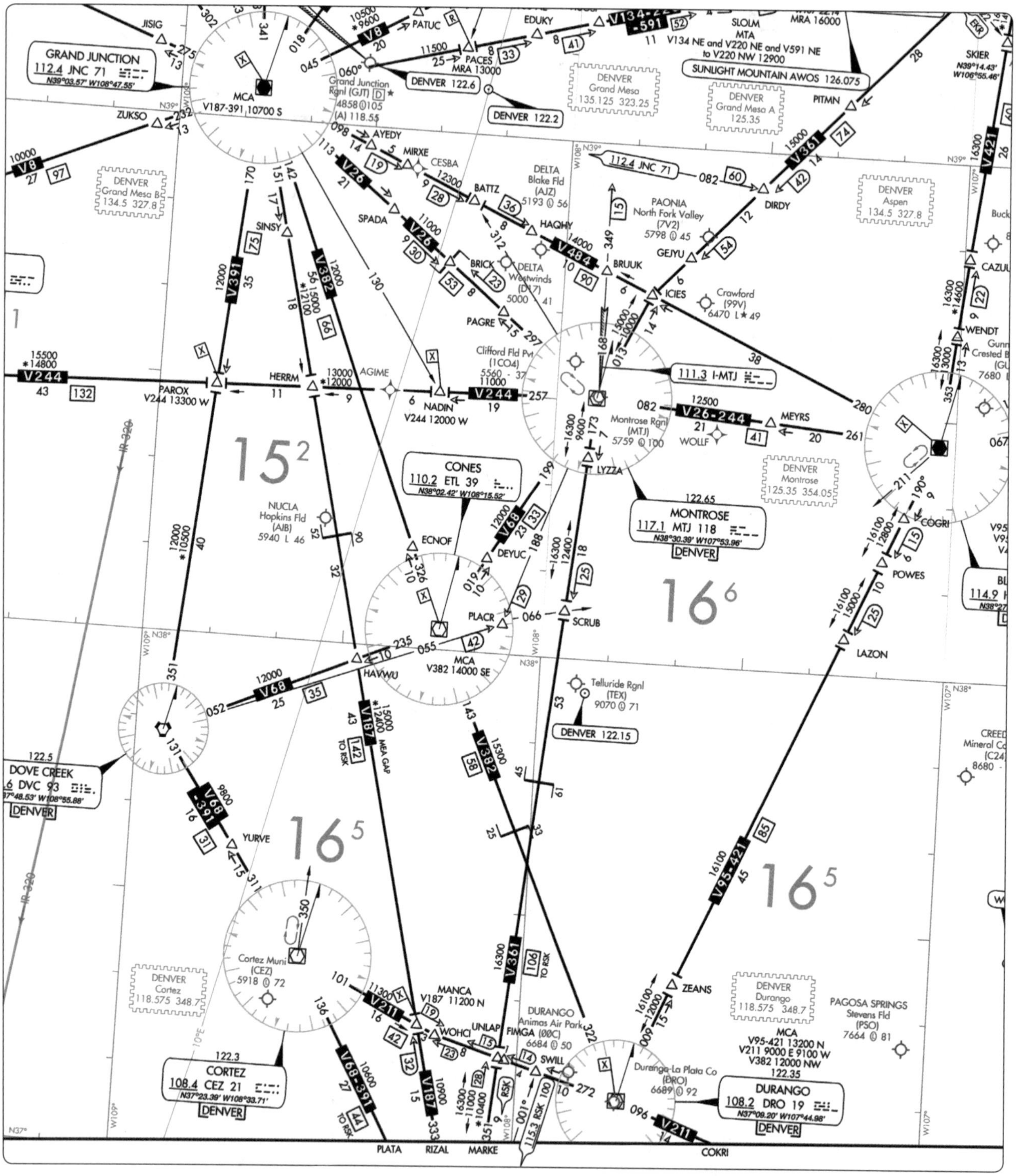

FIGURE 24.—En Route Low-Altitude Chart Segment.

NOTE: Chart is not to scale and should not be used for navigation. Chart is for testing purposes only.

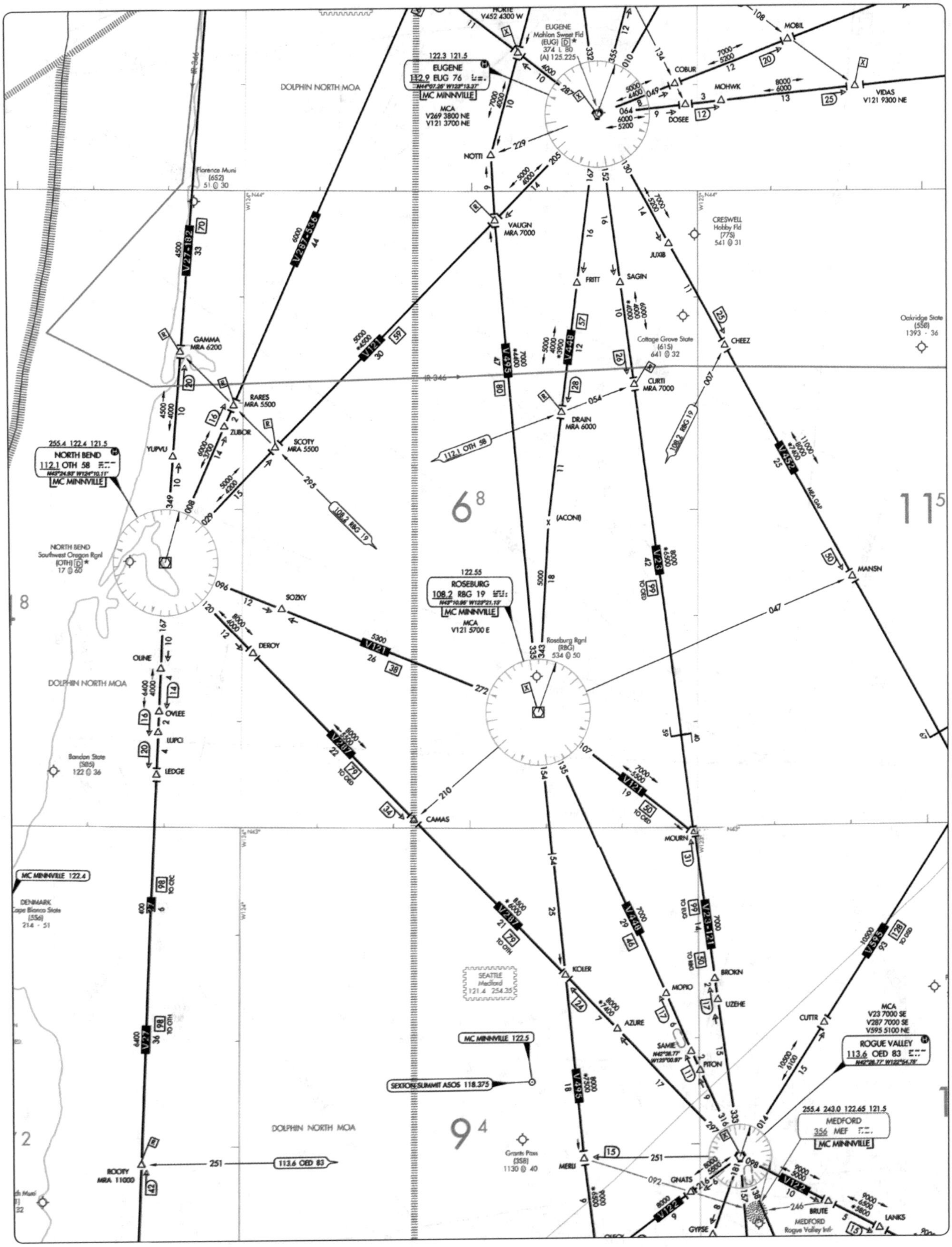

FIGURE 31.—En Route Low-Altitude Chart Segment.

NOTE: Chart is not to scale and should not be used for navigation. Chart is for testing purposes only.

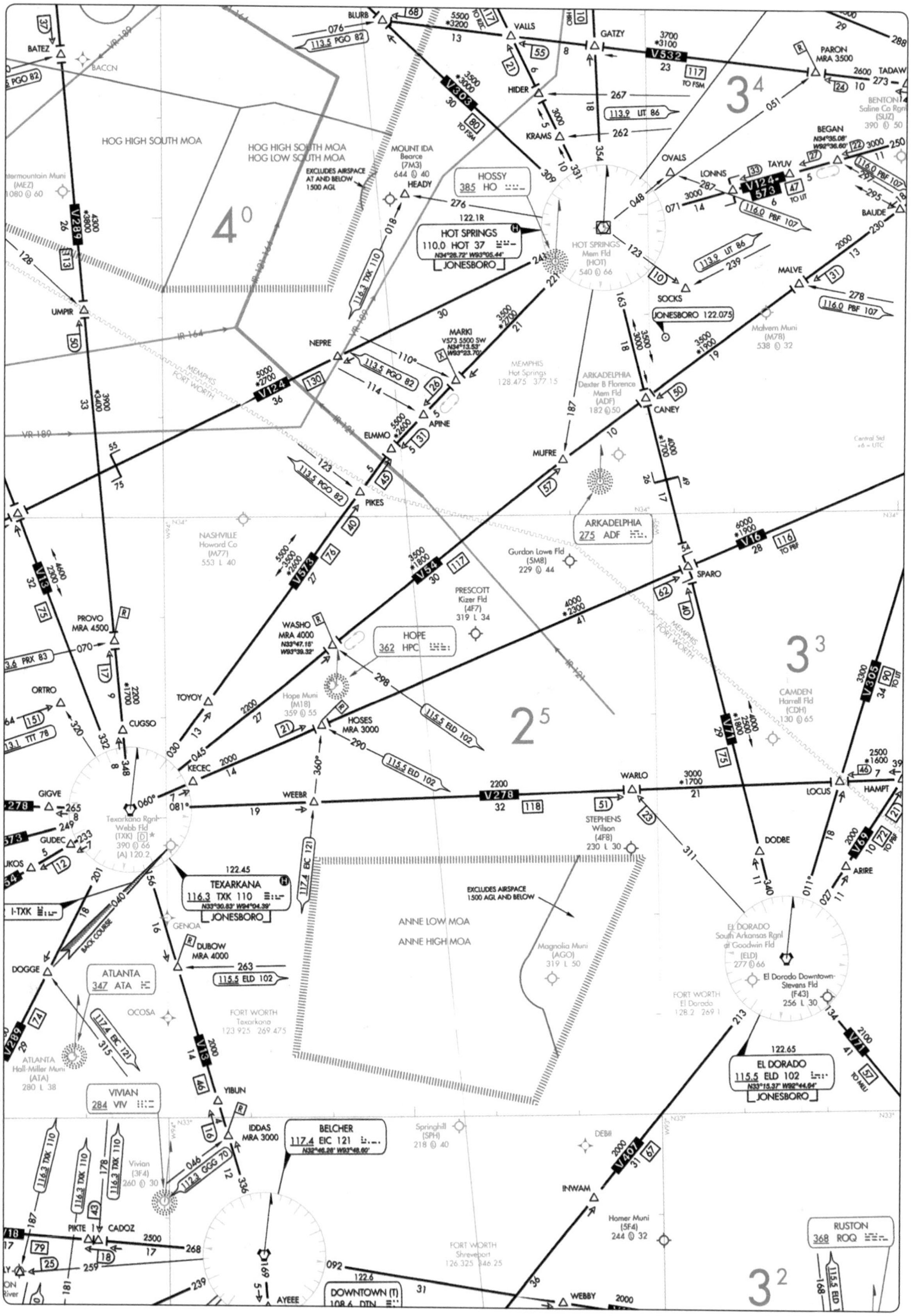

FIGURE 34.—En Route Low-Altitude Chart Segment.

NOTE: Chart is not to scale and should not be used for navigation. Chart is for testing purposes only.

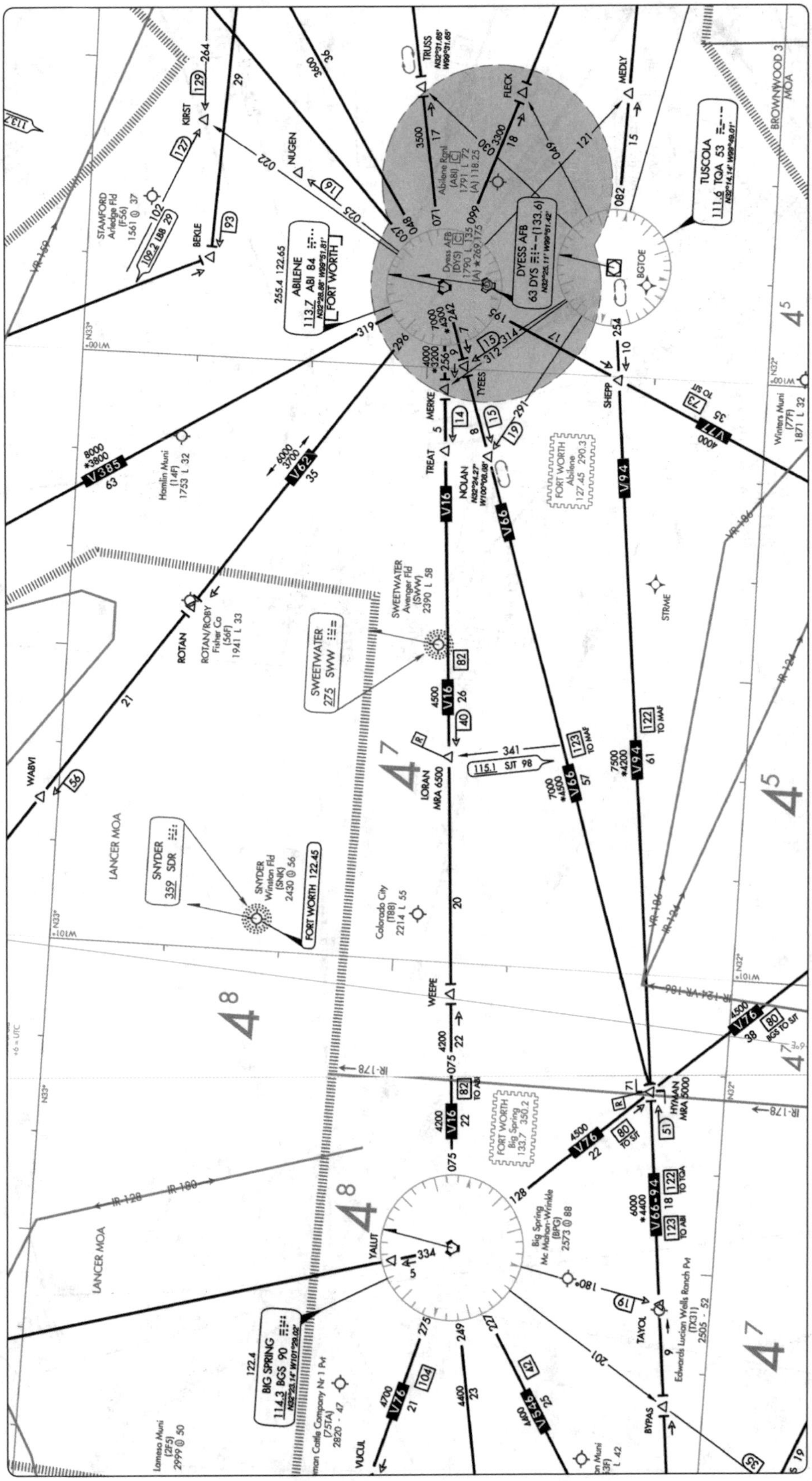

FIGURE 40.—En Route Low-Altitude Chart Segment.

NOTE: Chart is not to scale and should not be used for navigation. Chart is for testing purposes only.

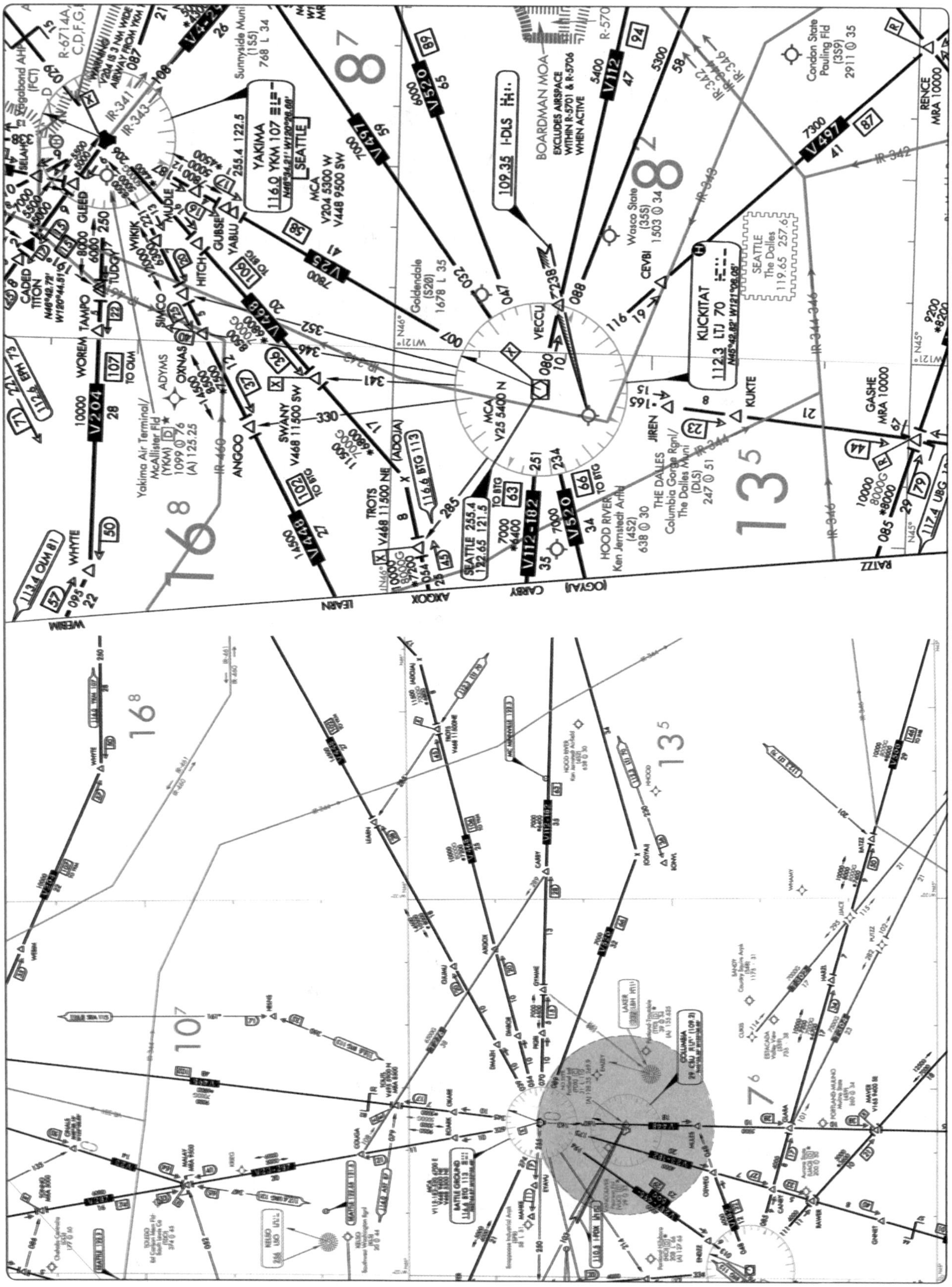

FIGURE 47.—En Route Low-Altitude Chart Segment.

NOTE: Chart is not to scale and should not be used for navigation. Chart is for testing purposes only.

NAV - 1

FREQ	N.M.	KNOTS	MIN
116.0	9.0	7	////

FIGURE 48.—CDI—NAV 1.

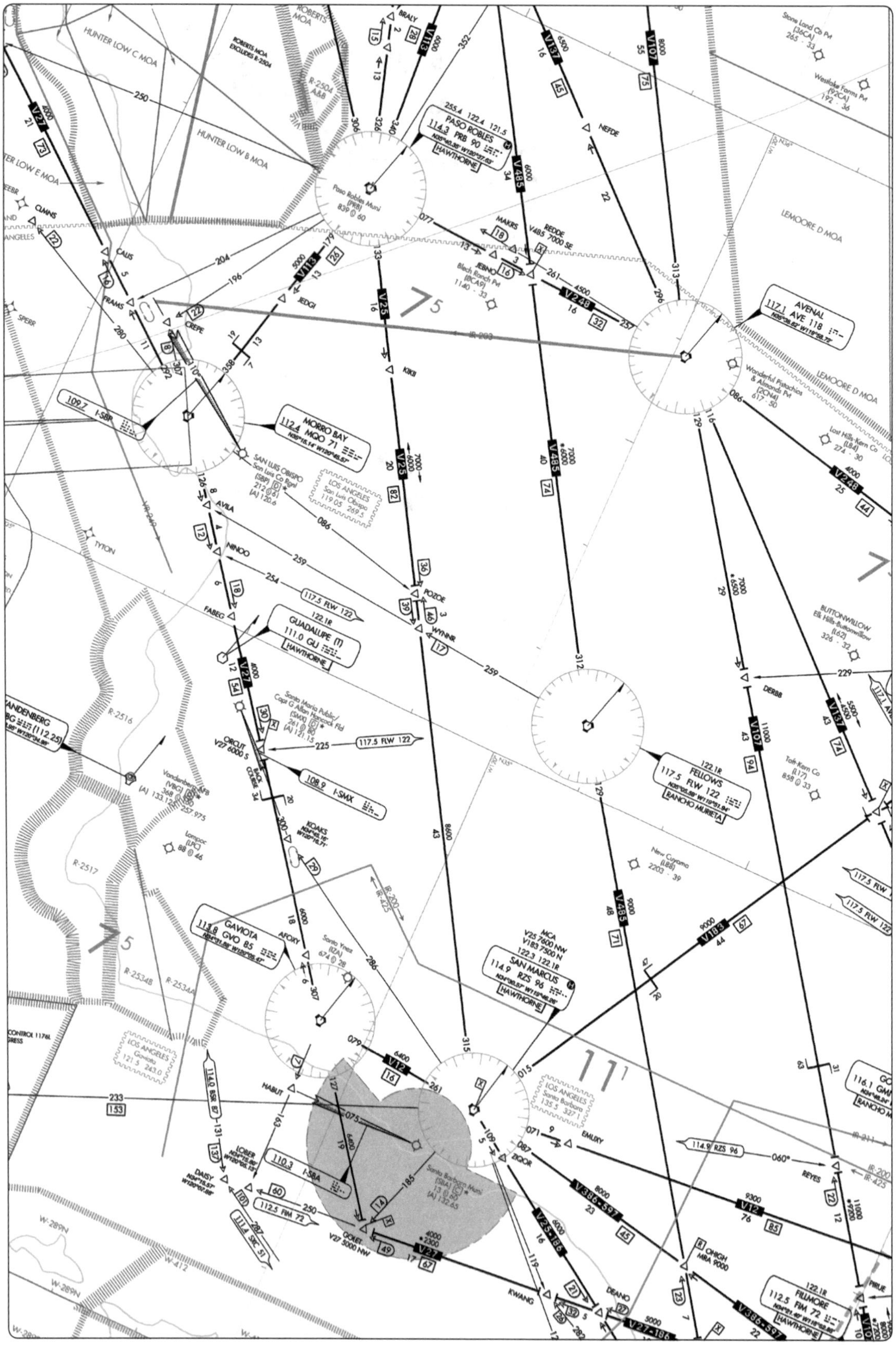

FIGURE 53.—En Route Low-Altitude Chart Segment.

NOTE: Chart is not to scale and should not be used for navigation. Chart is for testing purposes only.

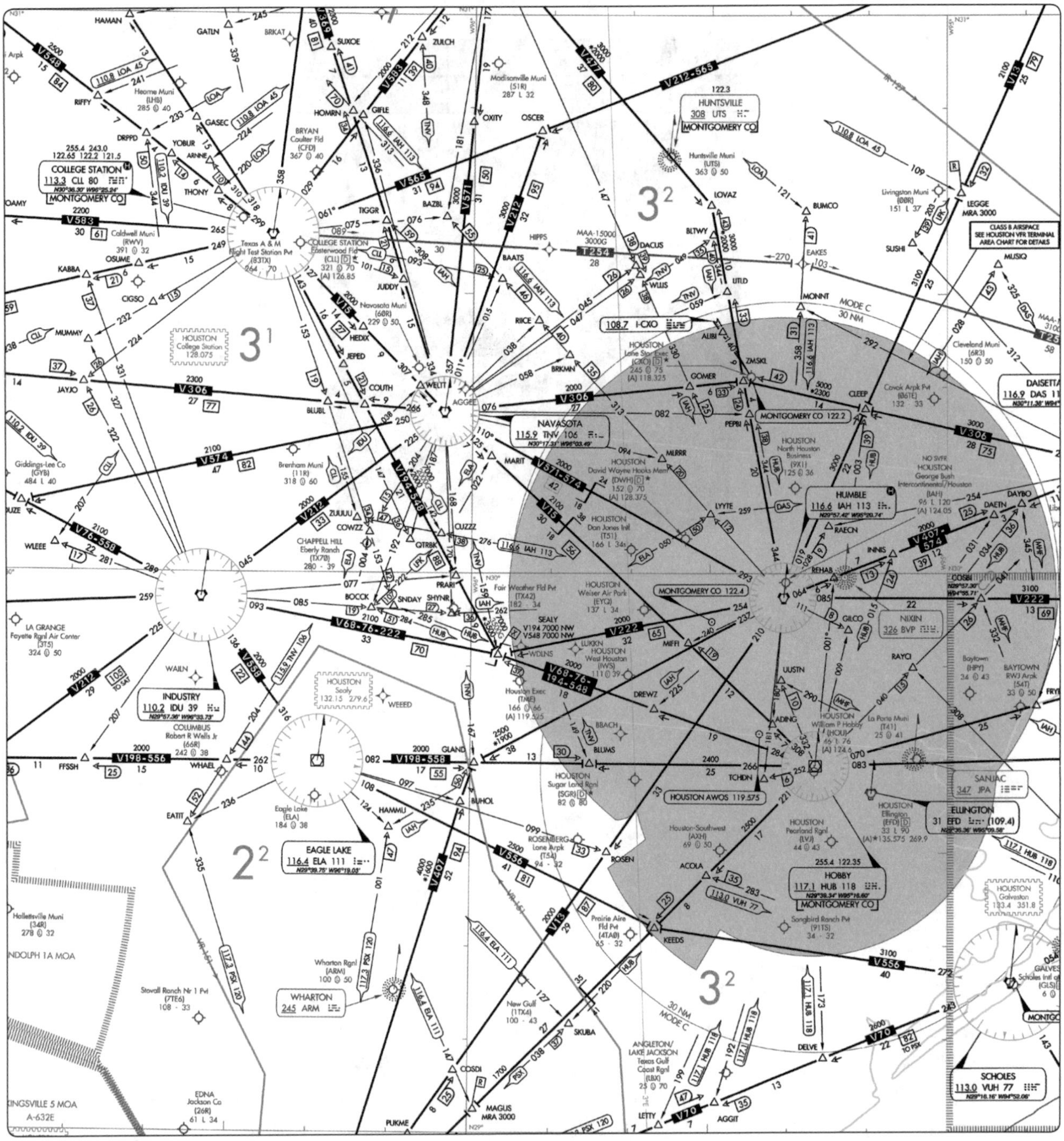

FIGURE 59.—En Route Low-Altitude Chart Segment.

NOTE: Chart is not to scale and should not be used for navigation. Chart is for testing purposes only.

FIGURE 61.—CDI Indicator.

LOUISIANA
VOR RECEIVER CHECKPOINTS

Facility Name (Arpt Name)	Freq/Ident	Type Check Pt. Gnd. AB/ALT	Azimuth from Fac. Mag	Dist. from Fac. N.M.	Checkpoint Description
Alexandria (Alexandria Intl)....................	116.1/AEX	G	328	4.3	On runup Rwy 32.
Baton Rouge (Baton Rouge Metro, Ryan).	116.5/BTR	A/1500	063	7.2	Over water tank W side of arpt.
Lafayette (Lafayette Rgnl/Paul Fournet Fld)	109.8/LFT	A/1000	343	22.1	Over rotating beacon at St. Landry Parish–Ahart Fld. arpt.
	109.8/LFT	G	355	0.5	On Twy F run up area Rwy 04L.
	109.8/LFT	G	341	0.9	On Twy B run up area Rwy 11.
	109.8/LFT	G	025	1.4	On Twy J run up area Rwy 22L.
	109.8/LFT	G	039	0.8	On Twy B run up area Rwy 29.
Lake Charles (Lake Charles Rgnl)	113.4/LCH	A/1000	253	6.2	Over rotg bcn on twr.
Monroe (Monroe Rgnl)...........................	117.2/MLU	G	212	0.7	On Twy G South of twr.
Natchez (Concordia Parish)....................	110.0/HEZ	A/1000	247	10.5	Over hangar NW end of fld.
Reserve (St John The Baptist Parish).......	110.8 RQR	A/1500	270	16.8	Over center of bridge.
Tibby (Houma–Terrebonne)	112.0/TBD	A/1000	121	10.7	Over intersection of Rwys 18–36 and 12–30.
Tibby (Thibodaux Muni).........................	112.0/TBD	A/1000	356	5.0	Over microwave twr near arpt.

84 **LOUISIANA**

LAFAYETTE RGNL (LFT) 2 SE UTC–6(–5DT) N30°12.30′ W91°59.27′ **HOUSTON**
42 B S4 **FUEL** 100LL, JET A OX 1, 4 Class I, ARFF Index B NOTAM FILE LFT **H–7D, L–21B, 22E, GOMC**
IAP, AD

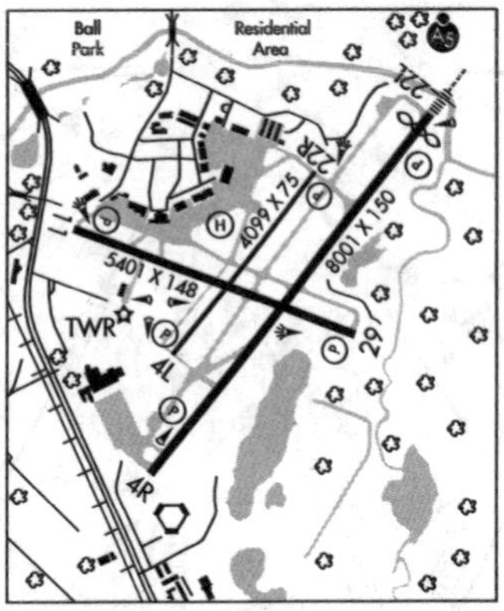

RWY 04R–22L: H8001X150 (ASPH–GRVD) S–140, D–170, 2S–175, 2D–290 HIRL
RWY 04R: REIL. PAPI(P4L)—GA 3.0° TCH 53′. Pole. Rgt tfc.
RWY 22L: MALSR. PAPI(P4L)—GA 3.0° TCH 52′. Thld dsplcd 342′. Trees.
RWY 11–29: H5401X148 (ASPH–GRVD) S–85, D–110, 2S–140, 2D–175 MIRL
RWY 11: REIL. PAPI(P4L)—GA 3.0° TCH 35′. Trees. Rgt tfc.
RWY 29: REIL. PAPI(P4L)—GA 3.0° TCH 35′. Tree.
RWY 04L–22R: H4099X75 (ASPH) S–25, D–32 MIRL
RWY 04L: REIL. PAPI(P2L)—GA 3.0° TCH 26′. Tree.
RWY 22R: REIL. PAPI(P2L)—GA 3.0° TCH 27′. Tree. Rgt tfc.
RUNWAY DECLARED DISTANCE INFORMATION

RWY 04L:	TORA–4099	TODA–4099	ASDA–4099	LDA–4099
RWY 04R:	TORA–8001	TODA–8001	ASDA–8001	LDA–8001
RWY 11:	TORA–5401	TODA–5401	ASDA–5401	LDA–5401
RWY 22L:	TORA–8001	TODA–8001	ASDA–8001	LDA–7659
RWY 22R:	TORA–4099	TODA–4099	ASDA–4099	LDA–4099
RWY 29:	TORA–5401	TODA–5401	ASDA–5401	LDA–5401

ARRESTING GEAR/SYSTEM
RWY 04R: EMAS
RWY 22L: EMAS

AIRPORT REMARKS: Attended continuously. Numerous birds on and invof arpt. PPR for unscheduled air carrier ops with more than 30 passenger seats call arpt manager 337–266–4400. Rwy 04L–22R not avbl for air carrier ops with more than 30 passenger seats. Ctc ground control prior to push back from terminal. 155′ oil rig 1 NM southeast of arpt. Rwy 22L runway visual range touchdown avbl. Twy B between Twy C and Twy D clsd to acft with wingspan over 80′. Twy F south of Twy B clsd to single wheel acft over 25,000 lbs and dual wheel acft over 32,000 lbs. Twy F south of Twy B reduces to 40′ wide. When twr clsd ACTIVATE MALSR Rwy 22L—CTAF, MIRL Rwy 04L–22R not avbl.
WEATHER DATA SOURCES: ASOS (337) 237–8153 **HIWAS** 109.8 LFT.
COMMUNICATIONS: CTAF 118.5 **ATIS** 134.05 **UNICOM** 122.95
RCO 122.35 (DE RIDDER RADIO)
Ⓡ **APP/DEP CON** 121.1 (020°–210°) 128.7 (211°–019°) (1130–0430Z‡)
Ⓡ **HOUSTON CENTER APP/DEP CON** 126.35 (0430–1130Z‡)
TOWER 118.5 (1130–0430Z‡) **GND CON** 121.8 **CLNC DEL** 125.55
AIRSPACE: CLASS C svc ctc **APP CON** svc 1130–0430Z‡ other times CLASS E.
RADIO AIDS TO NAVIGATION: NOTAM FILE LFT.
(L) VORTACW 109.8 LFT Chan 35 N30°11.63′ W91°59.55′ at fld. 36/3E. **HIWAS.**
LAFFS NDB (LOM) 375 LF N30°17.36′ W91°54.48′ 216° 6.5 NM to fld. Unmonitored when ATCT clsd.
ILS/DME 110.9 I–TYN Chan 46 Rwy 04R. Class IE.
ILS/DME 109.5 I–LFT Chan 32 Rwy 22L. Class IE. LOM LAFFS NDB. ILS and LOM unmonitored when ATCT clsd.
ASR (1130–0430Z‡)

FIGURE 64.—Excerpt from Chart Supplement (LFT).

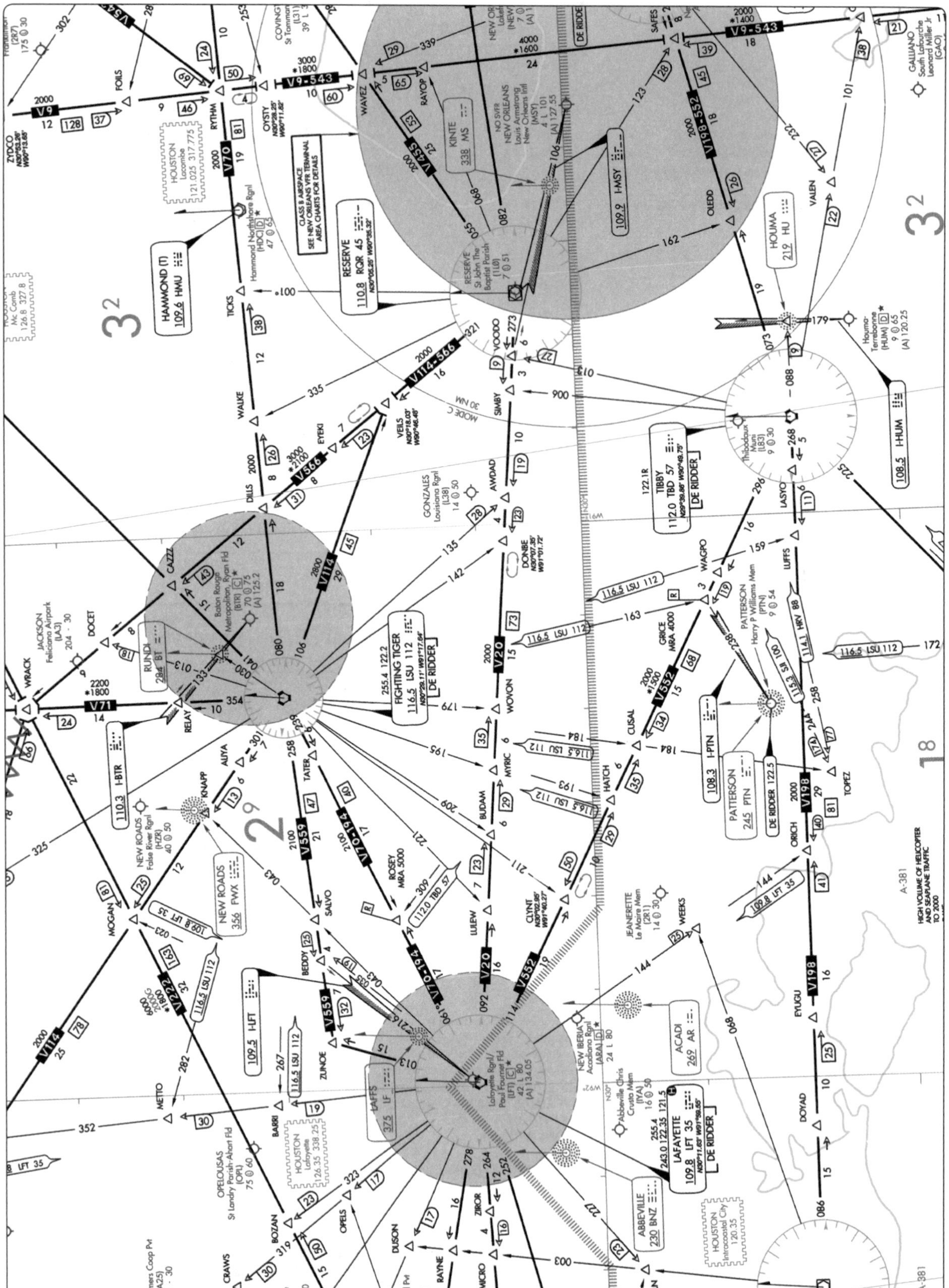

FIGURE 65.—En Route Low-Altitude Chart Segment.

NOTE: Chart is not to scale and should not be used for navigation. Chart is for testing purposes only.

FREQ	OBS	
112.0	116	TO

FREQ	OBS	
108.3	236	//////

FIGURE 66.—CDI and OBS Indicators.

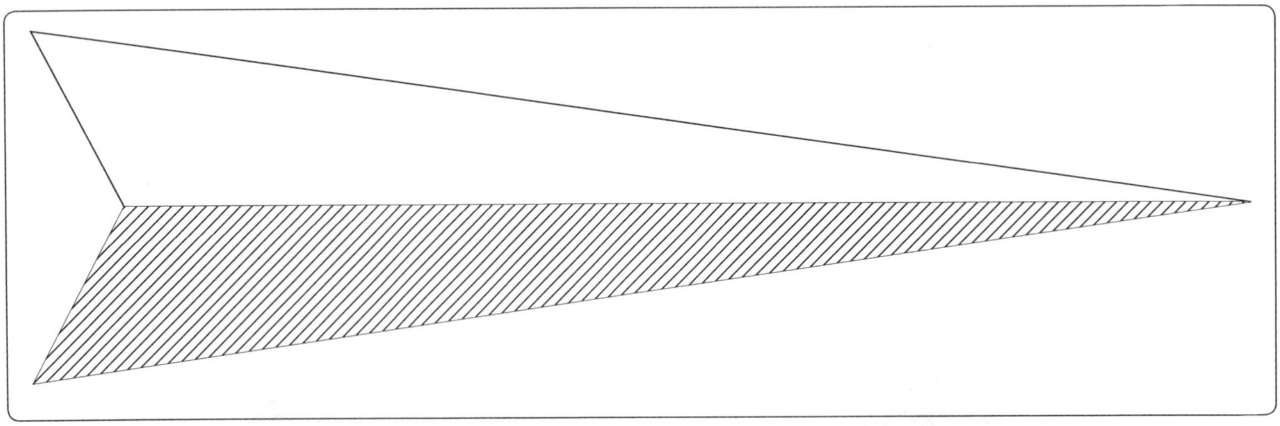

Figure 67.—Localizer Symbol.

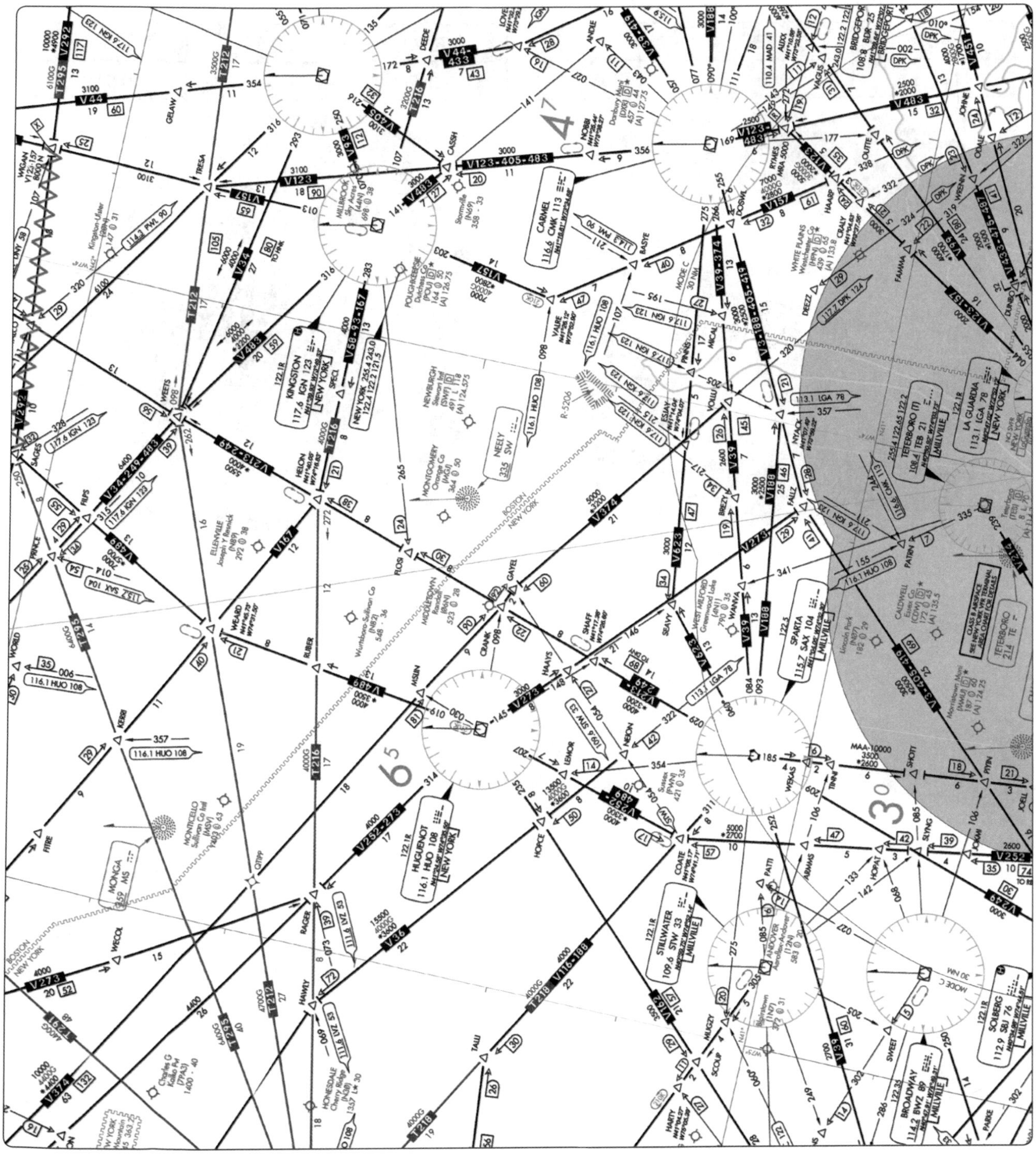

FIGURE 71.—En Route Low-Altitude Chart Segment.
NOTE: Chart is not to scale and should not be used for navigation. Chart is for testing purposes only.

FREQ	OBS	
117.6	265	FROM

FREQ	OBS	
115.7	029	FROM

FIGURE 71A.—CDI and OBS Indicators.

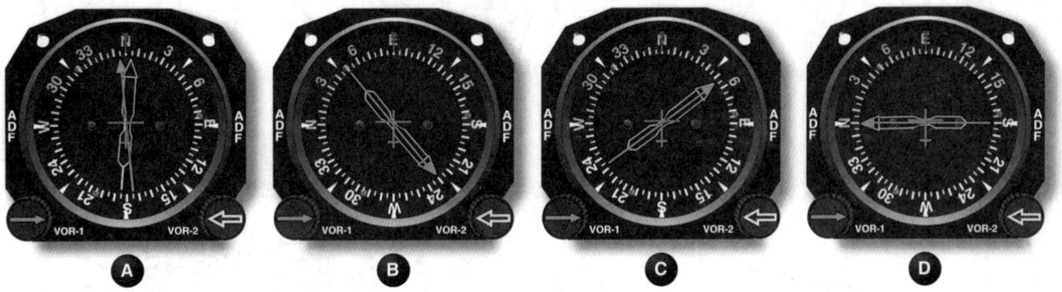

HELENA RGNL (HLN)(KHLN) P (ARNG) 2 NE UTC–7(–6DT) N46°36.41´ W111°58.97´ **GREAT FALLS**
3877 B S4 **FUEL** 80, 100, 100LL, JET A OX 1, 3 LRA Class I, ARFF Index B NOTAM FILE HLN **H–1D, L–13C**
IAP, DIAP, AD

RWY 09–27: H9000X150 (ASPH–PFC) S–100, D–160, 2S–175, 2D–250 HIRL
RWY 09: REIL. VASI(V4L)—GA 3.0° TCH 45´. Ground. 0.3% down.
RWY 27: MALSR. VASI(V4L)—GA 3.0° TCH 47´. Rgt tfc.
RWY 05–23: H4644X75 (ASPH–PFC) S–21, D–30 MIRL 1.2% up SW
RWY 05: Road.
RWY 23: PAPI(P2L)—GA 3.0° TCH 49´. Fence. Rgt tfc.
RWY 16–34: H2989X75 (ASPH–PFC) S–21, D–30 MIRL 1.7% up SE
RWY 34: Ground. Rgt tfc.
MILITARY SERVICE: FUEL A+, J8 (C406–442–2190. Opr 1200–0600Z‡, OT $150 fee, 90 min PPR.) (NC–80, 100, 100LL)
AIRPORT REMARKS: Attended 1200–0800Z‡. ARFF coverage provided for scheduled Part 121 air carriers only exc with prior approval—call 406–442–2821. Landing rights customs available call 406–449–5506. Rwy 16–34 and Rwy 05–23 (except between Twy F and Rwy 09–27) not available for air carrier use by acft with greater than 30 passenger seats. Twys A, B, and C between Twy A and Rwy 34 not available for air carrier use by acft with greater than 30 passenger seats. When tower closed ACTIVATE HIRL Rwy 09–27, MIRL Rwy 05–23 and Rwy 16–34, REIL Rwy 09. MALSR Rwy 27—CTAF. Ldg fee for all commercial acft and all acft over 10,000 pounds. Flight Notification Service (ADCUS) avbl. NOTE: See SPECIAL NOTICE.

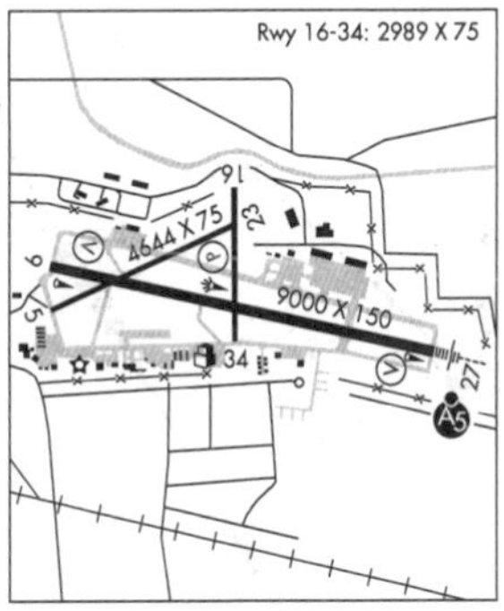

MILITARY REMARKS: ARNG Opr Mon–Fri 1400–0030Z‡, except holidays. Exercise caution while taxiing, AASF ramp not stressed for large acft. Ctc flight ops for ramp advisory 126.2, DSN 324–3055/56, C406–324–3055/56. No trans svc Sat, Sun, holidays or after 2300Z‡ Mon–Fri.
WEATHER DATA SOURCES: ASOS (406) 443–4317
COMMUNICATIONS: CTAF 118.3 **ATIS** 120.4 **UNICOM** 122.95
RCO 122.55 255.4 (GREAT FALLS RADIO)
APP/DEP CON 119.5 229.4 (1300–0500Z‡)
SALT LAKE CENTER APP/DEP CON 133.4 285.4 (0500–1300Z‡)
TOWER 118.3 257.8 (1300–0500Z‡) **GND CON** 121.9
ARNG OPS 40.65 126.2 321.45
AIRSPACE: CLASS D svc 1300–0500Z‡ other times CLASS E.
RADIO AIDS TO NAVIGATION: NOTAM FILE HLN.
(H) VORTACW 117.7 HLN Chan 124 N46°36.41´ W111°57.21´ 254° 1.2 NM to fld. 3823/16E.

VOR portion unusable:	TACAN DME unusable:	TACAN AZIMUTH unusable:
035°–050° byd 35 NM blo 12,000´	035°–070° byd 35 NM blo 13,000´	105°–150° byd 15 NM
105°–165° byd 25 NM blo 17,000´	105°–150° byd 25 NM	150°–165° byd 15 NM blo 17,000´
165°–185° byd 25 NM blo 13,500´	105°–210° byd 15 NM blo 11,100´	185°–210° byd 15 NM
185°–230° byd 25 NM blo 17,500´	105°–210° byd 20 NM blo 12,000´	210°–250° byd 15 NM blo 17,500´
203°–213° byd 22 NM blo 13,000´	150°–165° byd 25 NM blo 17,000´	
230°–270° byd 25 NM blo 12,500´	165°–185° byd 25 NM blo 13,500´	
TACAN AZIMUTH and DME unusable:	185°–210° byd 25 NM	
035°–070° byd 35 NM blo 13,000´	203°–213° byd 22 NM blo 13,000´	
165°–185° byd 25 NM blo 13,500´	210°–250° byd 15 NM blo 12,000´	
250°–300° byd 25 NM blo 14,000´	210°–250° byd 25 NM blo 17,500´	
320°–035° byd 25 NM blo 13,000´	250°–300° byd 25 NM blo 14,000´	
	320°–035° byd 25 NM blo 13,000´	

CAPITOL NDB (HW) 335 CVP N46°36.40´ W111°56.23´ 258° 1.9 NM to fld. NDB unmonitored when ATCT clsd.
HAUSER NDB (MHW) 386 HAU N46°34.13´ W111°45.48´ 268° 9.6 NM to fld. NDB unmonitored when HLN ATCT clsd.
ILS 110.1 I–HLN Rwy 27. Unmonitored when ATCT closed. Localizer backcourse unusable byd 22° rgt of course, unusable within 2.7 DME.

VOR RECEIVER CHECKPOINTS

Facility Name (Arpt Name)	Freq/Ident	Type Check Pt. Gnd. AB/ALT	Azimuth from Fac. Mag	Dist. from Fac. N.M.	Checkpoint Description
Helena (Helena Rgnl)	117.7/HLN	G	238	0.7	On Twy E on South side of Rwy 27.
Kalispell (Glacier Park Intl)	113.2/FCA	A/4000	316	6.4	Over apch end Rwy 30.
Lewistown (Lewistown Muni)	112.0/LWT	A/5200	075	5.6	Over apch end Rwy 07.
Livingston	116.1/LVM	A/6500	237	5.5	Over northern most radio twr NE of city.
Miles City (Frank Wiley Field)	112.1/MLS	G	036	4.2	On twy leading to Rwy 30.
Missoula (Missoula Intl)	112.8/MSO	G	344	0.6	Terminal ramp east of Twy D.

FIGURE 76.—VOR Indications and Excerpts from Chart Supplement (HLN).

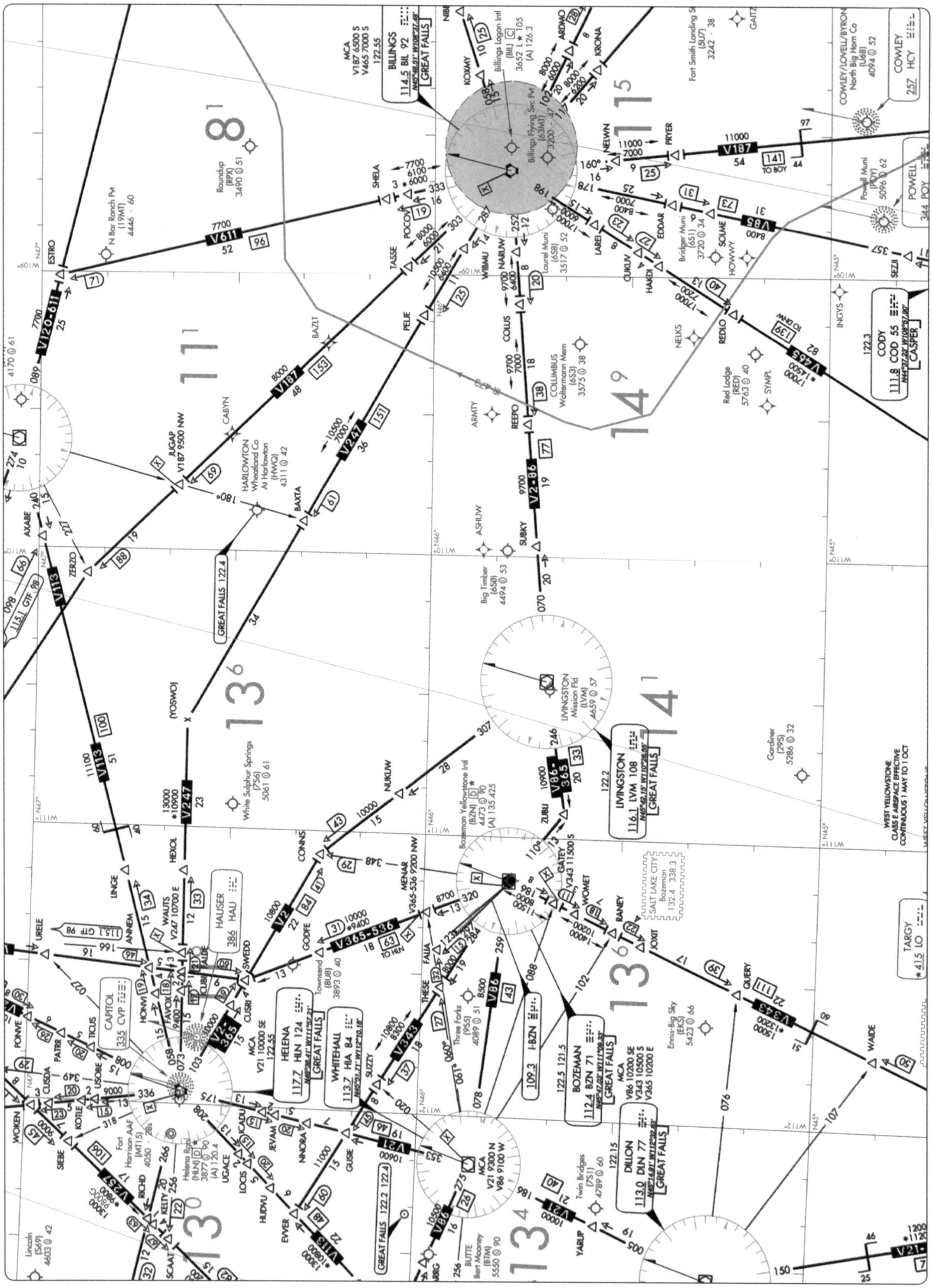

FIGURE 78.—En Route Low-Altitude Chart Segment.

NOTE: Chart is not to scale and should not be used for navigation. Chart is for testing purposes only.

FIGURE 81.—Dual VOR System, VOT Check.

FIGURE 82.—Dual VOR System, Accuracy Check.

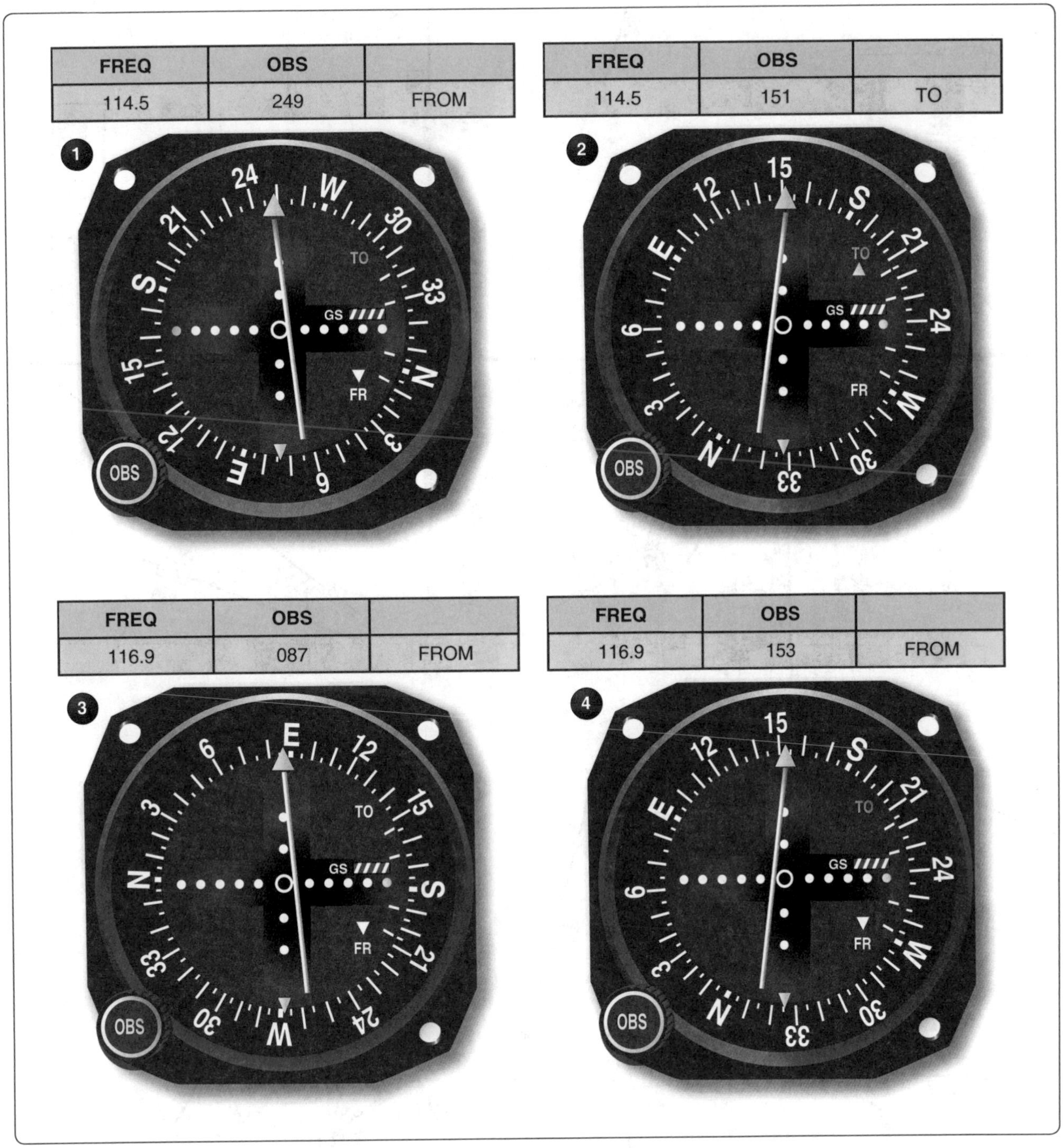

FIGURE 86.—CDI and OBS Indicators.

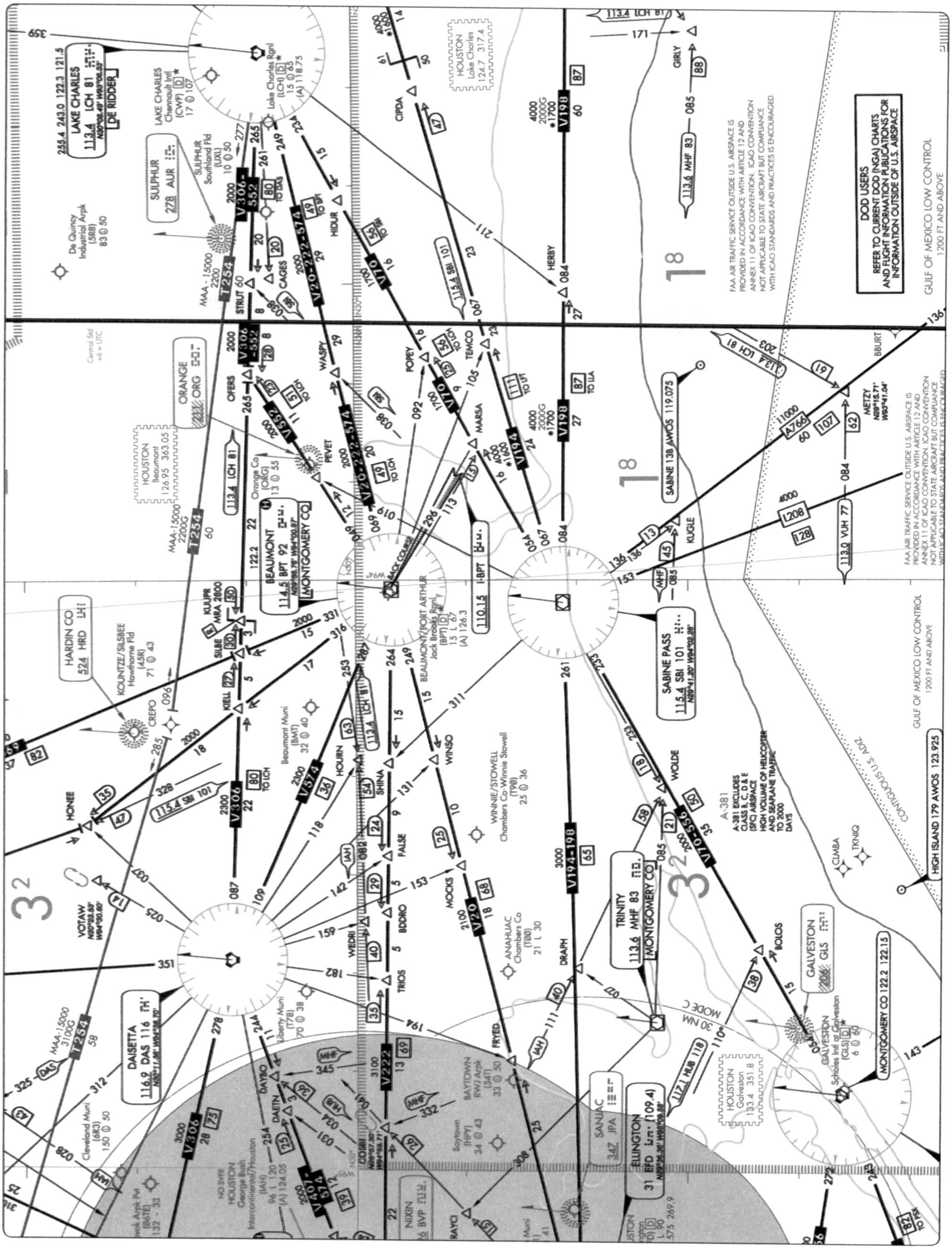

FIGURE 87.—En Route Low-Altitude Chart Segment.

NOTE: Chart is not to scale and should not be used for navigation. Chart is for testing purposes only.

FREQ	OBS	
114.5	264	FROM

FREQ	OBS	
116.9	139	FROM

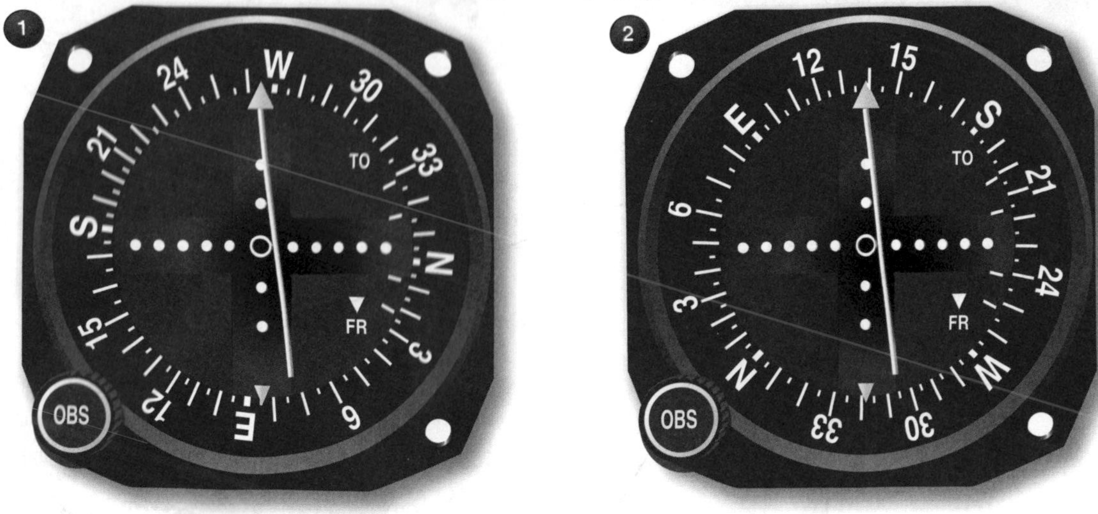

FIGURE 88.—CDI and OBS Indicators.

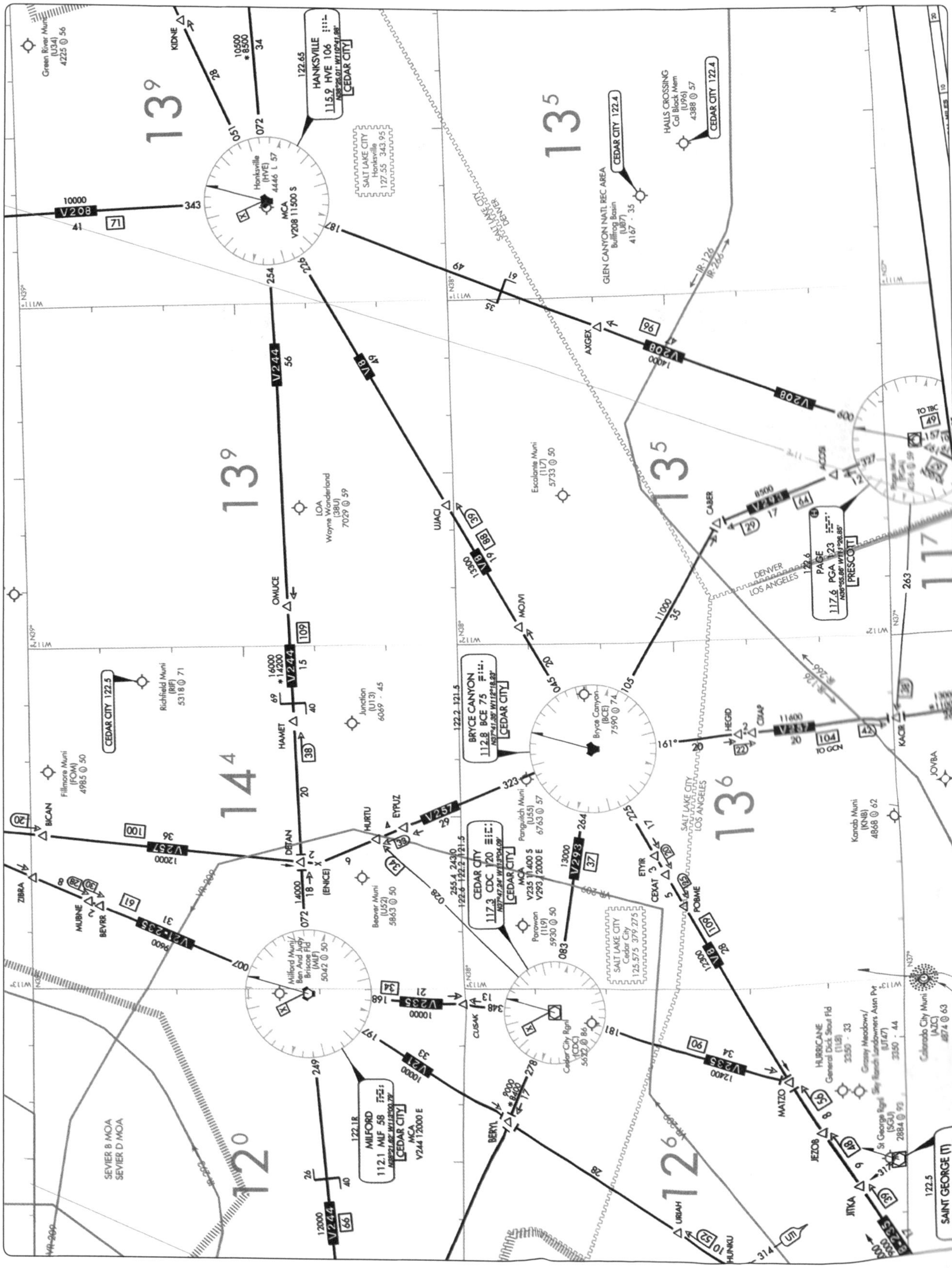

FIGURE 89.—En Route Low-Altitude Chart Segment.

NOTE: Chart is not to scale and should not be used for navigation. Chart is for testing purposes only.

FREQ	OBS	
112.8	033	FROM

FREQ	OBS	
115.9	046	TO

FIGURE 90.—CDI/OBS Indicators.

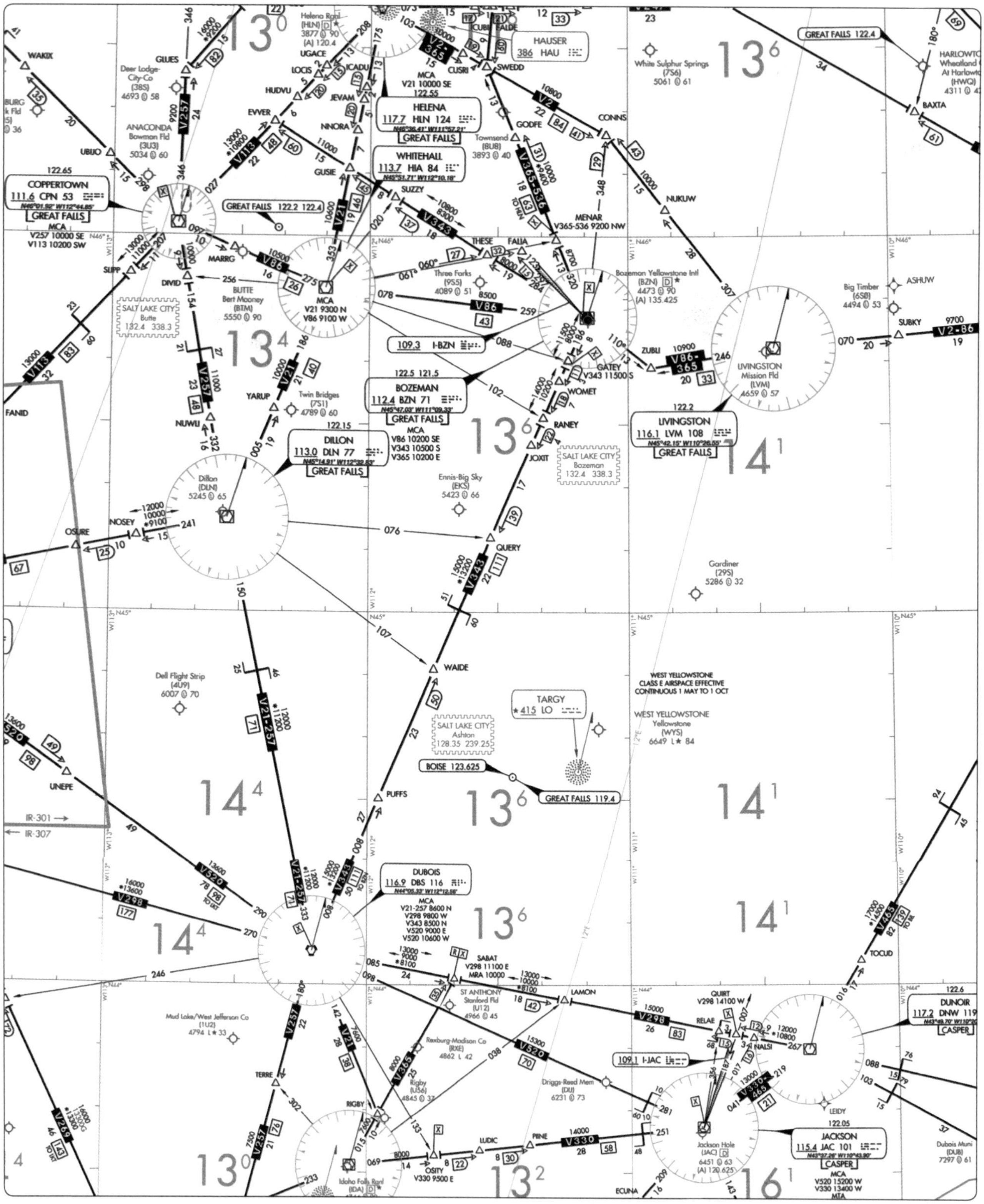

FIGURE 91.—En Route Low-Altitude Chart Segment.

NOTE: Chart is not to scale and should not be used for navigation. Chart is for testing purposes only.

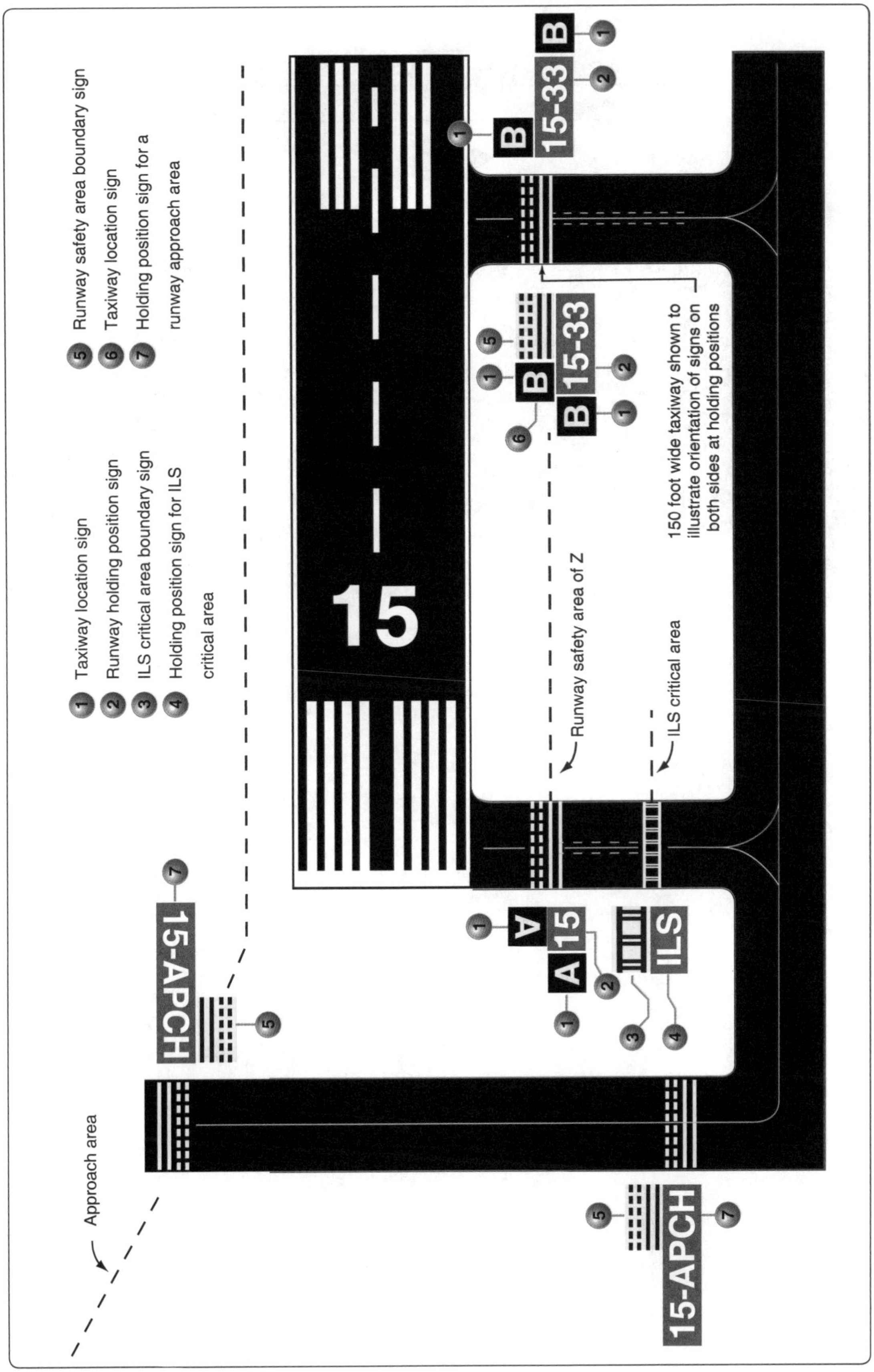

FIGURE 94.—Application Examples for Holding Positions.

FREQ	N.M.	KNOTS	MIN
115.0	60	180	20.0

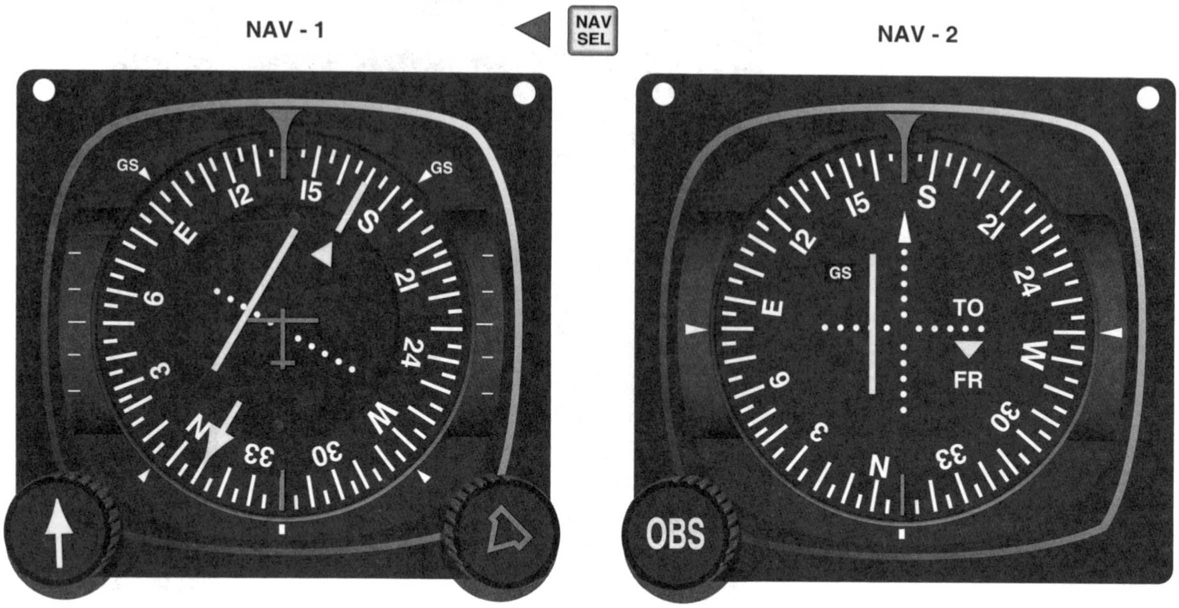

Figure 95.—No. 1 and No. 2 NAV Presentation.

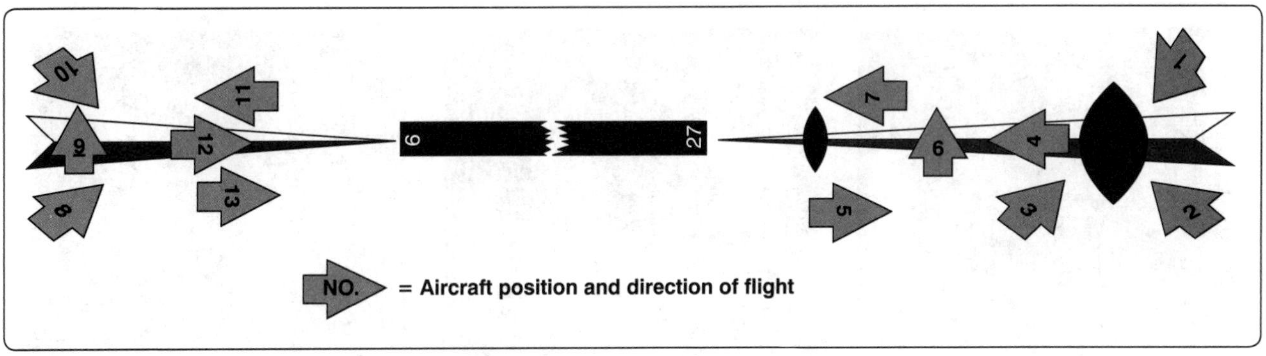

FIGURE 96.—Aircraft Position and Direction of Flight.

FIGURE 97.—HSI Presentation.

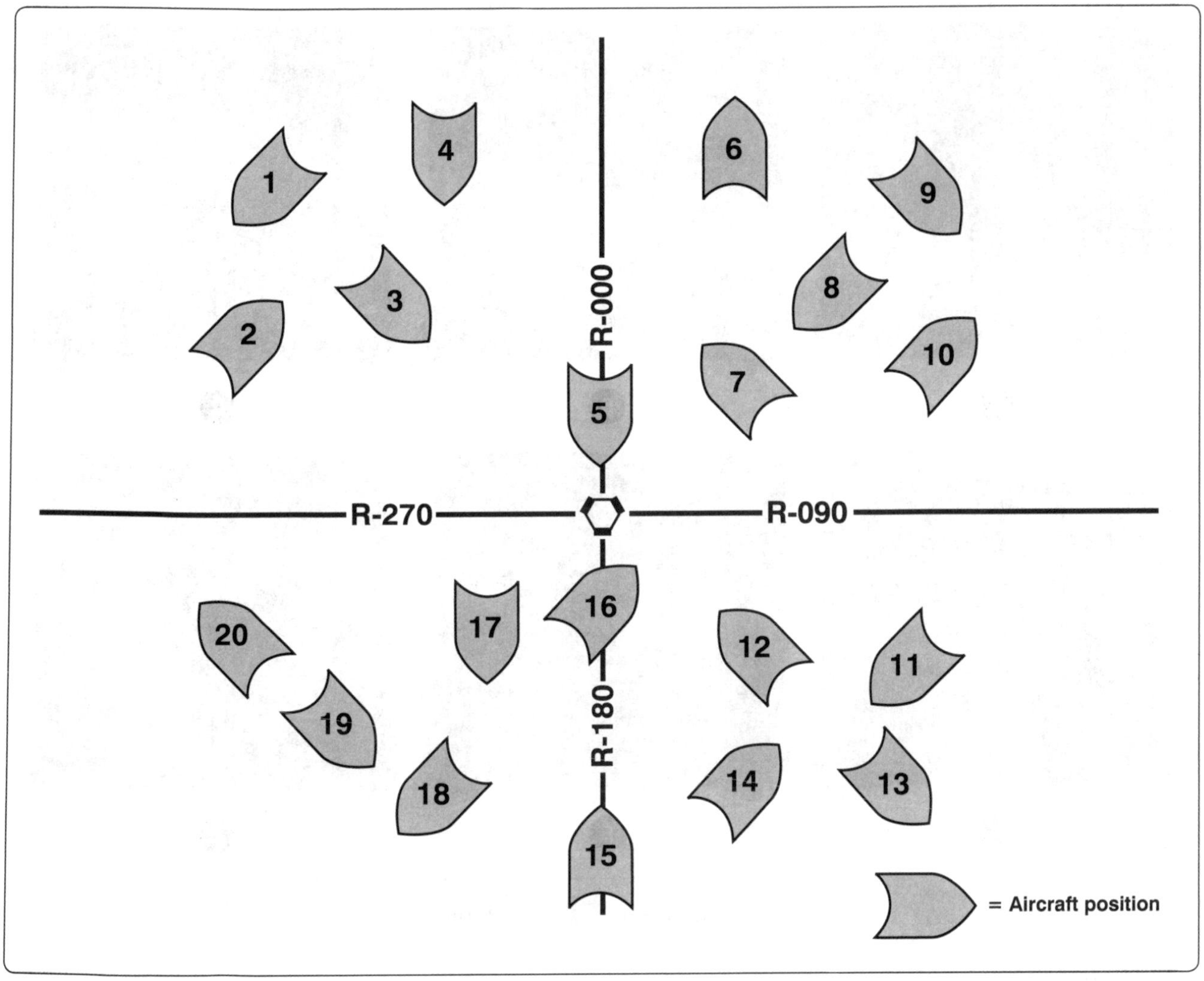

FIGURE 98.—Aircraft Position.

FIGURE 99.—HSI Presentation.

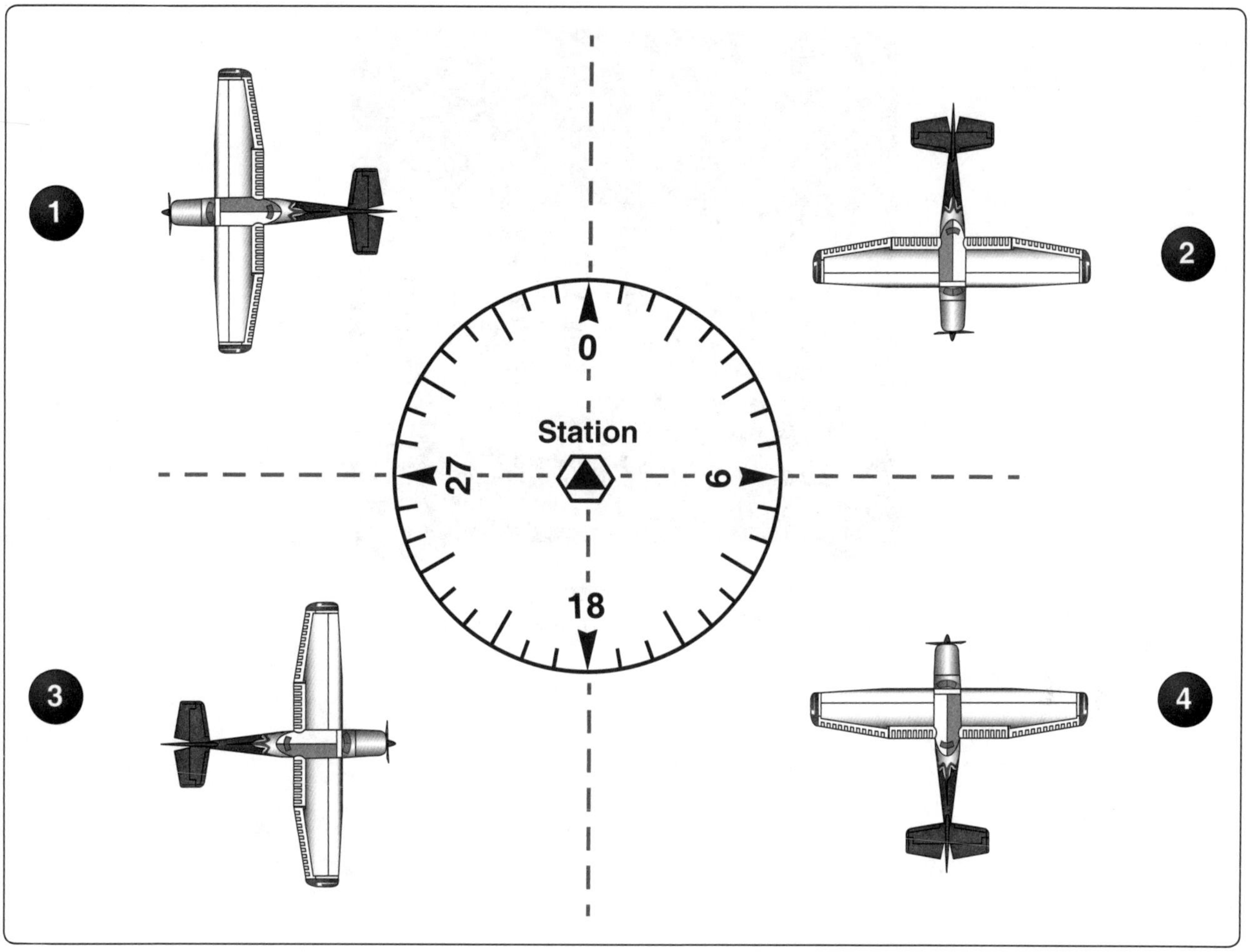

FIGURE 106.—Aircraft Location Relative to VOR.

FIGURE 109.—CDI Direction from VORTAC.

FIGURE 110.—CDI Direction from VORTAC.

FIGURE 111.—CDI Direction from VORTAC.

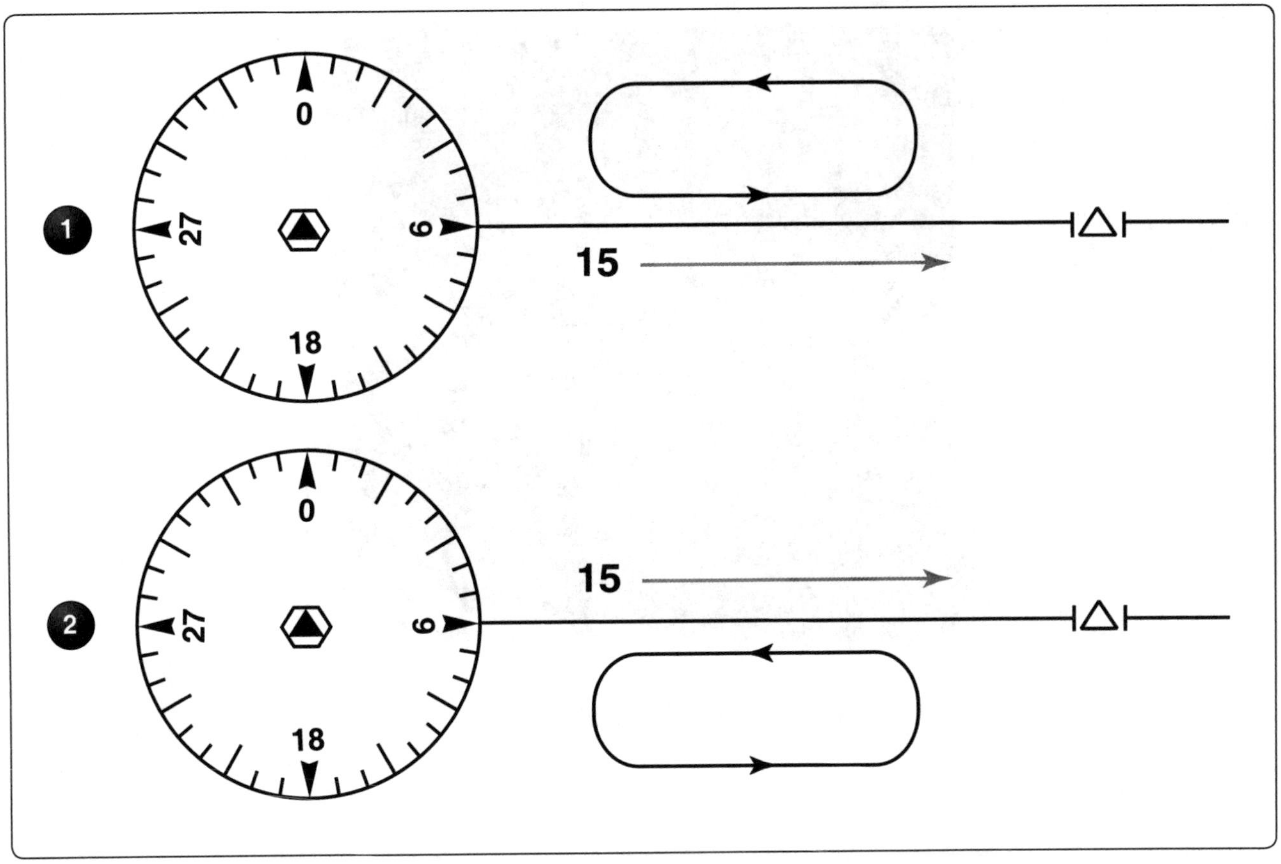

FIGURE 112.—Holding Entry Procedure.

FIGURE 113.—Aircraft Course and DME Indicator.

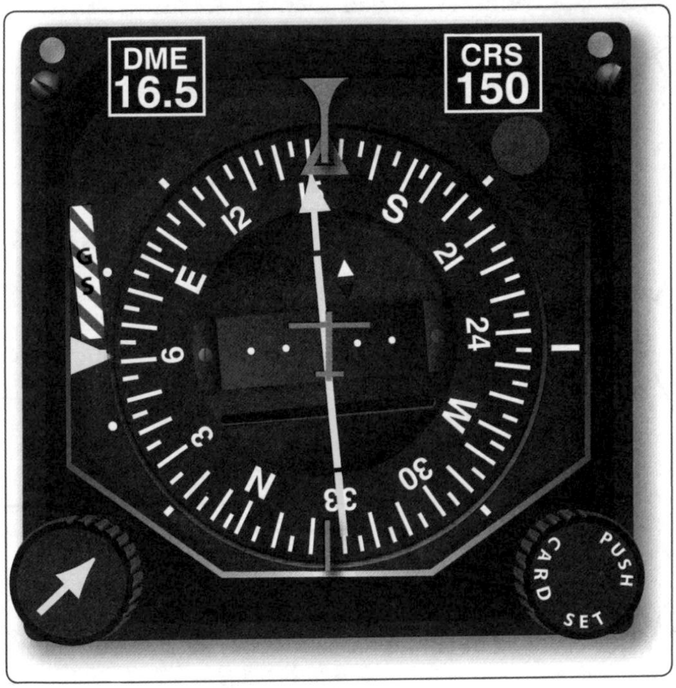

FIGURE 114.—Aircraft Course and DME Indicator.

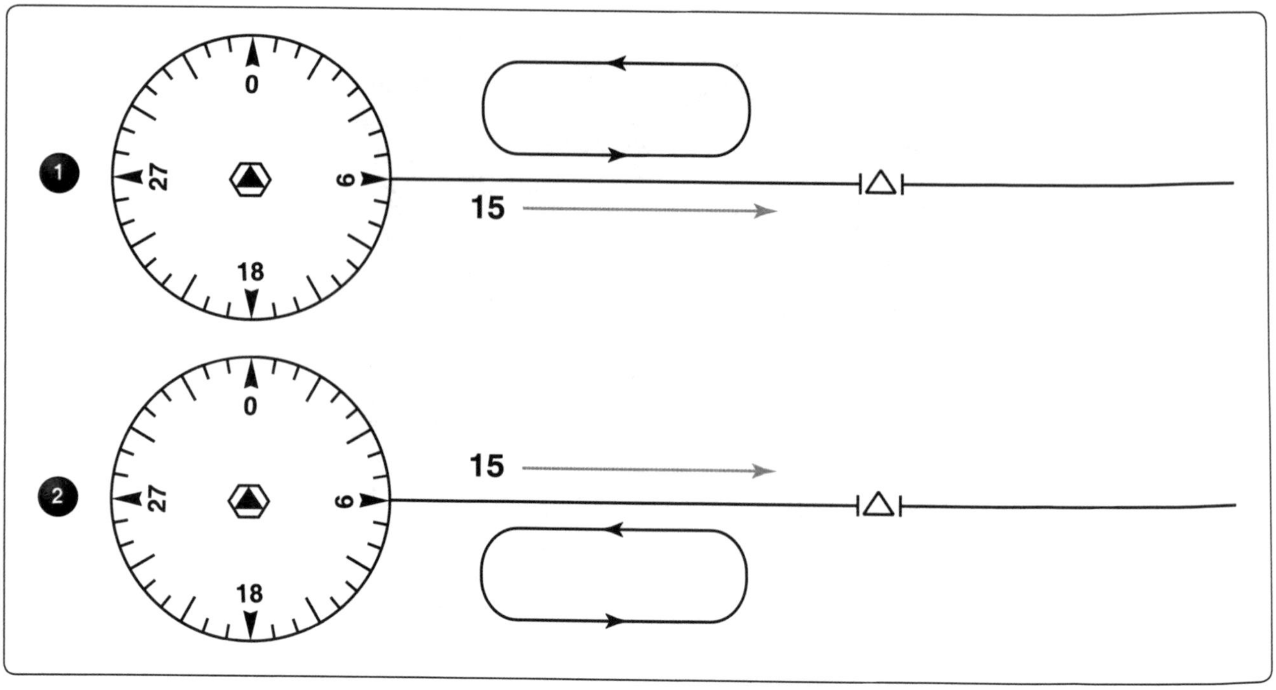

FIGURE 115.—DME Fix with Holding Pattern.

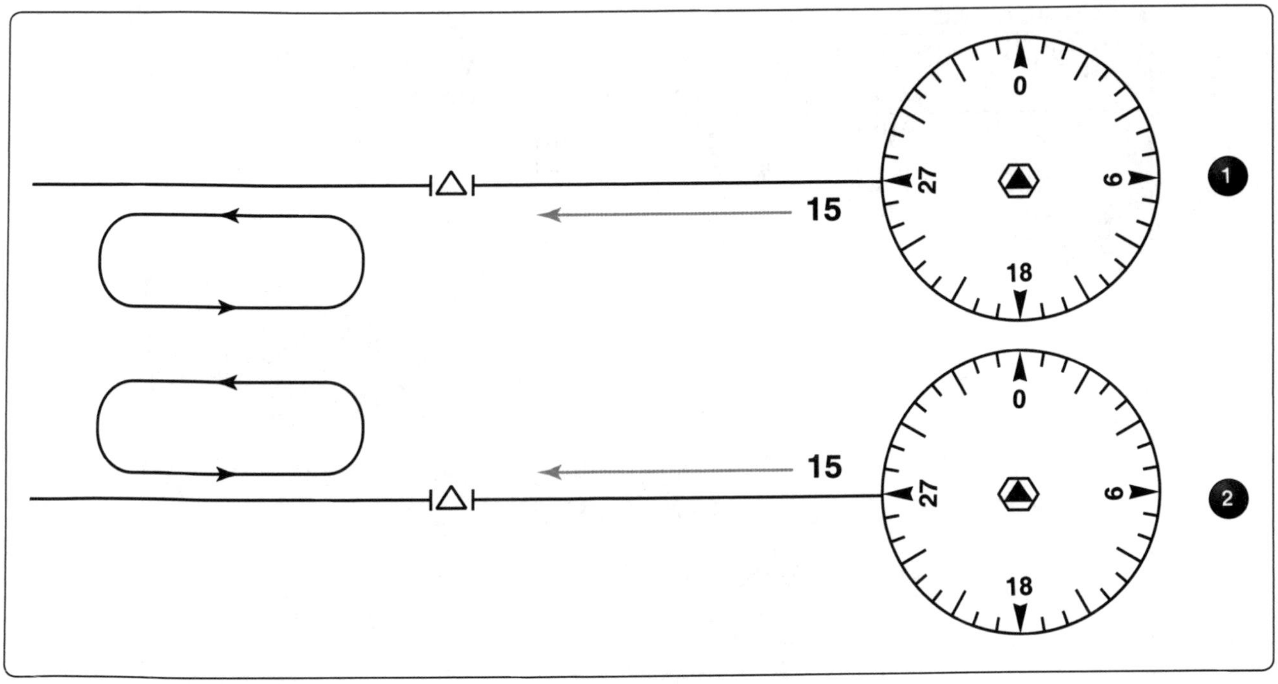

FIGURE 116.—Holding Entry Procedure.

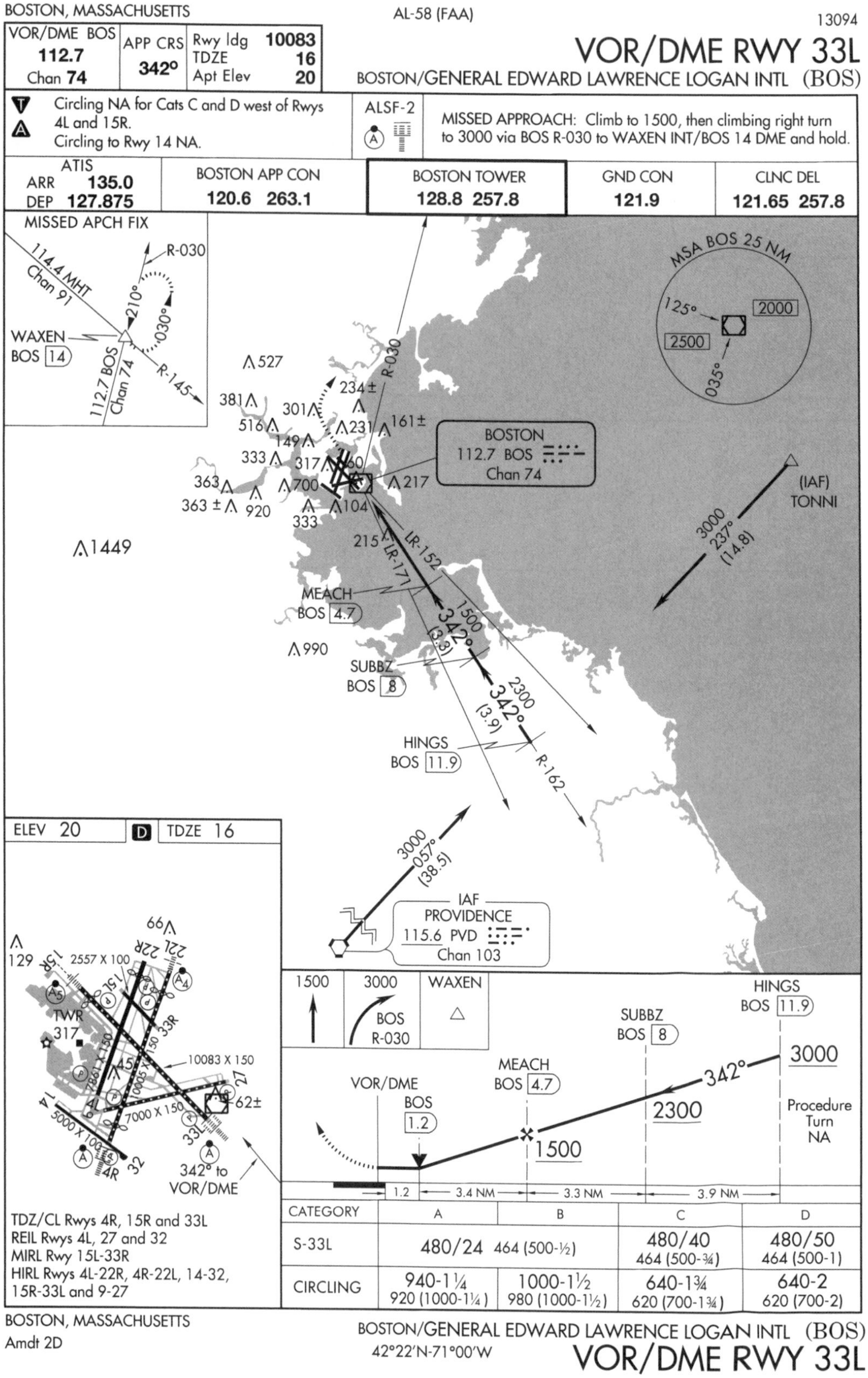

FIGURE 131.—VOR/DME RWY 33L.

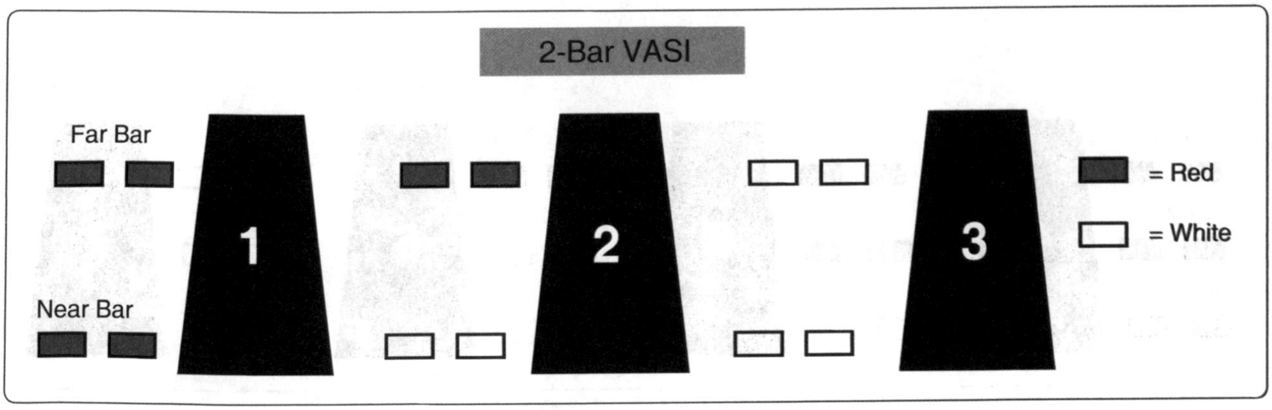

FIGURE 134.—2-BAR VASI.

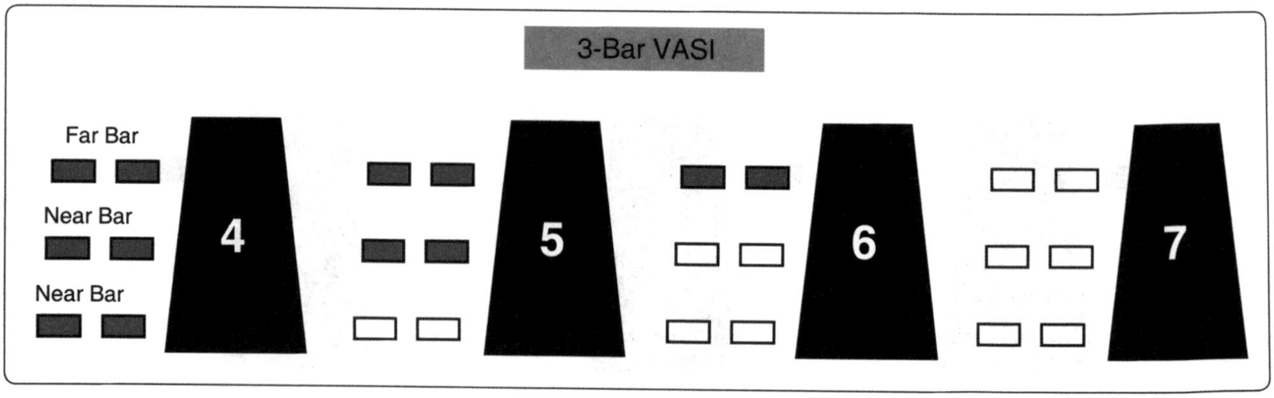

FIGURE 135.—3-BAR VASI.

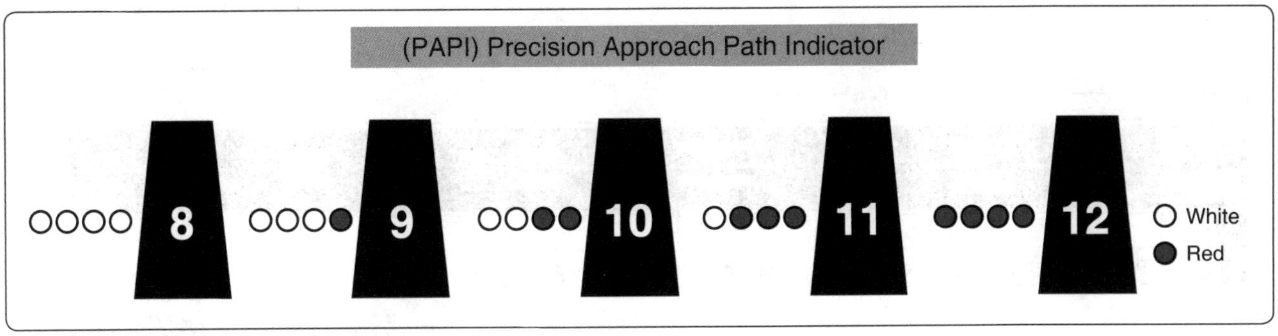

FIGURE 136.—Precision Approach Path Indicator (PAPI).

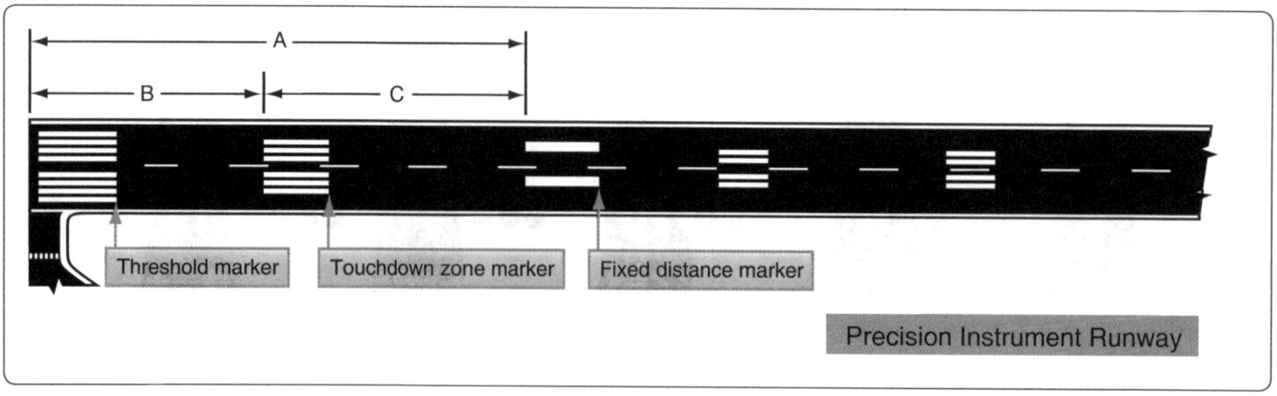

FIGURE 137.—Precision Instrument Runway.

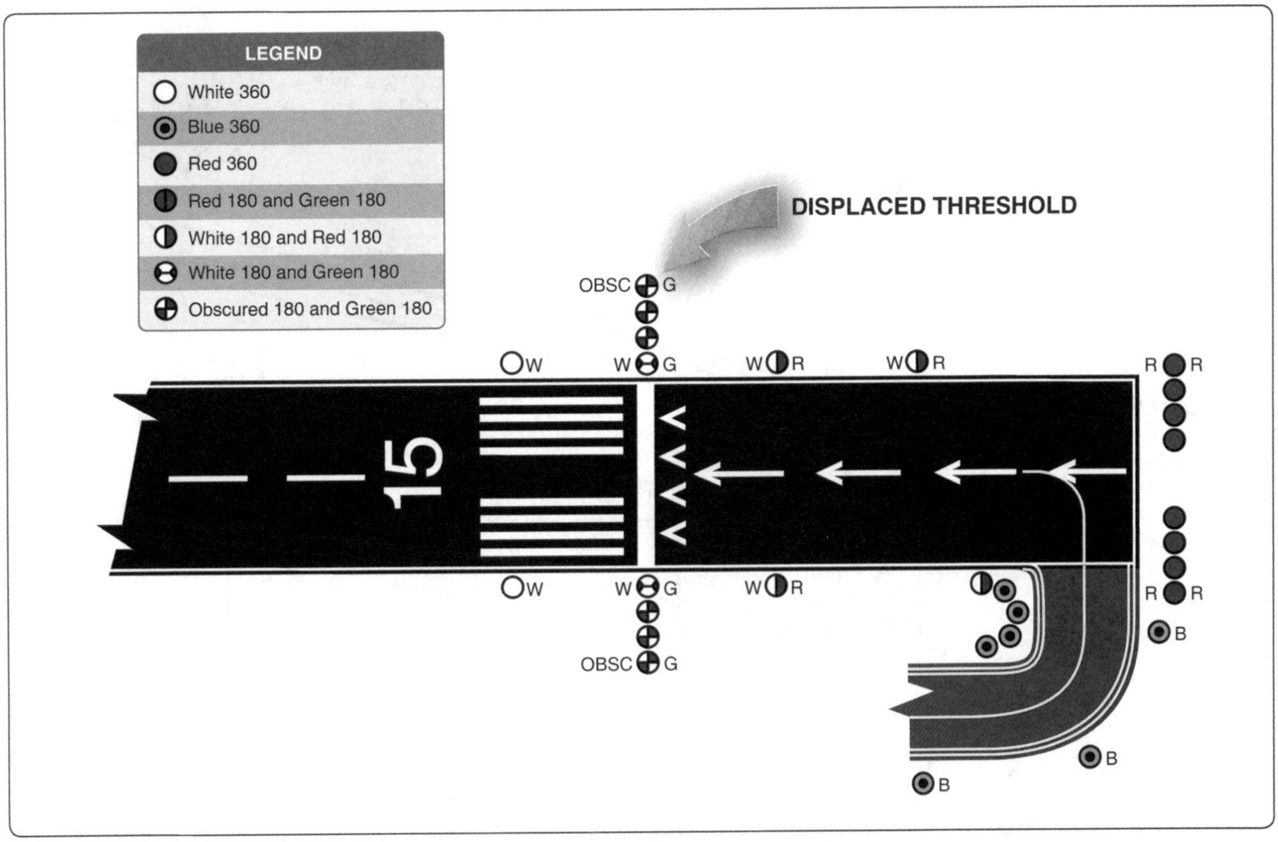

FIGURE 138.—Runway Legend.

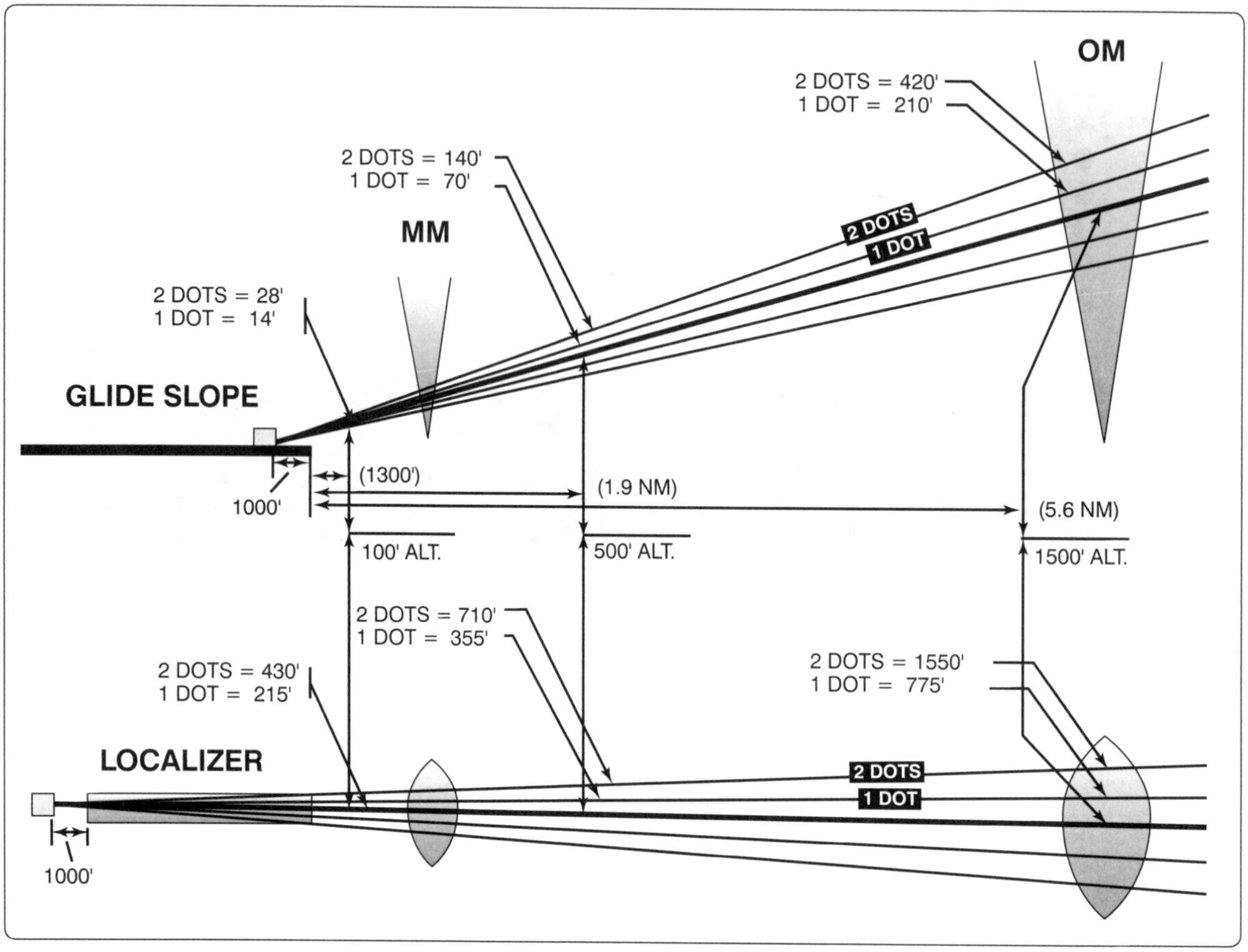

FIGURE 139.—Glide Slope and Localizer Illustration.

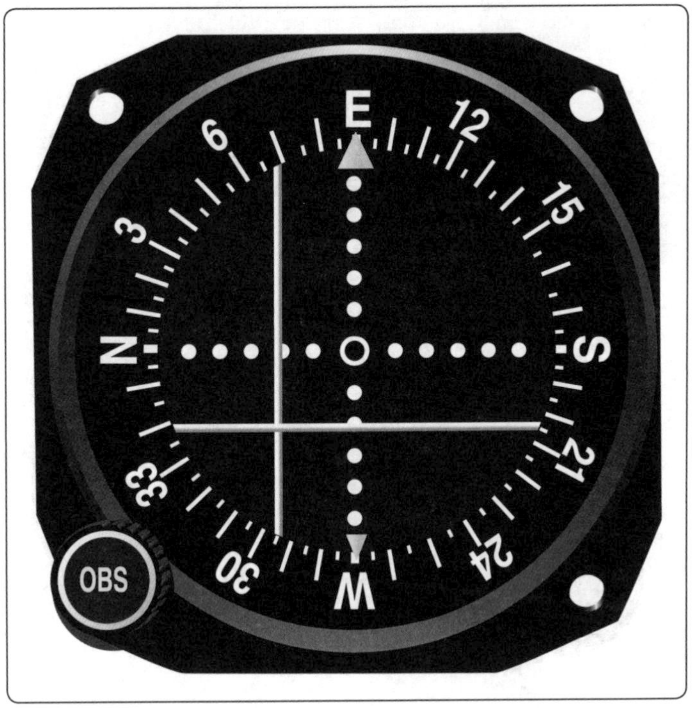

FIGURE 140.—OBS, ILS, and GS Displacement.

FIGURE 141.—OBS, ILS, and GS Displacement.

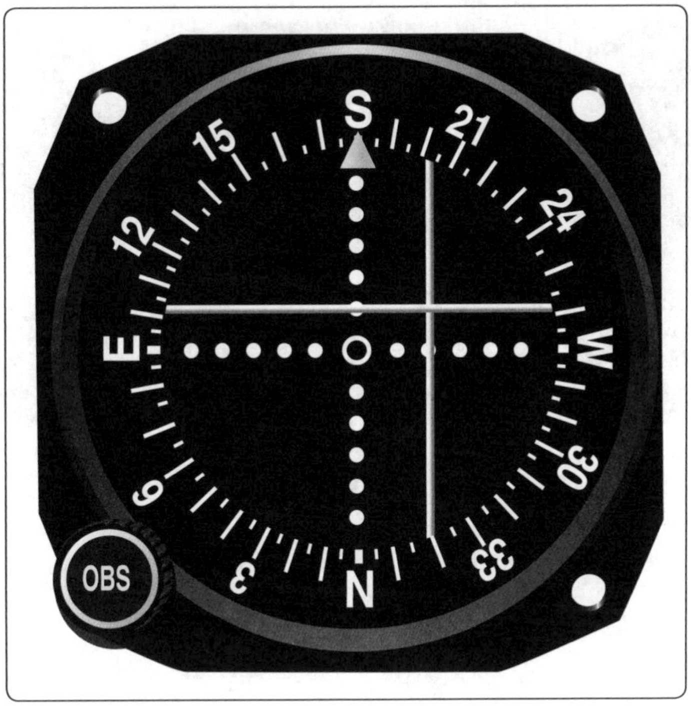

FIGURE 142.—OBS, ILS, and GS Displacement.

FIGURE 144.—Turn-and-Slip indicator.

FIGURE 145.—Instrument Sequence (Unusual Attitude).

FIGURE 146.—Instrument Sequence (System Failed).

FIGURE 147.—Instrument Sequence (Unusual Attitude).

FIGURE 148.—Instrument Interpretation (System Malfunction).

FIGURE 149.—Instrument Interpretation (System Malfunction).

FIGURE 150.—Instrument Interpretation (Instrument Malfunction).

FIGURE 151.—Instrument Interpretation (Instrument Malfunction).

(JNC6.JNC) 12320 SL-634 (FAA)

GRAND JUNCTION SIX DEPARTURE

GRAND JUNCTION RGNL (GJT)
GRAND JUNCTION, COLORADO

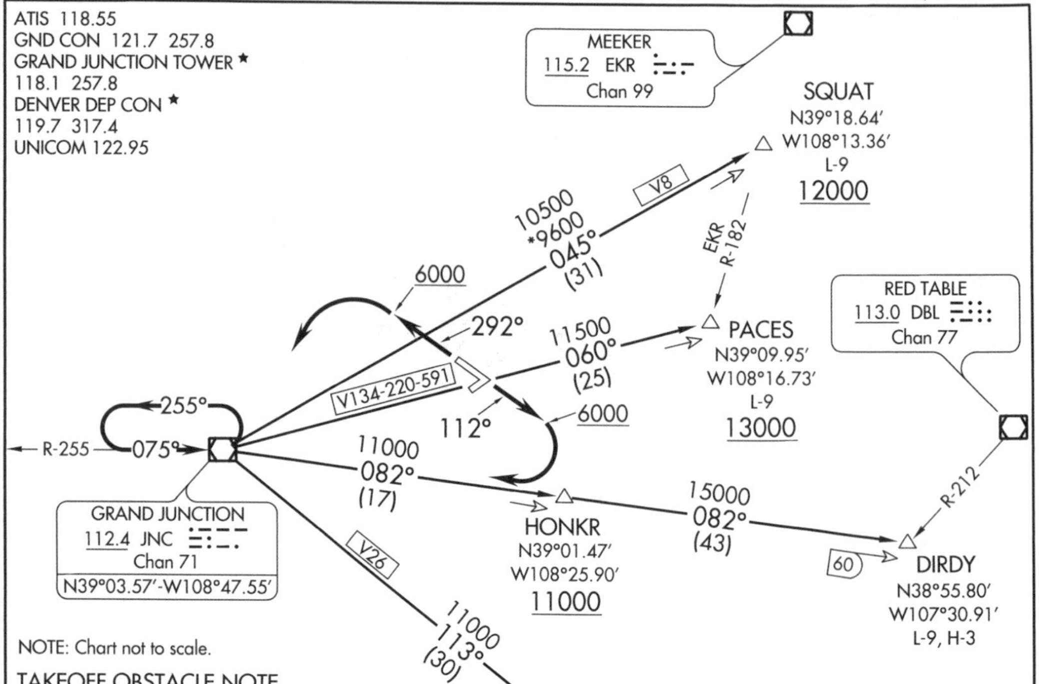

TAKEOFF OBSTACLE NOTE

Rwy 11: Pole 252′ from DER, 266′ left of centerline, up to 20′ AGL/4880′ MSL.
Tree 1691′ from DER, 437′ left of centerline, 100′ AGL/5019′ MSL.

TAKEOFF MINIMUMS

Rwy 4: NA - Obstacles.
Rwy 22: NA - Obstacles, facility reception (JNC VOR/DME).
Rwy 11: Standard with minimum climb of 300′ per NM to 9300.
Rwy 29: Standard with minimum climb of 300′ per NM to 8300.

DEPARTURE ROUTE DESCRIPTION

TAKEOFF RUNWAY 11: Climb heading 112° to 6000, then climbing right turn direct JNC VOR/DME, thence. . . .

TAKEOFF RUNWAY 29: Climb heading 292° to 6000, then climbing left turn direct JNC VOR/DME, thence. . . .

. . . .on transition/route.

BRICK TRANSITION (JNC6.BRICK): From over JNC VOR/DME via JNC R-113 to BRICK/JNC 30 DME.

DIRDY TRANSITION (JNC6.DIRDY): From over JNC VOR/DME via JNC R-082 to DIRDY INT/JNC 60 DME.

PACES TRANSITION (JNC6.PACES): From over JNC VOR/DME via JNC R-060 to PACES INT/JNC 25 DME.

SQUAT TRANSITION (JNC6.SQUAT): From over JNC VOR/DME via JNC R-045 to SQUAT INT/JNC 31 DME.

GRAND JUNCTION SIX DEPARTURE
(JNC6.JNC) 12320
GRAND JUNCTION, COLORADO
GRAND JUNCTION RGNL (GJT)

FIGURE 155.—Grand Junction Six Departure (JNC6.JNC).

HOT SPOTS

An "airport surface hot spot" is a location on an aerodrome movement area with a history or potential risk of collision or runway incursion, and where heightened attention by pilots/drivers is necessary.

A "hot spot" is a runway safety related problem area on an airport that presents increased risk during surface operations. Typically it is a complex or confusing taxiway/taxiway or taxiway/runway intersection. The area of increased risk has either a history of or potential for runway incursions or surface incidents, due to a variety of causes, such as but not limited to: airport layout, traffic flow, airport marking, signage and lighting, situational awareness, and training. Hot spots are depicted on airport diagrams as open circles or polygons designated as "HS 1", "HS 2", etc. and tabulated in the list below with a brief description of each hot spot. Hot spots will remain charted on airport diagrams until such time the increased risk has been reduced or eliminated.

CITY/AIRPORT	HOT SPOT	DESCRIPTION*
ALAMOGORDO, NM		
HOLLOMAN AFB (HMN)	HS1	Twy R, Twy G, and Twy L have multiple hold lines for Rwy 07-25 and Rwy 04-22. Contact tower if confused or lost.
	HS2	Hold line on Twy /EOR A and Twy/EOR H have multiple POV access roads, possibility of high vehicle traffic.
	HS3	Hold line on Twy /EOR B and Twy C for Rwy 07-25 have multiple POV access roads, possibility of high vehicle traffic.
	HS4	Multiple hold lines at intersecting rwys. Landing/departing aircraft disregard hold lines, taxiing aircraft contact tower prior to crossing hold lines.
	HS5	Multiple hold lines where rwys intersect. Hold line also at Twy D. Contact tower if confused or lost.
	HS6	POV crossing controlled by tower. Hold line located on each side of Rwy 07-25. Possibility of high vehicular traffic.
ALBUQUERQUE, NM		
ALBUQUERQUE INTL SUNPORT (ABQ)	HS 1	Hold Position Marking on Twy E1 for Rwy 08 and Rwy 12.
	HS 2	Twy G1 from Cutter Aviation ramp and Rwy 12-30.
	HS 3	Complex int at Twy F, Twy C, Twy G. Twy G and Rwy 03-21
ASPEN, CO		
ASPEN-PITKIN COUNTY / SARDY FIELD (ASE)	HS 1	Twy A2. Short taxi distance from ramp to rwy.
	HS 2	Twy A3. Short taxi distance from ramp to rwy.
	HS 3	Twy A4. Short taxi distance from ramp to rwy.
COLORADO SPRINGS, CO		
CITY OF COLORADO SPRINGS (COS)	HS 1	The apch ends of Rwy 13 and Rwy 17R; and Twy A1.
	HS 2	Twy A4 and Twy G at Rwy 17R-35L.
	HS 3	Int of Twy E4, Twy G, Twy H and Twy E.
	HS 4	Apch ends of Rwy 35R and Rwy 35L.
DENVER, CO		
CENTENNIAL (APA)	HS 1	Rwy 17L at Twy A1.
	HS 2	Twy A, Twy A8, Twy A9 and Twy C1 congested INT.
	HS 3	Twy C1 and Twy D1 close proximity to Rwy 10.
DENVER, CO		
DENVER INTL (DEN)	HS 1	Rwy 35L hold signs may not be visible from Twy SC or Twy A until entering Twy M, pilots sometimes enter Rwy 35L without authorization.
	HS 2	Rwy 17R Apch Hold Position.
DENVER, CO		
ROCKY MOUNTAIN METROPOLITAN (BJC)	HS 1	Frequent helicopter operations.
	HS 2	Multiple hold lines in close proximity. Hold line on Twy B south of Rwy 11R-29L is prior to Twy D.
EAGLE, CO		
EAGLE COUNTY RGNL (EGE)	HS 1	High density parking area.
GRAND JUNCTION, CO		
GRAND JUNCTION RGNL (GJT)	HS 1	Rwy 22 and Rwy 29 close proximity, wrong rwy departure risk.

FIGURE 156.—Grand Junction Hot Spots.

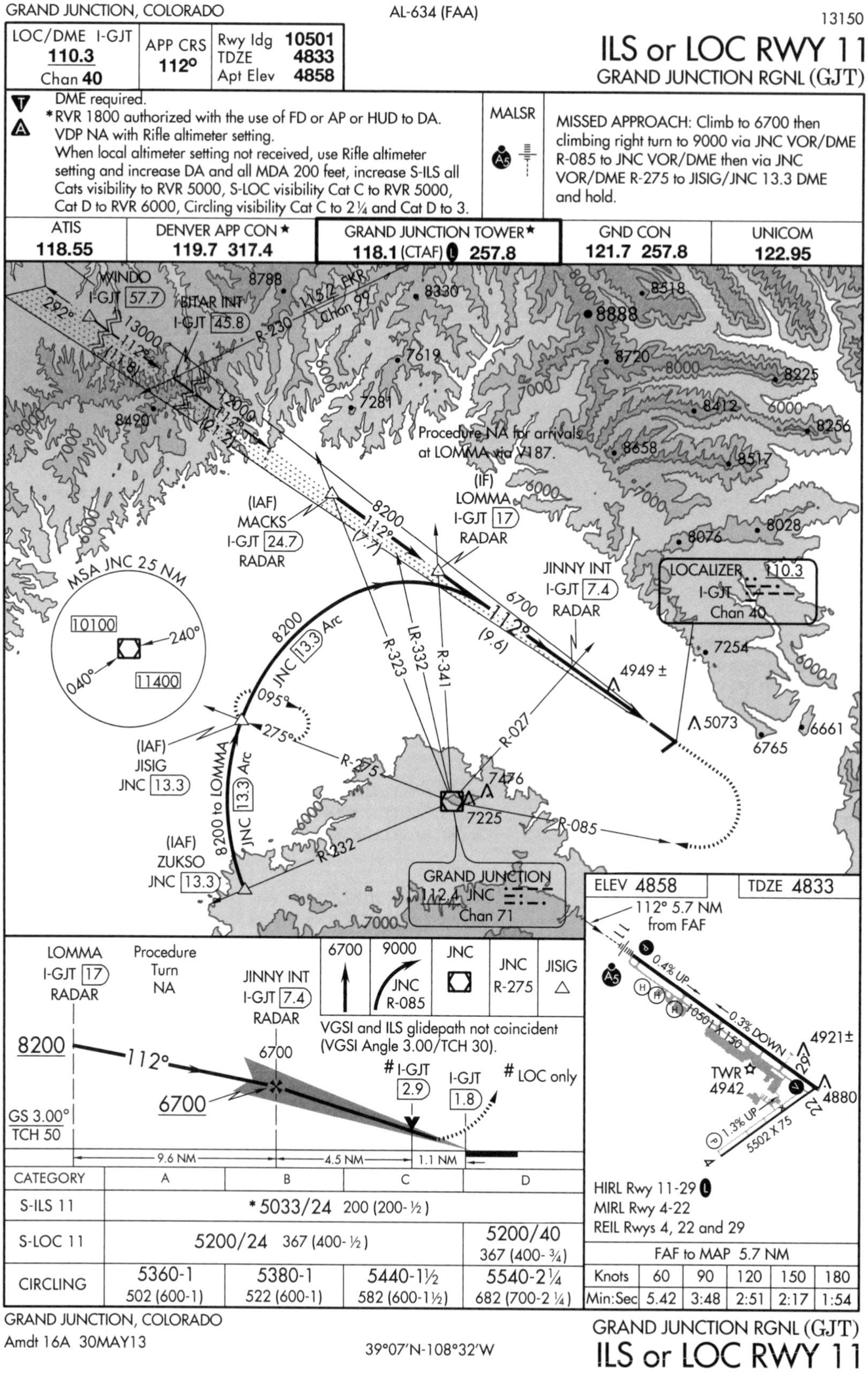

CATEGORY	A	B	C	D
S-ILS 11	*5033/24 200 (200-½)			
S-LOC 11	5200/24 367 (400-½)			5200/40 367 (400-¾)
CIRCLING	5360-1 502 (600-1)	5380-1 522 (600-1)	5440-1½ 582 (600-1½)	5540-2¼ 682 (700-2¼)

FAF to MAP 5.7 NM

Knots	60	90	120	150	180
Min:Sec	5.42	3:48	2:51	2:17	1:54

FIGURE 157.—ILS RWY 11 (GJT).

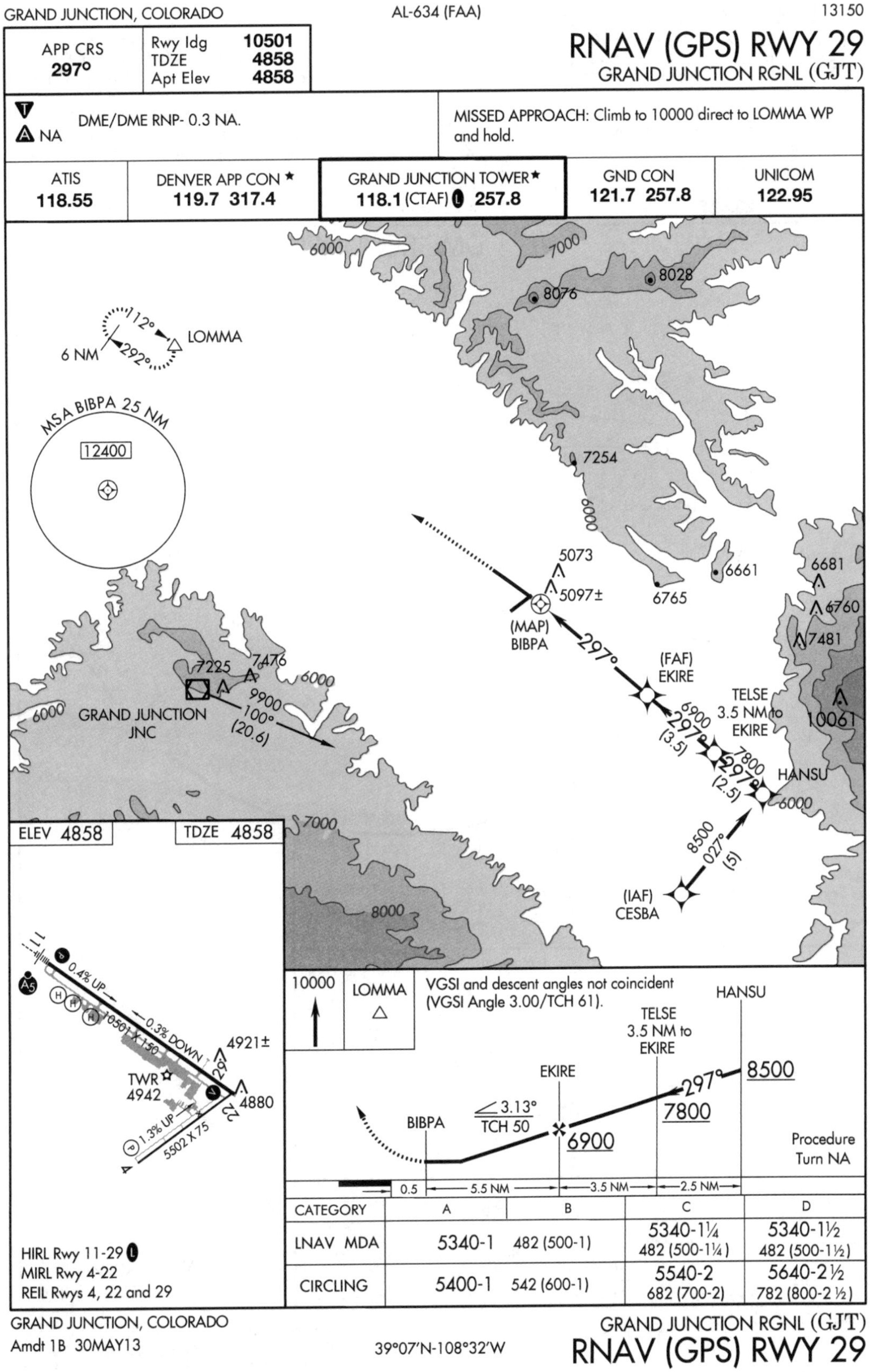

FIGURE 158.—ILS RWY 11 (GJT).

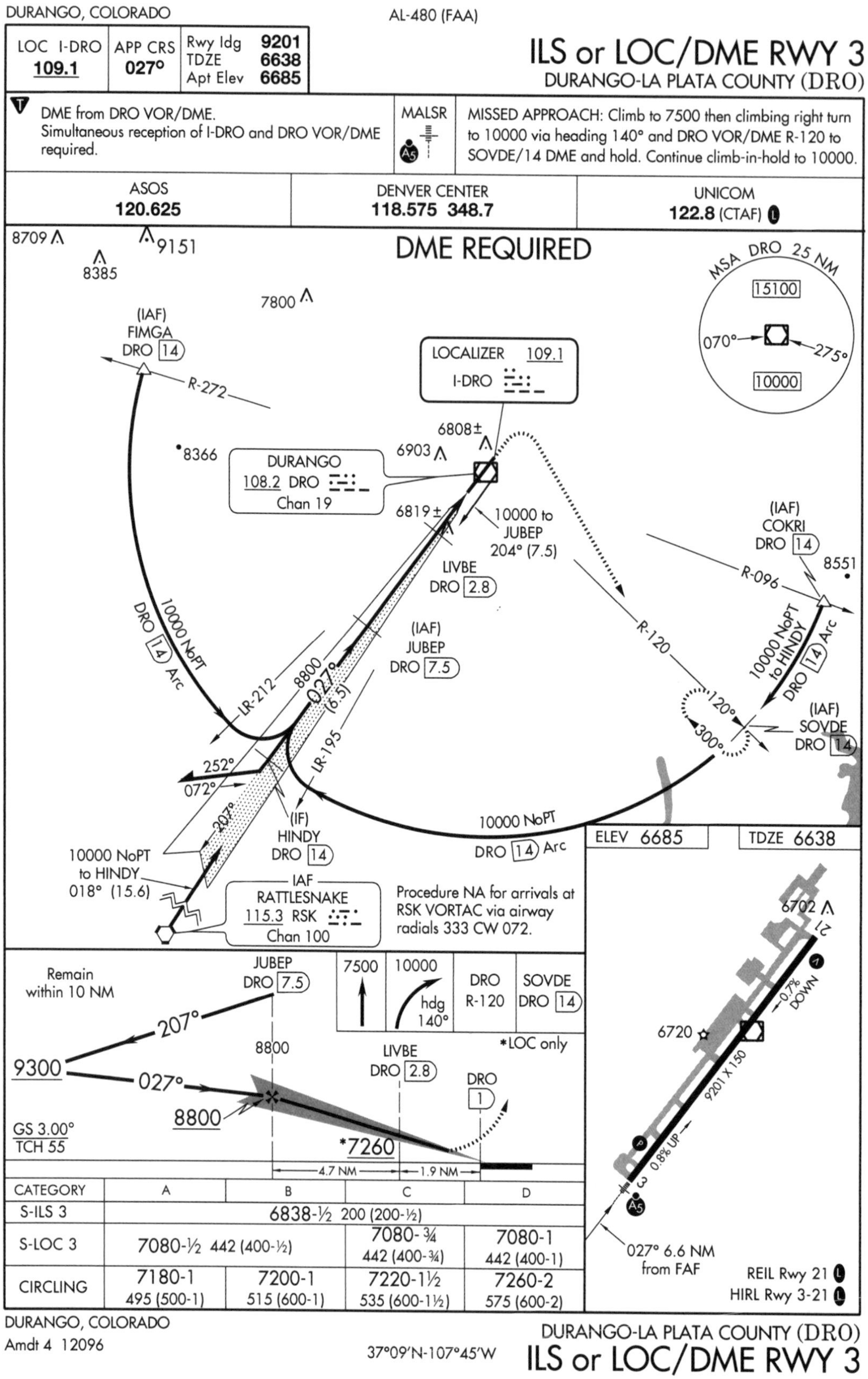

FIGURE 159.—ILS/DME RWY 3 (DRO).

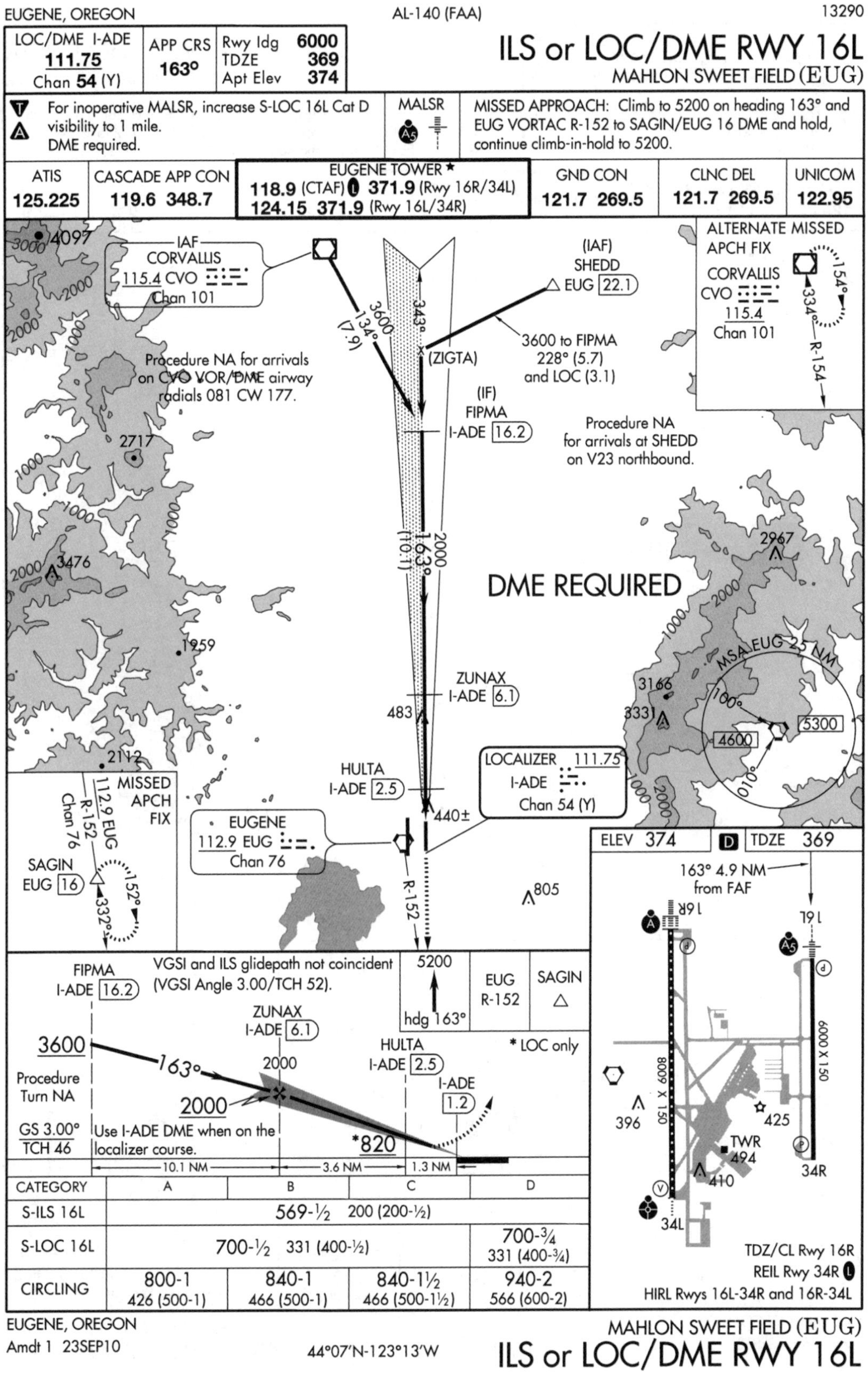

FIGURE 160.—ILS or LOC/DME RWY 16L (EUG).

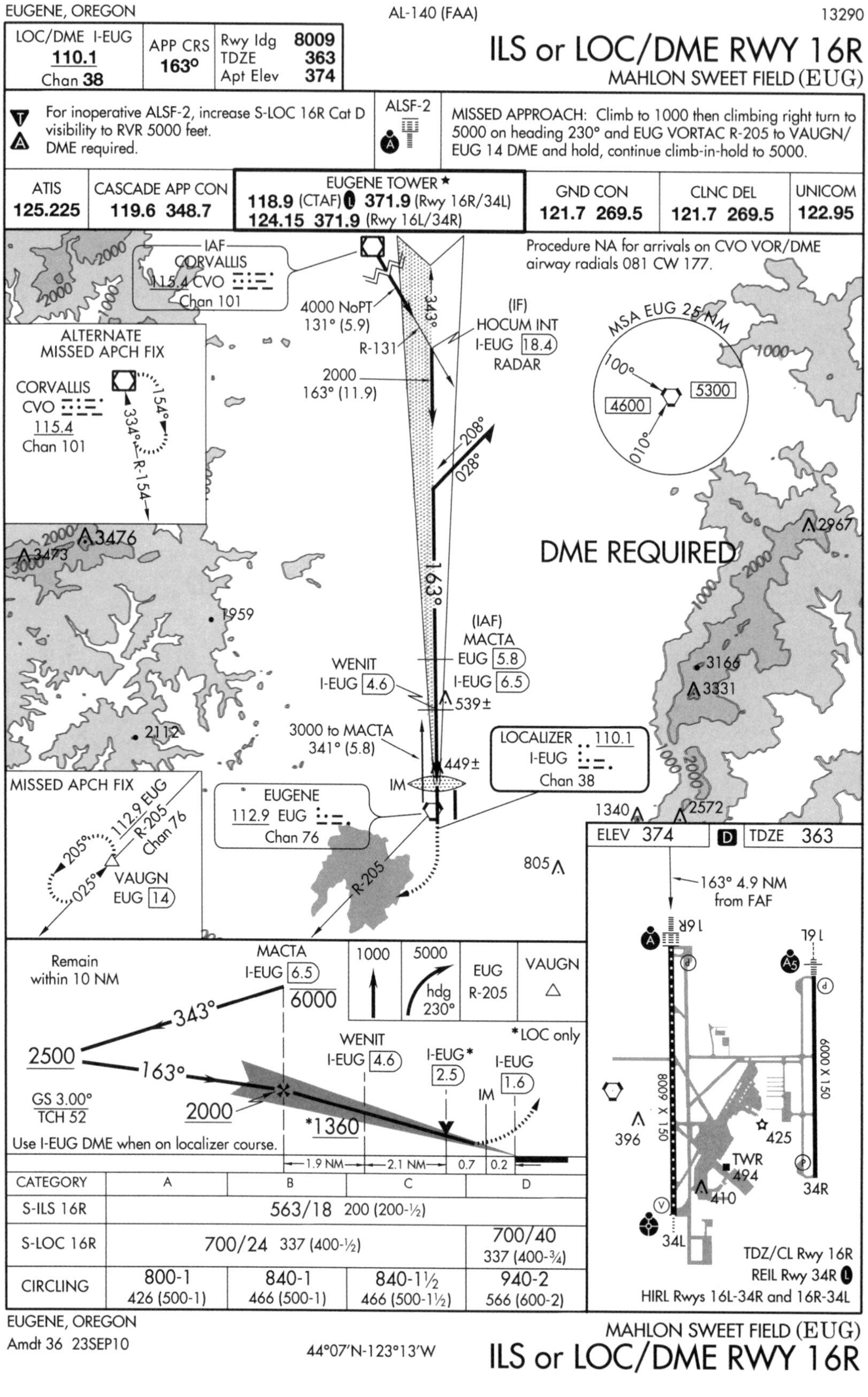

CATEGORY	A	B	C	D
S-ILS 16R	563/18 200 (200-½)			
S-LOC 16R	700/24 337 (400-½)			700/40 337 (400-¾)
CIRCLING	800-1 426 (500-1)	840-1 466 (500-1)	840-1½ 466 (500-1½)	940-2 566 (600-2)

FIGURE 161.—ILS or LOC/DME RWY 16R (EUG).

OREGON 119

EUGENE

MAHLON SWEET FLD (EUG) 7 NW UTC–8(–7DT) N44°07.48´ W123°12.72´ **KLAMATH FALLS**
374 B S4 **FUEL** 100LL, JET A OX 1, 2, 3, 4 TPA—1174(800) Class I, ARFF Index B **H–1B, L–1B**
NOTAM FILE EUG **IAP, AD**

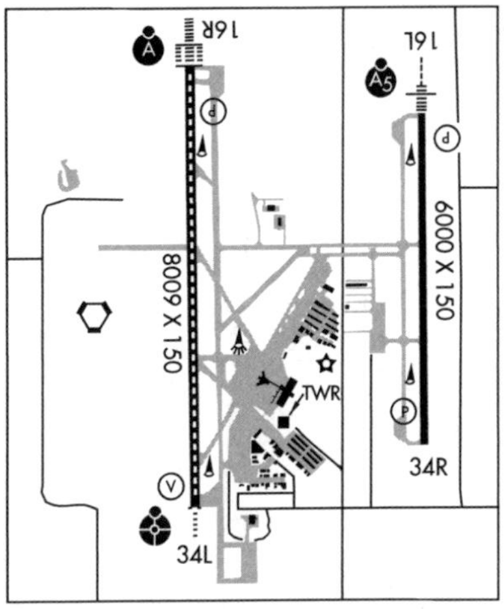

RWY 16R–34L: H8009X150 (ASPH–GRVD) S–75, D–200, 2D–400
HIRL CL
RWY 16R: ALSF2. TDZL. PAPI(P4L)—GA 3.0° TCH 50´.
RWY 34L: ODALS. VASI(V4L)—GA 3.0° TCH 53´.
RWY 16L–34R: H6000X150 (ASPH–GRVD) S–105, D–175, 2D–240
HIRL
RWY 16L: MALSR. PAPI(P4L)—GA 3.0° TCH 52´.
RWY 34R: REIL. PAPI(P4L)—GA 3.0° TCH 50´.
RUNWAY DECLARED DISTANCE INFORMATION
RWY 16L: TORA–6000 TODA–6000 ASDA–6000 LDA–6000
RWY 16R: TORA–8009 TODA–8009 ASDA–8009 LDA–8009
RWY 34L: TORA–8009 TODA–8009 ASDA–8009 LDA–8009
RWY 34R: TORA–6000 TODA–6000 ASDA–6000 LDA–6000
AIRPORT REMARKS: Attended continuously. Migratory waterfowl and other birds on and invof arpt. PPR for unscheduled air carrier ops with more than 30 passenger seats call 541–682–5430. ARFF svcs unavailable 0000–0500 local except PPR 541–682–5430. No access to Rwy 34L byd Twy A9. Helicopters ldg and departing avoid overflying the airline passenger terminal and ramp located E of Rwy 16R–34L. Helipad west of Rwy 16R restricted, PPR phone 541–682–5430. Twys H and K unavailable to acft 21,000 pounds single weight and 40,000 pounds dual gross weight. Terminal apron closed to acft except scheduled air carriers and flights with prior permission. PAPI Rwy 16R and Rwy 16L and 34R and VASI Rwy 34L opr 24 hrs. When twr clsd HIRL Rwy 16L–34R and Rwy 16R–34L preset medium ints. When twr clsd ACTIVATE ALSF2 Rwy 16R, ODALS Rwy 34L MALSR Rwy 16L and REIL Rwy 34R—CTAF.
WEATHER DATA SOURCES: ASOS (541) 461–3114 **HIWAS** 112.9 EUG.
COMMUNICATIONS: CTAF 118.9 **ATIS** 125.225 541–607–4699 **UNICOM** 122.95
EUGENE RCO 122.3 (MC MINNVILLE RADIO)
Ⓡ **CASCADE APP/DEP CON** 119.6 (340°–159°) 120.25 (160°–339°) (1400–0730Z‡)
Ⓡ **SEATTLE CENTER APP/DEP CON** 125.8 (0730–1400Z‡)
EUGENE TOWER 118.9 (Rwy 16R– 34L) 124.15 (Rwy 16L– 34R) (1400–0730Z‡) **GND CON** 121.7 **CLNC DEL** 121.7
AIRSPACE: CLASS D svc 1400–0730Z‡ other times CLASS E.
RADIO AIDS TO NAVIGATION: NOTAM FILE EUG.
EUGENE (H) VORTACW 112.9 EUG Chan 76 N44°07.25´ W123°13.37´ at fld. 364/20E. **HIWAS.**
ILS/DME 111.75 I–ADE Chan 54(Y) Rwy 16L. Class IE.
ILS/DME 110.1 I–EUG Chan 38 Rwy 16R. Class IIIE. Unmonitored when ATCT clsd.

FLORENCE

FLORENCE MUNI (6S2) 1 N UTC–8(–7DT) N43°58.97´ W124°06.68´ **KLAMATH FALLS**
51 B **FUEL** 100LL, JET A TPA—1051(1000) NOTAM FILE MMV **L–1A**

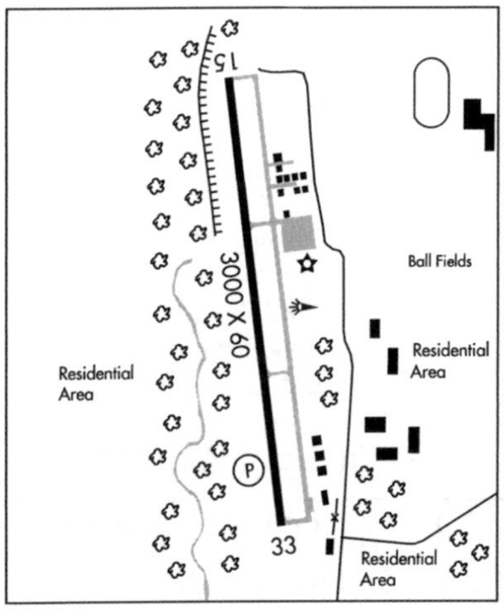

RWY 15–33: H3000X60 (ASPH) S–12.5 MIRL 0.4% up NW
RWY 15: Hill. Rgt tfc.
RWY 33: PAPI(P2L)—GA 3.0° TCH 40´. Trees.
AIRPORT REMARKS: Attended 1630–0030Z‡. Birds, deer and wildlife on and invof arpt. ACTIVATE MIRL Rwy 15–33—CTAF. PAPI Rwy 33 opr 24 hrs.
WEATHER DATA SOURCES: AWOS–3 118.225 (541) 997–8664.
COMMUNICATIONS: CTAF/UNICOM 122.8
RADIO AIDS TO NAVIGATION: NOTAM FILE OTH.
NORTH BEND (L) VORTACW 112.1 OTH Chan 58 N43°24.93´ W124°10.11´ 346° 34.1 NM to fld. 707/18E. **HIWAS.**
VORTAC unusable:
012°–087° byd 30 NM blo 5,000´

FIGURE 162.—Excerpt from Chart Supplement.

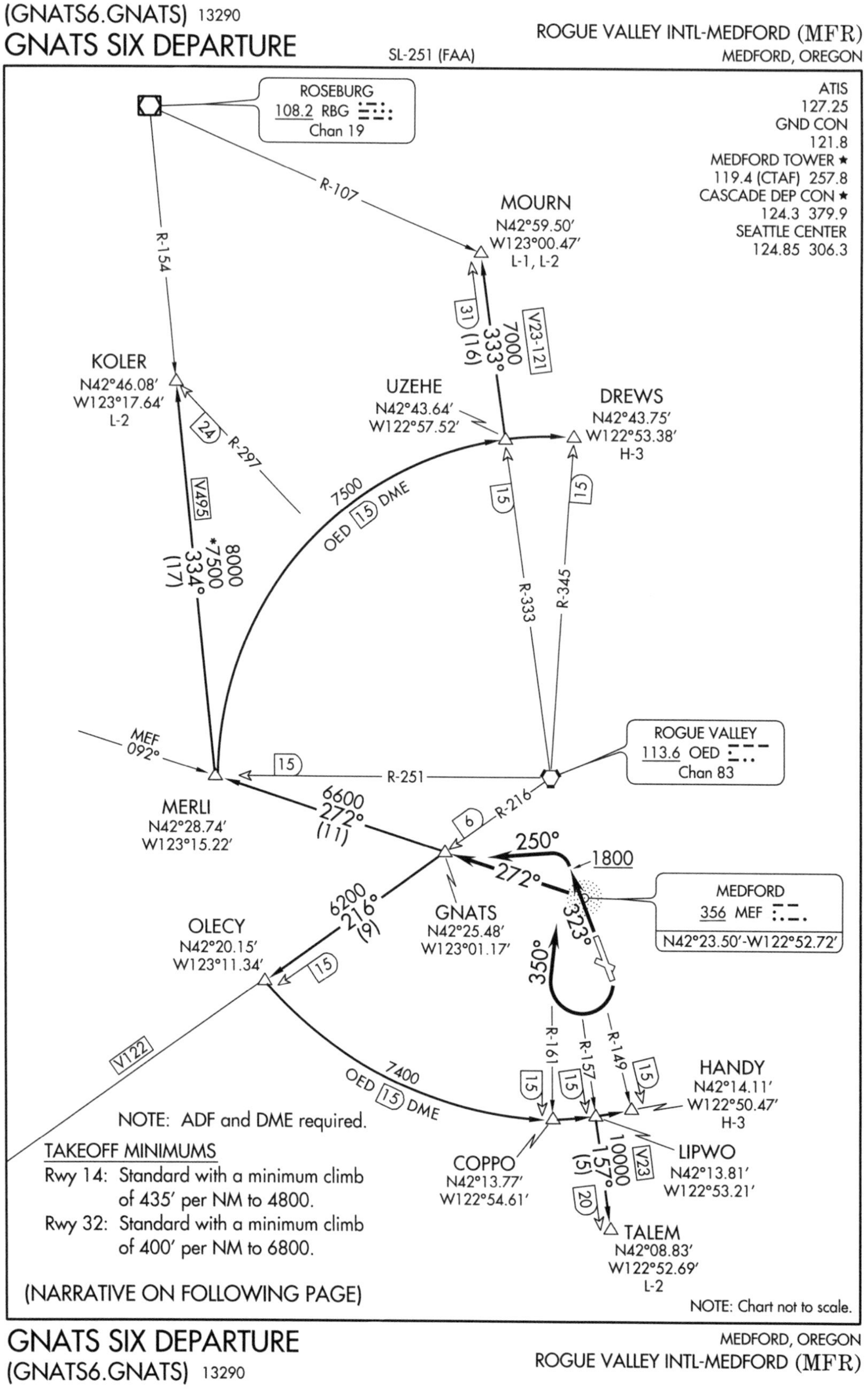

FIGURE 163.—GNATS Six Departure (GNATS6.GNATS).

(GNATS6.GNATS) 13290
GNATS SIX DEPARTURE SL-251 (FAA)

ROGUE VALLEY INTL-MEDFORD (MFR)
MEDFORD, OREGON

DEPARTURE ROUTE DESCRIPTION

TAKEOFF RUNWAY 14: Climbing right turn on heading 350° to intercept bearing 272° from MEF NDB to GNATS INT. Thence . . . .

TAKEOFF RUNWAY 32: Climb on heading 323° to 1800 then climbing left turn on heading 250° to intercept bearing 272° from MEF NDB to GNATS INT. Thence . . . .

. . . . via (transition) or (assigned route). Maintain 11000 or assigned lower altitude.

COPPO TRANSITION (GNATS6.COPPO): From over GNATS INT via OED VORTAC R-216 to OLECY DME, then via the OED VORTAC 15 DME Arc CCW to COPPO DME.

DREWS TRANSITION (GNATS6.DREWS): From over GNATS INT via MEF NDB 272° to MERLI INT, then via the OED VORTAC 15 DME Arc CW to DREWS DME.

HANDY TRANSITION (GNATS6.HANDY): From over GNATS INT via the OED VORTAC R-216 to OLECY DME, then via the OED VORTAC 15 DME Arc CCW to HANDY DME.

KOLER TRANSITION (GNATS6.KOLER): From over GNATS INT via MEF NDB 272° to MERLI INT, then via RBG VOR/DME R-154 to KOLER INT.

MOURN TRANSITION (GNATS6.MOURN): From over GNATS INT via MEF NDB 272° to MERLI INT, then via the OED VORTAC 15 DME Arc CW to UZEHE DME, then via OED VORTAC R-333 to MOURN INT.

TALEM TRANSITION (GNATS6.TALEM): From over GNATS INT via OED VORTAC R-216 to OLECY DME, then via the OED VORTAC 15 DME Arc CCW to LIPWO DME, then via OED VORTAC R-157 to TALEM DME.

GNATS SIX DEPARTURE
(GNATS6.GNATS) 13290

MEDFORD, OREGON
ROGUE VALLEY INTL-MEDFORD (MFR)

FIGURE 164.—GNATS Six Departure (GNATS6.GNATS).

OREGON **129**

MEDFORD

ROGUE VALLEY INTL – MEDFORD (MFR) 3 N UTC–8(–7DT) N42°22.45′ W122°52.41′ **KLAMATH FALLS**
1335 B S4 **FUEL** 100LL, JET A OX 1, 3 TPA—See Remarks Class I, ARFF Index B **H–3B, L–2I**
NOTAM FILE MFR **IAP, AD**

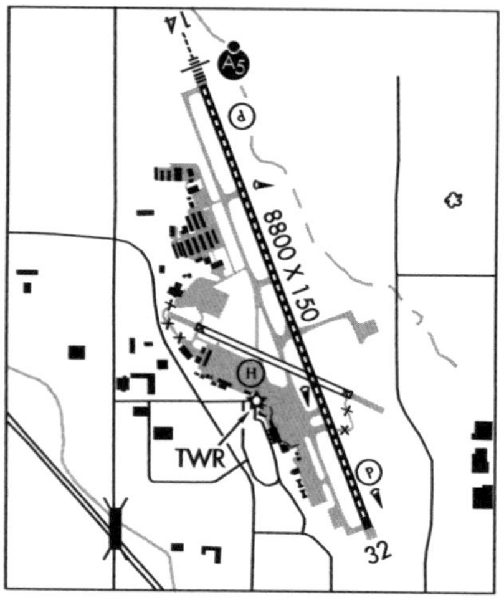

RWY 14–32: H8800X150 (ASPH–GRVD) S–200, D–200, 2S–175, 2D–400 HIRL CL
RWY 14: MALSR. TDZL. PAPI(P4L)—GA 3.0° TCH 73′. 0.4% up.
RWY 32: REIL. PAPI(P4R)—GA 3.0° TCH 50′. 0.5% down.
RUNWAY DECLARED DISTANCE INFORMATION
RWY 14: TORA–8800 TODA–8800 ASDA–8800 LDA–8800
RWY 32: TORA–8800 TODA–8800 ASDA–8800 LDA–8800
AIRPORT REMARKS: Attended 1300–0800Z‡. For fuel after hrs call 541–779–5451, or 541–842–2254. Bird haz large flocks of migratory waterfowl in vicinity Nov–May. Terminal apron clsd to acft exc scheduled air carrier and flts with prior permission. PPR for unscheduled ops with more than 30 passenger seats, call arpt ops 541–776–7228. Tran tie–downs avbl thru FBOs only. Rwy 32 preferred for tkfs and ldgs when twr clsd. TPA—2304(969) for propeller acft, 2804(1469) for turbo acft. PAPI Rwy 14 and VASI Rwy 32 on continuously. ACTIVATE HIRL Rwy 14–32, MALSR Rwy 14, REIL Rwy 32, TDZL Rwy 14, centerline lgts Rwy 14 and Rwy 32, and twy lgts—CTAF. Ldg fee applies to all corporate acft and all other acft with weight exceeding 12,500 lbs.
WEATHER DATA SOURCES: ASOS (541) 776–1238 SAWRS.
COMMUNICATIONS: CTAF 119.4 **ATIS** 127.25 **UNICOM** 122.95
MEDFORD RCO 122.65 (MC MINNVILLE RADIO)
Ⓡ **CASCADE APP/DEP CON** 124.3 (1400–0730Z‡)
SEATTLE CENTER APP/DEP CON 124.85 (0730–1400Z‡)
TOWER 119.4 (1400–0500Z‡) **GND CON** 121.8
AIRSPACE: CLASS D svc 1400–0500Z‡ other times CLASS E.
VOR TEST FACILITY (VOT) 117.2
RADIO AIDS TO NAVIGATION: NOTAM FILE MFR.
(H) VORTACW 113.6 OED Chan 83 N42°28.77′ W122°54.78′ 145° 6.6 NM to fld. 2083/19E. **HIWAS.**
VOR portion unusable:
260°–270° byd 35 NM blo 9,000′
290°–300° byd 35 NM blo 8,500′
MEDFORD NDB (MHW) 356 MEF N42°23.50′ W122°52.73′ 151° 1.1 NM to fld.
NDB unusable:
220°–240° byd 15 NM
PUMIE NDB (LOM) 373 MF N42°27.06′ W122°54.80′ 143° 4.9 NM to fld. LOM unusable 260°–270° beyond 10 NM. Unmonitored when ATCT closed.
ILS/DME 110.3 I–MFR Chan 40 Rwy 14. Class IA. LOM PUMIE NDB. LOM unusable 260°–270° beyond 10 NM. Unmonitored when ATCT closed. Localizer backcourse unusable byd 11 NM blo 7,000′, byd 13 NM blo 8,300′, byd 17 NM blo 8,700′. Localizer backcourse unusable byd 20° left of course.

MEMALOOSE (See IMNAHA on page 122)

MILLER MEM AIRPARK (See VALE on page 145)

MONUMENT MUNI (12S) 1 NW UTC–8(–7DT) N44°49.89′ W119°25.78′ **SEATTLE**
2323 TPA—3323(1000) NOTAM FILE MMV
RWY 14–32: H2104X29 (ASPH)
RWY 14: Hill.
AIRPORT REMARKS: Unattended. Intermittently clsd winters due to snow. Wildlife on and invof arpt. Rwy ends marked at each corner by a single white tire.
COMMUNICATIONS: CTAF 122.9

MULINO STATE (See PORTLAND–MULINO on page 137)

FIGURE 165.—Excerpt from Chart Supplement.

HOSSY N34°25.35′ W93°11.38′ NOTAM FILE HOT. **MEMPHIS**
NDB (HW/LOM) 385 HO 050° 5.7 NM to Mem Fld. **L–17E**

HOT SPRINGS

MEMORIAL FLD (HOT) 3 SW UTC–6(–5DT) N34°28.68′ W93°05.77′ **MEMPHIS**
540 B S4 **FUEL** 100LL, JET A Class II, ARFF Index A NOTAM FILE HOT **H–6I, L–17E**
IAP

RWY 05–23: H6595X150 (ASPH–GRVD) S–75, D–125, 2S–158, 2D–210, 2D/2D2–400 HIRL 0.6% up NE
RWY 05: MALSR. Rgt tfc.
RWY 23: PAPI(P4L)—GA 3.0° TCH 40′. Pole.
RWY 13–31: H4098X100 (ASPH) S–28, D–36, 2D–63 MIRL 0.4% up NW
RWY 13: REIL. Trees. Rgt tfc.
RWY 31: Pole.

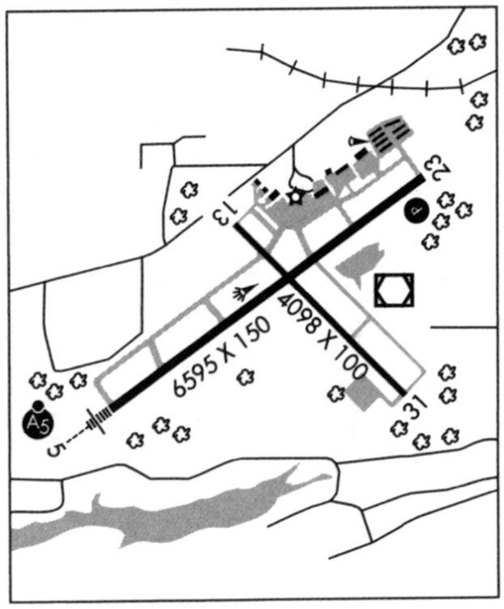

RUNWAY DECLARED DISTANCE INFORMATION
RWY 05: TORA–6595 TODA–6595 ASDA–6595 LDA–6595
RWY 13: TORA–4100 TODA–4100 ASDA–4100 LDA–4100
RWY 23: TORA–6595 TODA–6595 ASDA–6595 LDA–6595
RWY 31: TORA–4100 TODA–4100 ASDA–4100 LDA–4100

AIRPORT REMARKS: Attended 1100–0400Z‡. For fuel after hrs call 501–617–0324 or 501–617–4908. Rwy 23 PAPI OTS indef. ACTIVATE HIRL Rwy 05–23, MIRL Rwy 13–31, MALSR Rwy 05, PAPI Rwy 23 and REIL Rwy 13—CTAF.
WEATHER DATA SOURCES: ASOS 119.925 (501) 624–7633. **HIWAS** 110.0 HOT.
COMMUNICATIONS: CTAF/UNICOM 123.0
RCO 122.1R 110.0T (JONESBORO RADIO)
Ⓡ**MEMPHIS CENTER APP/DEP CON** 128.475
AIRSPACE: CLASS E svc 1200–0400Z‡ other times CLASS G.
RADIO AIDS TO NAVIGATION: NOTAM FILE HOT.
HOT SPRINGS (L) VOR/DME 110.0 HOT Chan 37 N34°28.72′ W93°05.44′ at fld. 529/4E. **HIWAS.**
VOR unusable:
056°–140° byd 20 NM blo 6,500′
141°–227° byd 20 NM blo 3,500′
141°–227° byd 26 NM blo 5,500′
228°–311° byd 20 NM blo 3,500′
312°–345° byd 15 NM blo 5,500′
312°–345° byd 32 NM blo 9,500′
346°–055° byd 20 NM blo 3,500′
DME unusable:
310°–035° byd 10 NM blo 11,000′
310°–035° byd 25 NM blo 12,000′
310°–035° byd 30 NM blo 17,000′
HOSSY NDB (LOM) 385 HO N34°25.36′ W93°11.38′ 050° 5.7 NM to fld. Unmonitored.
ILS/DME 111.5 I–HOT Chan 52 Rwy 05. Class IT. LOM HOSSY NDB. ILS and LOM unmonitored.

HOWARD CO (See NASHVILLE on page 55)

FIGURE 166.—Chart Supplement (HOT).

(BYP.BYP6) 13178 ST-6039 (FAA)

DALLAS-FORT WORTH INTL (DFW)
DALLAS-FORT WORTH, TEXAS

BONHAM SIX ARRIVAL Transition Routes

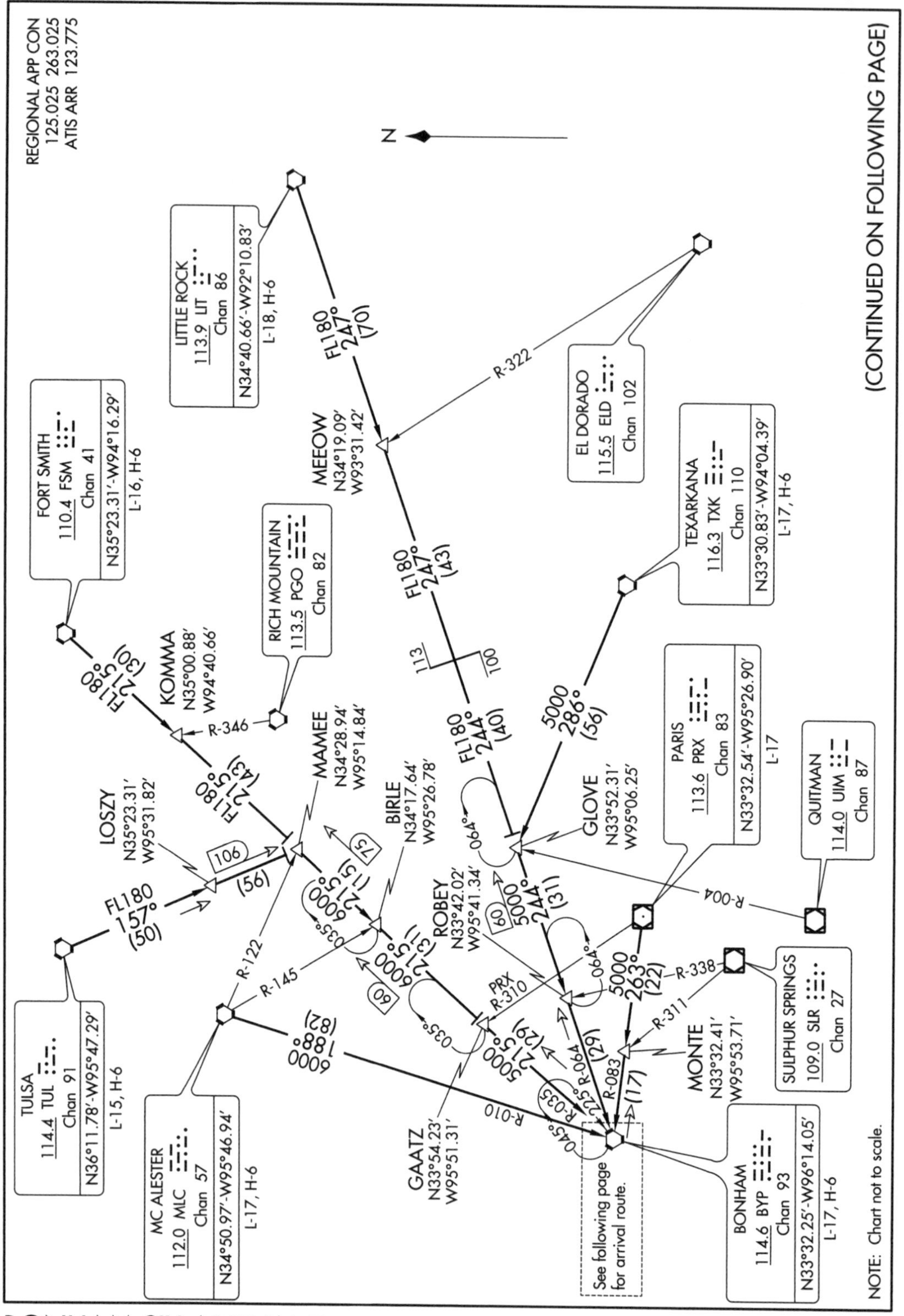

BONHAM SIX ARRIVAL Transition Routes
(BYP.BYP6) 13178

DALLAS-FORT WORTH, TEXAS
DALLAS-FORT WORTH INTL (DFW)

FIGURE 167.—BONHAM Six Arrival Transition Routes (BYP.BYP6) (DFW).

(BYP.BYP6) 13178 ST-6039 (FAA) DALLAS-FORT WORTH INTL (DFW)

BONHAM SIX ARRIVAL Arrival Routes

DALLAS-FORT WORTH, TEXAS

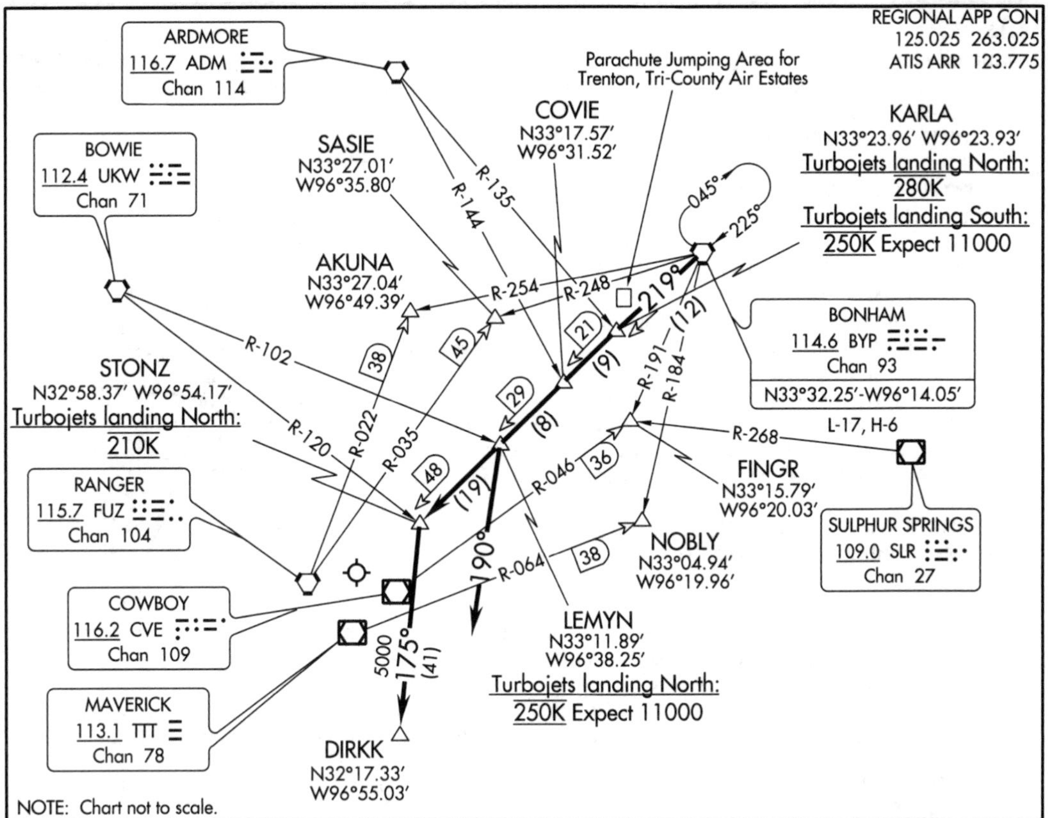

ARRIVAL DESCRIPTION

FORT SMITH TRANSITION (FSM.BYP6): From over FSM VORTAC on FSM R-215 to MAMEE INT, then on BYP R-035 to BYP VORTAC. Thence. . . .
LITTLE ROCK TRANSITION (LIT.BYP6): From over LIT VORTAC on LIT R-247 to MEEOW INT then on LIT R-247 and BYP R-064 to GLOVE INT, then on BYP R-064 to BYP VORTAC. Thence. . .
MC ALESTER TRANSITION (MLC.BYP6): From over MLC VORTAC on MLC R-188 and BYP R-010 to BYP VORTAC. Thence. . . .
PARIS TRANSITION (PRX.BYP6): From over PRX VOR/DME on PRX R-263 to MONTE INT then on BYP R-083 to BYP VORTAC. Thence. . . .
TEXARKANA TRANSITION (TXK.BYP6): From over TXK VORTAC on TXK R-286 to GLOVE INT then on BYP R-064 to BYP VORTAC. Thence. . . .
TULSA TRANSITION (TUL.BYP6): From over TUL VORTAC on TUL R-157 to MAMEE INT, then on BYP R-035 to BYP VORTAC. Thence. . . .

. . . . ALL AIRCRAFT: From over BYP VORTAC on BYP R-219, thence. . . .

ALL AIRCRAFT LANDING SOUTH: To LEMYN INT, expect vectors to final approach course.
JETS LANDING NORTH: FOR /E, /F, /G, and /R (RNP-2.0) EQUIPPED AIRCRAFT: From over STONZ INT direct DIRKK, expect vector to final approach course prior to DIRKK, if not received by DIRKK fly present heading.
ALL OTHERS: To STONZ depart STONZ heading 175° for vector to final approach course.
PROPS LANDING NORTH: Depart LEMYN INT heading 190°, expect vectors to final approach course.

BONHAM SIX ARRIVAL Arrival Routes DALLAS-FORT WORTH, TEXAS
DALLAS-FORT WORTH INTL (DFW)
(BYP.BYP6) 13178

FIGURE 168.—BONHAM Six Arrival Routes (BYP.BYP6) (DFW).

DALLAS

ADDISON (ADS) 9 N UTC–6(–5DT) N32°58.11´ W96°50.19´ **DALLAS–FT WORTH**
645 B S4 **FUEL** 100LL, JET A OX 2, 3 TPA—See Remarks LRA NOTAM FILE ADS **COPTER**
RWY 15–33: H7203X100 (ASPH–GRVD) S–60, D–120 HIRL **H–6H, L–17C, A**
RWY 15: MALSR. PAPI(P4R)—GA 3.0° TCH 60´. Thld dsplcd 979´. Pole. **IAP, AD**
RWY 33: REIL. PAPI(P4L)—GA 3.0° TCH 60´. Thld dsplcd 772´. Bldg.
RUNWAY DECLARED DISTANCE INFORMATION
RWY 15: TORA–7202 TODA–7202 ASDA–6592 LDA–5613
RWY 33: TORA–7202 TODA–7202 ASDA–7202 LDA–6431
AIRPORT REMARKS: Attended continuously. Birds on and invof arpt. No touch and go landings without arpt managers approval. Numerous 200´ buildings within 1 mile East, and South of arpt, transmission towers and water tanks West of arpt. Noise sensitive areas surround arpt. Pilots requested to use NBAA std noise procedures. TPA—1600 (956) for light acft, 2000 (1356) for large acft. Be alert: Rwy holding position markings located at the west edge of Twy A. ACTIVATE HIRL Rwy 15–33 and MALSR Rwy 15—CTAF. Flight Notification Service (ADCUS) available.
WEATHER DATA SOURCES: AWOS–3 (972) 386–4855 LAWRS.
COMMUNICATIONS: CTAF 126.0 **ATIS** 133.4 972–628–2439
UNICOM 122.95
Ⓡ**REGIONAL APP/DEP CON** 124.3
TOWER 126.0 (1200–0400Z‡) **GND CON** 121.6 **CLNC DEL** 119.55

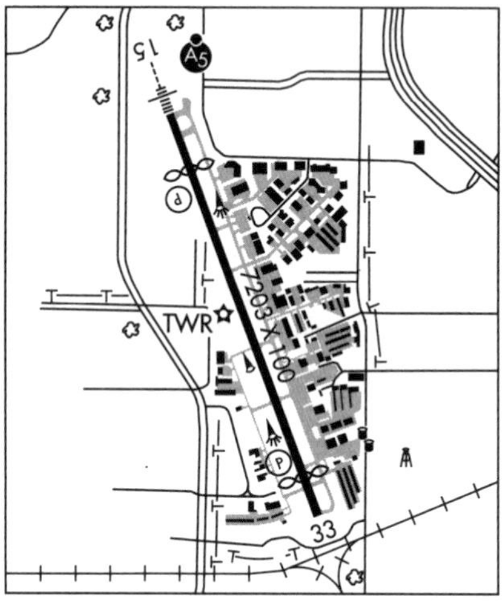

AIRSPACE: CLASS D svc 1200–0400Z‡, other times CLASS G.
RADIO AIDS TO NAVIGATION: NOTAM FILE FTW.
MAVERICK (H) VORW/DME 113.1 TTT Chan 78 N32°52.15´ W97°02.43´ 054° 11.9 NM to fld. 540/6E.
All acft arriving DFW are requested to turn DME off until departure due to traffic overload of Maverick DME
ILS/DME 110.1 I–ADS Chan 38 Rwy 15. Class IT. Unmonitored when ATCT closed. DME also serves Rwy 33.
ILS/DME 110.1 I–TBQ Chan 38 Rwy 33. Class IB. Localizer unmonitored when ATCT closed. DME also serves Rwy 15.

AIR PARK–DALLAS (F69) 16 NE UTC–6(–5DT) N33°01.41´ W96°50.22´ **DALLAS–FT WORTH**
695 S4 **FUEL** 100LL TPA—1890(1195) NOTAM FILE FTW **COPTER**
RWY 16–34: H3080X30 (ASPH) LIRL(NSTD) **L–17C, A**
RWY 16: Thld dsplcd 300´. Pole.
RWY 34: Tree. Rgt tfc.
AIRPORT REMARKS: Uattended. For fuel call 972–248–4265 prior to arrival. Rwy 16–34 extensive cracking, loose asph and stones rwy. Rwy 16–34 NSTD LIRL, south 2780´ of rwy lgtd. Rwy 16 and Rwy 34 NSTD centerline marking incorrect size and spacing, dsplcd thld yellow. Rwy numbers 25´ tall. ACTIVATE LIRL Rwy 16–34—CTAF.
COMMUNICATIONS: CTAF 122.9
RADIO AIDS TO NAVIGATION: NOTAM FILE FTW.
MAVERICK (H) VORW/DME 113.1 TTT Chan 78 N32°52.15´ W97°02.43´ 042° 13.8 NM to fld. 540/6E.
All acft arriving DFW are requested to turn DME off until departure due to traffic overload of Maverick DME

AIRPARK EAST (1F7) 23 E UTC–6(–5DT) N32°48.78´ W96°21.12´ **DALLAS–FT WORTH**
510 B S4 NOTAM FILE FTW **COPTER**
RWY 13–31: H2630X30 (ASPH) LIRL
RWY 13: Tree. Rgt tfc.
RWY 31: Tree.
AIRPORT REMARKS: Unattended. ACTIVATE LIRL Rwy 13–31—122.9.
COMMUNICATIONS: CTAF/UNICOM 122.7

FIGURE 169.—Excerpt from Chart Supplement (ADS).

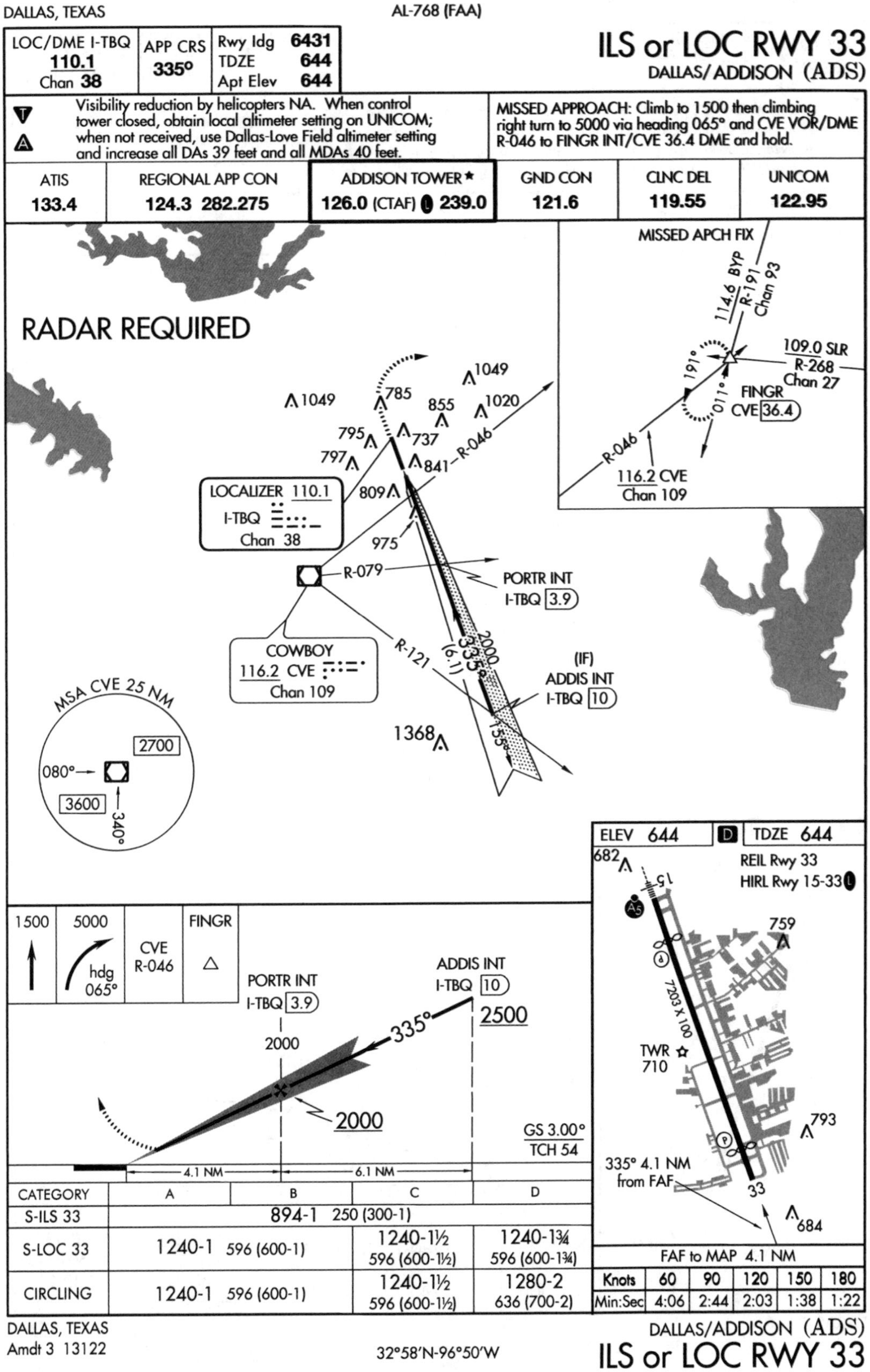

FIGURE 170.—ILS or LOC RWY 33 (ADS).

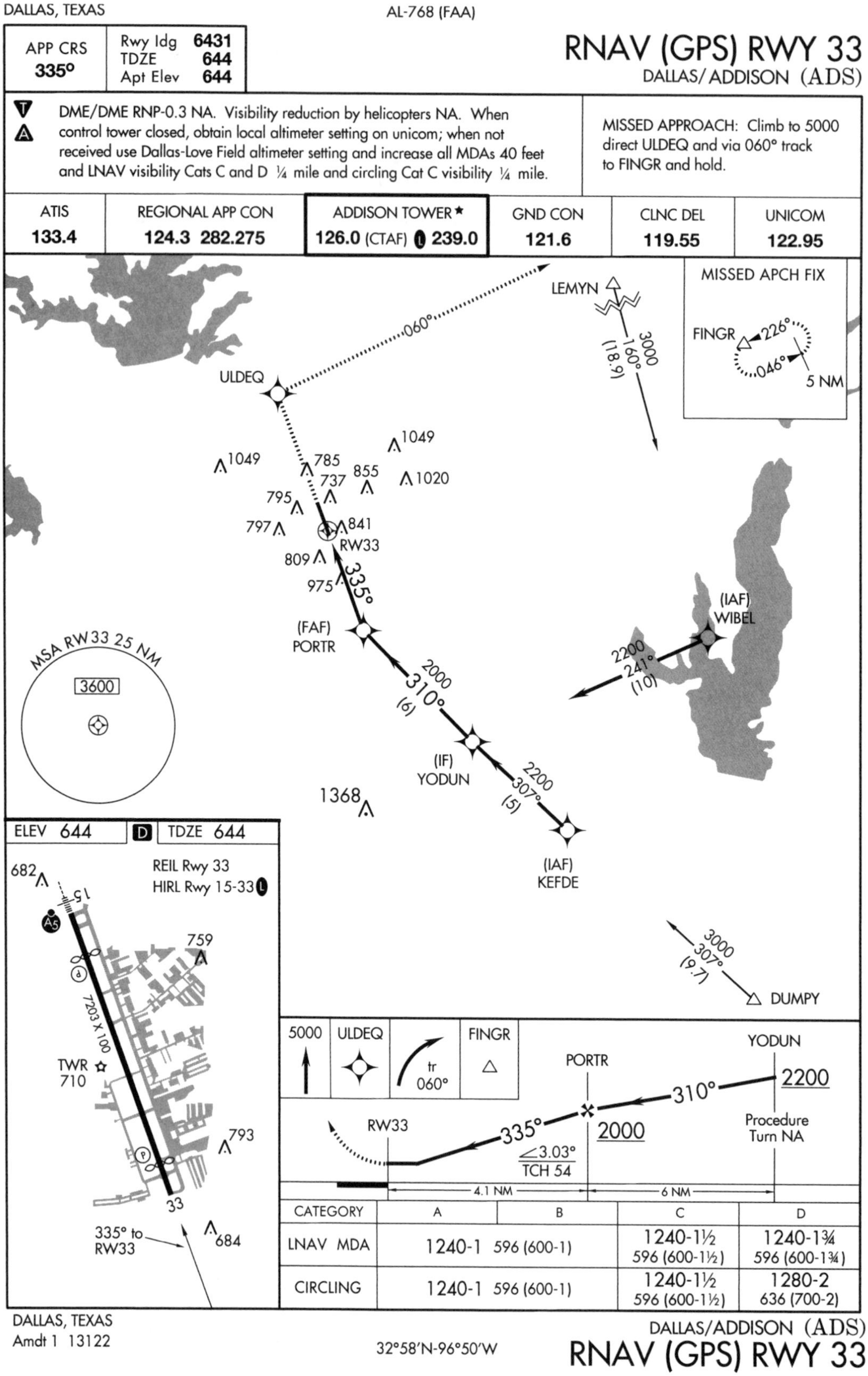

FIGURE 171.—RNAV (GPS) RWY 33 (ADS).

HELENA RGNL (HLN)(KHLN) P (ARNG) 2 NE UTC–7(–6DT) N46°36.41′ W111°58.97′ **GREAT FALLS**
3877 B S4 **FUEL** 80, 100, 100LL, JET A OX 1, 3 LRA Class I, ARFF Index B NOTAM FILE HLN **H–1D, L–13C**
RWY 09–27: H9000X150 (ASPH–PFC) S–100, D–160, 2S–175, 2D–250 HIRL **IAP, DIAP, AD**

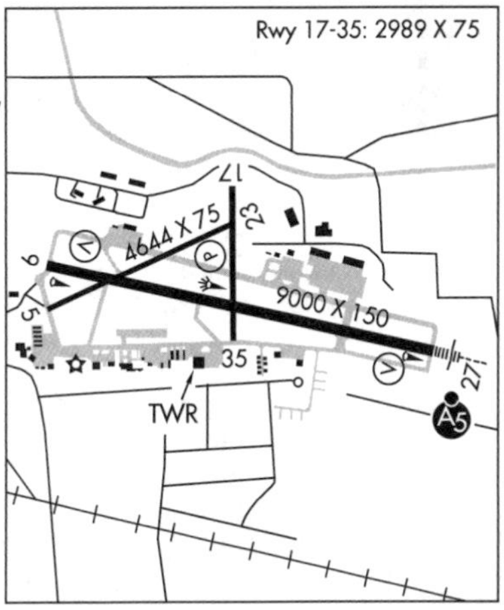

RWY 09: REIL. VASI(V4L)—GA 3.0° TCH 45′. Ground. 0.3% down.
RWY 27: MALSR. VASI(V4L)—GA 3.0° TCH 47′. Rgt tfc.
RWY 05–23: H4644X75 (ASPH–PFC) S–21, D–30 MIRL 1.2% up SW
RWY 05: Road.
RWY 23: PAPI(P2L)—GA 3.0° TCH 49′. Fence. Rgt tfc.
RWY 17–35: H2989X75 (ASPH–PFC) S–21, D–30 MIRL 1.7% up SE
RWY 35: Ground. Rgt tfc.
MILITARY SERVICE: LGT When twr clsd, ACTIVATE–HIRL Rwy 09–27, MIRL Rwy 05–23 and 16–34, REIL Rwy 09, MALSR Rwy 27 – CTAF. **FUEL** A+, J8 (C406–442–2190. Opr 1200–0600Z‡, OT $150 fee, 90 min PPR.) (NC–80, 100, 100LL)
AIRPORT REMARKS: Attended 1200–0800Z‡. ARFF coverage provided for scheduled Part 121 air carriers only exc with prior approval, call 406–442–2821. Ldg rights customs avbl call 406–449–5506. Rwy 17–35 and Rwy 05–23 (exc between Twy F and Rwy 09–27) not avbl for air carrier use by acft with greater than 30 passenger seats. Twy A, Twy B, and Twy C between Twy A and Rwy 35 not avbl for air carrier use by acft with greater than 30 passenger seats. When twr clsd ACTIVATE HIRL Rwy 09–27, MIRL Rwy 05–23 and Rwy 17–35, REIL Rwy 09, MALSR Rwy 27—CTAF. Ldg fee for all commercial acft and all acft over 10,000 lbs. Flight Notification Service (ADCUS) avbl. NOTE: See SPECIAL NOTICE.
MILITARY REMARKS: ARNG Opr Mon–Fri 1400–0030Z‡, exc holidays. Exercise caution while taxiing, AASF ramp not stressed for large acft. Ctc flt ops for ramp advisory 126.2, DSN 324–3055/56, C406–324–3055/56. No tran svc Sat, Sun, holidays or after 2300Z‡ Mon–Fri.
WEATHER DATA SOURCES: ASOS (406) 443–4317
COMMUNICATIONS: CTAF 118.3 **ATIS** 120.4 **UNICOM** 122.95
RCO 122.55 255.4 (GREAT FALLS RADIO)
APP/DEP CON 119.5 229.4 (1300–0500Z‡)
SALT LAKE CENTER APP/DEP CON 133.4 285.4 (0500–1300Z‡)
TOWER 118.3 257.8 (1300–0500Z‡) **GND CON** 121.9
ARNG OPS 40.65 126.2 321.45
AIRSPACE: CLASS D svc 1300–0500Z‡ other times CLASS E.
RADIO AIDS TO NAVIGATION: NOTAM FILE HLN.
(H) VORTACW 117.7 HLN Chan 124 N46°36.41′ W111°57.21′ 254° 1.2 NM to fld. 3823/16E.
VOR portion unusable:
035°–050° byd 35 NM blo 12,000′
105°–165° byd 25 NM blo 17,000′
165°–185° byd 25 NM blo 13,500′
185°–230° byd 25 NM blo 17,500′
203°–213° byd 22 NM blo 13,000′
230°–270° byd 25 NM blo 12,500′
TACAN AZIMUTH and DME unusable:
035°–070° byd 35 NM blo 13,000′
165°–185° byd 25 NM blo 13,500′
250°–300° byd 25 NM blo 14,000′
320°–035° byd 25 NM blo 13,000′
TACAN DME unusable:
035°–070° byd 35 NM blo 13,000′
105°–150° byd 25 NM
105°–210° byd 15 NM blo 11,100′
105°–210° byd 20 NM blo 12,000′
150°–165° byd 25 NM blo 17,000′
165°–185° byd 25 NM blo 13,500′
185°–210° byd 25 NM
203°–213° byd 22 NM blo 13,000′
210°–250° byd 15 NM blo 12,000′
210°–250° byd 25 NM blo 17,500′
250°–300° byd 25 NM blo 14,000′
320°–035° byd 25 NM blo 13,000′
TACAN AZIMUTH unusable:
105°–150° byd 15 NM
150°–165° byd 15 NM blo 17,000′
185°–210° byd 15 NM
210°–250° byd 15 NM blo 17,500′

CONTINUED ON NEXT PAGE

FIGURE 172.—Excerpt from Chart Supplement.

BIG SPRING MC MAHON–WRINKLE (BPG) 2 SW UTC–6(–5DT) N32°12.76′ W101°31.30′ **DALLAS–FT WORTH**
2573 B S4 **FUEL** 100LL, JET A NOTAM FILE BPG **H–6G, L–6H**
RWY 17–35: H8802X100 (CONC) S–60, D–150, 2D–200 MIRL **IAP**
RWY 17: SSALS. PAPI(P4L)—GA 3.0° TCH 45′. Rgt tfc.
RWY 35: PAPI(P4L)—GA 3.0° TCH 36′.
RWY 06–24: H4601X75 (ASPH) MIRL 0.6% up NE
RWY 06: PVASI(PSIL)—GA 2.97° TCH 47′. Rgt tfc.
RWY 24: PVASI(PSIL)—GA 3.55° TCH 35′.
AIRPORT REMARKS: Attended Mon–Sat 1400–2300Z‡. For fuel after hours call 432–267–8952 or 432–935–3395. Prairie dogs on rwys and twys. Extensive agricultural ops invof arpt. Sandhill Cranes crossing in the spring and fall. MIRL Rwy 06–24 and Rwy 17–35 preset low ints, to increase ints and ACTIVATE SSALS Rwy 17 and PVASI Rwy 06, Rwy 24, and PAPI Rwy 17 and Rwy 35—CTAF.
WEATHER DATA SOURCES: AWOS–3 118.025 (432) 263–3842.
COMMUNICATIONS: CTAF/UNICOM 122.8
RCO 122.4 (SAN ANGELO RADIO)
FORT WORTH CENTER APP/DEP CON 133.7
RADIO AIDS TO NAVIGATION: NOTAM FILE BPG.
(L) VORTACW 114.3 BGS Chan 90 N32°23.14′ W101°29.02′ 180° 10.5 NM to fld. 2670/11E.

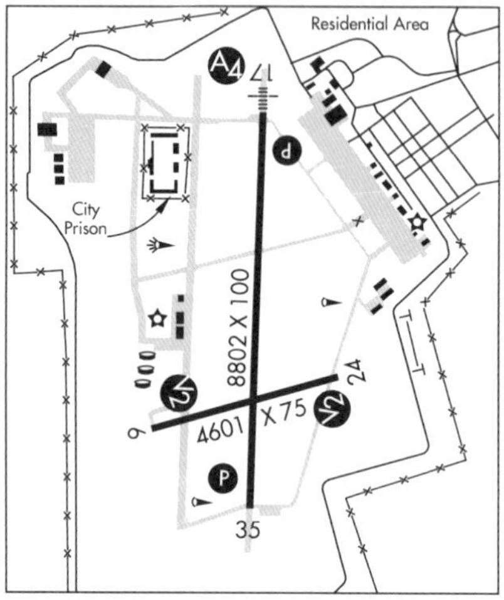

BIGGS AAF (FORT BLISS) (BIF)(KBIF) A 5 NE UTC–7(–6DT) N31°50.97′ W106°22.80′ **EL PASO**
3948 B TPA—See Remarks NOTAM FILE ABQ Not insp. **H–4L, L–6F**
RWY 03–21: H13554X150 (PEM) PCN 120 R/C/W/T HIRL **DIAP, AD**
RWY 03: PAPI(P4L)—GA 3.0° TCH 71′.
RWY 21: ALSF1. PAPI(P4L)—GA 3.0° TCH 71′. Rgt tfc. 0.3% down.
MILITARY SERVICE: LGT When unattended ACTIVATE 3–step HIRL Rwy 03–21, High Intensity ALS Category I configuration with sequenced Flashers (code) Rwy 21 and PAPI Rwy 21–127.9. **JASU** 4(A/M32A–86) 2(A/M32–95) **FUEL** A+ (Atlantic Avn, 1200–0400Z‡ Mon–Sun, C915–779–2831, 1 hr prior notice, after hr C915–861–2390, after hr call out fee $100.) **FLUID** SP **TRAN ALERT** 1300–0500Z‡ Mon–Sun, exc holidays.
MILITARY REMARKS: Attended Mon–Sun 1300–0500Z‡, except holidays. See FLIP AP/1 Supplementary Arpt Remark. **RSTD** PPR all acft. 24 hr prior notice, ctc Airfield Ops DSN 621–8811/8330, C915–744–8811/8330. Twr and svcs avbl for all acft with PPR. PPR time valid +/— 1 hr. All acft ctc Afld Ops via PTD 30 min prior to arr. Twr and svcs unavbl before 1 hr prior to PPR sked arr. **CAUTION** El Paso Intl Rwy 22 2 NM SE can be mistaken for Rwy 21. Coyote hazard. **TFC PAT** Fixed Wing 5002(1054), Fixed Wing Category BCDE turbo prop 5502(1554), Rotary Wing 4502(554), Jet 6002(2054). **NS ABTMT** VFR west arr/dep via mountain pass 15 NM NW of Biggs AAF. Avoid VFR over flight of city. Fly 1500′ AGL, 1500′ horizontal distance from mountain dwellings. **MISC** Approval required for access to ramp. Temporary storage of classified material avbl at Afld Ops. Intl garbage cap ltd. Expect delays unless placed in garbage bags prior to arrival. Hangar space extremely limited for transient acft. KBIF manual obsn and wx forecaster avbl Mon–Fri 1300–0500Z‡, clsd holidays. DSN 621–1215/1214, C915–744–1215/1214, OT 25th OWS, Davis Monthan AFB, DSN 228–6598/6599.
COMMUNICATIONS: ATIS 120.0 254.3 (C915–772–9412) **PTD** 122.7
Ⓡ **EL PASO APP CON** 119.15 353.5 (South of V16) 124.25 298.85 (North of V16)
TOWER 127.9 342.25 (Mon–Sun 1300–0500Z‡, except holidays). Advisory svc twr freq other times.
Ⓡ **EL PASO DEP CON** 121.3 263.0
EL PASO CLNC DEL 125.0 379.1
AIRSPACE: CLASS D svc 1300–0500Z‡ Mon–Sat except holidays other times CLASS E.
RADIO AIDS TO NAVIGATION: NOTAM FILE ABQ.
NEWMAN (L) VORTACW 112.4 EWM Chan 71 N31°57.10′ W106°16.34′ 210° 8.2 NM to fld. 4040/12E.
DME portion unusable:
220°–255° byd 25 NM blo 12,000′
COMM/NAV/WEATHER REMARKS: Radar—See Terminal FLIP for Radar Minima.

BIRD DOG AIRFIELD (See KRUM on page 297)

BISHOP (See DECATUR on page 245)

FIGURE 172A.—Excerpt from Chart Supplement.

MONTANA 85

CONTINUED FROM PRECEDING PAGE

CAPITOL NDB (HW) 335 CVP N46°36.40′ W111°56.23′ 258° 1.9 NM to fld. NDB unmonitored when ATCT clsd.
HAUSER NDB (MHW) 386 HAU N46°34.13′ W111°45.48′ 268° 9.6 NM to fld. NDB unmonitored when HLN ATCT clsd.
ILS 110.1 I–HLN Rwy 27. Unmonitored when ATCT closed. Localizer backcourse unusable byd 22° rgt of course, unusable within 2.7 DME.

HINSDALE (6U5) 0 SE UTC–7(–6DT) N48°23.28′ W107°05.00′ **BILLINGS**
2220 NOTAM FILE GTF
RWY 07–25: 2200X75 (TURF) LIRL(NSTD) 0.7% up W
RWY 07: Road.
RWY 10–28: 2160X200 (TURF) 0.3% up W
RWY 10: Road.
RWY 16–34: 1960X75 (TURF) 1.5% up S
RWY 16: P–line.
RWY 34: Fence.
AIRPORT REMARKS: Unattended. Rwys soft when wet. Hay bales and farm equipment adjacent to rwy. Rwys not clearly defined. Rwy 16–34, Rwy 07–25 and Rwy 10–28 marked with white cones full length of rwy. Rwy 16 p–lines marked with globes. Rwy 07–25 NSTD LIRL 335′ spacing between lgts, one thld lgt each end. For rwy lgts phone 406–364–2272/2387.
COMMUNICATIONS: CTAF 122.9

HOGELAND (6U6) 1 NW UTC–7(–6DT) N48°51.61′ W108°39.66′ **BILLINGS**
3139 B NOTAM FILE GTF
RWY 07–25: 3140X60 (TRTD) 0.6% up W
RWY 16–34: 1230X50 (TURF)
RWY 34: Bldg.
AIRPORT REMARKS: Unattended. Rwy 16–34 for emerg use only, road and drainage ditch parallel rwy on east side. Rwy 07–25 patches of loose aggregate and grvl.
COMMUNICATIONS: CTAF 122.9

HOT SPRINGS (SØ9) 2 E UTC–7(–6DT) N47°36.75′ W114°36.81′ **GREAT FALLS**
2763 B NOTAM FILE GTF
RWY 06–24: H3550X45 (ASPH–TRTD) MIRL
RWY 24: Thld dsplcd 411′. Road.
AIRPORT REMARKS: Unattended. Ultralights on and in vicinity of arpt. Occasional snow removal. Rwy 06–24 asph grvl composition full length. Rwy 24 has 411′ unlighted, 2169′ lgtd at ngt. Rwy 06–24 cones adjacent to MIRL full length and dsplcd thld marked with white cones. Rwy 06 and Rwy 24 numbers 4′x 8′ in measure, thld line and rwy lines NSTD.
COMMUNICATIONS: CTAF 122.9

HYSHAM (6U7) 2 E UTC–7(–6DT) N46°17.61′ W107°11.60′ **BILLINGS**
2624 B NOTAM FILE GTF
RWY 07–25: H3060X45 (ASPH–TRTD) LIRL
AIRPORT REMARKS: Unattended. 1030′ dirt extension east of Rwy 07 thld soft when wet. Rwy 07 basic markings NSTD numbers and stripes, markings are faded. Rwy 25 basic markings NSTD small numbers and stripes, markings are faded. Numerous rwy lgts inop. ACTIVATE LIRL Rwy 07–25—CTAF.
COMMUNICATIONS: CTAF 122.9

JORDAN (JDN) 2 NW UTC–7(–6DT) N47°19.73′ W106°57.16′ **BILLINGS**
2662 B NOTAM FILE JDN **L–13D**
RWY 10–28: H4300X75 (ASPH–PFC) S–12.5 MIRL
RWY 28: PAPI(P2L)—GA 3.0° TCH 29′.
AIRPORT REMARKS: Unattended. ACTIVATE MIRL Rwy 10–28 and PAPI Rwy 28—CTAF.
COMMUNICATIONS: CTAF 122.9
RADIO AIDS TO NAVIGATION: NOTAM FILE GGW.
GLASGOW (H) VORW/DME 113.9 GGW Chan 86 N48°12.92′ W106°37.53′ 180° 54.8 NM to fld. 2283/14E.
NDB (MHW) 263 JDN N47°20.00′ W106°56.29′ at fld. NOTAM FILE JDN. VFR only.

JUDITH MOUNTAIN N47°13.03′ W109°13.31′ **GREAT FALLS**
RCO 122.2 (GREAT FALLS RADIO) **L–13D**

FIGURE 173.—Excerpt from Chart Supplement.

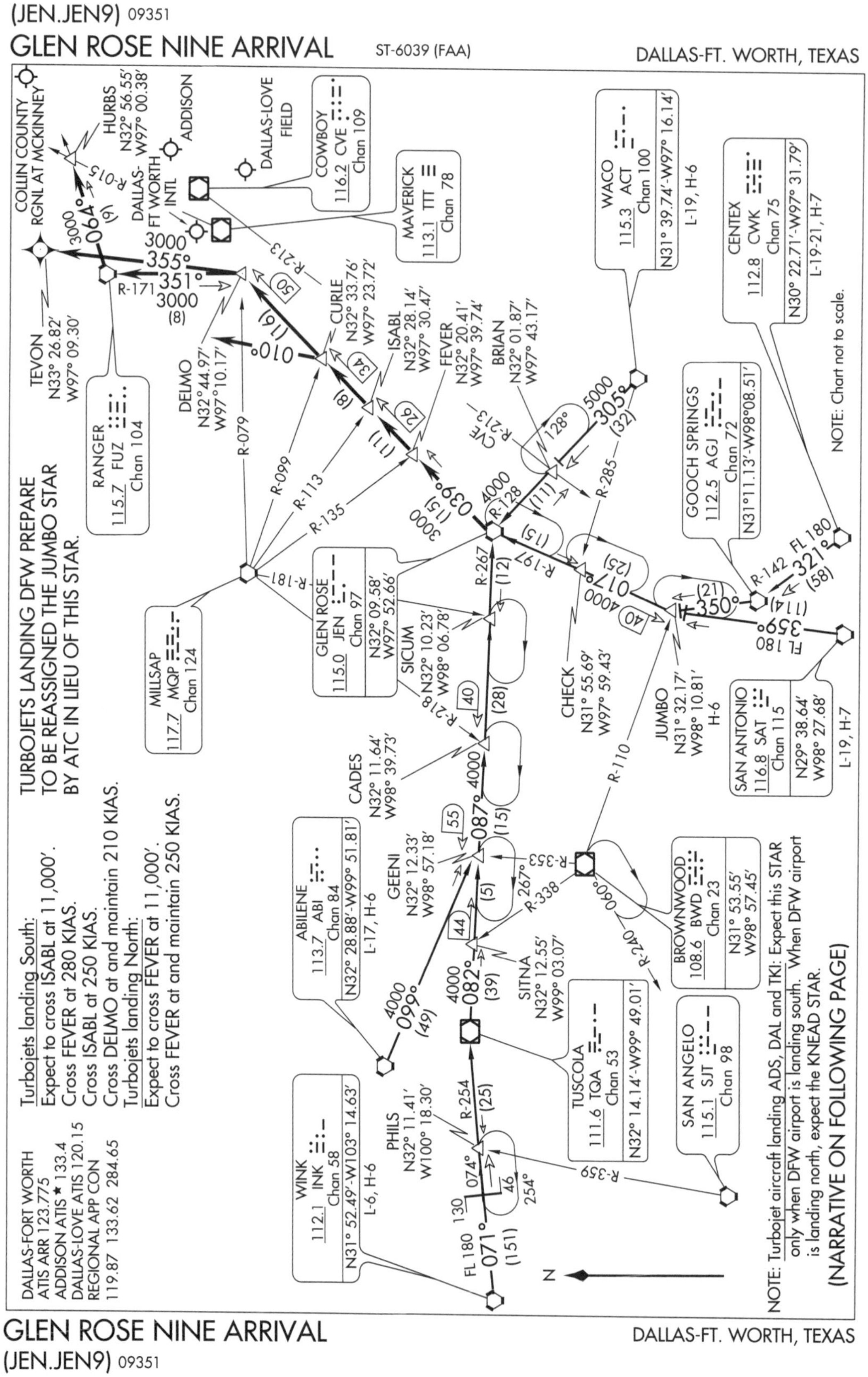

FIGURE 174.—GLEN ROSE Nine Arrival (JEN.JEN9).

(JEN.JEN9) 09351

GLEN ROSE NINE ARRIVAL ST-6039 (FAA) DALLAS-FT. WORTH, TEXAS

ARRIVAL DESCRIPTION

ABILENE TRANSITION (ABI.JEN9): From over ABI VORTAC via R-099 to GEENI INT, then via JEN R-267 to JEN VORTAC. Thence. . . .
CENTEX TRANSITION (CWK.JEN9): From over CWK VORTAC via CWK R-321 and AGJ R-142 to AGJ VORTAC, then via AGJ R-350 to JUMBO INT, then via JEN R-197 to JEN VORTAC. Thence . . . .
JUMBO TRANSITION (JUMBO.JEN9): From over JUMBO INT via JEN R-197 to JEN VORTAC. Thence . . . .
SAN ANTONIO TRANSITION (SAT.JEN9): From over SAT VORTAC via SAT R-359 to JUMBO INT, then via JEN R-197 to JEN VORTAC. Thence . . . .
WACO TRANSITION (ACT.JEN9): From over ACT VORTAC via ACT R-305 and JEN R-128 to JEN VORTAC. Thence. . . .
WINK TRANSITION (INK.JEN9): From over INK VORTAC via INK R-071 and TQA R-254 to TQA VOR/DME, then via TQA R-082 to GEENI INT, then via JEN R-267 to JEN VORTAC. Thence. . . .

. . . . ALL AIRCRAFT: From over JEN VORTAC via JEN R-039, thence . . . .

ALL AIRCRAFT LANDING NORTH: To CURLE INT, expect vectors to final approach course.

JETS LANDING SOUTH: To DELMO, depart DELMO heading 355°.
For /E, /F, /G and /R (RNP 2.0) EQUIPMENT SUFFIXED AIRCRAFT: From over DELMO WP direct TEVON WP, expect vector to final approach course prior to TEVON WP. If not received by TEVON fly present heading.
NON TURBOJETS LANDING SOUTH: To CURLE INT, depart CURLE heading 010° for vectors to final approach course.

AIRCRAFT LANDING DAL, ADS, TKI: To DELMO INT, depart DELMO via FUZ R-171 to FUZ VORTAC then FUZ R-064 to HURBS INT, expect vectors to final approach course.

GLEN ROSE NINE ARRIVAL DALLAS-FT. WORTH, TEXAS
(JEN.JEN9) 09351

FIGURE 175.—GLEN ROSE Nine Arrival (JEN.JEN9).

DALLAS–FORT WORTH

DALLAS/FORT WORTH INTL (DFW) 12 NW UTC–6(–5DT) N32°53.81´ W97°02.28´ **DALLAS–FT WORTH**
607 B **FUEL** 100LL, JET A OX 1, 3 AOE Class I, ARFF Index E NOTAM FILE DFW **COPTER**
RWY 17C–35C: H13401X150 (CONC–GRVD) S–120, D–200, 2S–175, 2D–600, 2D/2D2–850 HIRL CL **H–6H, L–17C, A IAP, AD**
RWY 17C: ALSF2. TDZL. PAPI(P4L)—GA 3.0° TCH 74´.
RWY 35C: ALSF2. TDZL. PAPI(P4L)—GA 3.0° TCH 76´.
RWY 17R–35L: H13401X200 (CONC–GRVD) S–120, D–200, 2S–175, 2D–600, 2D/2D2–850 HIRL CL
RWY 17R: MALSR. TDZL. PAPI(P4L)—GA 3.0° TCH 68´.
RWY 35L: MALSR. TDZL. PAPI(P4L)—GA 3.0° TCH 63´.
RWY 18L–36R: H13400X200 (CONC–GRVD) S–120, D–200, 2S–175, 2D–600, 2D/2D2–850 HIRL CL
RWY 18L: MALSR. TDZL. PAPI(P4L)—GA 3.0° TCH 70´.
RWY 36R: MALSR. TDZL. PAPI(P4L)—GA 3.0° TCH 66´.
RWY 18R–36L: H13400X150 (CONC–GRVD) S–120, D–200, 2S–175, 2D–600, 2D/2D2–850 HIRL CL
RWY 18R: ALSF2. TDZL. PAPI(P4L)—GA 3.0° TCH 74´.
RWY 36L: MALSR. TDZL. PAPI(P4L)—GA 3.0° TCH 72´.
RWY 13R–31L: H9301X150 (CONC–GRVD) S–120, D–200, 2S–175, 2D–600, 2D/2D2–850 HIRL CL
RWY 13R: MALSR. TDZL. PAPI(P4L)—GA 3.0° TCH 71´.
RWY 31L: REIL. PAPI(P4L)—GA 3.13° TCH 72´.
RWY 13L–31R: H9000X200 (CONC–GRVD) S–120, D–200, 2S–175, 2D–600, 2D/2D2–850 HIRL CL
RWY 13L: REIL. PAPI(P4L)—GA 3.0° TCH 82´. Thld dsplcd 625´. 0.5% down.
RWY 31R: MALSR. TDZL. PAPI(P4L)—GA 3.0° TCH 69´. 0.5% up.
RWY 17L–35R: H8500X150 (CONC–GRVD) S–120, D–200, 2S–175, 2D–600, 2D/2D2–850 HIRL CL
RWY 17L: ALSF2. TDZL. PAPI(P4L)—GA 3.0° TCH 77´. Antenna. 0.6% up.
RWY 35R: ALSF2. TDZL. PAPI(P4R)—GA 3.0° TCH 73´. 0.6% down.

LAND AND HOLD–SHORT OPERATIONS

LDG RWY	HOLD–SHORT POINT	AVBL LDG DIST
RWY 17C	TWY B	10460
RWY 18R	TWY B	10100
RWY 35C	TWY EJ	9050
RWY 36L	TWY Z	10650

RUNWAY DECLARED DISTANCE INFORMATION

RWY 13L:	TORA–9000	TODA–9000	ASDA–9000	LDA–8375
RWY 13R:	TORA–9301	TODA–9301	ASDA–9301	LDA–9301
RWY 17C:	TORA–13401	TODA–13401	ASDA–13401	LDA–13401
RWY 17L:	TORA–8500	TODA–8500	ASDA–8500	LDA–8500
RWY 17R:	TORA–13401	TODA–13401	ASDA–13401	LDA–13401
RWY 18L:	TORA–13400	TODA–13400	ASDA–13400	LDA–13400
RWY 18R:	TORA–13400	TODA–13400	ASDA–13400	LDA–13400
RWY 31L:	TORA–9301	TODA–9301	ASDA–9301	LDA–9301
RWY 31R:	TORA–8375	TODA–8375	ASDA–8375	LDA–8375
RWY 35C:	TORA–13401	TODA–13401	ASDA–13401	LDA–13401
RWY 35L:	TORA–13401	TODA–13401	ASDA–13401	LDA–13401
RWY 35R:	TORA–8500	TODA–8500	ASDA–8500	LDA–8500
RWY 36L:	TORA–13400	TODA–13400	ASDA–13400	LDA–13400
RWY 36R:	TORA–13400	TODA–13400	ASDA–13400	LDA–13400

CONTINUED ON NEXT PAGE

Figure 176.—ILS-1 RWY 36L, Dallas-Fort Worth Intl.

CONTINUED FROM PRECEDING PAGE

AIRPORT REMARKS: Attended continuously. Rwy 17L–35R CLOSED 0400–1200Z‡ except PPR. Rwy 13R–31L CLOSED 0400–1200Z‡ except PPR. Rwy 13L–31R CLOSED 0400–1200Z‡ except PPR. Rwy 31R last 625′ CLOSED indef. Visual screen 20′ AGL 1180′ south AER 35C. Visual screen 22′ AGL 1179′ south AER 35L. ASDE–X SURVEILLANCE system in use: Pilots should opr transponders with mode C on all twys and rwys. PPR for acft with wingspan 215′ or greater (GROUP VI), call arpt ops 972–973–3112 for follow me services while taxiing to and from ramp and rwys. Rwy 13L, Rwy 17L, Rwy 31R, and Rwy 35R rwy visual range touchdown, midpoint and rollout avbl. Rwy 31L and Rwy 31R runway visual range touchdown and rollout avbl. Arpt under construction, PAEW in movement areas. Birds on and in vicinity of arpt. Tkf distance for Rwy 17L from Twy Q2 is 8196′. Tkf distance for Rwy 35R from Twy Q9 is 8196′. Tkf distance for Rwy 17R from Twy EG is 13082′ and from Twy EH is 12816′. Tkf distance for Rwy 35L from Twy EQ is 13084′ and from Twy EP is 12811′. Tkf distance for Rwy 36R from Twy WP is 12815′, from Twy WQ is 13082′. Tkf distance for Rwy 18L from Twy WG is 13082′, from Twy WH is 12815′. Tkf distance for Rwy 17C from Twy EG is 13,082′. Tkf distance for Rwy 18R from Twy WG is 13,082′. Land and hold–short signs on Rwy 17C at Twy B 10,460′ south of Rwy 17C thld, Rwy 18R at Twy B 10,100′ south of Rwy 18R thld, Rwy 35C at Twy EJ 9050′ north of Rwy 35C thld, Rwy 36L at Twy Z 10,650′ north of Rwy 36L thld, lgtd and marked with in–pavement pulsating white lgts. Twy G11 east of Twy G clsd to acft with wingspan 125′ and greater. Acft using gates D6–D17 must obtain approval from DFW ramp twr 129.95 prior to entering ramp and prior to pushback 1130–0430Z‡. Use extreme care at other times. Apron Terminal E ramp work in progress, ctc DFW ramp on 131.0 1530–1200Z‡ for Terminal E procedure change. Apron entrance/exit Points 32, 33, 34, 35, 36, 37, 38 and 39 clsd to acft with wingspan greater than 135′. Acft pushing back or powering back on Terminal B Apron have right of way. Frequent ground support equip under escort crossing Twys A and B at Twy HA. Apron entrance/exit points 5, 7, 42 and 44 clsd to acft with wingspan 118′ and greater. Apron entrance/exit points 42 and 44 clsd to acft with wingspan greater than 118′. Terminal B apron taxilane btn apron entrance/exit point taxilanes 110 and 115 clsd to acft with wingspan 118′ and greater. Apron entrance/exit points 22, 24, 105, 107 and 122 clsd to acft with wingspan 125′ and greater. Apron entrance/exit point 124 clsd to acft with wingspan 200′ and greater. Twy A5 clsd to acft with wingspan 171′ and greater. Twys may require judgemental oversteering for large acft. Apron entrance/exit points 52 and 53 clsd to acft with wingspan 171′ and greater. Acft exiting via apron entrance/exit points 42, 43 and 44 ctc Gnd Con prior to taxiing. PPR general aviation ops 0400–1200Z‡, call arpt ops 972–973–3112. PPR from arpt ops for general aviation acft to proceed to airline terminal gate except to general aviation facility. PPR from the primary tenant airlines to operate within the central terminal area. Proper minimum object free area distances may not be maintained for ramp/apron taxi lanes. Twy edge reflectors along all twys. Landing fee. Flight Notification Service (ADCUS) available. NOTE: See Land and Hold Short Operations, Intersection Departures During Periods of Darkness, Noise Abatement Procedures and Continuous Power Facilities.

WEATHER DATA SOURCES: ASOS (972) 453–0992 LLWAS.

COMMUNICATIONS: D–ATIS ARR 123.775 (972) 615–2701 **D–ATIS DEP** 135.925 (972) 615–2701 **UNICOM** 122.95
Ⓡ **RGNL APP CON** 125.025 133.525 (E) 119.875 133.625 (W)
DFW TOWER 126.55 127.5 (E) 124.15 134.9 (W) **GND CON** 121.65 121.8 (E) 121.85 (W)
CLNC DEL 128.25
Ⓡ **RGNL DEP CON** 118.55 (E) 126.475 (W) 124.825 (N) 125.125 (S)

AIRSPACE: CLASS B See VFR Terminal Area Chart

RADIO AIDS TO NAVIGATION: NOTAM FILE FTW.
MAVERICK (H) VORW/DME 113.1 TTT Chan 78 N32°52.15′ W97°02.43′ 358° 1.7 NM to fld. 540/6E.
ILS/DME 109.5 I–LWN Chan 32 Rwy 13R. Class IE.
ILS/DME 110.3 I–FLQ Chan 40 Rwy 17C. Class IIIE. DME also serves Rwy 35C.
ILS/DME 111.75 I–PPZ Chan 54(Y) Rwy 17L. Class IIIE. DME also serves Rwy 35R.
ILS/DME 111.35 I–JHZ Chan 50(Y) Rwy 17R. Class IE. DME also serves Rwy 35L.
ILS/DME 110.55 I–CIX Chan 42(Y) Rwy 18L. Class IE. DME also serves Rwy 36R.
ILS/DME 111.9 I–VYN Chan 56 Rwy 18R. Class IIIE. DME also serves Rwy 36L.
ILS/DME 110.9 I–RRA Chan 46 Rwy 31R. Class IE.
ILS/DME 110.3 I–PKQ Chan 40 Rwy 35C. Class IIIE. DME also serves Rwy 17C. OM/comlo also serves Rwy 35L.
ILS/DME 111.35 I–UWX Chan 50(Y) Rwy 35L. Class IE. OM/comlo also serves Rwy 35R. LOC unusable byd 14 NM blo 3,400′. DME also serves Rwy 17R.
ILS/DME 111.75 I–AJQ Chan 54(Y) Rwy 35R. Class IIIE. DME also serves Rwy 17L. LOC unusable byd 16 NM 5° right of course.
ILS/DME 111.9 I–BXN Chan 56 Rwy 36L. Class ID. DME also serves Rwy 18R. OM also serves Rwy 36R. LOC unusable byd 15 NM 5° right of course.
ILS/DME 110.55 I–FJN Chan 42(Y) Rwy 36R. Class IE. OM also serves Rwy 36L. DME also serves Rwy 18L.

COMM/NAV/WEATHER REMARKS: All acft arriving DFW are requested to turn DME off until dep due to tfc overload of Maverick DME.

DALLAS/FORT WORTH INTL (See DALLAS–FORT WORTH on page 243)

DAN E RICHARDS MUNI (See PADUCAH on page 325)

DAN JONES INTL (See HOUSTON on page 279)

FIGURE 176A.—ILS-1 RWY 36L, Dallas-Fort Worth Intl.

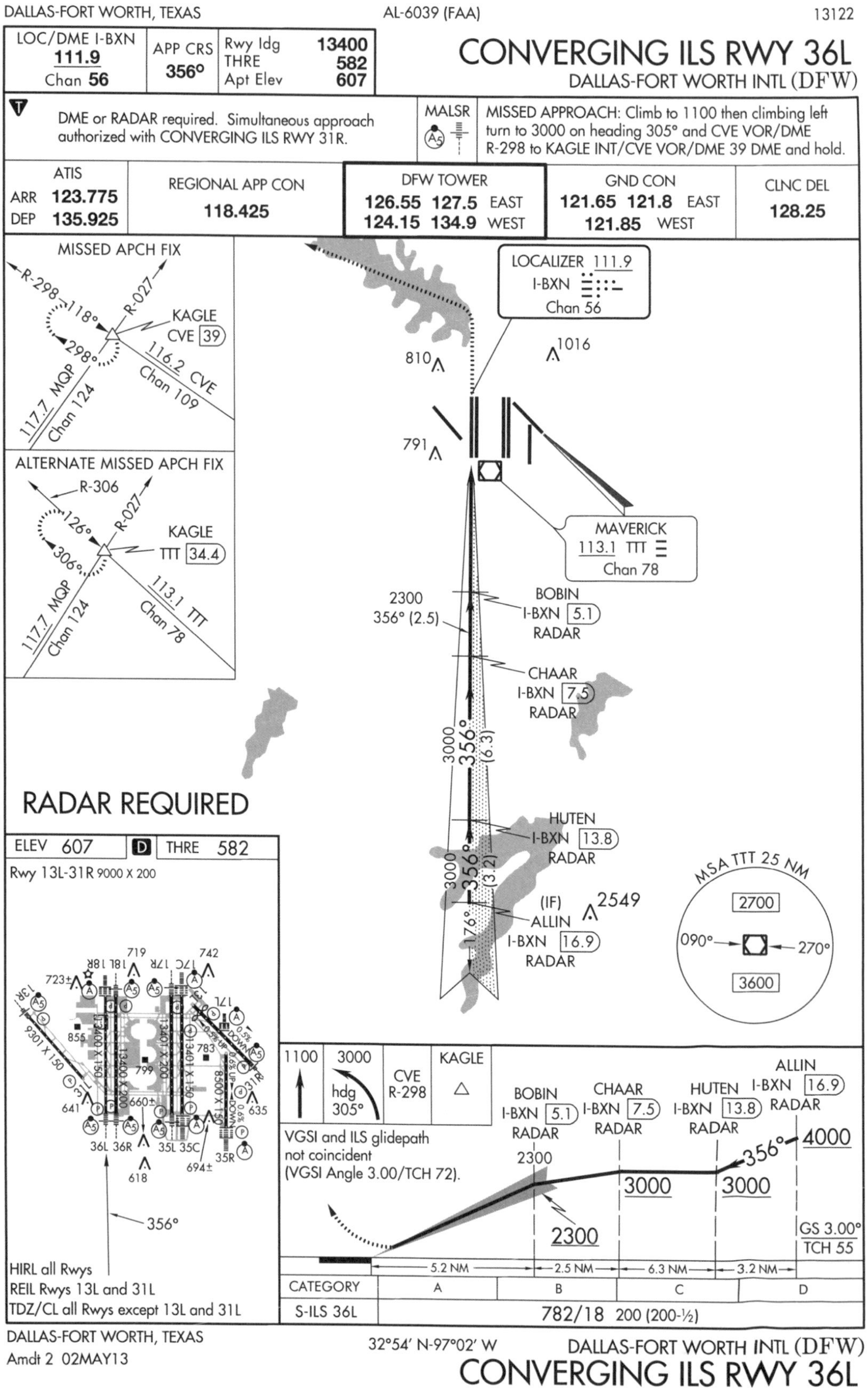

FIGURE 177.—Converging ILS RWY 36L (DFW).

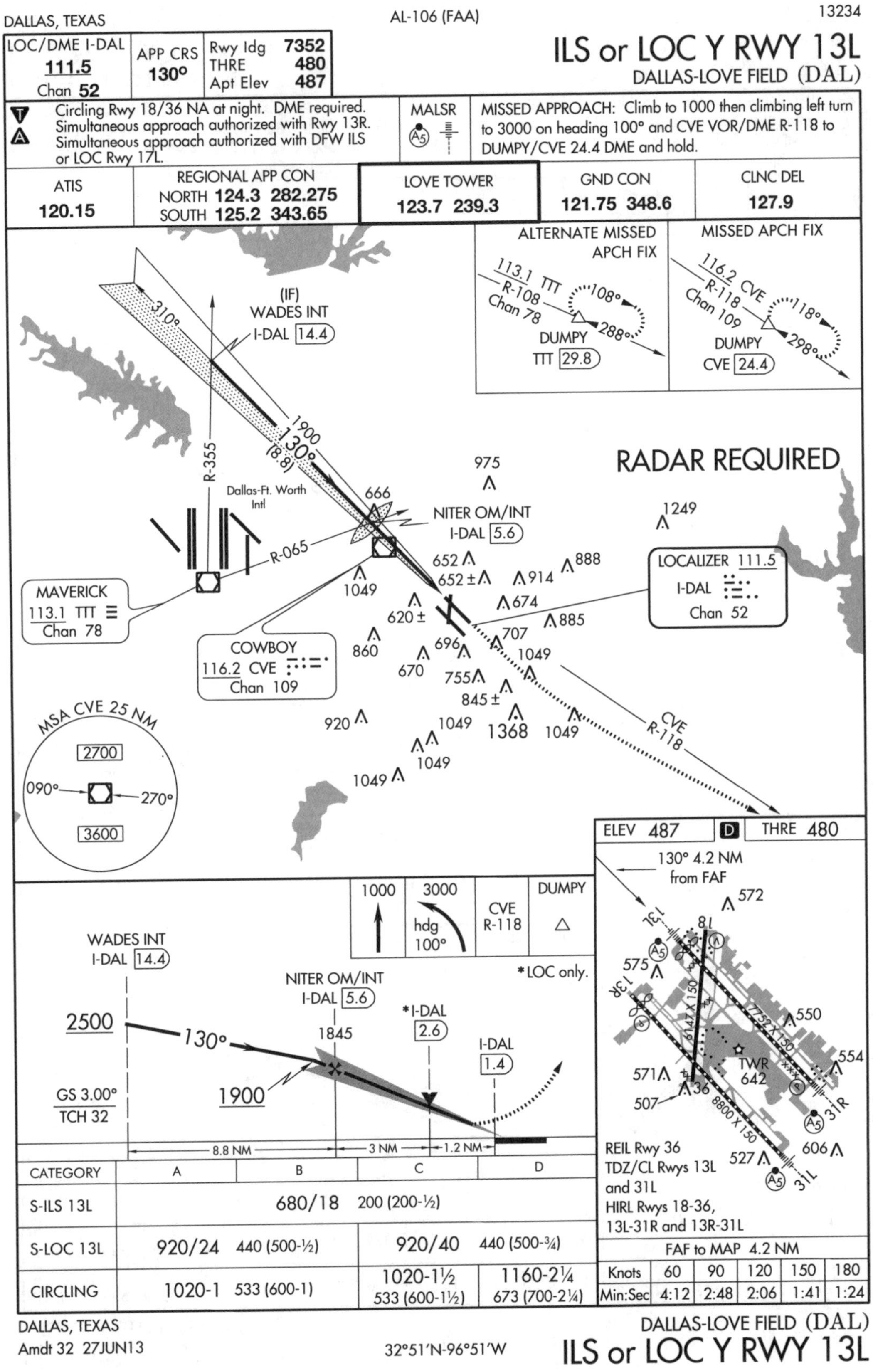

FIGURE 178.—ILS or LOC Y RWY 13L (DAL).

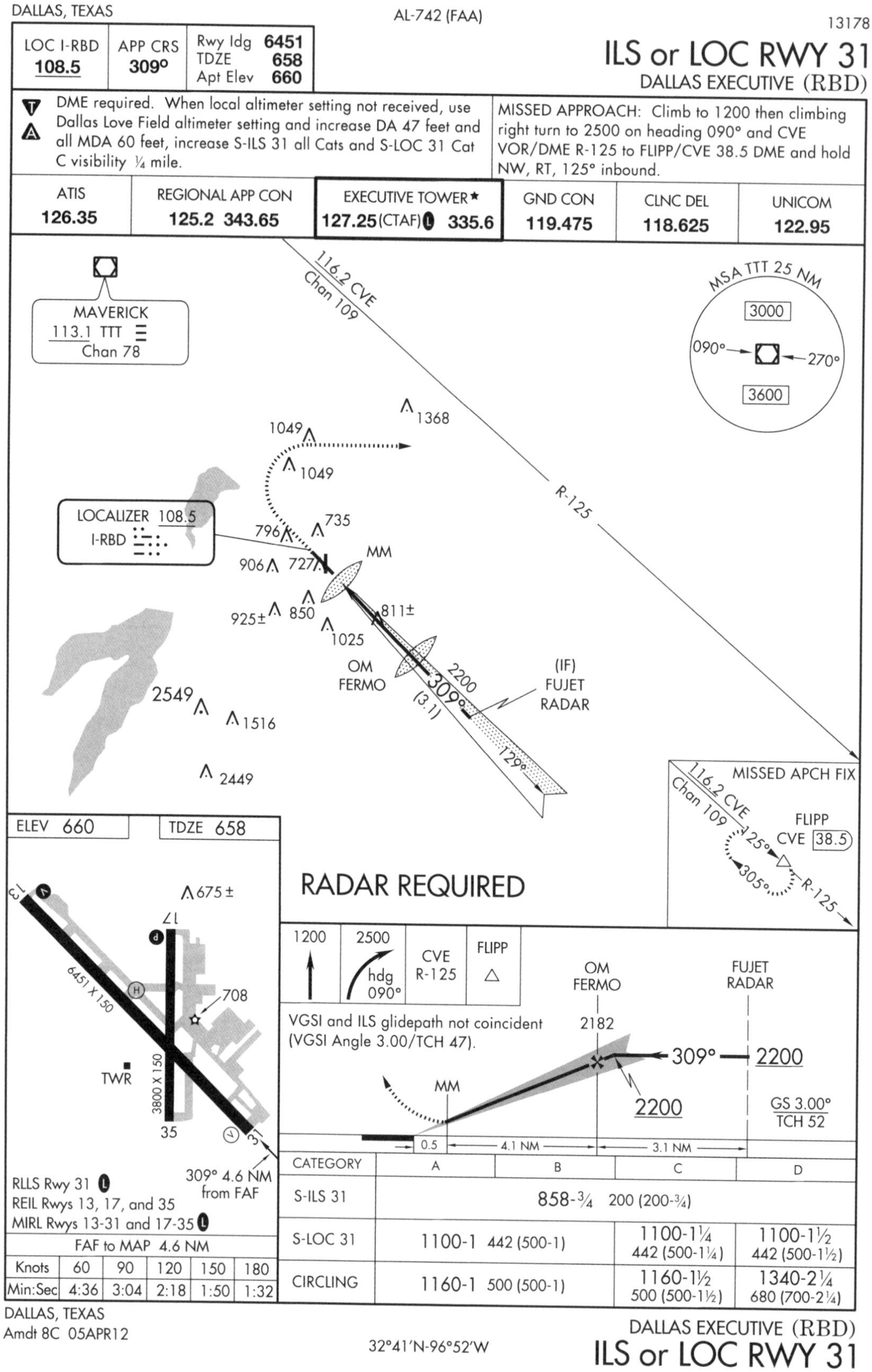

FIGURE 179.—ILS or LOC RWY 31 (RBD).

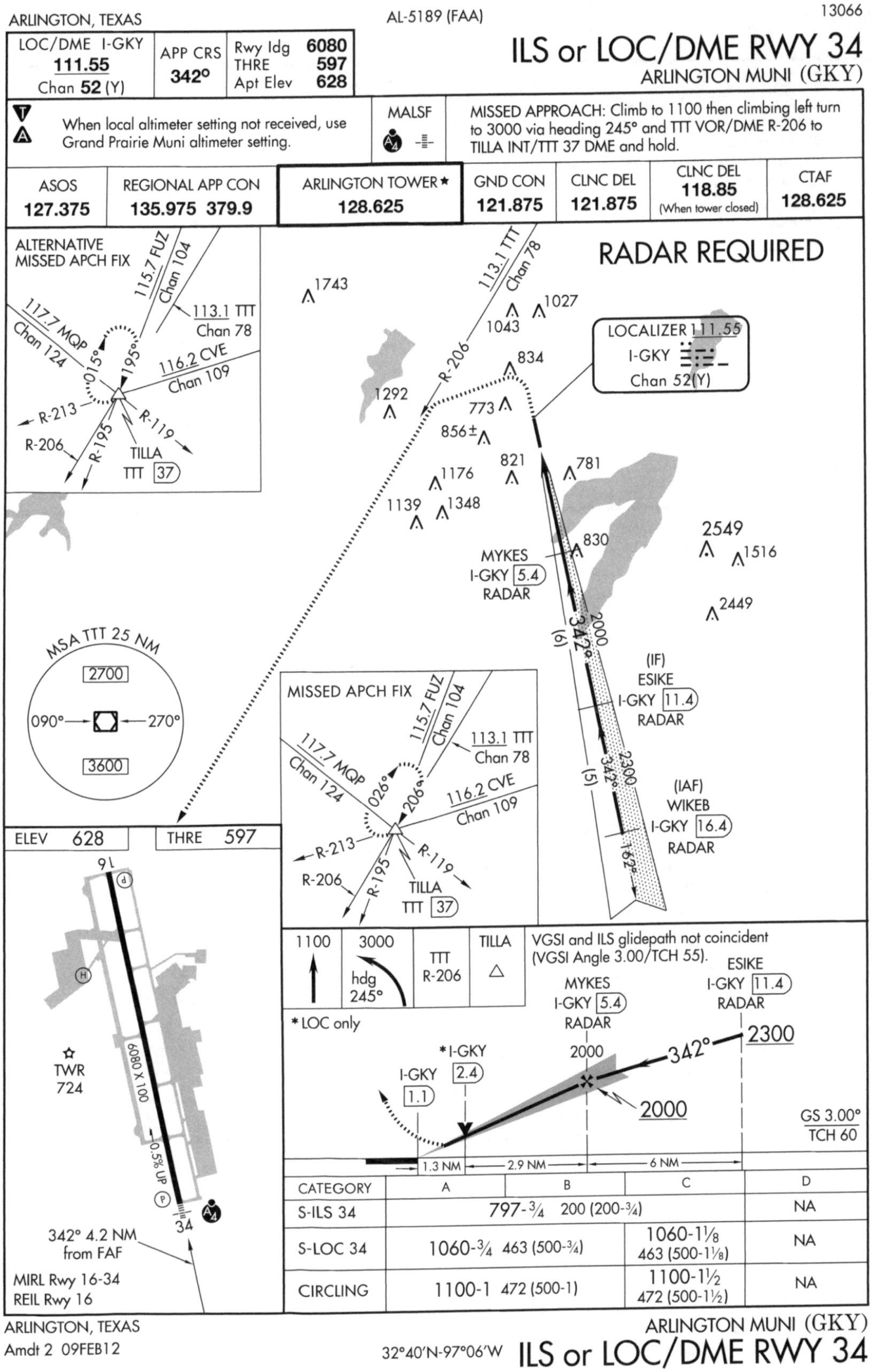

CATEGORY	A	B	C	D
S-ILS 34	797-¾ 200 (200-¾)			NA
S-LOC 34	1060-¾ 463 (500-¾)		1060-1⅛ 463 (500-1⅛)	NA
CIRCLING	1100-1 472 (500-1)		1100-1½ 472 (500-1½)	NA

FIGURE 180.—ILS or LOC/DME RWY 34 (GKY).

ARCHER CITY MUNI (T39) 1 SE UTC–6(–5DT) N33°34.94´ W98°37.12´ **DALLAS–FT WORTH**
1065 S2 NOTAM FILE FTW **L–17B**
RWY 17–35: H3200X60 (ASPH) S–12.5
RWY 17: Road.
AIRPORT REMARKS: Unattended. Wildlife on and invof arpt. 70´ AGL drilling rig 700´ northwest of Rwy 17–35. Rwy 17–35 loose grvl, tall grass and pot holes on rwy.
COMMUNICATIONS: CTAF 122.9
RADIO AIDS TO NAVIGATION: NOTAM FILE SPS.
WICHITA FALLS (H) VORTACW 112.7 SPS Chan 74 N33°59.24´ W98°35.61´ 173° 24.3 NM to fld. 1133/10E.

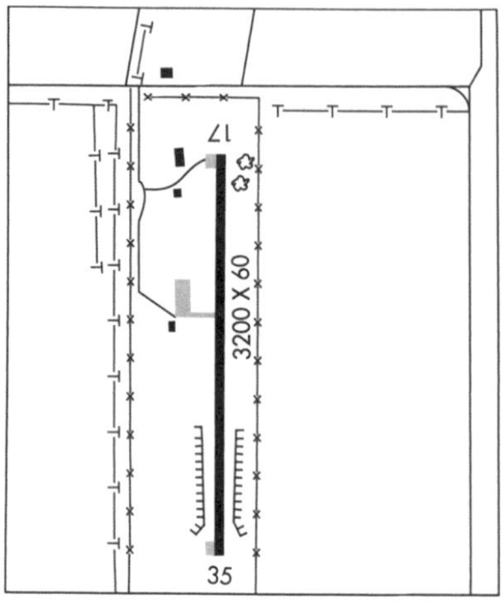

ARDYTH N27°38.54´ W99°27.48´ NOTAM FILE SJT. **BROWNSVILLE**
NDB (MHW) 405 AGH 174° 5.9 NM to Laredo Intl. **L–20G**

ARLEDGE FLD (See STAMFORD on page 351)

ARLINGTON MUNI (GKY) 4 S UTC–6(–5DT) N32°39.83´ W97°05.66´ **DALLAS–FT WORTH**
628 B S4 **FUEL** 100LL, JET A OX 4 TPA—1628(1000) NOTAM FILE GKY **COPTER**
RWY 16–34: H6080X100 (CONC) S–60 MIRL 0.5% up NW **H–6H, L–17C, A**
RWY 16: REIL. PAPI(P4L)—GA 3.0° TCH 42´. **IAP, AD**
RWY 34: MALSF. PAPI(P4L)—GA 3.0° TCH 55´.
AIRPORT REMARKS: Attended continuously. Self serve fuel with major credit card. Helicopter test facility at arpt mostly from private helipad adjoining ldg area. Extensive helicopter traffic west of rwy. Rwy 34 PAPI unusable byd 8° right of centerline. MIRL Rwy 16–34 preset medium ints, higher ints by twr request. When twr clsd ACTIVATE MALSF Rwy 34—CTAF. PAPI Rwy 16 and Rwy 34 opr continuously.
WEATHER DATA SOURCES: ASOS 127.375 (817) 557–0251.
COMMUNICATIONS: CTAF 128.625
Ⓡ **REGIONAL APP/DEP CON** 135.975
TOWER 128.625 (1300–0300Z‡) **GND CON/CLNC DEL** 121.875
CLNC DEL 118.85 (RGNL APP CON when twr clsd)
AIRSPACE: CLASS D svc 1300–0300Z‡ other times CLASS G.
RADIO AIDS TO NAVIGATION: NOTAM FILE FTW.
MAVERICK (H) VORW/DME 113.1 TTT Chan 78 N32°52.15´ W97°02.43´ 186° 12.6 NM to fld. 540/6E.
All acft arriving DFW are requested to turn DME off until departure due to traffic overload of Maverick DME
ILS/DME 111.55 I–GKY Chan 52(Y) Rwy 34. Class IE. LOC unusable byd 15° right of course. Unmonitored when ATCT clsd.

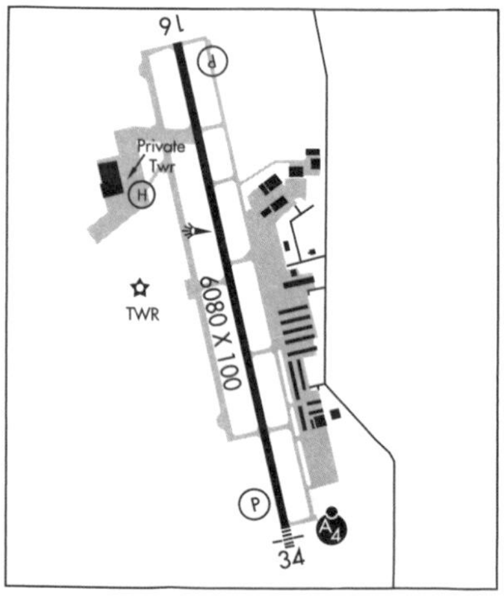

FIGURE 181.—Excerpt from Chart Supplement.

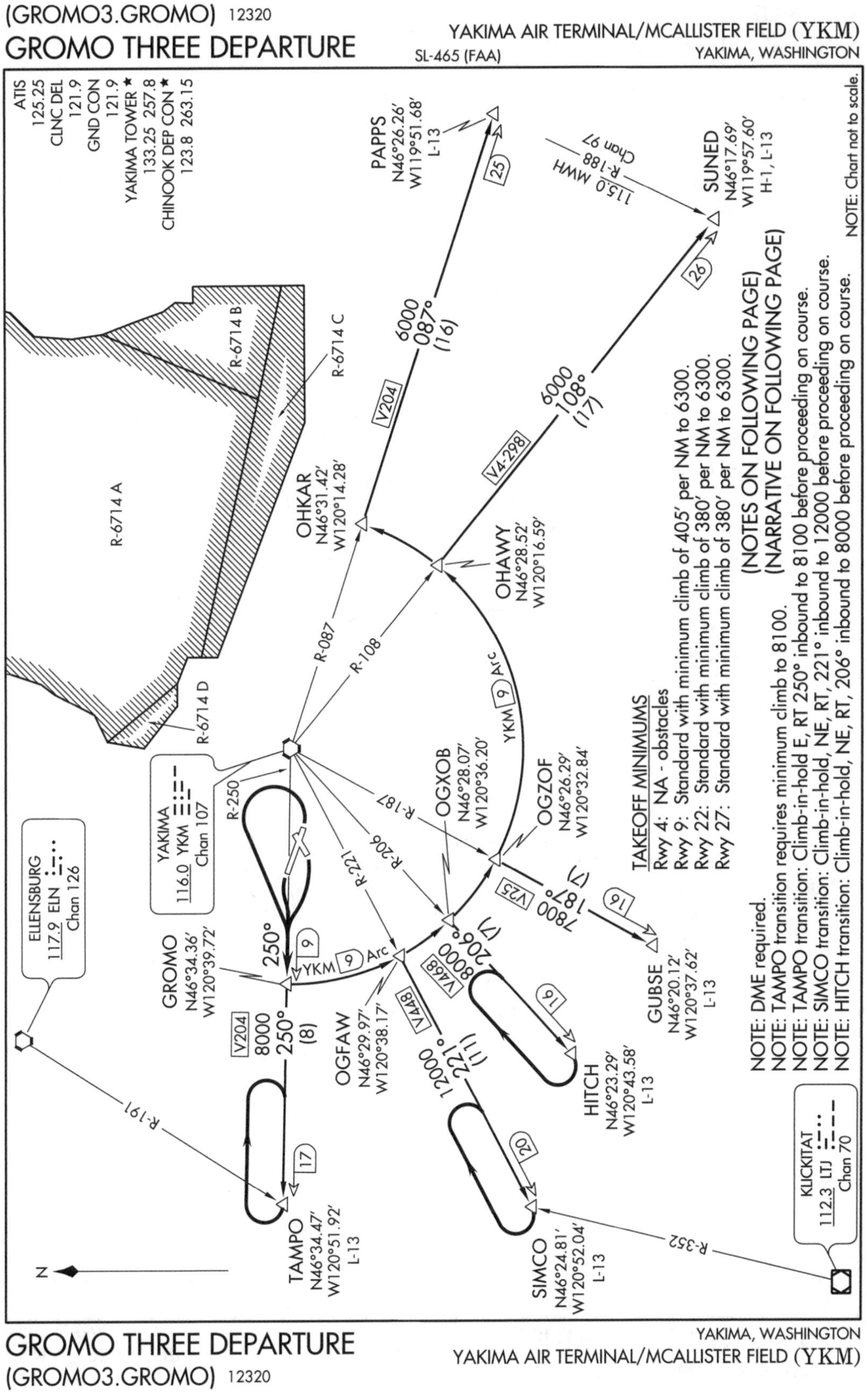

FIGURE 182.—GROMO Three Departure (GROMO3.GROMO).

(GROMO3.GROMO) 12208

GROMO THREE DEPARTURE

SL-465 (FAA)

YAKIMA AIR TERMINAL/MCALLISTER FIELD (YKM)

YAKIMA, WASHINGTON

DEPARTURE ROUTE DESCRIPTION

TAKEOFF RUNWAY 9,27: Climbing left turn thence. . . .

TAKEOFF RUNWAY 22: Climbing right turn thence. . . .

. . . . intercept and proceed via YKM R-250 to GROMO/YKM 9 DME, then on assigned transition.

GUBSE TRANSITION (GROMO3.GUBSE): From over GROMO DME Fix via YKM 9 DME Arc to OGZOF DME fix and YKM VORTAC R-187 to GUBSE DME fix.

HITCH TRANSITION (GROMO3.HITCH): From over GROMO DME Fix via YKM 9 DME Arc to OGXOB DME fix and YKM VORTAC R-206 to HITCH DME fix.

PAPPS TRANSITION (GROMO3.PAPPS): From over GROMO DME Fix via YKM 9 DME Arc to OKHAR DME fix and YKM VORTAC R-087 to PAPPS DME fix.

SIMCO TRANSITION (GROMO3.SIMCO): From over GROMO DME Fix via YKM 9 DME Arc to OGFAW DME fix and YKM VORTAC R-221 to SIMCO INT.

SUNED TRANSITION (GROMO3.SUNED): From over GROMO DME Fix via 9 DME Arc to OHAWY DME fix and KM R-108 to SUNED INT.

TAMPO TRANSITION (GROMO3.TAMPO): From over GROMO DME Fix via YKM VORTAC R-250 to TAMPO INT.

TAKEOFF OBSTACLE NOTES

Rwy 9: OL on building 27′ from DER, 507′ right of centerline, 34′ AGL/1074′ MSL.
Pole 388′ from DER, 561′ right of centerline, 34′ AGL/1073′ MSL.
Trees beginning 586′ from DER, 550′ right of centerline, up to 100′ AGL/1139′ MSL.

Rwy 22: Fence beginning 27′ from DER, 435′ right of centerline, up to 10′ AGL/1085′ MSL.
Trees beginning 570′ from DER, 228′ left of centerline, up to 100′ AGL/1199′ MSL.
Trees beginning 3195′ from DER, 202′ right of centerline, up to 100′ AGL/1199′ MSL.
Trees beginning 1 NM from DER, 732′ left of centerline, up to 100′ AGL/1239′ MSL.

Rwy 27: Ant on building 398′ from DER, 282′ left of centerline, 15′ AGL/1117′ MSL.
Trees beginning 3893′ from DER, 1341′ right of centerline, up to 100′ AGL/1239′ MSL.

GROMO THREE DEPARTURE

(GROMO3.GROMO) 12208

YAKIMA, WASHINGTON

YAKIMA AIR TERMINAL/MCALLISTER FIELD (YKM)

FIGURE 183.—GROMO Three Departure (GROMO3.GROMO).

YAKIMA AIR TERMINAL/MCALLISTER FLD (YKM) 3 S UTC–8(–7DT) N46°34.09′ W120°32.64′ **SEATTLE**
1099 B S4 **FUEL** 100LL, JET A OX 1, 3 Class I, ARFF Index A NOTAM FILE YKM **H–1C, L–13A**
RWY 09–27: H7604X150 (ASPH–GRVD) S–95, D–160, 2S–175, 2D–220, 2D/2D2–550 PCN 33 F/C/X/T **IAP, DIAP, AD**
HIRL 0.7% up W
RWY 09: REIL. VASI(V4L)—GA 3.0° TCH 50′.
RWY 27: MALSR. PAPI(P4L)—GA 3.0° TCH 57′.
RWY 04–22: H3835X150 (ASPH–PFC) S–70, D–80, 2S–102, 2D–120 PCN 28 F/C/X/T MIRL 0.5% up SW
RWY 04: REIL. PAPI(P4L)—GA 3.0° TCH 57′.
RWY 22: REIL. PAPI(P4L)—GA 3.0° TCH 45′.
RUNWAY DECLARED DISTANCE INFORMATION
RWY 04: TORA–3835 TODA–3835 ASDA–3835 LDA–3835
RWY 09: TORA–7604 TODA–7604 ASDA–7604 LDA–7604
RWY 22: TORA–3835 TODA–3835 ASDA–3535 LDA–3835
RWY 27: TORA–7604 TODA–7604 ASDA–7604 LDA–7604
AIRPORT REMARKS: Attended 1400–0400Z‡. Sfc conditions unmonitored 0800–1330Z‡. Be alert, birds invof Yakima River 5 NM east of apch to Rwy 27. Reflectors on Twy C only. Rwy 04–22 some spalling and raveling. PPR for unscheduled air carrier ops with more than 30 passenger seats, call arpt manger 509–575–6149/6150. Twy B from apch end of Rwy 22 to Twy A rstd to acft with wingspans 79′ or less. MIRL Rwy 04–22, REIL Rwy 04 and Rwy 22, PAPI Rwy 04 and Rwy 22 OTS when twr clsd. Twy B1 and Twy B2 twy lgts OTS when twr clsd. Twy B lgts south of Rwy 09–27 OTS when twr clsd. When twr clsd ACTIVATE HIRL Rwy 09–27 and MALSR Rwy 27—CTAF.
WEATHER DATA SOURCES: ASOS (509) 248–1502
COMMUNICATIONS: CTAF 133.25 **ATIS** 125.25 **UNICOM** 122.95
RCO 122.5 (SEATTLE RADIO)
Ⓡ **CHINOOK APP/DEP CON** 123.8 (1400–0600Z‡)
Ⓡ **SEATTLE CENTER APP/DEP CON** 132.6 (0600–1400Z‡)
TOWER 133.25 (1400–0600Z‡) **GND CON** 121.9 **CLNC DEL** 121.9
AIRSPACE: CLASS D svc 1400–0600Z‡ other times CLASS E.
RADIO AIDS TO NAVIGATION: NOTAM FILE YKM.
(H) VORTACW 116.0 YKM Chan 107 N46°34.21′ W120°26.68′ 247° 4.1 NM to fld. 984/21E.
DME unusable:
095°–115° byd 26 NM blo 8,000′
095°–115° byd 35 NM
115°–207° byd 20 NM blo 8,500′
115°–207° byd 36 NM blo 10,000′
207°–230° byd 20 NM blo 10,000′
290°–315° byd 20 NM blo 11,000′
315°–080° byd 12 NM blo 15,000′
VOR portion unusable:
025°–035° byd 5 NM blo 6,000′
080°–105° byd 35 NM blo 6,000′
105°–107° byd 25 NM blo 6,000′
109°–135° byd 25 NM blo 6,000′
135°–180° byd 30 NM blo 7,500′
195°–225° byd 30 NM blo 8,500′
305°–335° byd 30 NM blo 9,000′
350°–080° byd 25 NM blo 9,000′
DONNY NDB (LOM) 371 YK N46°31.54′ W120°22.33′ 274° 7.6 NM to fld. Unmonitored when ATCT closed.
ILS 110.1 I–YKM Rwy 27. LOM DONNY NDB. Unmonitored when ATCT closed.
COMM/NAV/WEATHER REMARKS: During hrs twr is clsd all ops in vicinity of arpt rstd to acft with VHF radio capability, unless an emerg exist necessitating UHF equipped acft to land.

FIGURE 184.—Excerpt from Chart Supplement.

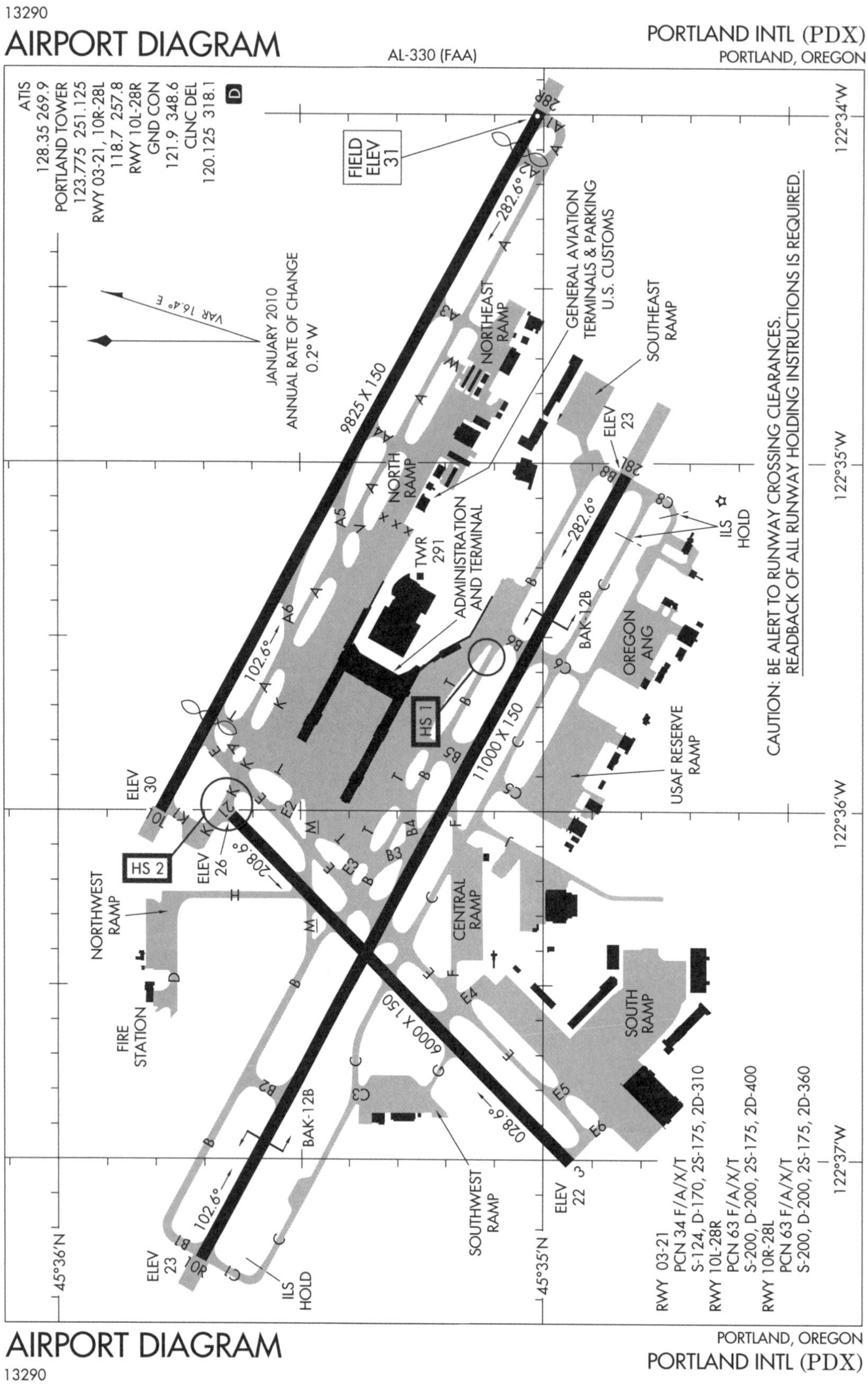

FIGURE 185.—Airport Diagram - Portland INTL (PDX).

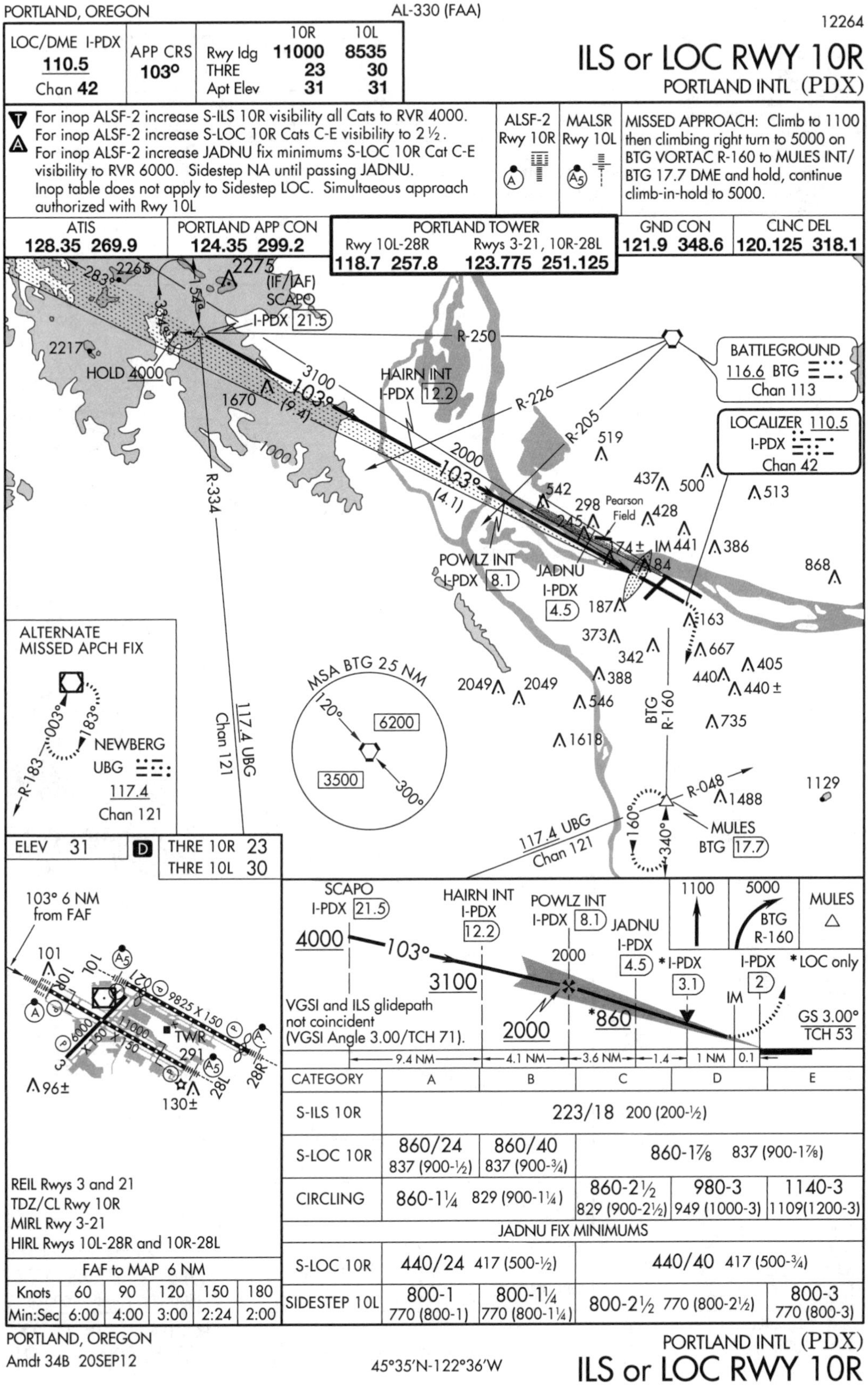

FIGURE 186.—ILS or LOC RWY 10R (PDX).

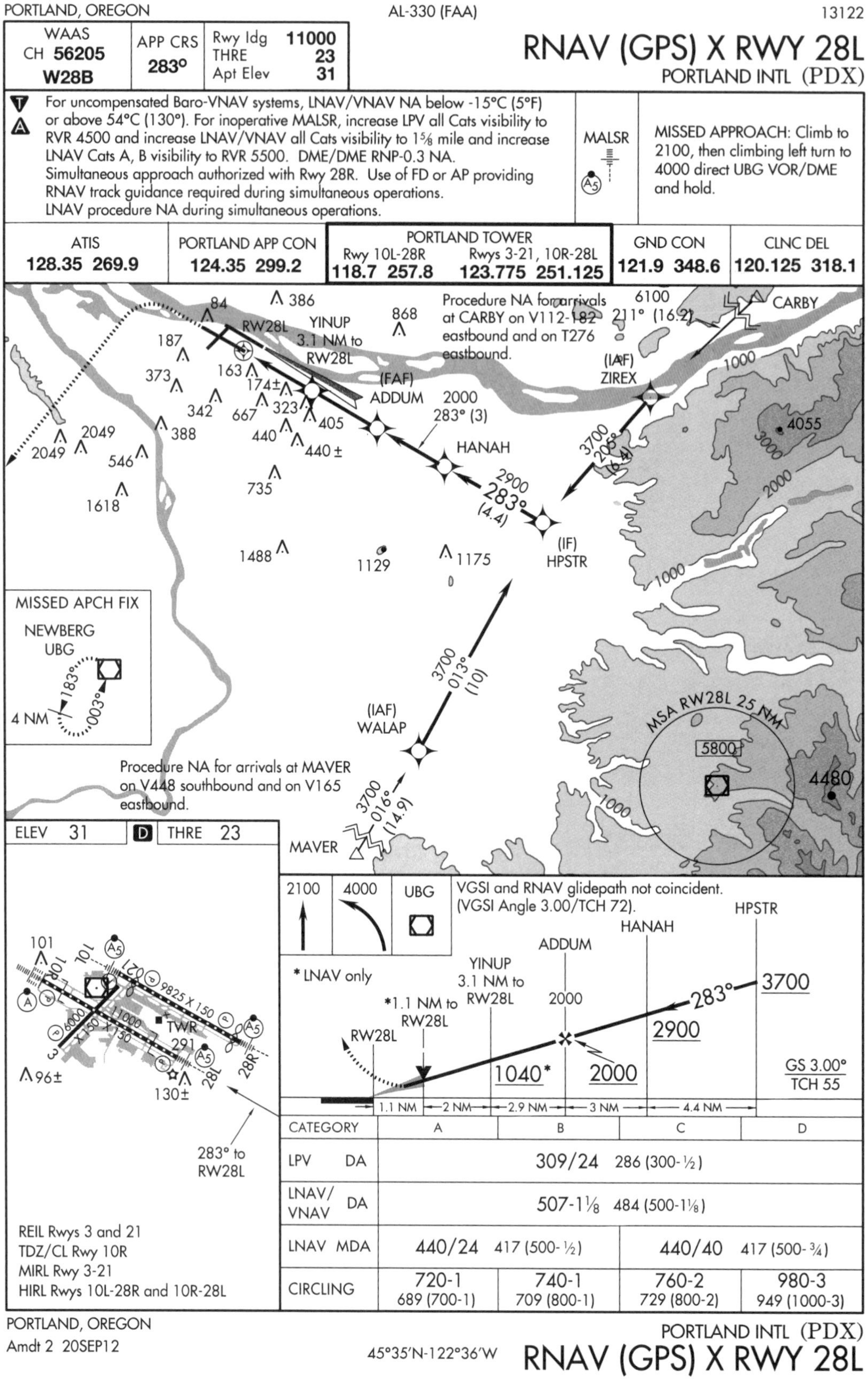

FIGURE 187.—RNAV (GPS) X RWY 28L (PDX).

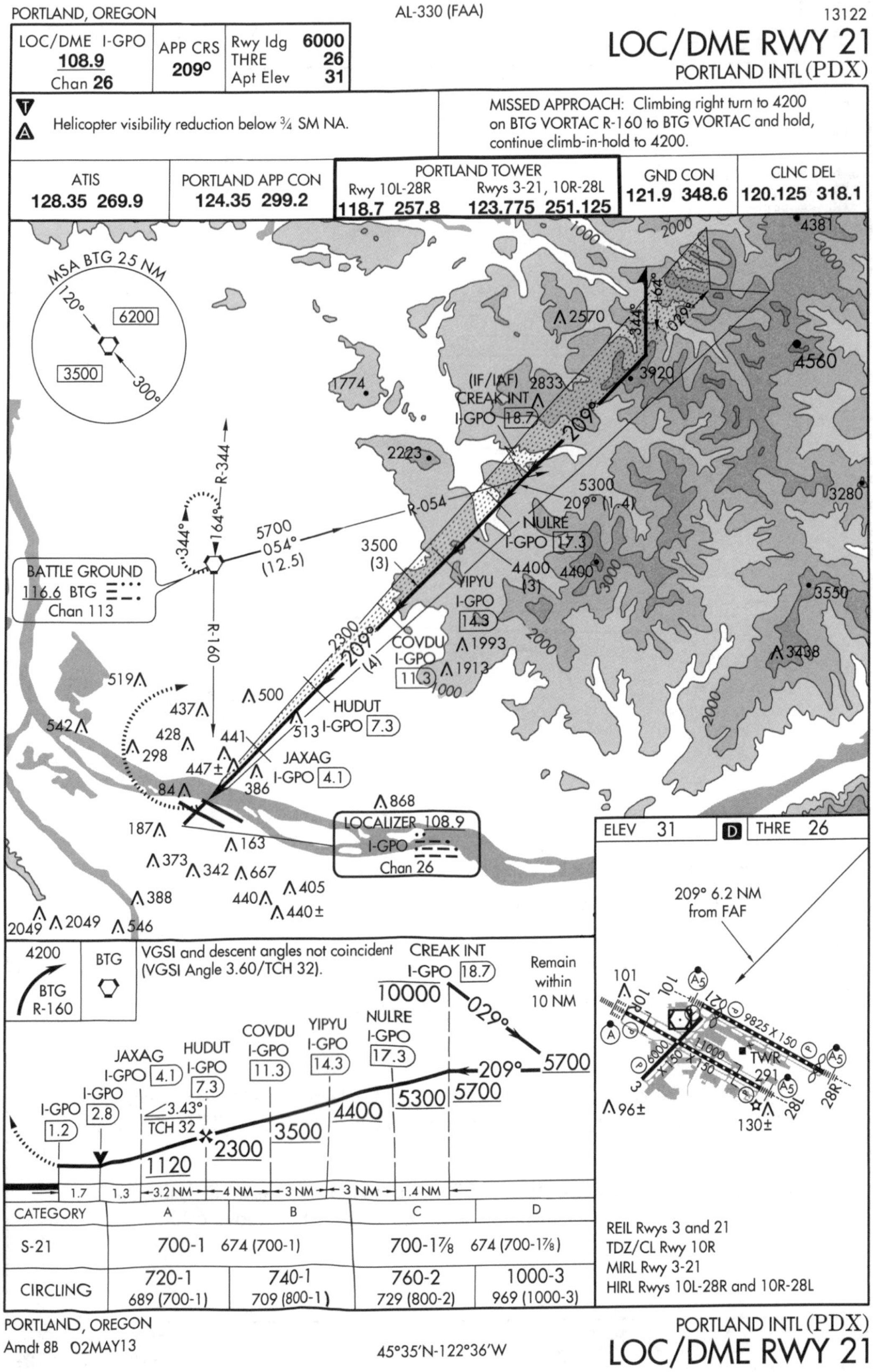

CATEGORY	A	B	C	D
S-21	700-1 674 (700-1)		700-1⅞ 674 (700-1⅞)	
CIRCLING	720-1 689 (700-1)	740-1 709 (800-1)	760-2 729 (800-2)	1000-3 969 (1000-3)

FIGURE 188.—LOC/DME RWY 21 (PDX).

(HABUT4.GVO) 13122

HABUT FOUR DEPARTURE SL-378 (FAA)

SANTA BARBARA MUNI (SBA)
SANTA BARBARA, CALIFORNIA

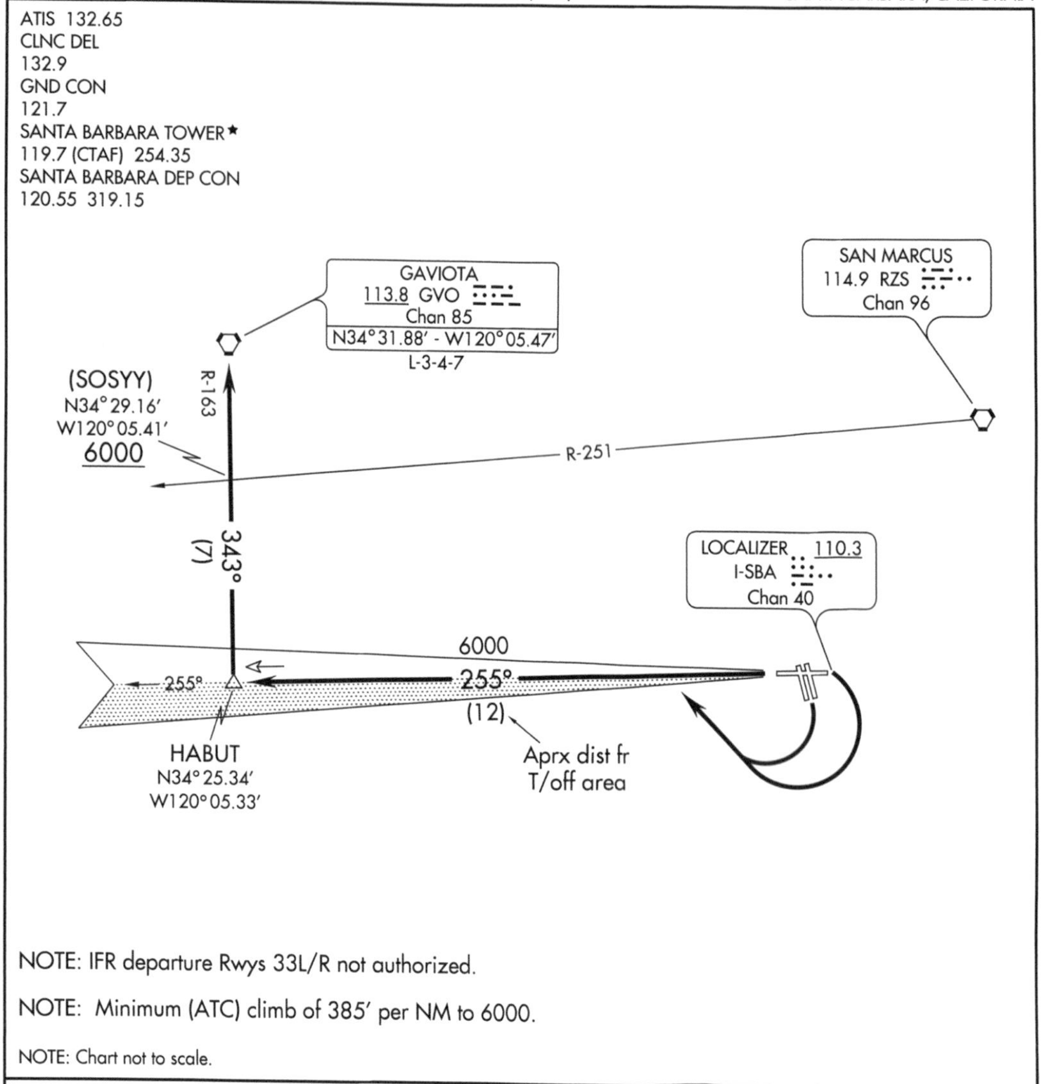

DEPARTURE ROUTE DESCRIPTION

TAKE-OFF RUNWAYS 7 and 15L/R: Turn right, intercept I-SBA west course to HABUT INT, thence via GVO R-163 to GVO VORTAC. Cross RZS R-251 at or above 6000′.

TAKE-OFF RUNWAY 25: Intercept I-SBA west course to HABUT INT, thence via GVO R-163 to GVO VORTAC. Cross RZS R-251 at or above 6000′.

HABUT FOUR DEPARTURE
(HABUT4.GVO) 13122

SANTA BARBARA, CALIFORNIA
SANTA BARBARA MUNI (SBA)

FIGURE 189.—HABUT Four Departure (HABUT4.GVO) (SBA).

SANTA BARBARA MUNI (SBA) 7 W UTC–8(–7DT) N34°25.57′ W119°50.49′ **LOS ANGELES**
13 B S4 **FUEL** 100LL, JET A OX 1, 2, 3, 4 TPA—See Remarks LRA Class I, ARFF Index C **H–4H, L–3D, 4F, 7A**
NOTAM FILE SBA **IAP, AD**

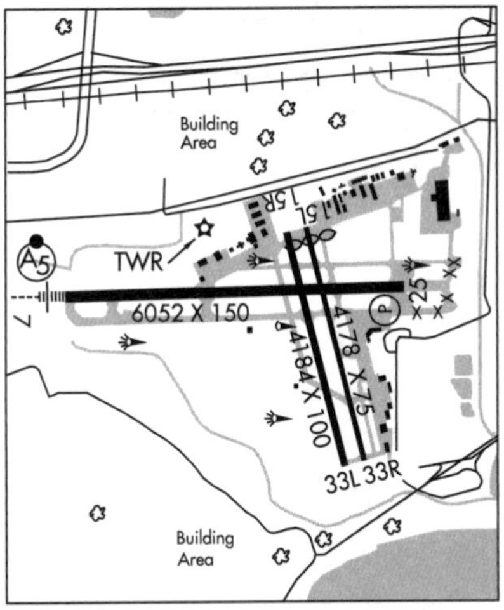

RWY 07–25: H6052X150 (ASPH–PFC) S–110, D–160, 2S–175, 2D–245 HIRL
RWY 07: MALSR. Tree. Rgt tfc.
RWY 25: REIL. PAPI(P4L)—GA 3.0° TCH 50′. Fence.
RWY 15R–33L: H4184X100 (ASPH) S–48, D–63, 2S–80, 2D–100 MIRL
RWY 15R: REIL. Tree.
RWY 33L: Tree. Rgt tfc.
RWY 15L–33R: H4178X75 (ASPH) S–35, D–41, 2S–80, 2D–63
RWY 15L: Thld dsplcd 217′. Bldg.
RWY 33R: Rgt tfc.
AIRPORT REMARKS: Attended 1330–0600Z‡. 100LL fuel 24 hr credit card svc avbl. Fee for Jet A fuel after hrs call 805–964–6733 or 967–5608. Numerous flocks of birds on and invof arpt. Deep creek located 300′ from rwy end Rwy 07, Rwy 33L and Rwy 33R. Rwy 15L–33R dalgt hrs only. Arpt has noise abatement procedures ctc arpt ops 805–692–6005. Due to ltd ramp space at the airline terminal non–scheduled transport category acft with more than 30 passenger seats are required to ctc arpt ops 805–692–6005 24 hour PPR to arrival. Commercial airline ramp clsd to all General Aviation acft. No customs personnel or facilities are avbl and international acft will not be allowed to land unless an emerg exists. TPA—1003(990) small acft, 1503(1490) large acft. Pure jet touch/go or low approaches prohibited. When twr clsd ACTIVATE MIRL Rwy 15R–33L, REIL Rwy 15R—CTAF. MALSR Rwy 07, PAPI Rwy 25 and REIL Rwy 25 opr continuously. CTAF. Ldg fee for all PART 135 opr and transient acft with maximum gross weight 10,000 lbs or more. Fees collected at FBO.
WEATHER DATA SOURCES: ASOS (805) 681–0583
COMMUNICATIONS: CTAF 119.7 **ATIS** 132.65 **UNICOM** 122.95
Ⓡ **APP/DEP CON** 120.55 (151°–329°) 125.4 (330°–150°) 124.15 127.725 (1400–0700Z‡)
Ⓡ **L.A. CENTER APP/DEP CON** 119.05 (0700–1400Z‡)
TOWER 119.7 (1400–0700Z‡) **GND CON** 121.7 **CLNC DEL** 132.9
AIRSPACE: CLASS C svc ctc **APP CON** svc 1400–0700Z‡ other times CLASS E.
RADIO AIDS TO NAVIGATION: NOTAM FILE HHR.
SAN MARCUS (H) VORTAC 114.9 RZS Chan 96 N34°30.57′ W119°46.26′ 201° 6.1 NM to fld. 3623/14E.
HIWAS.
VOR unusable:
140°–178° byd 27 NM
GAVIOTA (L) VORTACW 113.8 GVO Chan 85 N34°31.88′ W120°05.47′ 101° 13.9 NM to fld. 2616/16E.
VORTAC unusable:
117°–137° byd 35 NM
310°–095° byd 10 NM blo 8,500′
360°–095° byd 20 NM blo 12,500′
ILS/DME 110.3 I–SBA Chan 40 Rwy 07. Class IA. Unmonitored when ATCT clsd.

SANTA CATALINA N33°22.50′ W118°25.19′ NOTAM FILE HHR. **LOS ANGELES**
(L) VORTACW 111.4 SXC Chan 51 352° 1.8 NM to Catalina. 2090/15E. **H–4I, L–3E, 4G**

FIGURE 190.—Excerpt from Chart Supplement.

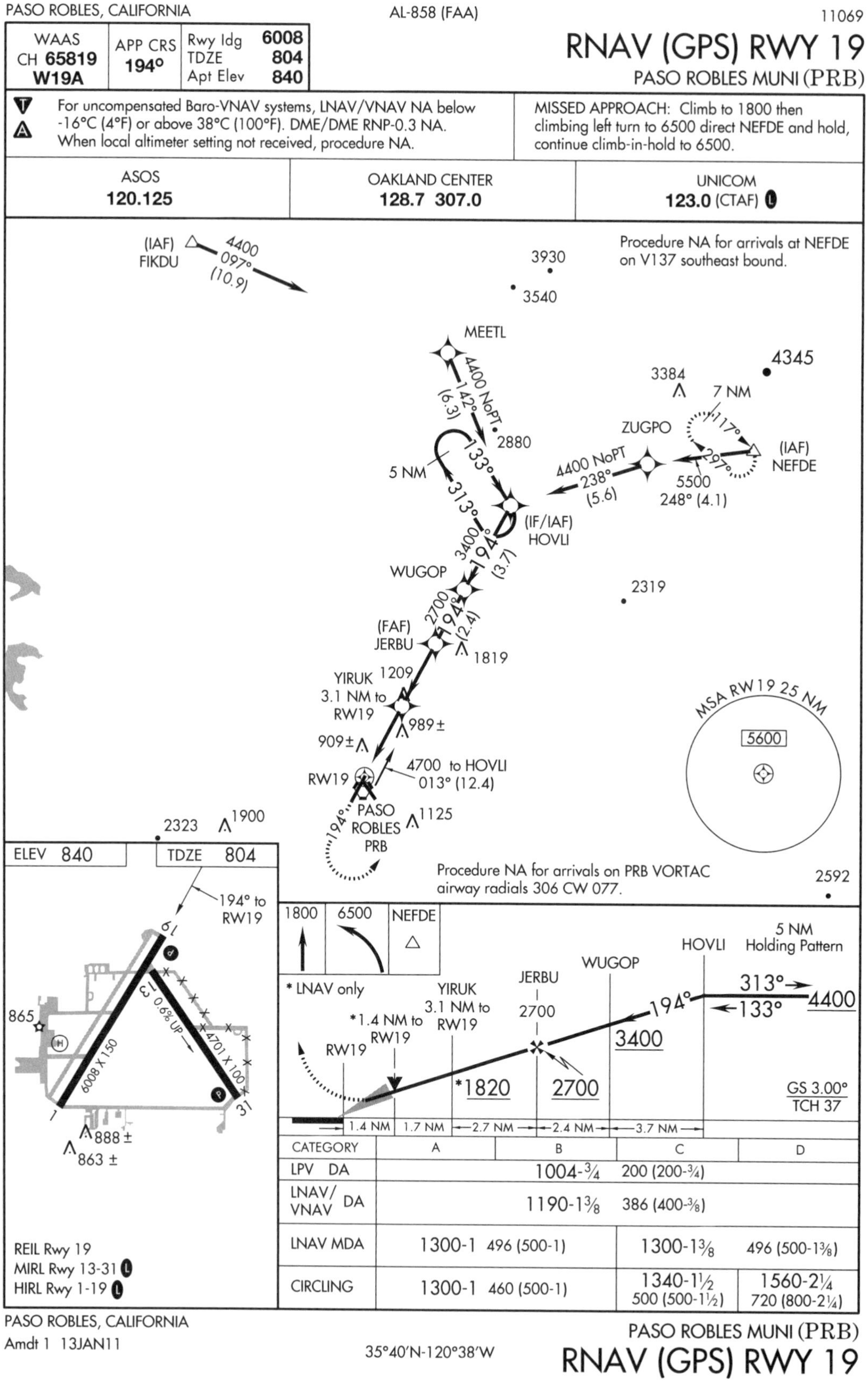

FIGURE 191.—RNAV (GPS) RWY 19 (PRB).

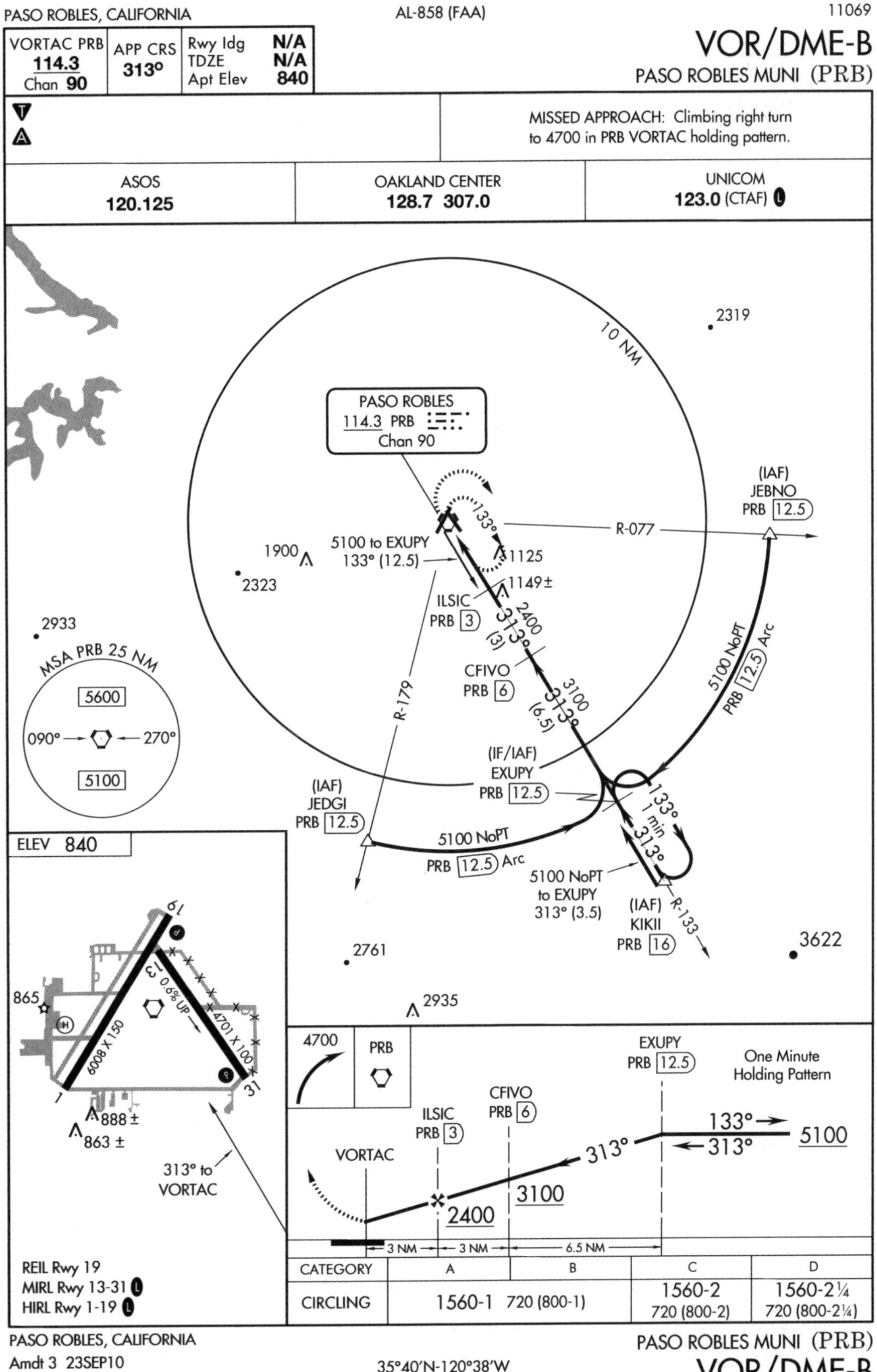

FIGURE 192.—VOR/DME-B (PRB).

COLLEGE STATION

EASTERWOOD FLD (CLL) 3 SW UTC–6(–5DT) N30°35.32´ W96°21.83´ **HOUSTON**
321 B S4 **FUEL** 100LL, JET A Class I, ARFF Index A NOTAM FILE CLL **H–7C, L–19D, 21A**
RWY 16–34: H7000X146 (ASPH–CONC–GRVD) S–70, D–90, 2S–114, 2D–150 HIRL **IAP, AD**
RWY 16: VASI(V4R)—GA 3.0° TCH 51´. Tree.
RWY 34: MALSR.
RWY 10–28: H5158X150 (ASPH–GRVD) S–27, D–50, 2D–87 MIRL
RWY 10: VASI(V4L)—GA 3.0° TCH 50´. Tree.
RWY 28: REIL. VASI(V4L)—GA 3.0° TCH 54´. Tree.
RWY 04–22: H5150X150 (CONC) S–27, D–50, 2D–87
RWY 04: Tree.
RWY 22: Tree.

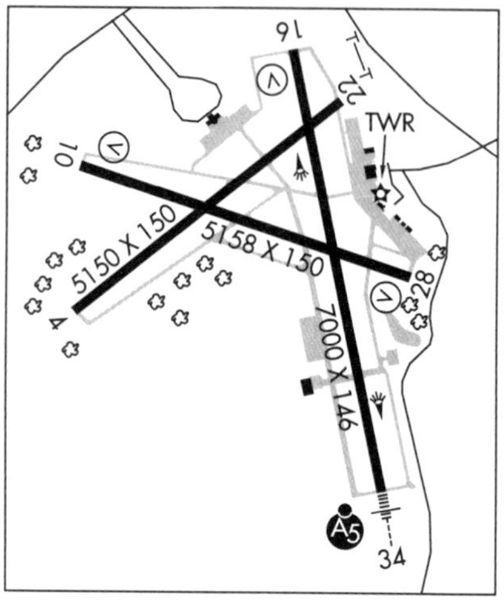

RUNWAY DECLARED DISTANCE INFORMATION

RWY 04:	TORA–5149	TODA–5149	ASDA–5149	LDA–5149
RWY 10:	TORA–5159	TODA–5159	ASDA–5159	LDA–5159
RWY 16:	TORA–7000	TODA–7000	ASDA–7000	LDA–7000
RWY 22:	TORA–5149	TODA–5149	ASDA–5149	LDA–5149
RWY 28:	TORA–5159	TODA–5159	ASDA–5159	LDA–5159
RWY 34:	TORA–7000	TODA–7000	ASDA–7000	LDA–7000

AIRPORT REMARKS: Attended 1200–0400Z‡. For fuel after hours PPR call 979–845–4811 or ctc Texas A and M University police 979–845–2345; late ngt fee. CLOSED to unscheduled air carrier ops with more than 30 passenger seats except 24 hours PPR call arpt manager 979–845–4811. Rwy 04–22 day VFR ops only. Rwy 10–28 mandatory hold short sign on Rwy 16–34 unlgtd. Itinerant acft park in front of twr, overnight parking fee. Ldg fee scheduled FAR 135 and all FAR 121 ops. Rwy 04–22 and Twy E S of Rwy 10–28 not avbl for air carrier acft with over 30 passenger seats. Rwy 16–34 first 1850´ Rwy 34 conc. PAEW adjacent all twys 1200–2200Z‡. When twr clsd ACTIVATE HIRL Rwy 16–34 and MALSR Rwy 34—CTAF. MIRL Rwy 10–28 and REIL Rwy 28 preset low ints only.
WEATHER DATA SOURCES: **ASOS** (979) 846–1708 **HIWAS** 113.3 CLL.
COMMUNICATIONS: **CTAF** 118.5 **ATIS** 126.85 **UNICOM** 122.95
COLLEGE STATION RCO 122.65 122.2 (MONTGOMERY COUNTY RADIO).
Ⓡ **HOUSTON APP/DEP CON** 134.3
TOWER 118.5 (1400–0300Z‡) **GND CON/CLNC DEL** 128.7 **CLNC DEL** 120.4 (when twr clsd)
AIRSPACE: **CLASS D** svc 1400–0300Z‡ other times CLASS E.

VOR RECEIVER CHECK

TEXAS
VOR RECEIVER CHECKPOINTS

Facility Name (Arpt Name)	Freq/Ident	Type Check Pt. Gnd. AB/ALT	Azimuth from Fac. Mag	Dist. from Fac. N.M.	Checkpoint Description
Abilene (Abilene Rgnl)	113.7/ABI	A/2800	047	10.1	Over silos in center of Ft Phantom Lake.
Alice (Alice International)	114.5/ALI	G	272	0.5	On twy near FBO.
Borger (Hutchinson Co)	108.6/BGD	G	173	6.7	On twy intersection at N end of ramp.
Brownsville (Brownsville/South Padre Island Intl)	116.3/BRO	G	247	3.2	3.2 NM on hold line Rwy 13R.
Brownwood (Brownwood Rgnl)	108.6/BWD	A/2600	169	6.2	Over rotating bcn.
Childress Muni	117.6/CDS	G	353	3.7	At the apron and the twy from Rwy 04–22.
College Station (Easterwood Fld)	113.3/CLL	G	97	3.2	On west edge of parking ramp.
Corpus Christi (Alfred C 'Bubba' Thomas)	115.5/CRP	A/1000	318	9.3	Over Rwy 32 thld.
Corpus Christi (Corpus Christi Intl)	115.5/CRP	A/1100	187	7.5	Over grain elevator.
Daisetta (Liberty Muni)	116.9/DAS	A/1200	195	7.5	Over hangar S of arpt.
Dalhart (Dalhart Muni)	112.0/DHT	A/5000	176	4.1	Over water tower on arpt.
Eagle Lake (Eagle Lake)	116.4/ELA	A/1200	180	4.1	Over water tank 0.4 NM SW of arpt.

FIGURE 193.—Excerpts from Chart Supplement.

CONTINUED FROM PRECEDING PAGE

RADIO AIDS TO NAVIGATION: NOTAM FILE CLL.
COLLEGE STATION (L) VORTACW 113.3 CLL Chan 80 N30°36.30′ W96°25.24′ 100° 3.1 NM to fld. 264/8E.
HIWAS.
DME unusable:
101°–130° byd 25 NM blo 2,500′
131°–148° byd 30 NM blo 2,500′
149°–160° byd 30 NM blo 2,000′
325°–349° byd 30 NM blo 2,500′
350°–100° byd 25 NM blo 3,500′
VOR portion unusable:
131°–189° blo 7,000′
ROWDY NDB (LOM) 260 CL N30°29.62′ W96°20.26′ 341° 5.8 NM to fld. Unmonitored when ATCT clsd.
ILS/DME 111.7 I–CLL Chan 54 Rwy 34. Class IB. LOM ROWDY NDB. Unmonitored when ATCT clsd. DME unmonitored. Glideslope unusable for coupled apchs blo 1,050′ MSL.

COLLIN CO RGNL AT MC KINNEY (See DALLAS on page 241)

COLLINSVILLE

SUDDEN STOP (T32) 1 NE UTC–6(–5DT) N33°34.29′ W96°54.43′ **DALLAS–FT WORTH**
720 NOTAM FILE FTW
RWY 17–35: 1550X60 (TURF)
RWY 17: Trees.
RWY 35: Road.
AIRPORT REMARKS: Attended continuously. Student training prohibited.
COMMUNICATIONS: **CTAF** 122.9

COLORADO CITY (T88) 6 NW UTC–6(–5DT) N32°28.11′ W100°55.27′ **DALLAS–FT WORTH**
2214 B NOTAM FILE FTW **H–6G, L–17A**
RWY 17–35: H5479X60 (ASPH) S–50 LIRL
RWY 35: Tree.
AIRPORT REMARKS: Attended irregularly. Rwy 17–35 pavement from Rwy 35 thld lgts southward used as a twy and not maintained.
COMMUNICATIONS: **CTAF** 122.9
RADIO AIDS TO NAVIGATION: NOTAM FILE BPG.
BIG SPRING (L) VORTACW 114.3 BGS Chan 90 N32°23.14′ W101°29.02′ 069° 29.0 NM to fld. 2670/11E.

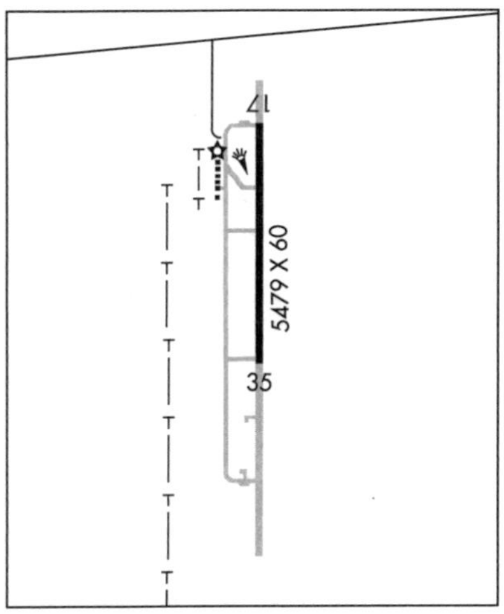

COLUMBUS

ROBERT R WELLS JR (66R) 3 S UTC–6(–5DT) N29°38.49′ W96°30.96′ **HOUSTON**
242 B **FUEL** 100LL, JET A NOTAM FILE CXO **L–19D, 21A**
RWY 15–33: H3800X60 (ASPH) S–12.5 MIRL
RWY 15: REIL. PAPI(P2L). Thld dsplcd 305′. Fence.
RWY 33: REIL. PAPI(P2L). Thld dsplcd 177′. Brush.
AIRPORT REMARKS: Unattended. Self svc fuel with major credit card. Ultra–light activity on and invof arpt. Rwy 33 REIL OTS indef. ACTIVATE MIRL Rwy 15–33—CTAF.
COMMUNICATIONS: **CTAF** 122.9
RADIO AIDS TO NAVIGATION: NOTAM FILE CXO.
INDUSTRY (L) VORTACW 110.2 IDU Chan 39 N29°57.36′ W96°33.73′ 165° 19.0 NM to fld. 419/8E.

FIGURE 194.—Excerpts from Chart Supplement.

WESTHEIMER AIR PARK (O07) 20 W UTC–6(–5DT) N29°41.68´ W95°47.68´ **HOUSTON**
117 B S2 **FUEL** 100LL NOTAM FILE CXO
RWY 11–29: H2500X28 (CONC) LIRL
RWY 11: Trees.
RWY 29: Tree.
AIRPORT REMARKS: Attended 1400–0000Z‡. 90´ P–line 1500´ from Rwy 11 thld. Grass in cracks on rwy sfc. ACTIVATE rotating bcn—CTAF. ACTIVATE LIRL Rwy 11–29—CTAF.
COMMUNICATIONS: CTAF/UNICOM 122.7

WILLIAM P HOBBY (HOU) 8 SE UTC–6(–5DT) N29°38.73´ W95°16.73´ **HOUSTON**
46 B S2 **FUEL** 100LL, JET A, A1 OX 1, 2, 3, 4 LRA Class I, ARFF Index C **COPTER**
NOTAM FILE HOU **H–7C, L–19E, 21A, GOMW**
RWY 04–22: H7602X150 (CONC–GRVD) S–75, D–200, 2S–168, 2T–461, 2D–400, 2D/D1–444, C5–717 HIRL CL **IAP, AD**
RWY 04: ALSF2. TDZL. PAPI(P4R)—GA 3.0° TCH 57´.
RWY 22: MALS. VASI(V4L)—GA 3.0° TCH 52´. Pole.
RWY 12R–30L: H7602X150 (ASPH–GRVD) S–75, D–195, 2S–168, 2T–461, 2D–220, 2D/D1–444, C5–717 HIRL CL
RWY 12R: MALSR. TDZL. PAPI(P4R)—GA 3.0° TCH 52´. Thld dsplcd 1034´. Pole.
RWY 30L: TDZL. REIL. PAPI(P4L)—GA 3.0° TCH 71´. Road.
RWY 17–35: H6000X150 (ASPH–CONC–GRVD) S–75, D–121, 2S–153, 2D–195 MIRL
RWY 17: VASI(V4L)—GA 3.0° TCH 38´. Antenna.
RWY 35: REIL. VASI(V4R)—GA 3.0° TCH 41´. Bldg.
RWY 12L–30R: H5148X100 (CONC–GRVD) S–30, D–45, 2D–80 MIRL
RWY 12L: PAPI(P4L)—GA 3.0° TCH 60´.

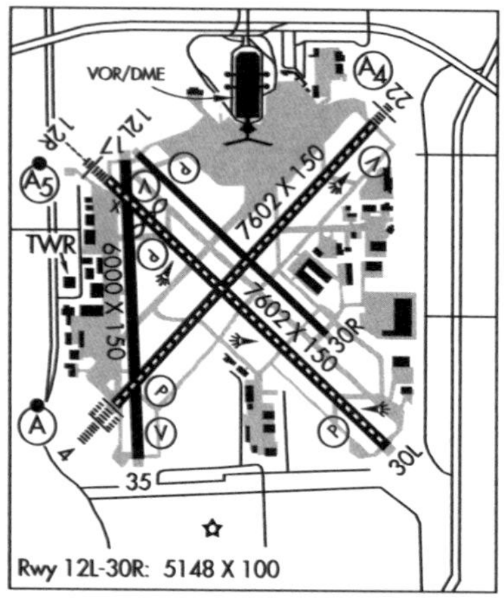

RUNWAY DECLARED DISTANCE INFORMATION

RWY 04:	TORA–7602	TODA–7602	ASDA–7602	LDA–7602
RWY 12L:	TORA–5148	TODA–5148	ASDA–5148	LDA–5148
RWY 12R:	TORA–7602	TODA–7602	ASDA–7602	LDA–6568
RWY 17:	TORA–6000	TODA–6000	ASDA–6000	LDA–6000
RWY 22:	TORA–7602	TODA–7602	ASDA–7602	LDA–7602
RWY 30L:	TORA–7602	TODA–7602	ASDA–7602	LDA–7602
RWY 30R:	TORA–5148	TODA–5148	ASDA–5148	LDA–5148
RWY 35:	TORA–6000	TODA–6000	ASDA–6000	LDA–6000

AIRPORT REMARKS: Attended continuously. Arpt CLOSED to acft with wingspan over 125´ except 24 hours PPR, call arpt manager 713–640–3000. Numerous birds on and invof arpt. ASDE–X Surveillance System in use: pilots should operate transponders with Mode C on all twys and rwys. Customs ramp has multiple obstructions, recommend large acft use customs overflow ramp. Acft in tkf position on Rwy 22 be alert for possible radio interference or null on frequency 118.7. Use upper antenna if so equipped. Rwy 04 runway visual range touchdown, midfield, rollout avbl. Rwy 22 runway visual range touchdown, midfield, rollout avbl. Rwy 12R runway visual range touchdown avbl. Rwy 30L runway visual range touchdown avbl. Twy G centerline to parked acft on W side only 68´. Twy G centerline to edge of adjacent svc vehicle road on W side only 48´. Due to complex rwy configuration, when taxiing to thlds 12L and 12R and 17 check compass heading before departing. Acft southbound on Twy C to Rwy 30L thld use extreme care, Twy C makes a 45° dogleg to the left crossing Twy K. PAPI Rwy 30L unusable byd 8° left and right of course. Flight Notification Service (ADCUS) available. NOTE: See Special Notices—U.S. Special Customs Requirement.
WEATHER DATA SOURCES: ASOS (713) 847–1462 TDWR.
COMMUNICATIONS: D–ATIS 124.6 (713) 847–1491 **UNICOM** 122.95
HOBBY RCO 122.35 (MONTGOMERY COUNTY RADIO)
Ⓡ **HOUSTON APP CON** 134.45 (South) 124.35 (West) 120.05 (East)
HOBBY TOWER 118.7
HOUSTON GND CON 121.9 **CLNC DEL** 125.45 **PRE–TAXI CLNC** 125.45
Ⓡ **HOUSTON DEP CON** 134.45 (South) 123.8 (West) 119.7 (North)
AIRSPACE: CLASS B See VFR Terminal Area Chart
VOR TEST FACILITY (VOT) 108.4
RADIO AIDS TO NAVIGATION: NOTAM FILE HOU.
HOBBY (H) VORW/DME 117.1 HUB Chan 118 N29°39.34´ W95°16.60´ at fld. 47/5E.
ILS/DME 109.9 I–HUB Chan 36 Rwy 04. Class IIIE. DME also serves Rwy 22.
ILS/DME 111.3 I–PRQ Chan 50 Rwy 12R. Class IE. DME also serves Rwy 30L.
LOC/DME 109.9 I–OIB Chan 36 Rwy 22. DME also serves Rwy 04. DME unusable byd 17° right of course.
ILS/DME 111.3 I–UPU Chan 50 Rwy 30L. Class IE. DME also serves Rwy 12R.

HOUSTON MCJ N29°42.83´ W95°23.80´ **HOUSTON**
AWOS–3 119.575 **H–7C, L–19E, 21A, GOMW**

FIGURE 195.—Excerpt from Chart Supplement.

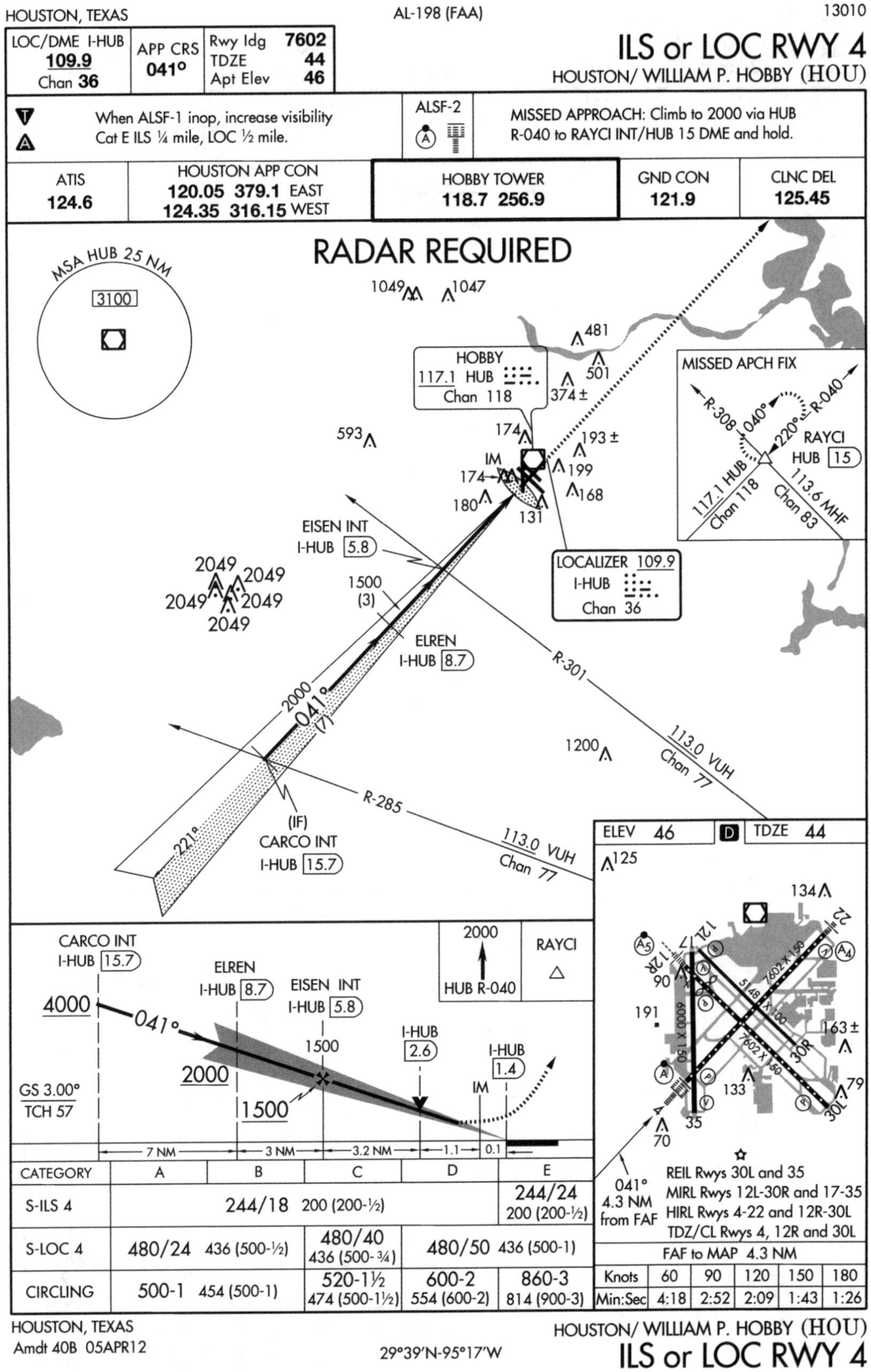

FIGURE 196.—ILS or LOC RWY 4 (HOU).

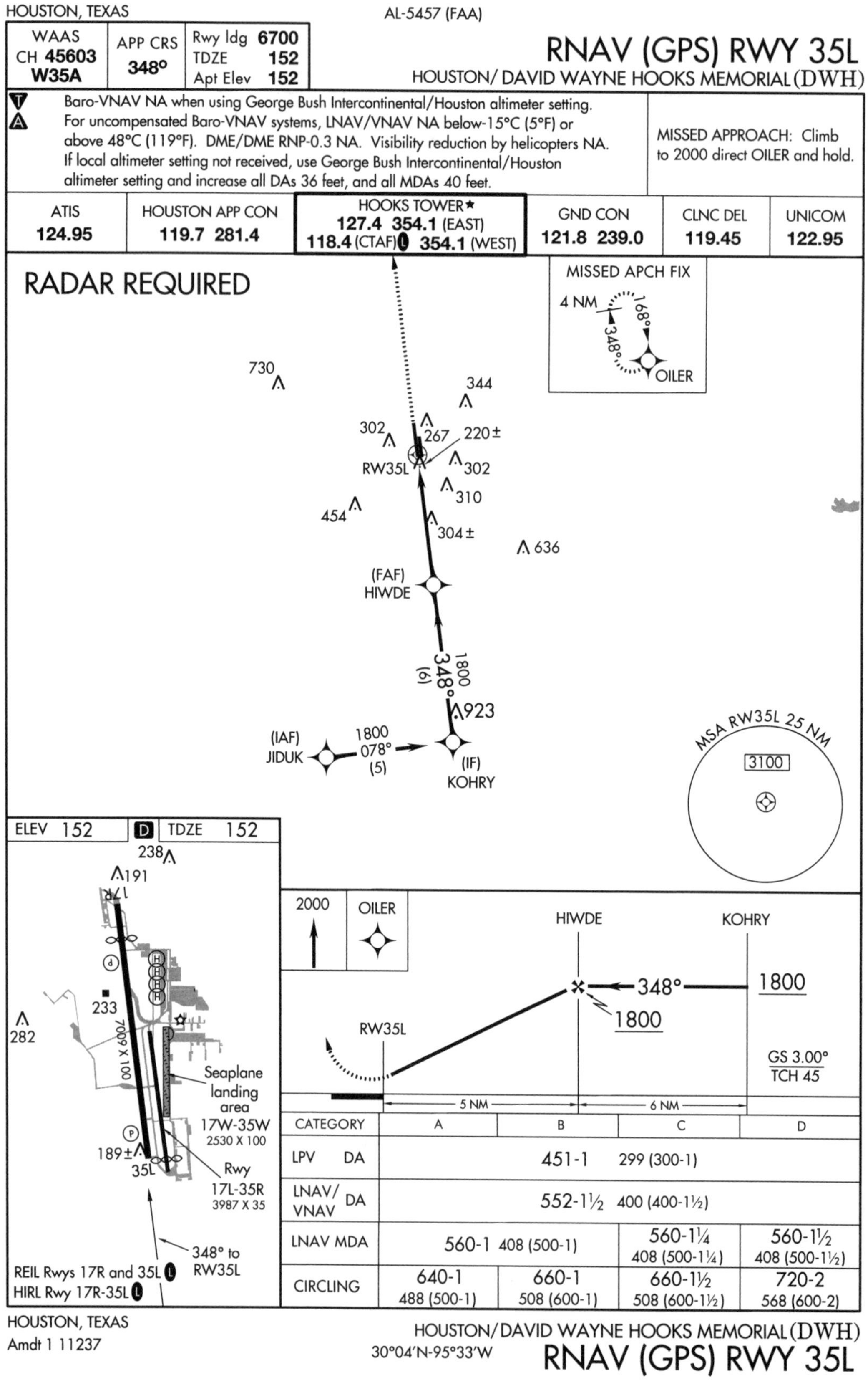

CATEGORY	A	B	C	D
LPV DA	451-1 299 (300-1)			
LNAV/VNAV DA	552-1½ 400 (400-1½)			
LNAV MDA	560-1 408 (500-1)		560-1¼ 408 (500-1¼)	560-1½ 408 (500-1½)
CIRCLING	640-1 488 (500-1)	660-1 508 (600-1)	660-1½ 508 (600-1½)	720-2 568 (600-2)

FIGURE 197.—RNAV (GPS) RWY 35L(DWH).

LOUISIANA

LAFAYETTE RGNL (LFT) 2 SE UTC–6(–5DT) N30°12.30′ W91°59.27′ **HOUSTON**
42 B S4 **FUEL** 100LL, JET A OX 1, 4 Class I, ARFF Index B NOTAM FILE LFT **H–7D, L–21B, 22E, GOMC**
RWY 04R–22L: H8001X150 (ASPH–GRVD) S–140, D–170, 2S–175, 2D–290 HIRL **IAP, AD**
RWY 04R: REIL. PAPI(P4L)—GA 3.0° TCH 53′. Pole. Rgt tfc.
RWY 22L: MALSR. PAPI(P4L)—GA 3.0° TCH 52′. Thld dsplcd 342′. Trees.
RWY 11–29: H5401X148 (ASPH–GRVD) S–85, D–110, 2S–140, 2D–175 MIRL
RWY 11: REIL. PAPI(P4L)—GA 3.0° TCH 35′. Trees. Rgt tfc.
RWY 29: REIL. PAPI(P4L)—GA 3.0° TCH 35′. Tree.
RWY 04L–22R: H4099X75 (ASPH) S–25, D–32 MIRL
RWY 04L: REIL. PAPI(P2L)—GA 3.0° TCH 26′. Tree.
RWY 22R: REIL. PAPI(P2L)—GA 3.0° TCH 27′. Tree. Rgt tfc.

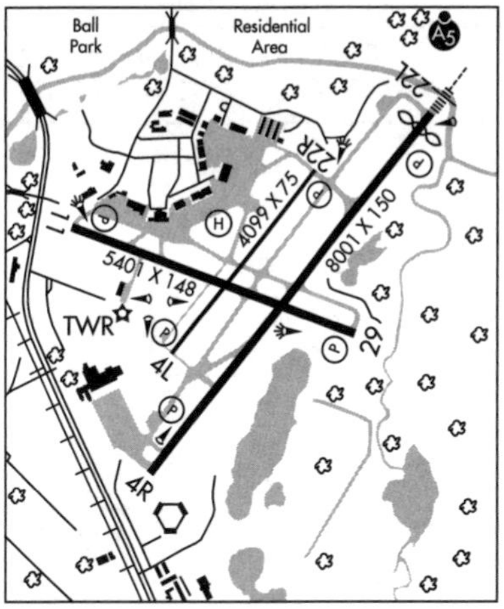

RUNWAY DECLARED DISTANCE INFORMATION
RWY 04L: TORA–4099 TODA–4099 ASDA–4099 LDA–4099
RWY 04R: TORA–8001 TODA–8001 ASDA–8001 LDA–8001
RWY 11: TORA–5401 TODA–5401 ASDA–5401 LDA–5401
RWY 22L: TORA–8001 TODA–8001 ASDA–8001 LDA–7659
RWY 22R: TORA–4099 TODA–4099 ASDA–4099 LDA–4099
RWY 29: TORA–5401 TODA–5401 ASDA–5401 LDA–5401
ARRESTING GEAR/SYSTEM
RWY 04R: EMAS
RWY 22L: EMAS
AIRPORT REMARKS: Attended continuously. Numerous birds on and invof arpt. PPR for unscheduled air carrier ops with more than 30 passenger seats call arpt manager 337–266–4400. Rwy 04L–22R not avbl for air carrier ops with more than 30 passenger seats. Ctc ground control prior to push back from terminal. 155′ oil rig 1 NM southeast of arpt. Rwy 22L runway visual range touchdown avbl. Twy B between Twy C and Twy D clsd to acft with wingspan over 80′. Twy F south of Twy B clsd to single wheel acft over 25,000 lbs and dual wheel acft over 32,000 lbs. Twy F south of Twy B reduces to 40′ wide. When twr clsd ACTIVATE MALSR Rwy 22L—CTAF, MIRL Rwy 04L–22R not avbl.
WEATHER DATA SOURCES: ASOS (337) 237–8153 **HIWAS** 109.8 LFT.
COMMUNICATIONS: CTAF 118.5 **ATIS** 134.05 **UNICOM** 122.95
RCO 122.35 (DE RIDDER RADIO)
® **APP/DEP CON** 121.1 (020°–210°) 128.7 (211°–019°) (1130–0430Z‡)
® **HOUSTON CENTER APP/DEP CON** 126.35 (0430–1130Z‡)
TOWER 118.5 (1130–0430Z‡) **GND CON** 121.8 **CLNC DEL** 125.55
AIRSPACE: CLASS C svc ctc **APP CON** svc 1130–0430Z‡ other times CLASS E.
RADIO AIDS TO NAVIGATION: NOTAM FILE LFT.
(L) VORTACW 109.8 LFT Chan 35 N30°11.63′ W91°59.55′ at fld. 36/3E. **HIWAS.**
LAFFS NDB (LOM) 375 LF N30°17.36′ W91°54.48′ 216° 6.5 NM to fld. Unmonitored when ATCT clsd.
ILS/DME 110.9 I–TYN Chan 46 Rwy 04R. Class IE.
ILS/DME 109.5 I–LFT Chan 32 Rwy 22L. Class IE. LOM LAFFS NDB. ILS and LOM unmonitored when ATCT clsd.
ASR (1130–0430Z‡)

• • • • • • • • • • • • • • • • • • • •

HELIPAD H1: H50X50 (ASPH)
HELIPAD H1: RLLS.
HELIPORT REMARKS: Rwy H1 circular pad. Helipad H1 perimeter lgts. Heliport ops to/from helipad between Twys B and F and the terminal ramp, avoid overflight of the terminal and other buildings in the 270°–020° quadrant from the helipad. Lead–in lgts two ingress paths. Helicopter parking pads avbl.

LAFFS N30°17.36′ W91°54.48′ NOTAM FILE LFT. **HOUSTON**
NDB (LOM) 375 LF 216° 6.5 NM to Lafayette Rgnl. Unmonitored when ATCT clsd. **L–21B, 22E**

FIGURE 198.—Excerpt from Chart Supplement.

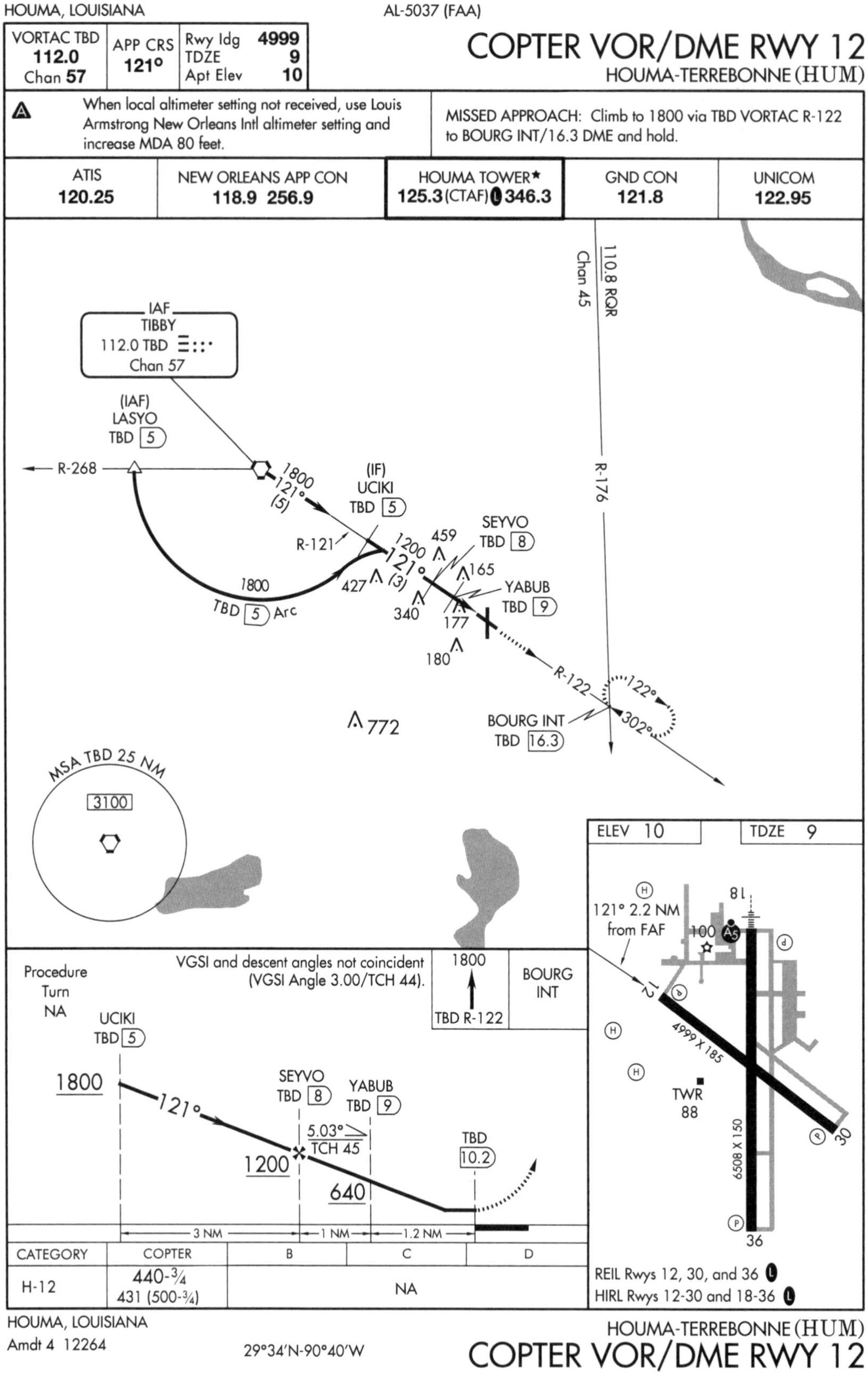

FIGURE 199.—COPTER VOR/DME RWY 12 (HUM).

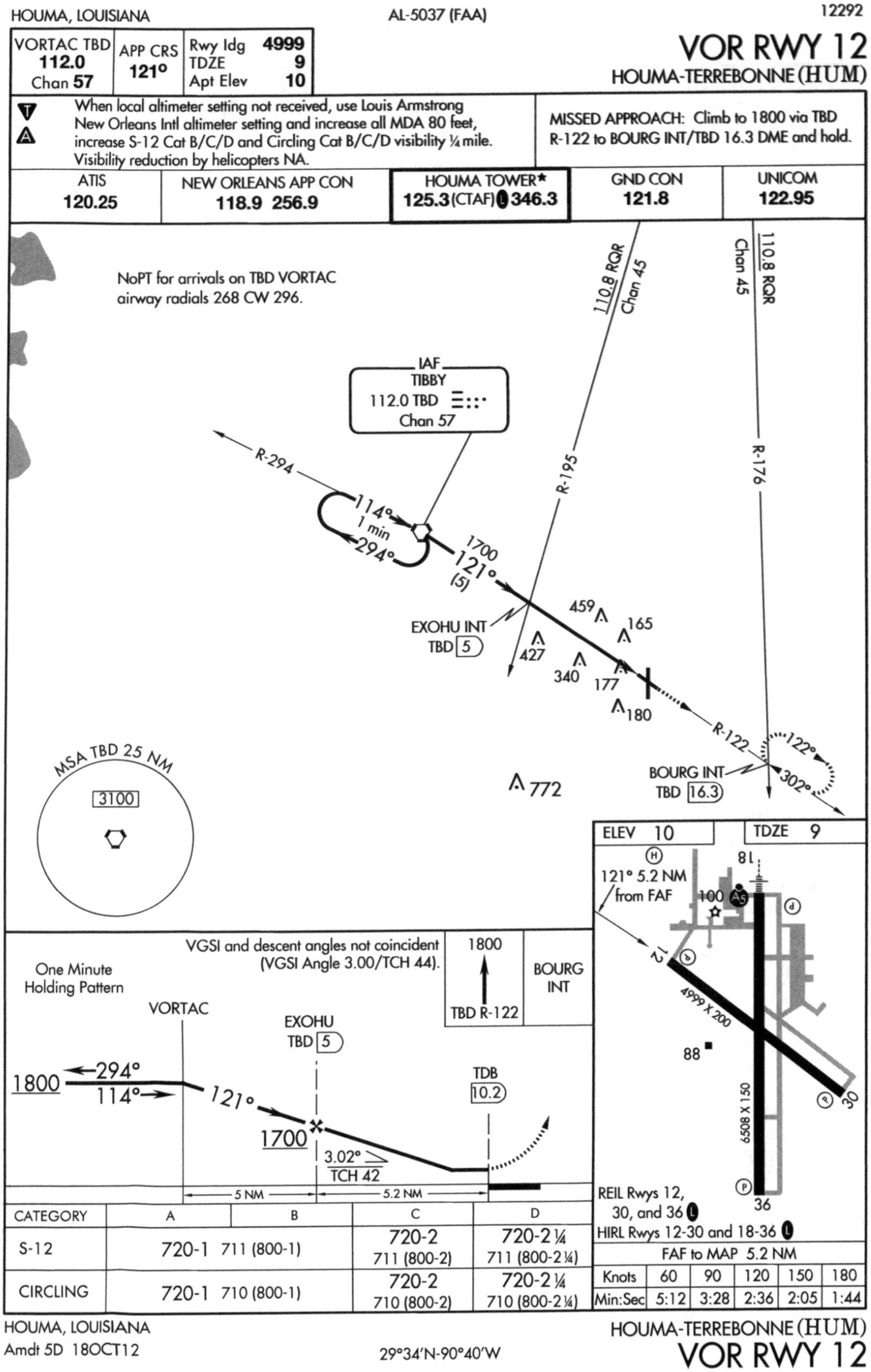

CATEGORY	A	B	C	D
S-12	720-1 711 (800-1)		720-2 711 (800-2)	720-2¼ 711 (800-2¼)
CIRCLING	720-1 710 (800-1)		720-2 710 (800-2)	720-2¼ 710 (800-2¼)

Knots	60	90	120	150	180
Min:Sec	5:12	3:28	2:36	2:05	1:44

FIGURE 200.—VOR RWY 12 (HUM).

HOUMA–TERREBONNE (HUM) 3 SE UTC–6(–5DT) N29°33.99′ W90°39.63′ **NEW ORLEANS**
9 B S4 **FUEL** 100LL, JET A OX 1, 2, 3, 4 TPA—1009(1000) NOTAM FILE HUM **H–7D, L–21B, 22F**
RWY 18–36: H6508X150 (CONC–GRVD) S–50, D–70, 2S–89, 2D–137 HIRL **IAP, AD**
RWY 18: MALSR. PAPI(P2L)—GA 3.0° TCH 52′. Trees.
RWY 36: REIL. PAPI(P2L)—GA 3.0° TCH 50′. Trees.
RWY 12–30: H4999X185 (CONC) S–50, D–70, 2S–89, 2D–137 HIRL
RWY 12: REIL. PAPI(P2L)—GA 3.0° TCH 44′. Trees.
RWY 30: REIL. PAPI(P2L)—GA 3.0° TCH 39′.

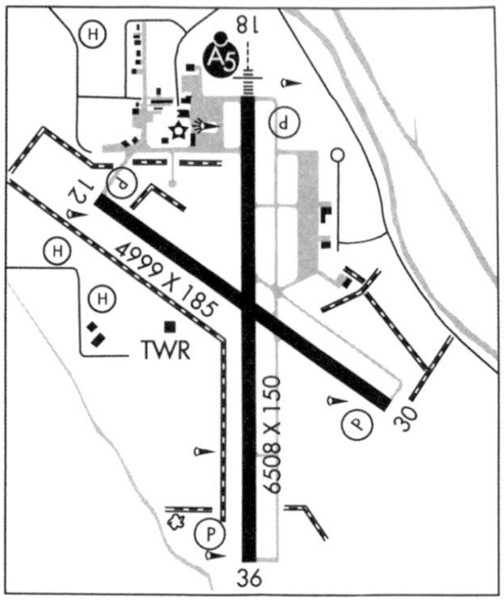

AIRPORT REMARKS: Attended 1200–0100Z‡. Fuel avbl 24 hrs with credit card. Birds on and invof arpt. Numerous birds 500′AGL and blo 2.8 NM south southwest AER 36, avoidance advised. Extensive helicopter ops south thru west of arpt. Rwy 12–30 surface skid resistance fair when wet. ACTIVATE HIRL Rwy 12–30 and Rwy 18–36 and MALSR Rwy 18 and REIL Rwy 12, Rwy 30 and Rwy 36—CTAF.
WEATHER DATA SOURCES: AWOS–3PT 120.25 (985) 876–4055. LAWRS.
COMMUNICATIONS: CTAF 125.3 **ATIS** 120.25 **UNICOM** 122.95
RCO 122.45 (DE RIDDER RADIO)
Ⓡ**NEW ORLEANS APP/DEP CON** 118.9
TOWER 125.3 (1200–0100Z‡) **GND CON** 121.8
AIRSPACE: CLASS D svc 1200–0100Z‡ other times CLASS G.
RADIO AIDS TO NAVIGATION: NOTAM FILE DRI.
TIBBY (L) VORTAC 112.0 TBD Chan 57 N29°39.86′ W90°49.75′ 122° 10.6 NM to fld. 10/2E.
VORTAC unusable:
byd 30 NM blo 2,000′
TACAN DME unusable:
byd 30 NM blo 2,000′
HOUMA NDB (LOM) 219 HU N29°39.80′ W90°39.58′ 179° 5.8 NM to fld. LOM unmonitored. Unmonitored when ATCT clsd.
ILS 108.5 I–HUM Rwy 18. LOM HOUMA NDB. LOM unmonitored. Unmonitored when ATCT clsd.

IDA'S HELIPORT (L87) 0 N UTC–6(–5DT) N33°00.26′ W93°53.59′ **MEMPHIS**
286 NOTAM FILE DRI
HELIPAD H1: H40X40 (CONC)
HELIPORT REMARKS: Attended continuously. Helipad H1 perimeter lgts. Helipad H1 100′ water twr 300′ E and 149′ radio twr 500′ S of pad. For perimeter lgts call 318–284–3231. Helipad H1 apch 180°–departure 000°.
COMMUNICATIONS: CTAF 122.9

INDEPENDENCE IPN N28°05.10′ W87°59.15′
AWOS–3 118.125 Winds unreliable.

JEANERETTE

LE MAIRE MEM (2R1) 1 S UTC–6(–5DT) N29°53.94′ W91°39.96′ **HOUSTON**
14 B **FUEL** 100LL NOTAM FILE DRI **L–21B, 22F**
RWY 04–22: H3000X75 (ASPH) S–6 MIRL
RWY 04: REIL. PAPI(P2L)—GA 3.0° TCH 50′. Trees.
RWY 22: REIL. PAPI(P2L)—GA 3.0° TCH 50′. Thld dsplcd 603′. Tree.
AIRPORT REMARKS: Unattended. For arpt attended call 337–365–7202. Fuel avbl 24 hrs self svc with credit card. MIRL Rwy 04–22 and REIL Rwys 04 and 22 preset low ints dusk to dawn, to incr ints ACTIVATE–CTAF.
COMMUNICATIONS: CTAF 122.9
RADIO AIDS TO NAVIGATION: NOTAM FILE LFT.
LAFAYETTE (L) VORTACW 109.8 LFT Chan 35 N30°11.63′ W91°59.55′ 133° 24.5 NM to fld. 36/3E. **HIWAS.**

FIGURE 201.—Excerpt from Chart Supplement.

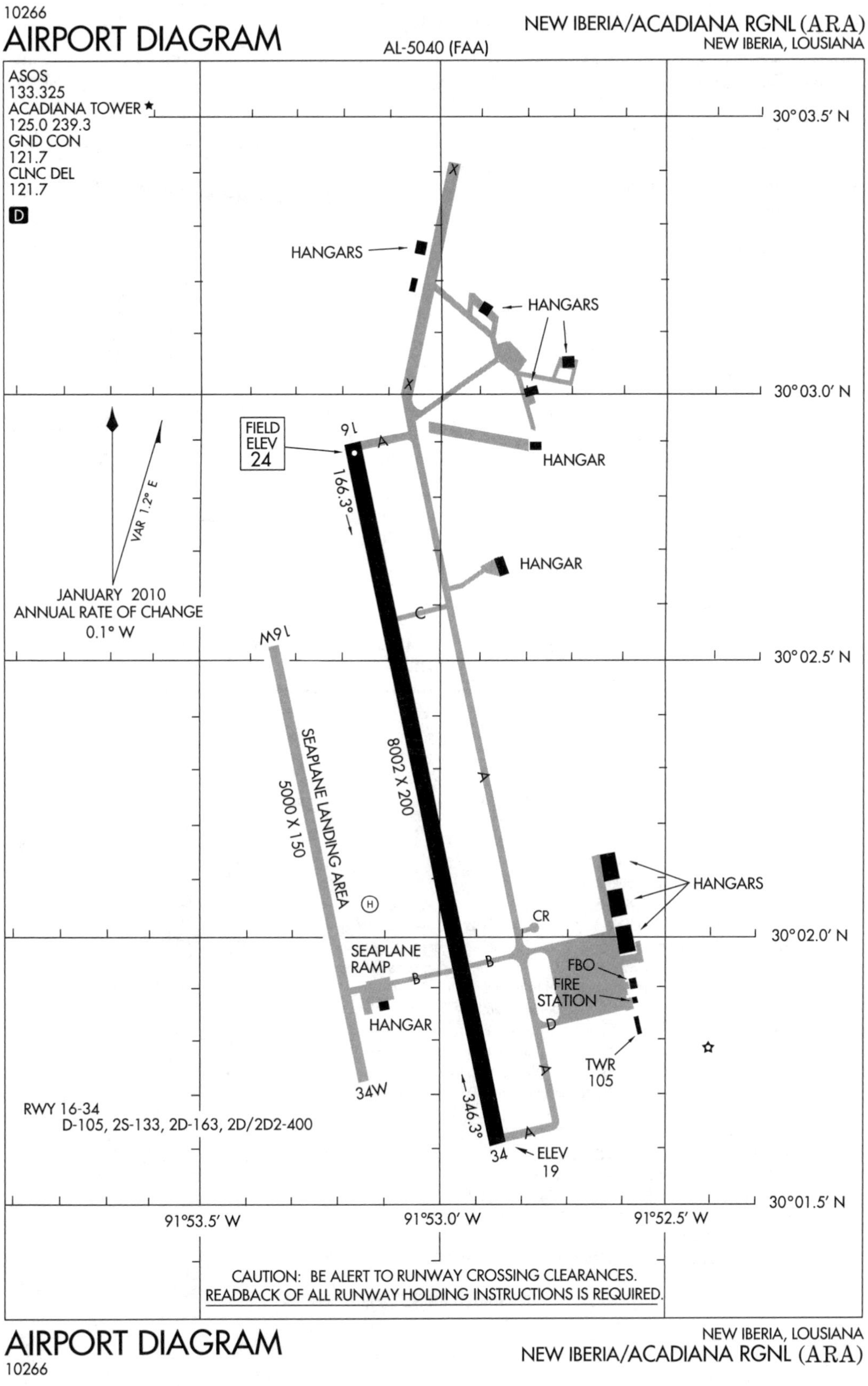

FIGURE 202.—Airport Diagram: New Iberia/Acadiana RGNL (ARA).

NATCHITOCHES RGNL (IER) 2 S UTC–6(–5DT) N31°44.14′ W93°05.95′ **HOUSTON**
121 B S4 **FUEL** 100LL, JET A1+ NOTAM FILE IER **H–6I, L–22E**
RWY 17–35: H5003X150 (ASPH) S–30 MIRL **IAP**
RWY 17: REIL. PAPI(P4L)—GA 3.0° TCH 45′. Tree.
RWY 35: ODALS. PAPI(P4L)—GA 3.0° TCH 43′. Trees.
RWY 07–25: H4000X100 (ASPH) S–21 MIRL
RWY 07: Trees.
RWY 25: P–line.
AIRPORT REMARKS: Attended dawn–dusk. For arpt attendant after hrs call 318–471–2106. Fuel avbl 24 hr with credit card. MIRL Rwy 17–35 and REIL Rwy 17 preset low ints dusk to dawn, to increase ints and ACTIVATE MIRL Rwy 07–25—CTAF. Rwy 35 ODALS operate low ints continuously, to increase ints ACTIVATE—CTAF.
WEATHER DATA SOURCES: AWOS–3 119.025 (318) 352–1575.
COMMUNICATIONS: CTAF/UNICOM 122.8
® **POLK APP/DEP CON** 125.4
GCO 135.075 (FORT POLK APCH AND DE RIDDER FSS)
RADIO AIDS TO NAVIGATION: NOTAM FILE AEX.
ALEXANDRIA (H) VORTACW 116.1 AEX Chan 108 N31°15.40′ W92°30.06′ 310° 42.0 NM to fld. 80/3E. **HIWAS.**
VOR unusable:
035°–065° blo 2,000′
066°–094° byd 35 NM blo 3,000′
185°–200° byd 35 NM blo 3,000′
201°–214° byd 35 NM blo 2,000′
215°–260° blo 2,000′
261°–285° byd 35 NM blo 2,000′
357°–034° byd 35 NM blo 3,000′
NDB (MHW) 407 OOC N31°39.45′ W93°04.66′ 343° 4.8 NM to fld. NOTAM FILE IER.
LOC 110.5 I–IER Rwy 35. LOC unmonitored 0000–1200Z‡.

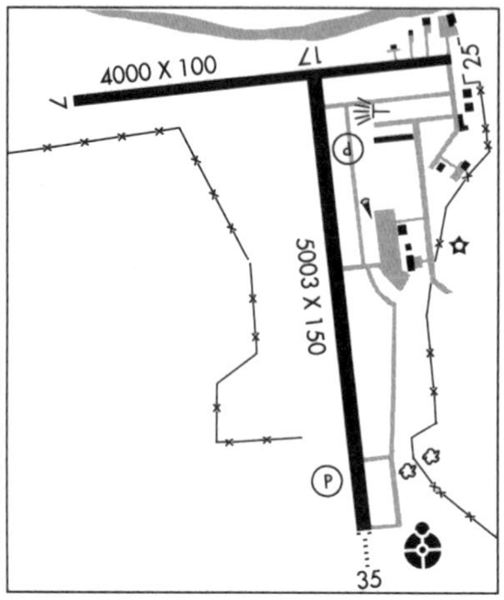

NEW IBERIA

ACADIANA RGNL (ARA) 4 NW UTC–6(–5DT) N30°02.27′ W91°53.03′ **HOUSTON**
24 B S2 **FUEL** 100LL, JET A OX 4 TPA—1024(1000) Class IV, ARFF Index A **H–7D, L–21B, 22E, GOMC**
NOTAM FILE ARA **IAP, AD**
RWY 16–34: H8002X200 (CONC) D–105, 2S–133, 2D–163, 2D/2D2–400 HIRL
RWY 16: ODALS. PAPI(P4L)—GA 3.0° TCH 51′.
RWY 34: MALSR. PAPI(P4L)—GA 3.0° TCH 52′. Rgt tfc.
RUNWAY DECLARED DISTANCE INFORMATION
RWY 16: TORA–8002 TODA–8002 ASDA–8002 LDA–8002
RWY 34: TORA–8002 TODA–8002 ASDA–8002 LDA–8002
AIRPORT REMARKS: Attended 1300–0300Z‡. For fuel after hrs call 337–367–1401, FAX 337–367–1404. Seaplane landing area (water channel) West of and adjacent/parallel to runway. Rwy 16W–34W seaway edge lgts green; thld lgts amber. Bird activity on and invof arpt. ARFF PPR for more than 30 passenger seats call arpt manager 337–365–7202. Rotor wing movement and landing area between the rwy and seaway. Intensive helicopter training. When twr closed HIRL Rwy 16–34 preset low ints, to increase ints and ACTIVATE MALSR Rwy 34—CTAF.
WEATHER DATA SOURCES: ASOS 133.325 (337) 365–0128.
COMMUNICATIONS: CTAF 125.0 **UNICOM** 122.95
® **LAFAYETTE APP/DEP CON** 121.1 (1130–0430Z‡)
HOUSTON CENTER APP/DEP CON 126.35 (0430–1130Z‡)
TOWER 125.0 (1200–0300Z‡) **GND CON** 121.7 **CLNC DEL** 121.7
LAFAYETTE CLNC DEL 118.05
AIRSPACE: CLASS D svc 1200–0300Z‡ other times CLASS G.

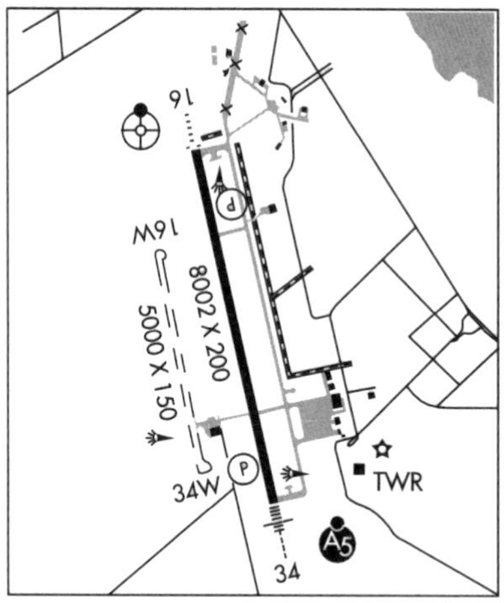

CONTINUED ON NEXT PAGE

FIGURE 203.—Excerpt from Chart Supplement.

LOUISIANA 91

CONTINUED FROM PRECEDING PAGE

RADIO AIDS TO NAVIGATION: NOTAM FILE LFT.
LAFAYETTE (L) VORTACW 109.8 LFT Chan 35 N30°11.63′ W91°59.55′ 146° 10.9 NM to fld. 36/3E. **HIWAS.**
ACADI NDB (MHW/LOM) 269 AR N29°57.38′ W91°51.80′ 345° 5.0 NM to fld. NOTAM FILE ARA.
ILS 108.9 I–ARA Rwy 34. Class IA. LOM ACADI NDB.

• • • • • • • • • • • • • • • • • • • •

WATERWAY 16W–34W: 5000X150 (WATER) MIRL
WATERWAY 16W: Rgt tfc.
RUNWAY DECLARED DISTANCE INFORMATION
RWY 16W:TORA–5000 TODA–5000 ASDA–5000 LDA–5000
RWY 34W:TORA–5000 TODA–5000 ASDA–5000 LDA–5000
SEAPLANE REMARKS: Waterway 16–34 seaway edge lgts green, thld lgts amber. ACTIVATE seaway edge lgts Waterway 16–34—122.7. 3 clicks on 7 clicks off.

NEW ORLEANS

LAKEFRONT (NEW) 4 NE UTC–6(–5DT) N30°02.55′ W90°01.70′
NEW ORLEANS
H–7E, 8F, L–21B, 22F, GOMC
IAP, AD

7 B S4 **FUEL** 100LL, JET A OX 1, 3 LRA NOTAM FILE NEW
RWY 18R–36L: H6879X150 (ASPH–GRVD) S–60, D–175, 2S–175, 2D–200, 2D/2D2–350 MIRL
RWY 18R: MALSF. PAPI(P4L)—GA 3.0° TCH 51′. Thld dsplcd 239′. Pier. Rgt tfc.
RWY 36L: REIL. PAPI(P4L)—GA 3.0° TCH 50′. Thld dsplcd 820′. Wall.
RWY 18L–36R: H3697X75 (ASPH) S–35, D–55, 2D–80 MIRL
RWY 18L: REIL.
RWY 36R: REIL. PAPI(P4L)—GA 3.0° TCH 45′. Bldg. Rgt tfc.
RWY 09–27: H3114X75 (ASPH) S–50, D–80, 2S–102, 2D–100 MIRL
RWY 09: REIL. PAPI(P4L)—GA 3.0° TCH 40′. Berm.
RWY 27: PAPI(P4R)—GA 3.0° TCH 40′. Road. Rgt tfc.
RUNWAY DECLARED DISTANCE INFORMATION
RWY 09: TORA–3113 TODA–3113 ASDA–3113 LDA–3113
RWY 18L:TORA–3697 TODA–3697 ASDA–3697 LDA–3697
RWY 18R:TORA–6880 TODA–6880 ASDA–6035 LDA–5510
RWY 27: TORA–3113 TODA–3113 ASDA–3113 LDA–3113
RWY 36L:TORA–6880 TODA–6880 ASDA–5955 LDA–5135
RWY 36R:TORA–3697 TODA–3697 ASDA–3697 LDA–3697

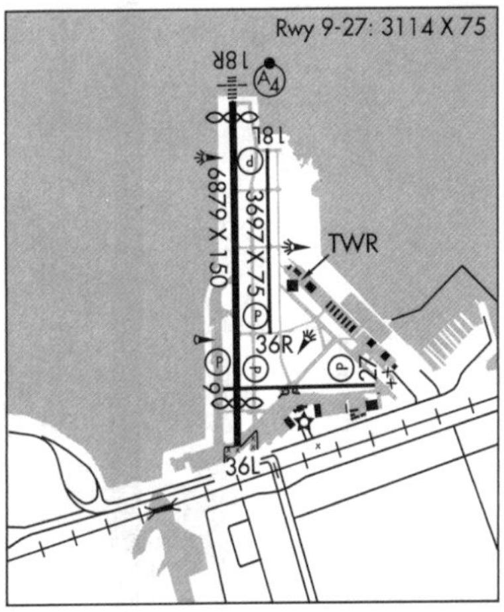

AIRPORT REMARKS: Attended continuously. For field conditions after 2200Z‡ ctc arpt manager on 504–914–5721. Birds on and invof arpt. Boats as high as 80′ pass within 400′ of Rwy 09 thld. Rwy 18R–36L few low spots near intersection of Rwy 09–27 holding water. When twr clsd MIRL Rwy 18R–36L preset med ints and twy lgts for Twys A, B, D, E, F and H preset on medium. ARFF capability equivalent to Index B. Acft transporting any items listed in Part 175 title 49 PPR to land. Landing fee. Landing fee waived with minimum fuel purchase. Flight Notification Service (ADCUS) temporarily not available. NOTE: See Special Notices—U.S. Special Customs Requirement.
WEATHER DATA SOURCES: ASOS (504) 245–4366 LAWRS.
COMMUNICATIONS: CTAF 119.9 **ATIS** 124.9
NEW ORLEANS RCO 122.6 (DE RIDDER RADIO)
® **NEW ORLEANS APP/DEP CON** 133.15 (North) 123.85 (South)
TOWER 119.9 (1400–0000Z‡) **GND CON** 121.7 **CLNC DEL** 127.4 (NEW ORLEANS APP/DEP CON when twr clsd)
AIRSPACE: CLASS D svc 1400–0000Z‡ other times CLASS E.
RADIO AIDS TO NAVIGATION: NOTAM FILE NEW.
HARVEY (H) VORTACW 114.1 HRV Chan 88 N29°51.01′ W90°00.18′ 351° 11.6 NM to fld. 2/2E.
VORTAC unusable:
004°–125° byd 30 NM blo 2,000′
126°–136° byd 25 NM blo 3,000′
137°–174° byd 30 NM blo 2,000′
175°–190° byd 30 NM blo 3,000′
191°–239° byd 30 NM blo 2,000′
240°–255° byd 25 NM blo 6,000′
256°–279° byd 30 NM blo 2,000′
280°–290° byd 30 NM
291°–352° byd 30 NM blo 2,000′
353°–003° byd 30 NM blo 3,000′
ILS/DME 111.3 I–NEW Chan 50 Rwy 18R.

FIGURE 203A.—Excerpt from Chart Supplement.

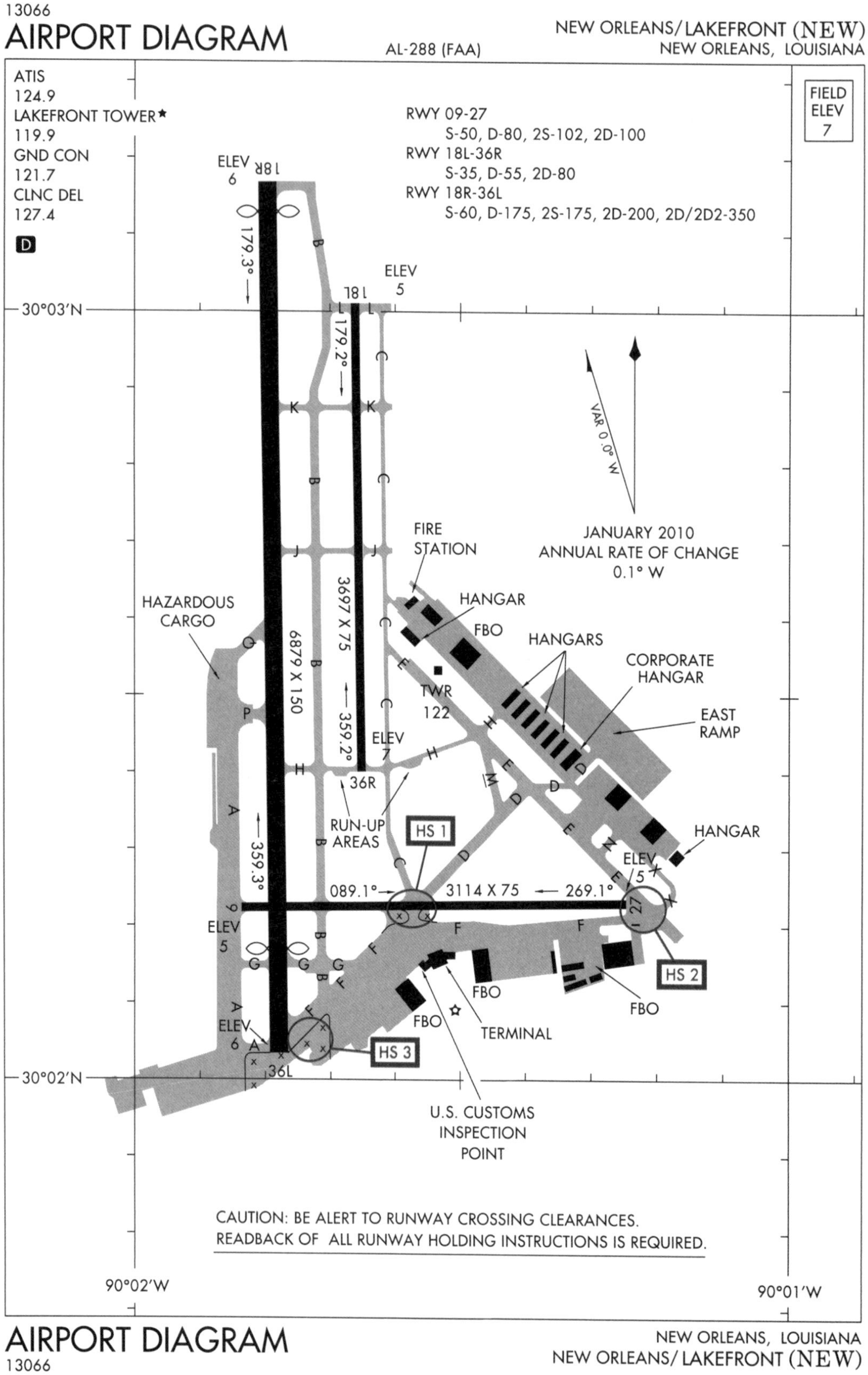

FIGURE 204.—Airport Diagram: New ORLEANS/LAKEFRONT (NEW).

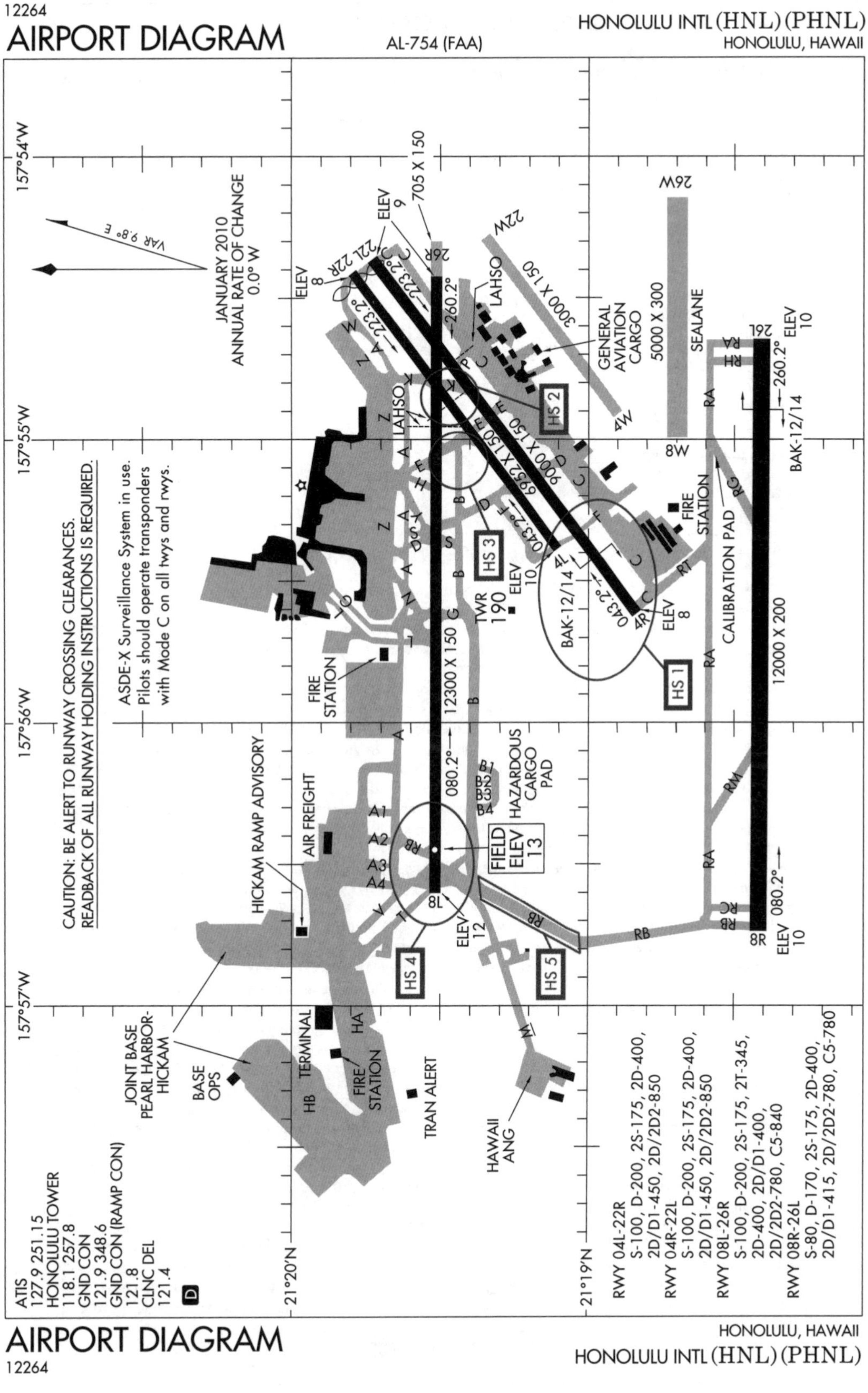

FIGURE 205.—Airport Diagram: Honolulu Intl (HNL) (PHNL).

HONOLULU INTL (JOINT BASE PEARL HARBOR–HICKAM) (HNL)(PHNL) 3 NW UTC–10 **HAWAIIAN–MARIANA**
N21°19.12′ W157°55.35′ **P–1C, 2G**
13 B S4 **FUEL** 80, 100, JET A, A1+, B OX 1, 2, 3, 4 TPA—See Remarks **IAP**
LRA Class I, ARFF Index E NOTAM FILE HNL
RWY 08L–26R: H12300X150 (ASPH–GRVD) S–100, D–200, 2S–175, 2T–345, 2D–400, 2D/D1–400, D2D/2D2–780 HIRL
RWY 08L: MALSR. PAPI(P4L)—GA 3.0° TCH 80′.
RWY 26R: REIL. PAPI(P4L)—GA 3.0 TCH 71′.
RWY 08R–26L: H12000X200 (ASPH–GRVD) S–80, D–170, 2S–175, 2D–400, D/2D2–780 HIRL
RWY 08R: REIL. PAPI(P4L)—GA 3.25° TCH 99′.
RWY 26L: MALSF. PAPI(P4L)—GA 3.0° TCH 75′. 3 cranes.
RWY 04R–22L: H9000X150 (ASPH–GRVD) S–100, D–200, 2S–175, 2D–400, D/2D2–850 HIRL
RWY 04R: MALSR. PAPI(P4L)—GA 3.0° TCH 71′. Tree.
RWY 22L: REIL. PAPI(P4L)—GA 3.44° TCH 80′. Stack.
RWY 04L–22R: H6952X150 (ASPH) S–100, D–200, 2S–175, 2D–400, D/2D2–850 MIRL
RWY 04L: REIL. PAPI(P4L)—GA 3.0° TCH 50′. **RWY 22R:** REIL. Antenna. Thld dsplcd 150′.
LAND AND HOLD-SHORT OPERATIONS

LDG RWY	HOLD-SHORT POINT	AVBL LDG DIST
RWY 04L	08L–26R	3700
RWY 04R	08L–26R	6250
RWY 08L	04L–22R	9300

RUNWAY DECLARED DISTANCE INFORMATION
RWY 04R: TORA–9000 TODA–9000 ASDA–8950 LDA–8950
RWY 22L: TORA–9000 TODA–9000 ASDA–8937 LDA–8937
ARRESTING GEAR/SYSTEMS
RWY 04R BAK–14 BAK–12B (1500′)
HOOK MB 60 (200′) → **RWY 26R**
BAK–14 BAK 12B(B) (1500) **RWY 26L**

AIRPORT REMARKS: Attended continuously. 80 and 100 octane fuel avbl thru FBO. Bird strike hazard all runways. Mil acft opr during Bird Watch Condition MODERATE (initial tkof or full stop ldg only, no multiple IFR/VFR approaches) and SEVERE (tkof and ldg prohibited w/o 15 OG/CC approval or 154 OG/CC approval for HIANG acft) ctc HIK ramp, PTD, 15 WG command post, 735 AMC command post, 154 WG command post for current conditions. See FLIP AP/3 Supplementary arpt information, route and area rstd, and Oakland FIR flt haz. Use caution for obstruction 76′ from Twy M centerline on Oceanside, approximately 200′ from parking apron. Crane 290′ AGL approximately 2,600′ north of Rwy 08L, 2500′ west of Inter Island Terminal 1630–0330Z daily. PAEW 600′–1300′E Rwy 22L and Rwy 22R thld, 1700–0130Z Mon–Fri. Rwys CLOSED 1730–0630 every month as follows: Rwy 04R–22L first Tue; Rwy 08R–26L second Tue; and Rwy 08L–26R third Tue. Rwy 08R–26L 200′ pavement width with lgts outside, pavement striped 150′ wide. Thld of Rwy 08L difficult to determine due to Twy T. All jet acft ctc ramp control prior to engine start at gate or hard stand. Foreign object debris hazard exits on all movement areas east of Twy S. Fighter acft exercise extreme caution when taxiing. To minimize foreign object damage potential, all acft should use minimum thrust, especially outboard engines, when taxiing past the F–22 alert facility on Twy T. Twys G and L between Twy A and Inter–Island ramp clsd to wide–bodied and 4–engine turbo–jet acft under power without PPR from arpt ops manager 808–836–6428 Mon–Fri 1745–0230Z. Twy K not a high speed exit twy. Wide body and 4 engine turbojets ldg on Rwy 04R roll to end of rwy, no left turn at Twy K without approval. Tfc pattern overhead altitude 2000(1987), restricted to HIANG acft. Rwy 04R–22L and Rwy 08R–26L sfc grvd within 10′ of A–G system. Potential for fighter acft tail hook skip exists. Due to sensitivities of citizens, fighter acft and water–augmented acft dep only authorized from Mon–Sat 1700–0700Z, and Sun and holidays 1800–0700Z. All request for waivers will be sent to the 15/OG/CC at least 5 working days in advance. Waivers will be granted on extreme necessary. If short notice mission essential waivers are necessary, ctc 15OG/CC by phone thru 15 WG Comd Post (15 WG/CP). 15 WG Comd Post will pass approval to Hickam flight svc and Hickam ramp advisory. Tfc pattern altitude for small acft entering from NW 800(787). Tfc pattern altitude for small acft entering from S 1000(987). Tfc pattern altitude for large acft entering from S 1500(1487). No F–16 transient support avbl in accordance with Area Control Center LSET flash safety 06–02. Transient F–16 units should provide their own maintenance support. PPR all acft units planning to stage ops from Hickam AFB must ctc 15 OSS/OSX DSN 315–449–1596/1597 at least 60 days prior to arrival. All military acft rqr Customs/Agriculture/Immigration inspection must ctc 15 WG command post or if Air Mobility Command ctc Hickam AMCC, no later than 3 hrs prior to arrival with departure location estimated block time, number of aircrew, Civilian/Military Passengers/Foreign Nationals/and Distinguished Visitor codes. JBPH–H is PPR to all non–AMC acft and AMC trng msn (QEN, KEN, PEN, AEN, and ANC C130's). All tran acft not on an AMC/TWCF msn and home stn acft terminating at JBPH–H, will provide a 3 hr out call (COMM 808–448–6900) as well as a 20–30 min out call on 292.5 to the 15 WG/CP (KOA CONTROL). All transient acft, not on an Air Mobility Command mission, will provide a 2–3 hr out call, as well as 20–30 minute out call on 292.5 to the 15 WG/CP (KOA Control). 15 WG can provide eqpt but crews must provide own pers when needed. Upon arrival, crews will proceed directly to Command Post (Bldg 2050) and complete an outbound setup sheet to facilitate departure requirements. No COMSEC material avbl thru Hickam Airfield Ops. Transient aircrews should plan to arrive with appropriate amount of COSMEC to complete entire mission. Arfld

CONTINUED ON NEXT PAGE

FIGURE 206.—Excerpt from Chart Supplement.

This page is intentionally left blank

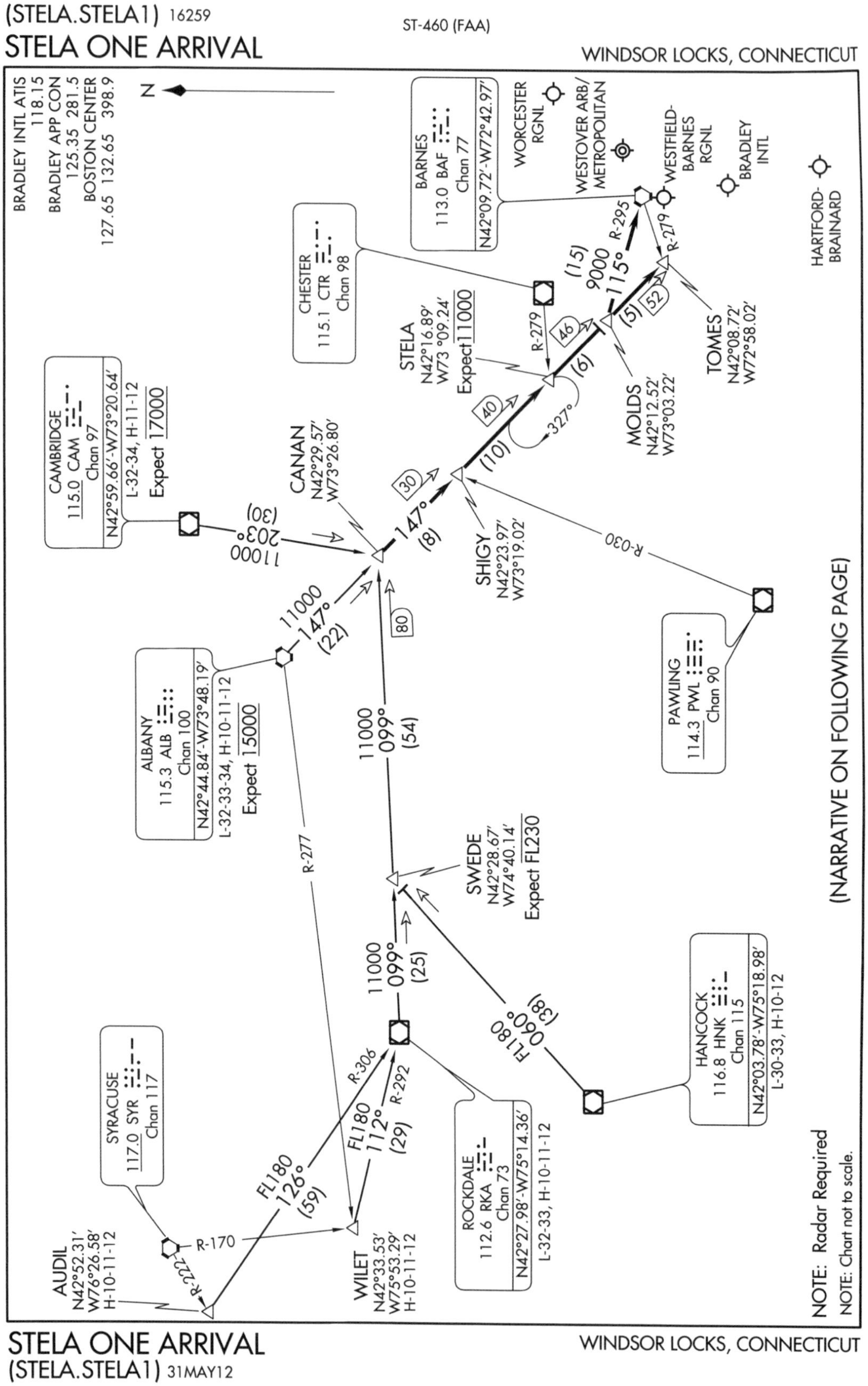

FIGURE 208.—STELA One Arrival (STELA.STELA1).

(STELA.STELA1) 16259 ST-460 (FAA)

STELA ONE ARRIVAL WINDSOR LOCKS, CONNECTICUT

ARRIVAL ROUTE DESCRIPTION

ALBANY TRANSITION (ALB.STELA1): From over ALB VORTAC via ALB R-147 to CANAN INT. Thence. . . .
AUDIL TRANSITION (AUDIL.STELA1): From over AUDIL INT via RKA R-306 to RKA VOR/DME, then via RKA R-099 to CANAN INT. Thence. . . .
CAMBRIDGE TRANSITION (CAM.STELA1): From over CAM VOR/DME via CAM R-203 to CANAN INT. Thence. . . .
HANCOCK TRANSITION (HNK.STELA1): From over HNK VOR/DME via HNK R-060 to SWEDE INT, then via RKA R-099 to CANAN INT. Thence. . . .
WILET TRANSITION (WILET.STELA1): From over WILET INT via RKA R-292 to RKA VOR/DME, then via RKA R-099 TO CANAN INT. Thence. . . .

KBDL and KHFD ARRIVALS: From over CANAN INT via ALB R-147 to TOMES INT. Expect radar vectors to final approach course prior to TOMES INT.

KBAF, KCEF and KORH ARRIVALS: From over CANAN INT via ALB R-147 to MOLDS INT. Then via BAF R-295 to BAF VORTAC. Expect radar vectors to final approach course prior to BAF VORTAC.

STELA ONE ARRIVAL WINDSOR LOCKS, CONNECTICUT

(STELA.STELA1) 31MAY12

FIGURE 209.—STELA One Arrival (STELA.STELA1).

WINDSOR LOCKS, CONNECTICUT — AL-460 (FAA) — 16203

ILS or LOC RWY 6
BRADLEY INTL (BDL)

LOC/DME I-BDL	APP CRS	Rwy ldg 9509
111.1 Chan **48**	**058°**	TDZE **173** / Apt Elev **173**

For inoperative ALSF-2, increase S-ILS 6 all Cats visibility to RVR 4000. JETIX Fix Minimums: For inoperative ALSF-2, increase S-LOC 6 Cat C, D visibility to RVR 6000.

ALSF-2

MISSED APPROACH: Climb to 4000 then left turn direct BAF VORTAC and hold.

ATIS	BRADLEY APP CON	BRADLEY TOWER	GND CON	CLNC DEL	CPDLC
118.15	123.95 290.55 (061°-240°) 125.35 281.5 (241°-060°)	120.3 351.8	121.9 348.6	121.75 322.3	

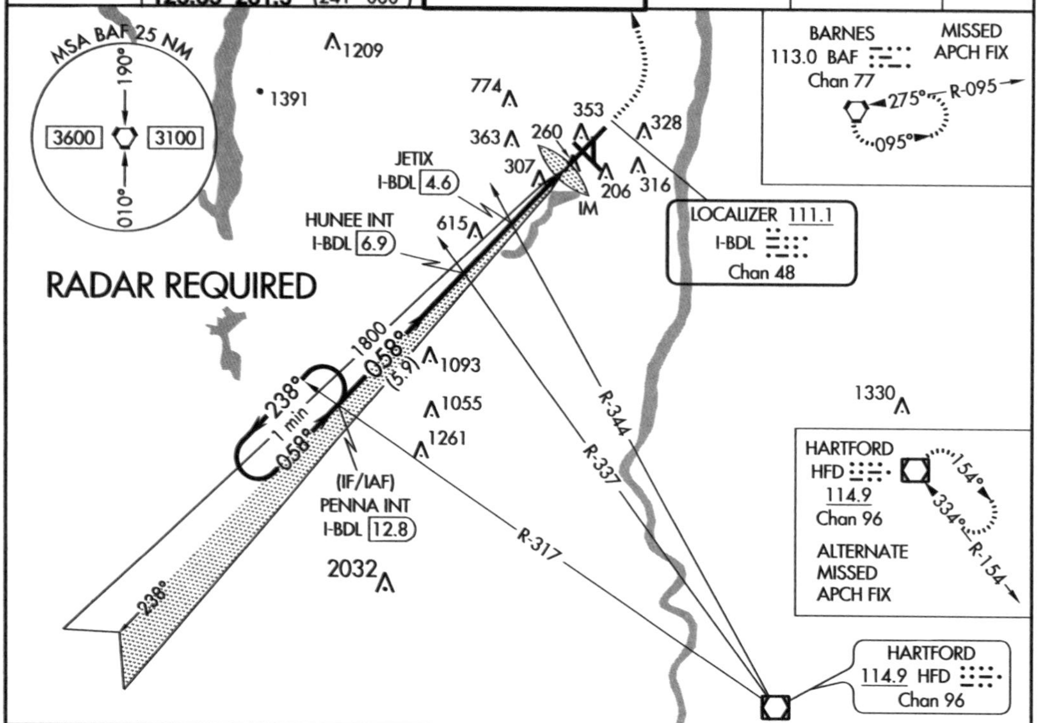

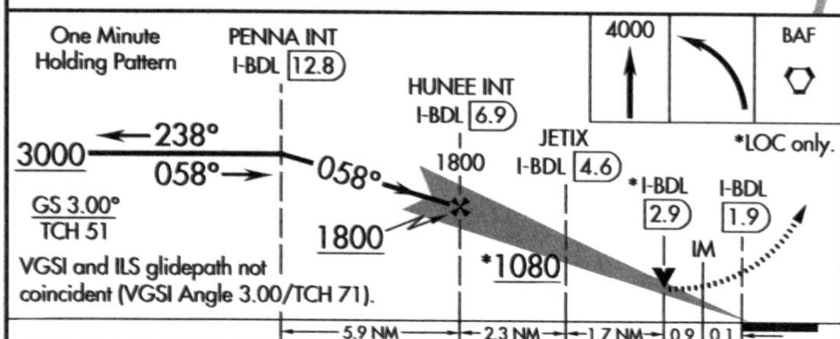

CATEGORY	A	B	C	D
S-ILS 6	373/18 200 (200-½)			
S-LOC 6	1080/40 907 (1000-¾)		1080-2 907 (1000-2)	
CIRCLING	1080-1¼ 907 (1000-1¼)		1080-2¾ 907 (1000-2¾)	1080-3 907 (1000-3)
JETIX FIX MINIMUMS				
S-LOC 6	560/24 387 (400-½)		560/35 387 (400-¾)	
CIRCLING	680-1 507 (600-1)		680-1½ 507 (600-1½)	940-2½ 767 (800-2½)

ELEV 173 — D — TDZE 173

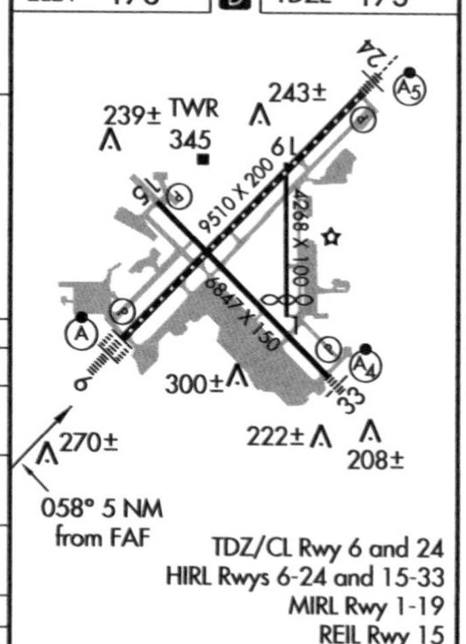

FAF to MAP 5 NM

Knots	60	90	120	150	180
Min:Sec	5:00	3:20	2:30	2:00	1:40

WINDSOR LOCKS, CONNECTICUT
Amdt 37A 18SEP14 — 41°56′N-72°41′W

BRADLEY INTL (BDL)
ILS or LOC RWY 6

FIGURE 210.—ILS or LOC RWY 6 (CAT I) (BDL).

(STAKK3.STAKK) 12040

STAKK THREE DEPARTURE

SL-192 (FAA)

HELENA RGNL (HLN)
HELENA, MONTANA

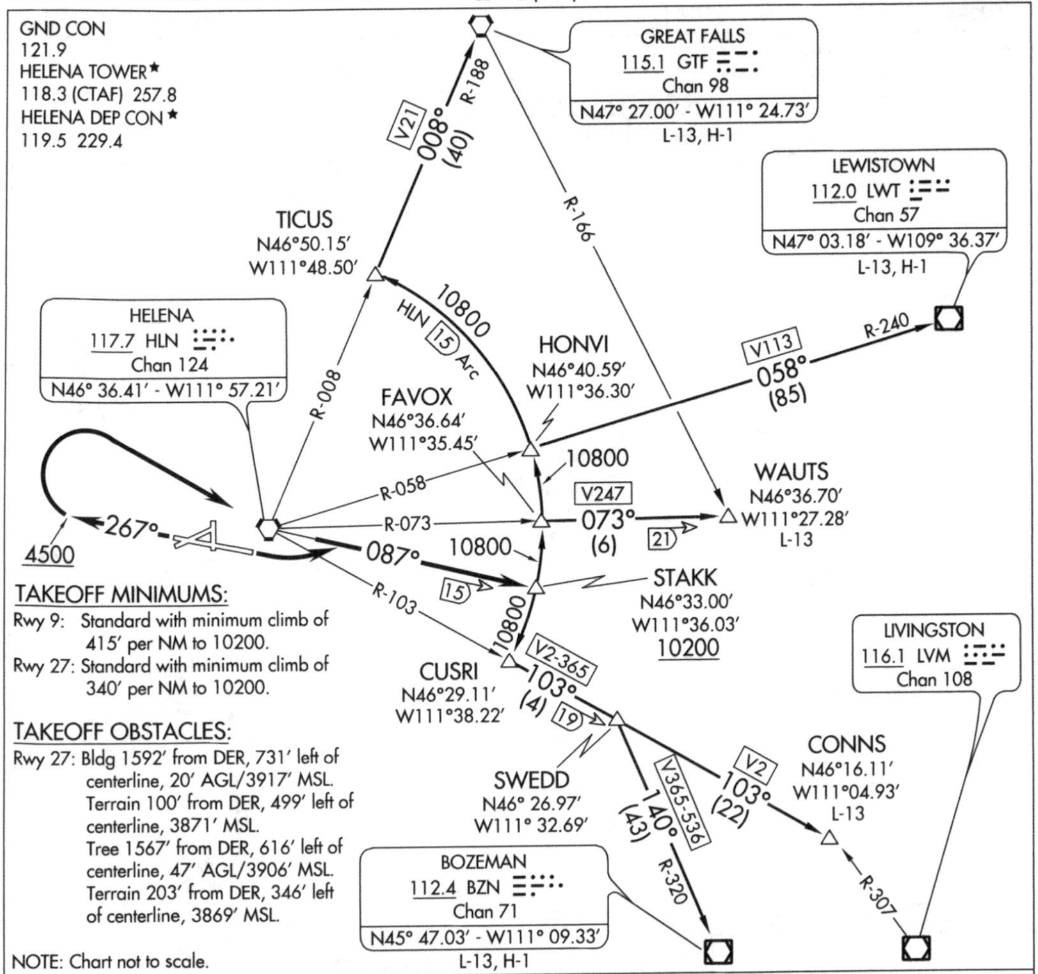

DEPARTURE ROUTE DESCRIPTION

TAKEOFF RUNWAY 9: Climbing left turn to intercept HLN R-087 to cross STAKK at or above 10200. Thence via transition.

TAKEOFF RUNWAY 27: Climb heading 267° to 4500 then climbing right turn direct HLN VORTAC. Continue climb on HLN R-087 to cross STAKK at or above 10200. Thence via transition.

BOZEMAN TRANSITION (STAKK3.BZN): From over STAKK via 15 DME Arc to CUSRI INT, then via HLN R-103 to SWEDD INT, then via BZN R-320 to BZN VOR/DME.

CONNS TRANSITION (STAKK3.CONNS): From over STAKK via 15 DME Arc to CUSRI INT, then via HLN R-103 to SWEDD INT, then via HLN R-103 to CONNS INT.

GREAT FALLS TRANSITION (STAKK3.GTF): From over STAKK via 15 DME Arc to FAVOX, then via 15 DME Arc to HONVI, then via 15 DME Arc to TICUS, then via HLN R-008 and GTF R-188 to GTF VORTAC.

LEWISTOWN TRANSITION (STAKK3.LWT): From over STAKK via 15 DME Arc to FAVOX, then via 15 DME Arc to HONVI, then via HLN R-058 and LWT R-240 to LWT VOR/DME.

WAUTS TRANSITION (STAKK3.WAUTS): From over STAKK via 15 DME Arc to FAVOX, then via HLN R-073 to WAUTS INT.

STAKK THREE DEPARTURE
(STAKK3.STAKK) 12040

HELENA, MONTANA
HELENA RGNL (HLN)

FIGURE 211.—STAKK Three Departure (STAKK3.STAKK) (HLN).

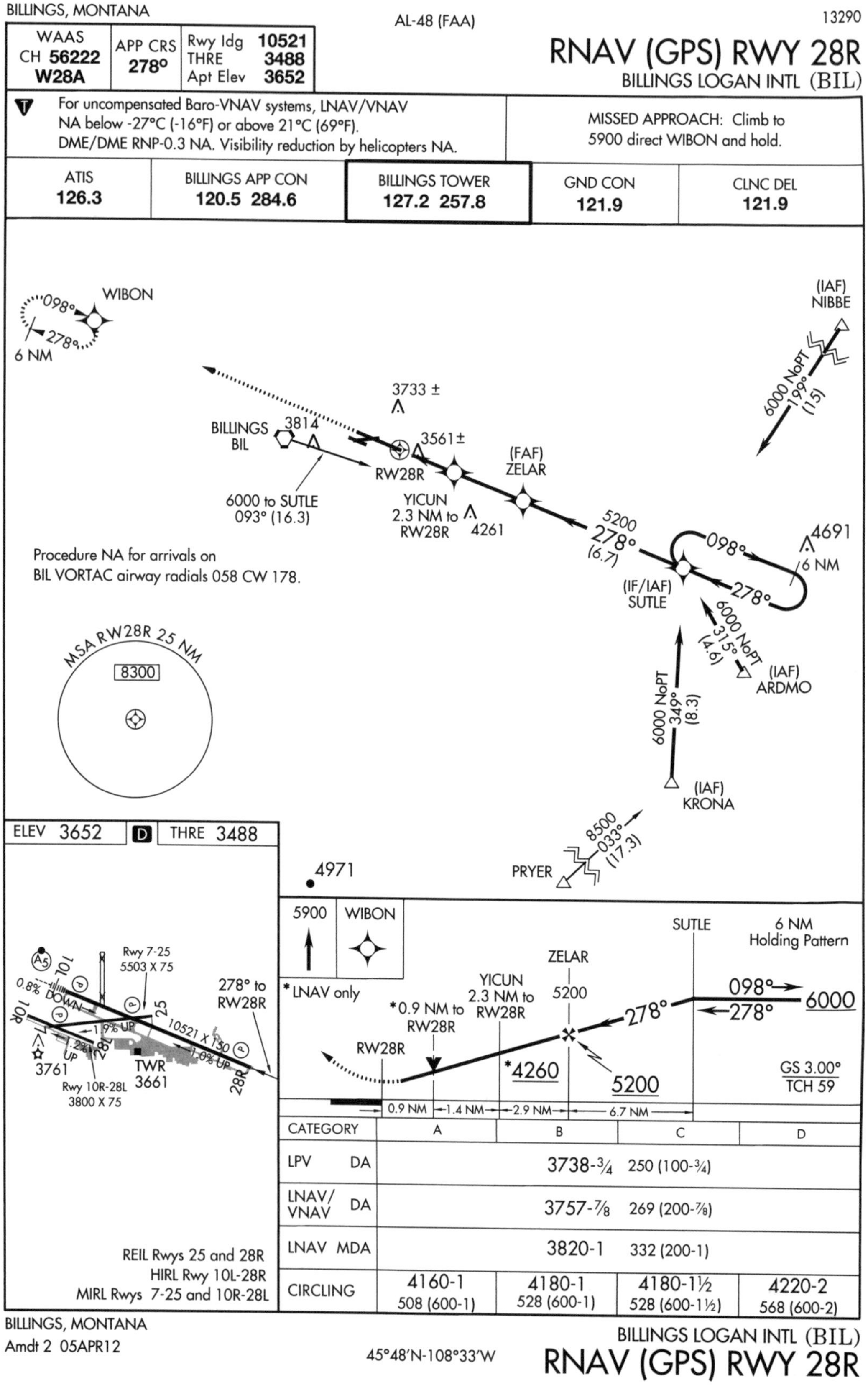

FIGURE 212.—RNAV (GPS) RWY 28R (BIL).

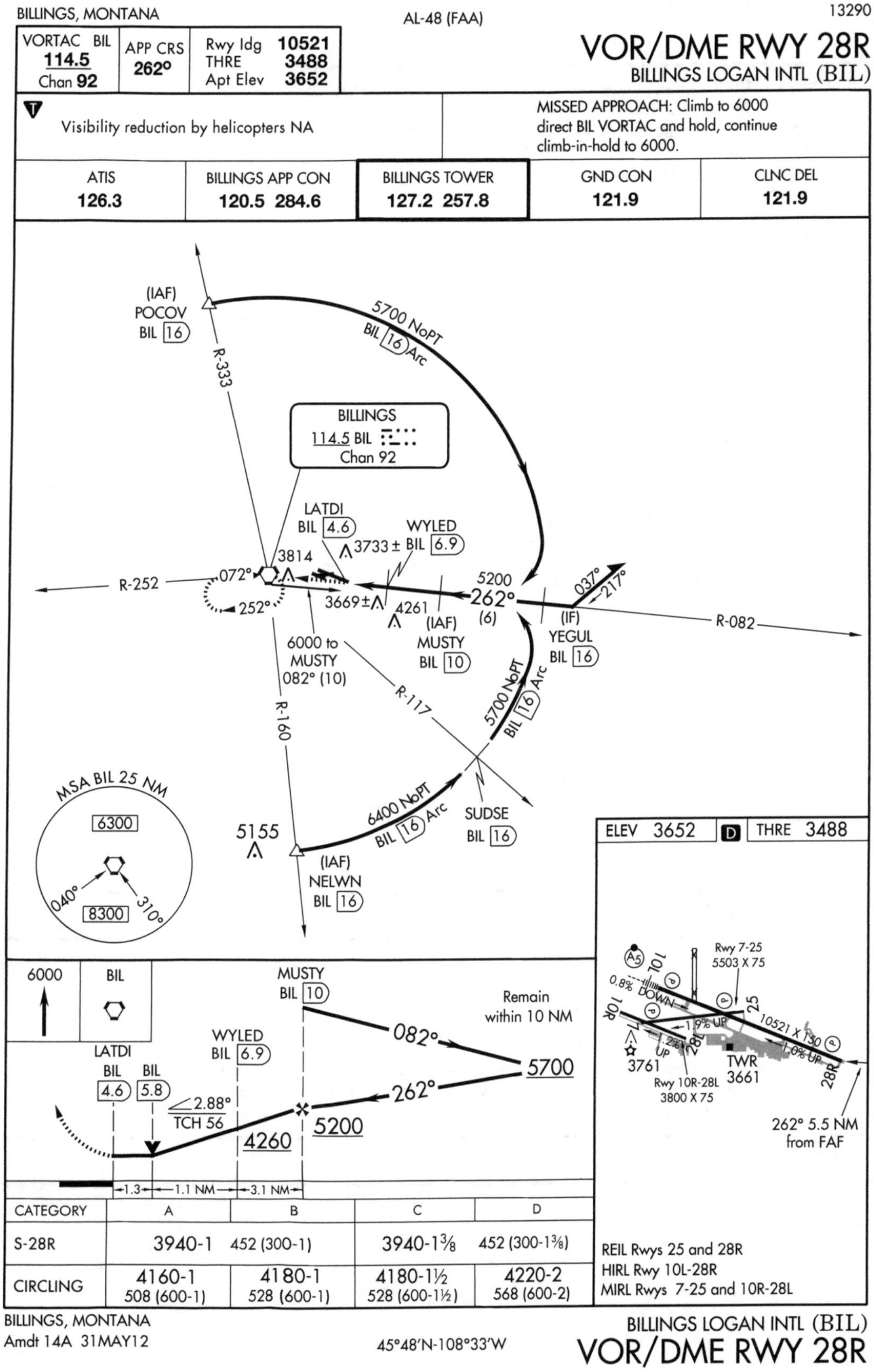

FIGURE 213.—VOR/DME RWY 28R (BIL).

BILLINGS LOGAN INTL (BIL) 2 NW UTC–7(–6DT) N45°48.46´ W108°32.57´ **BILLINGS**
3652 B S4 **FUEL** 100LL, JET A OX 1, 2, 3, 4 ARFF Index—See Remarks NOTAM FILE BIL **H–1E, L–13D**
RWY 10L–28R: H10521X150 (ASPH-GRVD) S–130, D–170, 2S–175, 2D–285 HIRL **IAP, AD**
RWY 10L: MALSR. PAPI(P4L)—GA 3.0° TCH 51´. 0.8% down.
RWY 28R: REIL. PAPI(P4R)—GA 3.0° TCH 56´. Ground. 1.0% up.
RWY 07–25: H5503X75 (ASPH-GRVD) S–12.5 MIRL 1.9% up SW
RWY 07: PAPI(P4L)—GA 3.0° TCH 31´. Ground.
RWY 25: REIL. PAPI(P4R)—GA 3.0° TCH 36´.
RWY 10R–28L: H3800X75 (ASPH) S–12.5 MIRL 1.2% up NW
RWY 10R: Ground.
RUNWAY DECLARED DISTANCE INFORMATION
RWY 07: TORA–5503 TODA–5503 ASDA–5503 LDA–5503
RWY 10L: TORA–10521 TODA–10521 ASDA–10521 LDA–10521
RWY 10R: TORA–3800 TODA–3800 ASDA–3800 LDA–3800
RWY 25: TORA–5503 TODA–5503 ASDA–5503 LDA–5503
RWY 28L: TORA–3800 TODA–3800 ASDA–3800 LDA–3800
RWY 28R: TORA–10521 TODA–10521 ASDA–10521 LDA–10521

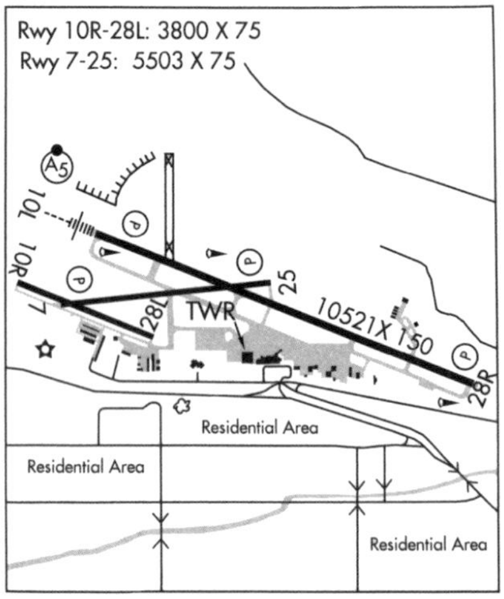

AIRPORT REMARKS: Attended continuously. Rwy 07–25 and Rwy 10R–28L CLOSED to acft over 12,500 lbs. No customs, remote acft parking, ltd ground handling svc. Migratory waterfowl invof arpt. Twy D 35´ wide clsd to acft over 12,500 lbs. Class I, ARFF Index C. PPR unscheduled air carrier ops with more than 30 passenger seats ctc arpt ops 406–657–8496. ARFF Index B from 0900–1300Z‡. 180° turns Rwy 10L–28R by acft over 25,000 lbs prohibited. For MIRL Rwy 10R–28L and Rwy 07–25, HIRL Rwy 10L–28R, MALSR Rwy 10L and REIL Rwy 25 and Rwy 28R ctc twr.
WEATHER DATA SOURCES: ASOS (406) 248–2773 LLWAS.
COMMUNICATIONS: ATIS 126.3 **UNICOM** 122.95
RCO 122.55 (GREAT FALLS RADIO)
® **APP/DEP CON** 119.2 (EAST) 120.5 (WEST)
TOWER 127.2 **GND CON** 121.9 **CLNC DEL** 121.9
PRE TAXI CLNC 121.9
AIRSPACE: CLASS C svc ctc **APP CON**
RADIO AIDS TO NAVIGATION: NOTAM FILE BIL.
(H) VORTACW 114.5 BIL Chan 92 N45°48.51´ W108°37.48´ 077° 3.4 NM to fld. 3811/14E.
SAIGE NDB (LOM) 251 BI N45°51.13´ W108°41.67´ 099° 6.9 NM to fld.
ILS 110.3 I–BIL Rwy 10L. Class IB. LOM SAIGE NDB.
ILS/DME 111.5 I–BMO Chan 52 Rwy 28R. Class IA. Localizer unusable beyond 20° left and right of course.

BLACK BUTTE NORTH (See WINIFRED on page 106)

BOULDER (3U9) 2 S UTC–7(–6DT) N46°12.70´ W112°06.46´ **GREAT FALLS**
4968 NOTAM FILE GTF
RWY 11–29: 3675X72 (TURF) 1.6% up W
RWY 11: Hill.
RWY 29: Road.
AIRPORT REMARKS: Unattended. No snow removal. Rwy 11–29 thlds marked with faded red cones, edges marked with white cones. –2´ drainage ditch +1´ berm W side of rwy full length, 43´ from Rwy 11–29 centerline.
COMMUNICATIONS: CTAF 122.9

BOWMAN FLD (See ANACONDA on page 62)

FIGURE 214.—Excerpt from Chart Supplement.

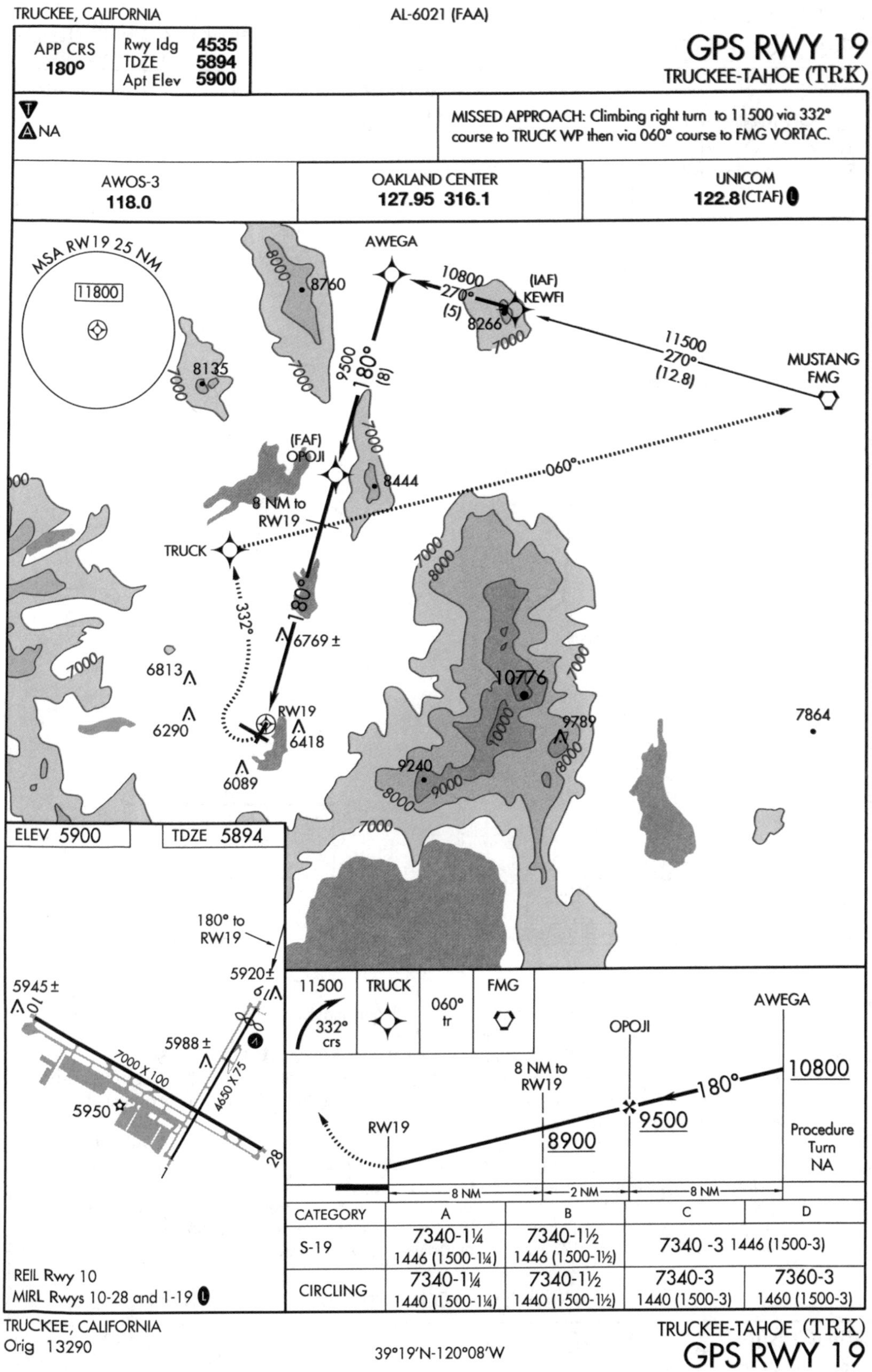

FIGURE 215.—GPS RWY 19 (TRK).

(RENO9.FMG) 16035

RENO NINE DEPARTURE

SL-346 (FAA)

RENO/TAHOE INTL (RNO)
RENO, NEVADA

TOP ALTITUDE:
FL190

ATIS
135.8 363.0
CLNC DEL
124.9 370.85
GND CON
121.9 348.6
RENO TOWER
118.7 257.8

TAKEOFF MINIMUMS

Rwy 7: NA- Obstacles.
Rwy 16L: Standard with minimum climb of 730′ per NM to 10900,
or 600-1¼ with minimum climb of 352′ per NM to 10900.
Rwy 16R: Standard with minimum climb of 460′ per NM to 10900,
or 300-1 with minimum climb of 395′ per NM to 10900.
Rwy 25: Standard with minimum climb of 500′ per NM to 9700.
Rwys 34L/R: Standard with mimimum climb of 480′ per NM to 8700,
or 500-1½ with minimum climb of 430′ per NM to 8700.

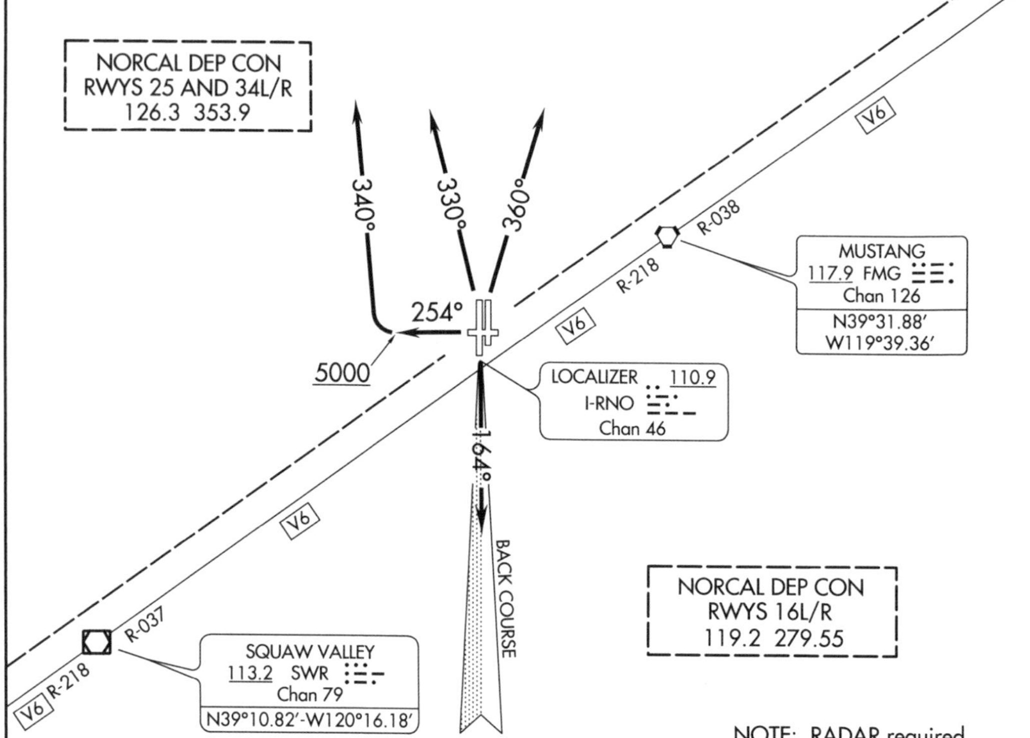

NOTE: RADAR required.

TAKEOFF OBSTACLE NOTES

Rwy 16L: Multiple poles, trees, bushes, terrain and buildings with antennas and cameras beginning 618′ from DER, 131′ left of centerline, up to 20′ AGL/4959′ MSL.
Rwy 16R: Multiple trees beginning 2784′ from DER, 171′ right of centerline, 20′ AGL/4510′ MSL.
Multiple trees and terrain beginning 746′ from DER, 380′ left of centerline, up to 20′ AGL/4723′ MSL.
Rwy 25: Multiple trees, poles, fence, and vent on building beginning 222′ from DER, 201′ right of centerline, up to 103′ AGL/4608′ MSL.
Multiple trees, poles and sign beginning 500′ from DER, 31′ left of centerline, up to 20′ AGL/4506′ MSL.
Rwy 34L: Multiple trees and pole beginning 1229′ from DER, 180′ right of centerline, up to 20′ AGL/4498′ MSL.
Multiple trees beginning 1193′ from DER, 331′ left of centerline, up to 20′ AGL/4489′ MSL.
Rwy 34R: Multiple trees and poles beginning 1067′ from DER, 172′ right of centerline, up to 20′ AGL/4497′ MSL.
Multiple trees beginning 1230′ from DER, 350′ left of centerline, up to 20′ AGL/4498′ MSL.
Building 1.2 NM from DER, 1730′ right of centerline, 363′ AGL/4780′ MSL.

(NARRATIVE ON FOLLOWING PAGE)

NOTE: Chart not to scale.

RENO NINE DEPARTURE
(RENO9.FMG) 04FEB16

RENO, NEVADA
RENO/TAHOE INTL (RNO)

FIGURE 216.—RENO Nine Departure (RENO9.FMG) (RNO).

(RENO9.FMG) 16035

RENO/TAHOE INTL (RNO)

RENO NINE DEPARTURE SL-346 (FAA) RENO, NEVADA

DEPARTURE ROUTE DESCRIPTION

TAKEOFF RUNWAYS 16L/R: Climb on heading 164° and I-RNO localizer south course. Thence. . . .

TAKEOFF RUNWAY 25: Climb heading 254° to 5000 then climbing right turn heading 340°. Thence. . . .

TAKEOFF RUNWAYS 34L/R: Climb heading 330° CW 360° as assigned by ATC. Thence. . . .

. . . .All aircraft maintain FL190 or assigned altitude. Expect clearance to requested altitude 5 minutes after departure. Expect RADAR vectors to assigned route/fix.

LOST COMMUNICATIONS: If not in contact with departure control within one minute after takeoff, maintain assigned heading until passing 10000, thence. . . .

. . . .RUNWAYS 16L/R DEPARTURES: Turn left direct FMG VORTAC, then via assigned route.

. . . .RUNWAYS 25 and 34L/R DEPARTURES: Turn right direct FMG VORTAC, then via assigned route.

RENO NINE DEPARTURE RENO, NEVADA

RENO/TAHOE INTL (RNO)

(RENO9.FMG) 04FEB16

FIGURE 216A.—RENO Nine Departure (RENO9.FMG) (RNO).

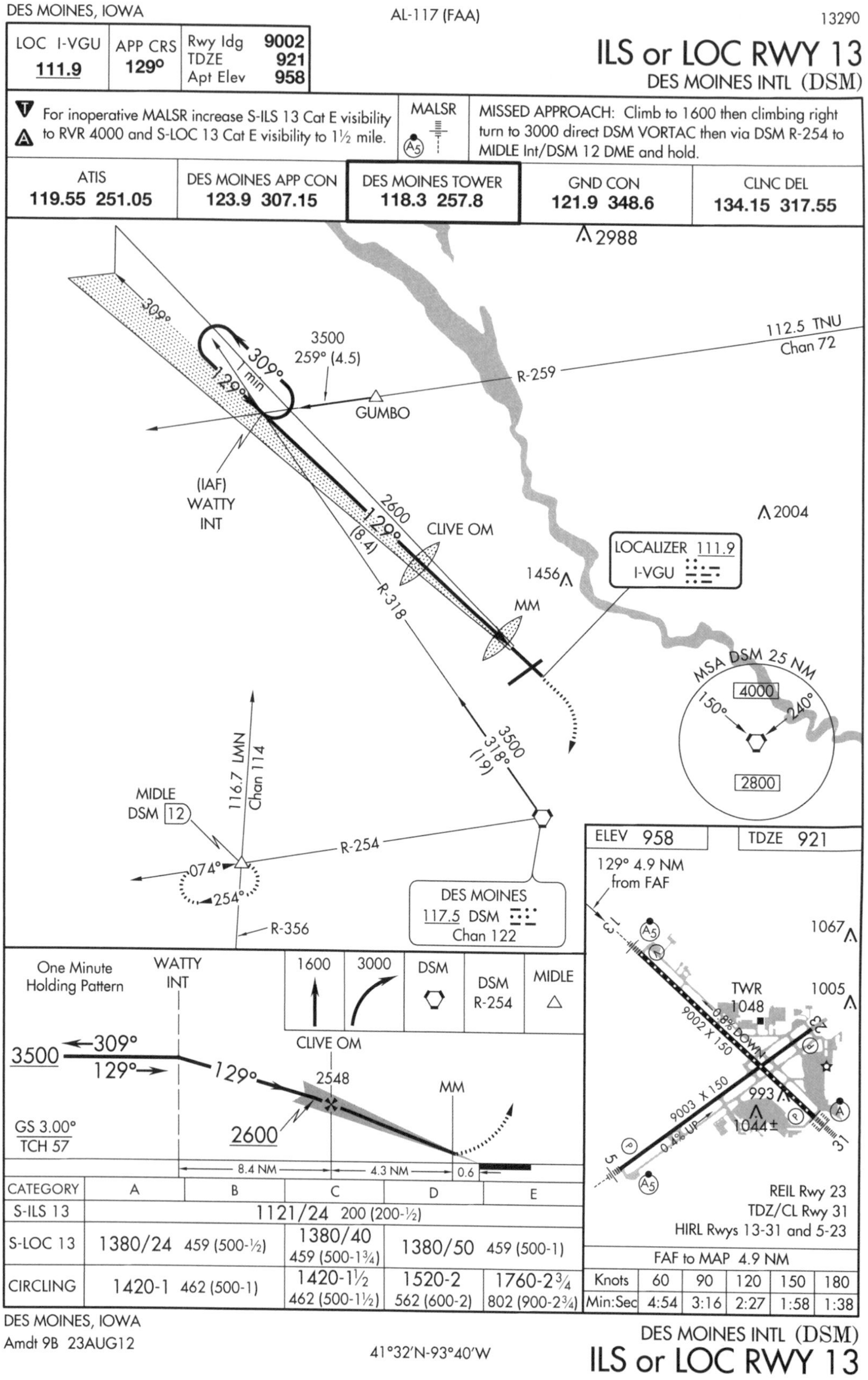

FIGURE 217.—ILS or LOC RWY 13 (DSM).

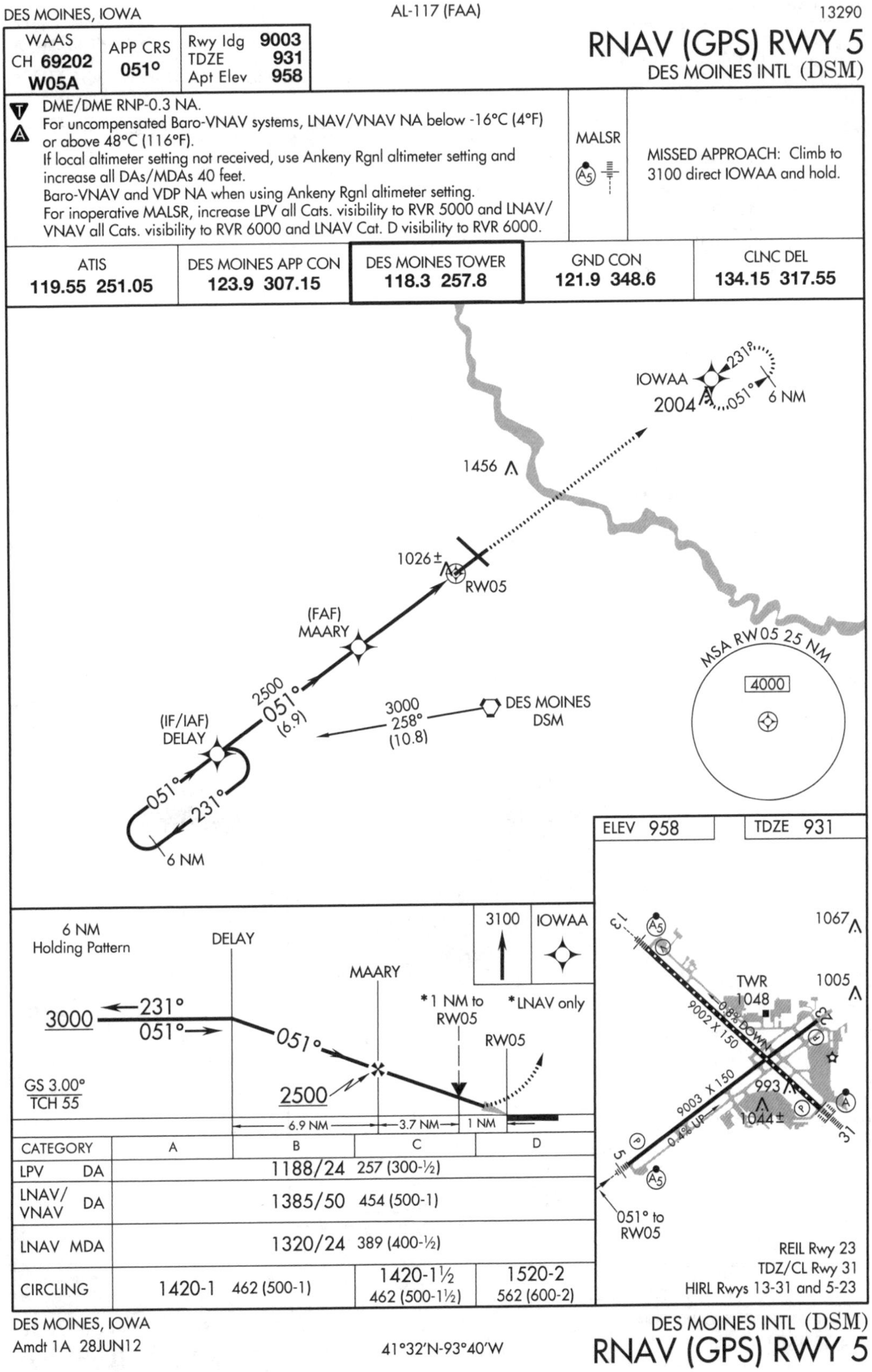

FIGURE 218.—RNAV (GPS) RWY 5 (DSM).

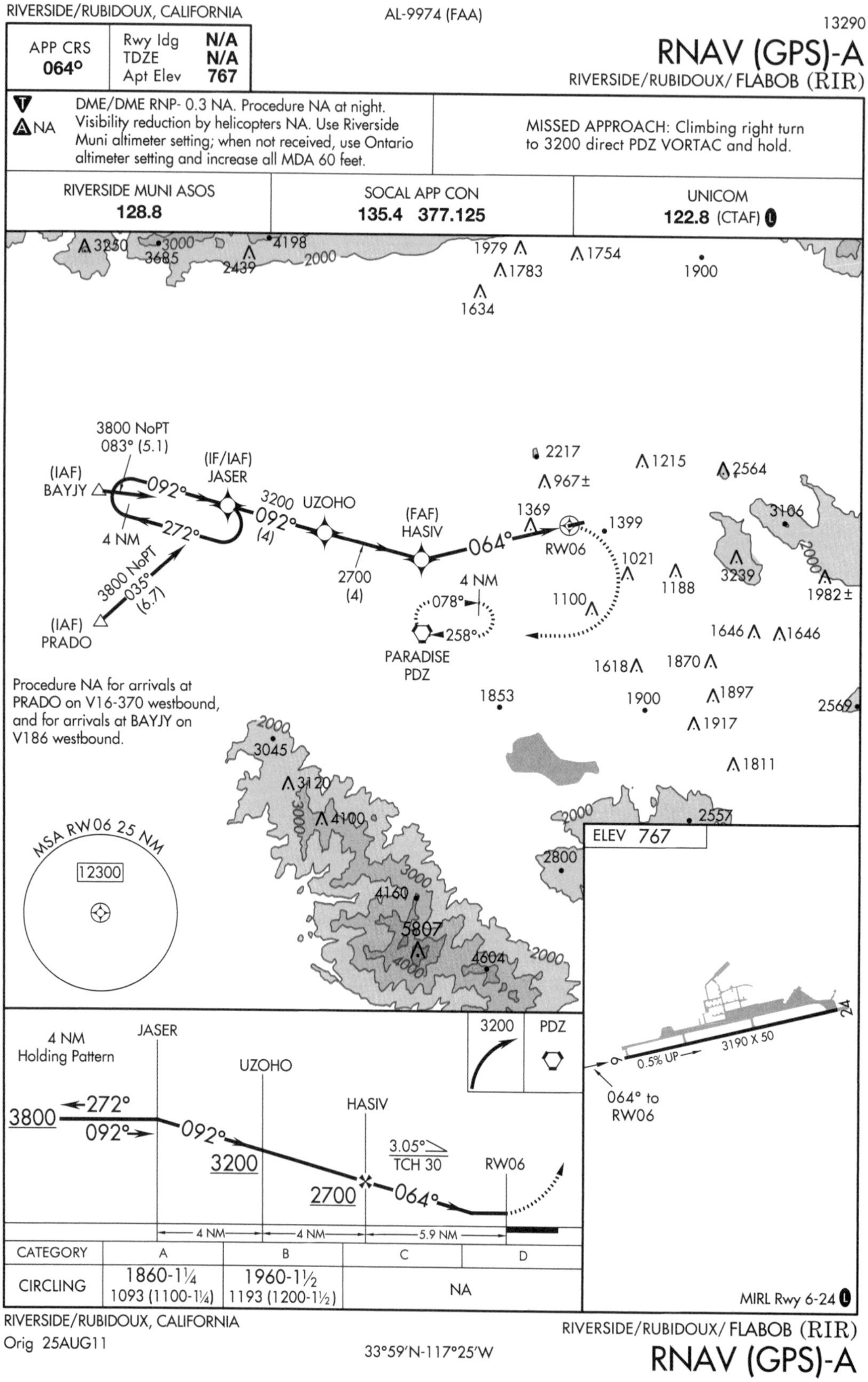

CATEGORY	A	B	C	D
CIRCLING	1860-1¼ 1093 (1100-1¼)	1960-1½ 1193 (1200-1½)	NA	

FIGURE 219.—RNAV (GPS)-A (RIR).

L11

TAKEOFF MINIMUMS AND (OBSTACLE) DEPARTURE PROCEDURES

13234

RIVERSIDE/RUBIDOUX, CA

FLABOB (RIR)
ORIG 11181 (FAA)

TAKEOFF MINIMUMS: **Rwy 6,** std. w/min. climb of 670' per NM to 4000 or 400-2 w/min. climb of 480' per NM to 4000 or 2100-3 for climb in visual conditions. **Rwy 24,** std. w/min. climb of 630' per NM to 3000 or 800-2¾ w/min. climb of 305' per NM to 4600 or 2100-3 for climb in visual conditions.

DEPARTURE PROCEDURE: **Rwy 6,** climb via heading 064° to 4000 then right turn direct PDZ VORTAC, or for climb in visual conditions cross Flabob Airport Southwest bound at or above 2700 then via PDZ R-039 to PDZ VORTAC. **Rwy 24,** climb via heading 244° and PDZ R-031 to PDZ VORTAC, or for climb in visual conditions cross Flabob airport Southwest bound at or above 2700 then via PDZ R-039 to PDZ VORTAC.

All aircraft climb in PDZ VORTAC holding pattern (hold East, right turns, 258° inbound) to cross PDZ VORTAC at or above MEA for direction of flight before proceeding on course.

NOTE: **Rwy 6,** trees beginning 3763' from DER, 1152' right of centerline, up to 40' AGL/1119' MSL. **Rwy 24,** antenna on tank 6193' from DER, 2057' right of centerline, 38' AGL/1237' MSL. Trees beginning 2494' from DER, 434' right of centerline, up to 40' AGL/1519' MSL. Pole 6261' from DER, 1950' right of centerline, 30' AGL/1230' MSL. Building 1.52 NM from DER, 1154' right of centerline, up to 29' AGL/1369' MSL. Antenna on tank 1.26 NM from DER, 2047' right of centerline, 54' AGL/1254' MSL. Tank 4043' from DER, 794' right of centerline, 66' AGL/961' MSL. Tree 1.79 NM from DER, 434' right of centerline, 58' AGL/1138' MSL.

SAN BERNARDINO, CA

SAN BERNARDINO INTL (SBD)
ORIG 93343 (FAA)

TAKEOFF MINIMUMS: **Rwy 6,** CAT A,B 2100-2 or std. with a min. climb of 340' per NM to 3700. CAT C,D 3100-2 or std. with a min. climb of 480' per NM to 4600.

DEPARTURE PROCEDURE: **Rwy 6,** climbing right turn. **Rwy 24,** climbing left turn. **All aircraft** climb direct PDZ VORTAC. Aircraft departing PDZ R-091 CW R-140 and R-231 CW R-280 climb on course. All others continue climb in PDZ holding pattern (Hold NE, right turns, 210° inbound) to cross PDZ VORTAC at or above: R-281 CW R-090, 7700; R-141 CW R-230, 4900.

SAN CLEMENTE ISLAND NALF (FREDERICK SHERMAN FLD)(KNUC)

SAN CLEMENTE ISLAND, CA 12208

Rwy 5: Diverse departures authorized 090° to 233° CCW.

Rwy 23: Diverse departures authorized 160° to 053° CW.

TAKE-OFF OBSTACLES: **Rwy 5,** Pylon 198' MSL, 44' from DER, 274' left of centerline. Terrain 192' MSL, 50' from DER, 500' right of centerline. Terrain 194' MSL, 264' from DER, 509' right of centerline. Terrain 209' MSL, 824' from DER, 721' right of centerline. Terrain 199' MSL, 957' from DER, 612' right of centerline.

SAN DIEGO, CA

BROWN FIELD MUNI (SDM)
AMDT 4 10154(FAA)

TAKEOFF MINIMUMS: **Rwy 8L,** std. w/ min. climb of 570' per NM to 3100. **Rwys 8R,26L,** NA - ATC.

DEPARTURE PROCEDURE: **Rwy 8L,** climbing left turn, thence...**Rwy 26R,** climbing right turn, thence...

...via heading 280° to intercept MZB R-160 to MZB VORTAC.

NOTE: **Rwy 26R,** tree 1284' from DER, 778' left of centerline, 52' AGL/561' MSL.

MONTGOMERY FIELD (MYF)
AMDT 3A 10210 (FAA)

TAKEOFF MINIMUMS: **Rwy 5,** 1500-2 or std. with a min. climb of 290' per NM to 1700.

DEPARTURE PROCEDURE: **Rwys 5, 10L/R,** climbing right turn. **Rwys 28L/R,** climbing left turn. **All aircraft** climb direct to MZB VORTAC. Aircraft departing MZB R-090 CW R-360 climb on course. All others climb in MZB holding pattern (W, right turns, 075° inbound) to cross MZB VORTAC at or above 1800.

NOTE: **Rwy 5,** trees and bushes beginning 244' from DER, 161' left of centerline, up to 99' AGL/524' MSL. Tree 1287' from DER, 103' right of centerline, up to 49' AGL/474' MSL. **Rwy 23,** tree, flag pole, and transmission towers beginning 1594' from DER, 82' right of centerline, up to 125' AGL/545' MSL. Transmission towers beginning 2627' from DER, 414' left of centerline up to 125' AGL/524' MSL. **Rwy 10L,** trees beginning 230' from DER, 494' left of centerline, up to 57' AGL/486' MSL. Trees beginning 1172' from DER, 591' right of centerline, up to 69' AGL/488' MSL. **Rwy 10R,** rod on electrical equipment 40' from DER, 66' left of centerline, 7' AGL/426' MSL. Trees beginning 2107' from DER, 199' right of centerline, up to 69' AGL/488' MSL. **Rwy 28L,** bushes and poles beginning 35' from DER, 160' right of centerline, up to 37' AGL/451' MSL. Trees beginning 1008' from DER, 7' left of centerline, up to 37' AGL/451' MSL.**Rwy 28R,** bushes, trees, and poles beginning 34' from DER, 162' left of centerline, up to 38' AGL/451' MSL. Trees, signs, and poles beginning 768' from DER, 98' right of centerline, up to 67' AGL/488' MSL.

13234

TAKEOFF MINIMUMS AND (OBSTACLE) DEPARTURE PROCEDURES

FIGURE 220.—Takeoff Minimums and (Obstacle) Departure Procedures.

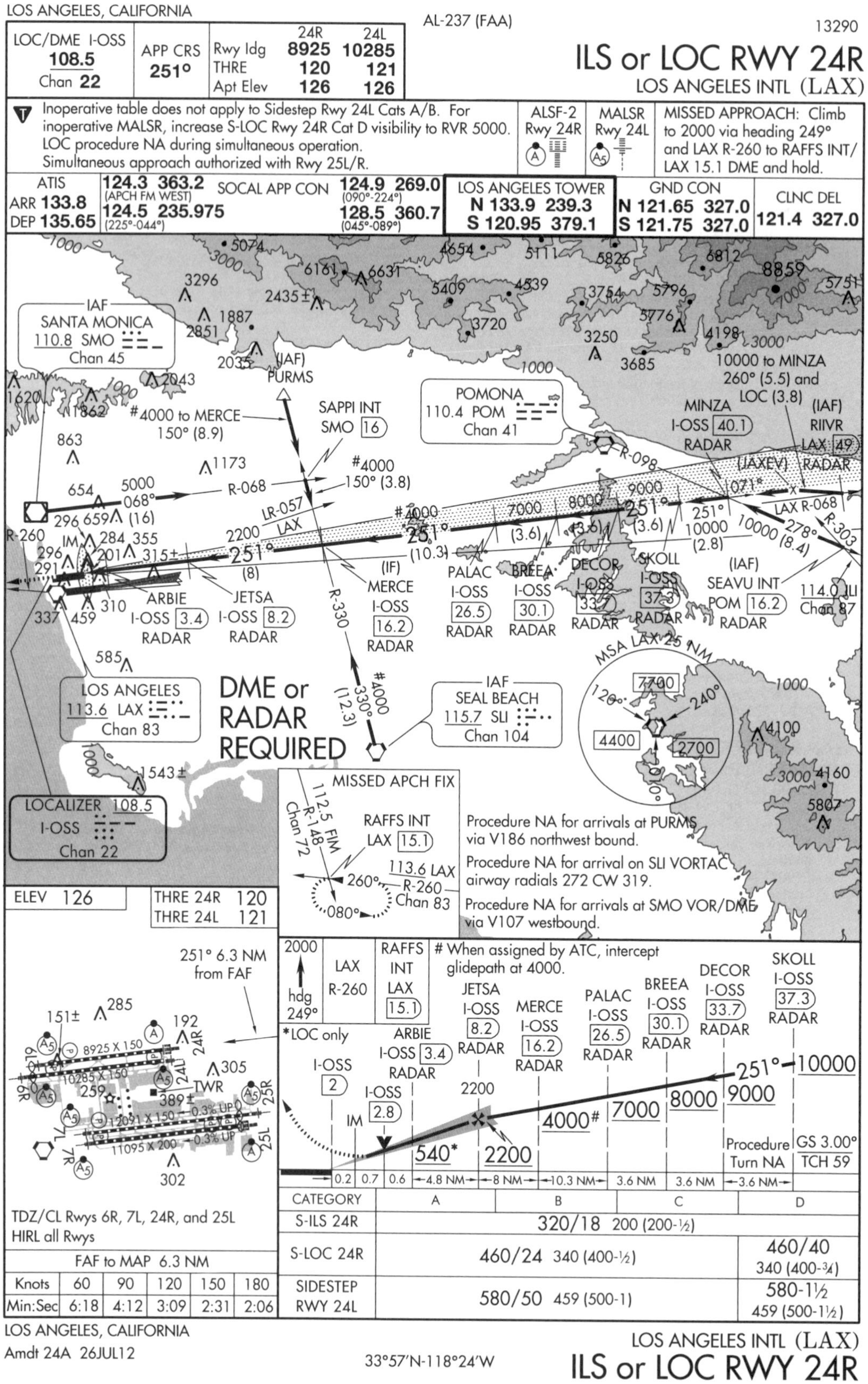

CATEGORY	A	B	C	D
S-ILS 24R	320/18 200 (200-½)			
S-LOC 24R	460/24 340 (400-½)			460/40 340 (400-¾)
SIDESTEP RWY 24L	580/50 459 (500-1)			580-1½ 459 (500-1½)

FAF to MAP 6.3 NM					
Knots	60	90	120	150	180
Min:Sec	6:18	4:12	3:09	2:31	2:06

FIGURE 221.—ILS or LOC RWY 24R (LAX).

BURBANK, CALIFORNIA AL-67 (FAA) 13290

LOC I-BUR	APP CRS	Rwy ldg	5801
109.5	**076°**	THRE	727
		Apt Elev	778

ILS or LOC Z RWY 8

BOB HOPE (BUR)

Circling to Rwy 26 NA at night. When VGSI inop, Circling Rwy 15, 33 NA at night. Inoperative table does not apply to S-LOC 8 Cats A, B. Inoperative table does not apply to S-ILS 8. When VGSI inop, Straight-in/Circling Rwy 8 procedure NA at night. Circling NA northeast of Rwys 15 and 26. Autopilot coupled approach NA below 1007. Visibility reduction by helicopters NA. For inoperative MALSR increase S-LOC 8 Cat C/D visibility to 1⅜ miles. ILS unusable from VINEE NDB inbound. Missed approach requires minimum climb of 372 feet per nautical mile to 2500; if unable to meet climb gradient, see LOC Y RWY 8.

MALSR

MISSED APPROACH: Climb to 1300 then climbing right turn to 4000 direct VNY VOR/DME and on VNY VOR/DME R-242 to SILEX INT/VNY 6.1 DME and hold.

ATIS	SOCAL APP CON	BURBANK TOWER	GND CON	CLNC DEL
134.5	134.2 338.2	118.7 254.3	123.9 348.6	118.0 348.6

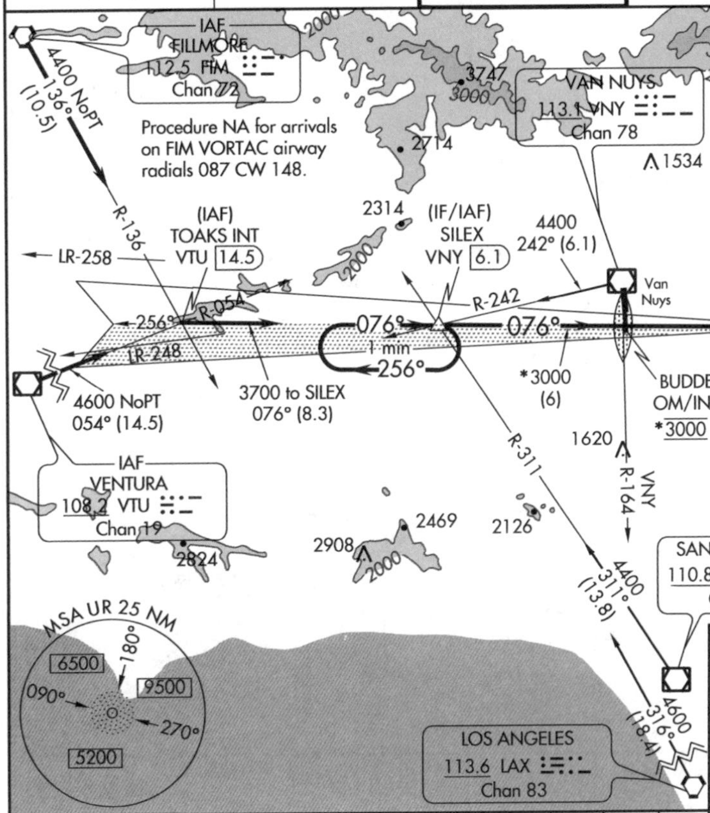

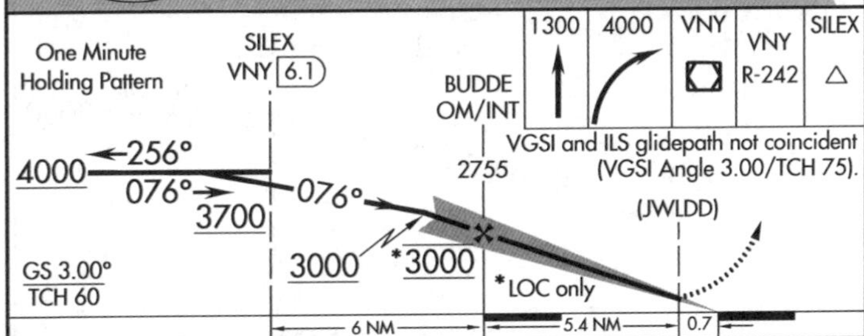

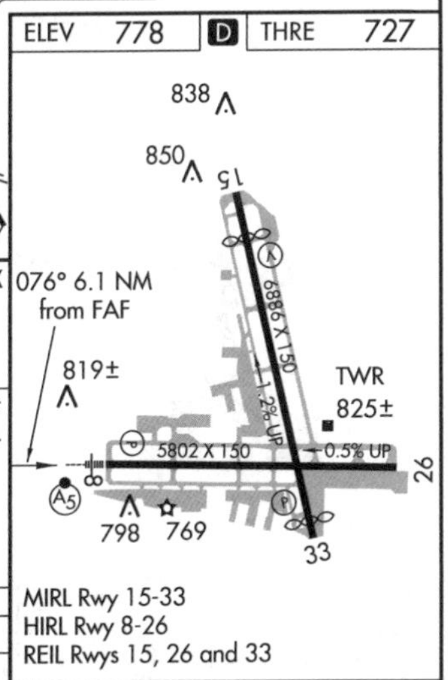

CATEGORY	A	B	C	D
S-ILS 8	1007/50 280 (300-1)			
S-LOC 8	1240/50 513 (500-1)		1240/55 513 (500-1¼)	
CIRCLING	1240-1 462 (500-1)	1280-1 502 (600-1)	1280-1½ 502 (600-1½)	1440-2 662 (700-2)

FAF to MAP 5.4 NM

Knots	60	90	120	150	180
Min:Sec	5:24	3:36	2:42	2:10	1:48

BURBANK, CALIFORNIA
Amdt 37 05APR12

34°12′N-118°22′W

BOB HOPE (BUR)
ILS or LOC Z RWY 8

FIGURE 222.—ILS or LOC Z RWY 8 (BUR).

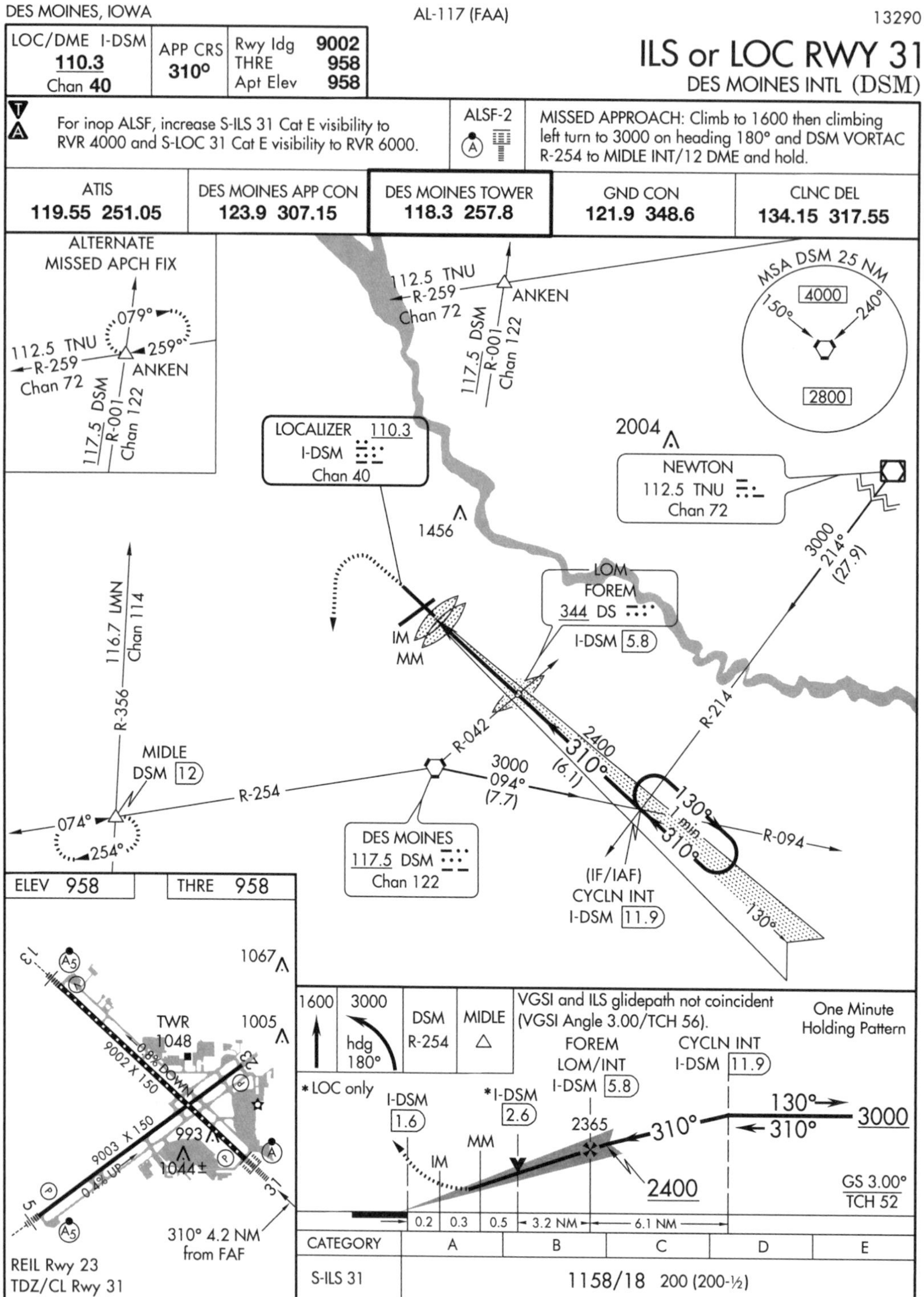

CATEGORY	A	B	C	D	E
S-ILS 31	1158/18 200 (200-½)				
S-LOC 31	1320/24 362 (400-½)		1320/35 362 (400-¾)		
CIRCLING	1420-1 462 (500-1)		1420-1½ 462 (500-1½)	1520-2 562 (600-2)	1760-2¾ 802 (900-2¾)

FAF to MAP 4.2 NM					
Knots	60	90	120	150	180
Min:Sec	4:12	2:48	2:06	1:41	1:24

DES MOINES, IOWA
Amdt 23A 26JUL12
41°32′N-93°40′W
DES MOINES INTL (DSM)
ILS or LOC RWY 31

FIGURE 223.—ILS or LOC RWY 31 (DSM).

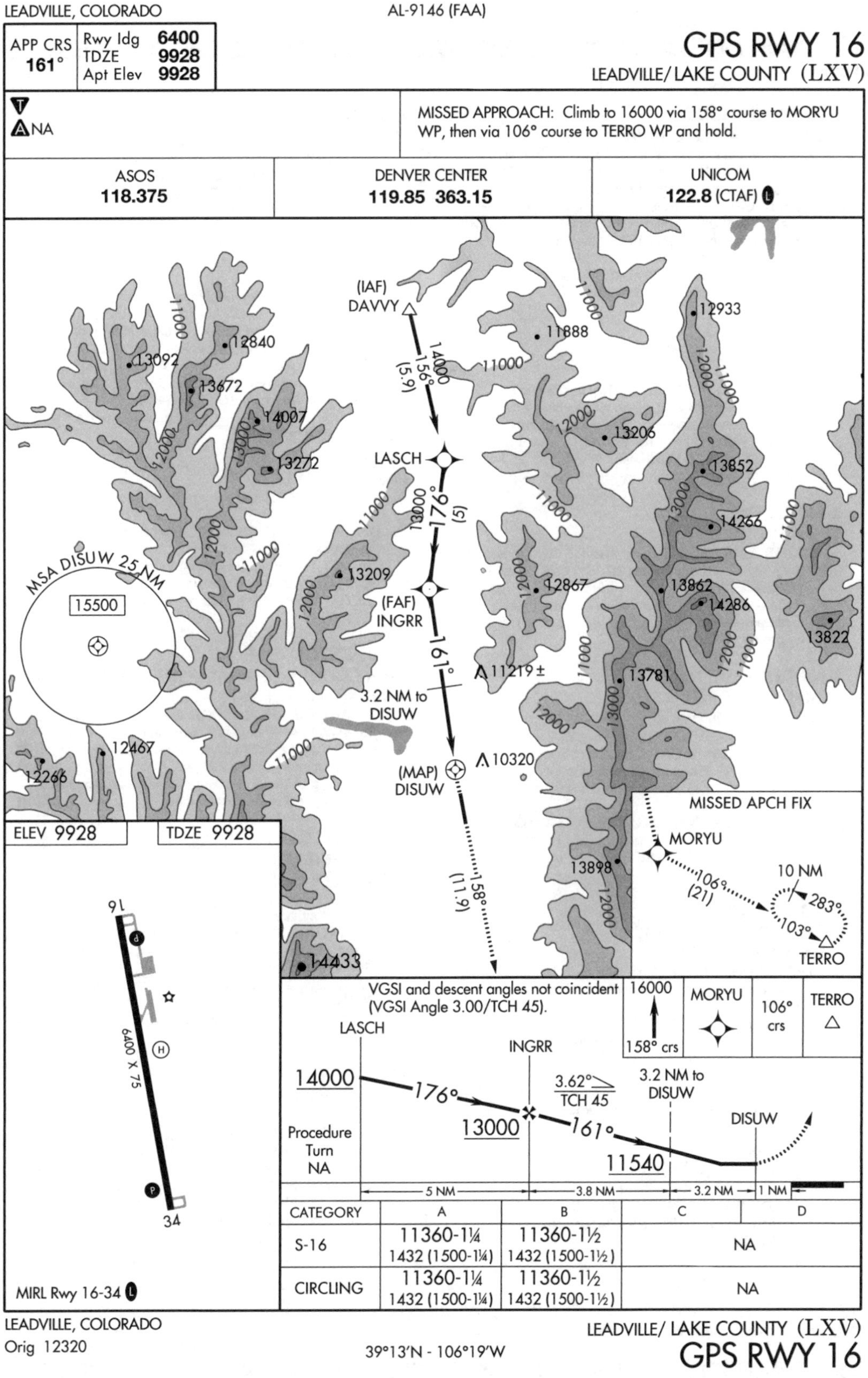

FIGURE 224.—GPS RWY 16 (LXV).

L8

TAKEOFF MINIMUMS AND (OBSTACLE) DEPARTURE PROCEDURES

13262

KREMMLING, CO
MC ELROY AIRFIELD (20V)

TAKEOFF MINIMUMS: **Rwy 9,** 2600-2 or std. with a min. climb of 370' per NM to 12700. **Rwy 27,** 3200-2 or std. with a min. climb of 500' per NM to 12700.

DEPARTURE PROCEDURE: **Rwy 9,** climb runway heading to 10000, then climbing right turn. **Rwy 27,** climb runway heading to 10900, then climbing left turn. **All aircraft** proceed direct RLG VOR/DME. Continue climb to 13,000 in RLG holding pattern (hold SW, left turns, 051° inbound).

LA JUNTA, CO
LA JUNTA MUNI (LHX)
AMDT 3 03191 (FAA)

DEPARTURE PROCEDURE: **Rwy 8,** climb via heading 080°. **Rwy 12,** climb via heading 120°. **Rwy 26,** turn left heading 160°. **Rwy 30,** turn left heading 140°. **All aircraft,** intercept LAA R-238 (V210) to LAA VOR/DME. When at or above 8000 proceed on course.

LAMAR, CO
LAMAR MUNI (LAA)

DEPARTURE PROCEDURE: **Rwys 8,36,** turn left. **Rwy 18,** turn left/right. **Rwy 26,** turn right. Direct LAA VOR/DME. Aircraft departing LAA R-048 CW R-118 climb on course. All others continue climbing in LAA holding pattern (N, right turns, 169° inbound) to 6000 before proceeding on course.

LAS CRUCES, NM
LAS CRUCES INTL (LRU)
AMDT 1 96340 (FAA)

DEPARTURE PROCEDURE: **Rwys 4, 8,** climbing right turn. **Rwy 12,** CAT A,B, climb runway heading CAT C,D, NA. **Rwys 22, 26,** climbing left turn. **Rwy 30,** climbing runway heading to 5100 then climbing left turn.

All aircraft climb direct HAWKE LOM. Continue climb in HAWKE holding pattern (SE, left turns, 304° inbound) to cross HAWKE LOM at or above 10000 before proceeding on course.

LAS VEGAS, NM
LAS VEGAS MUNI (LVS)
AMDT 1 06103 (FAA)

DEPARTURE PROCEDURE: **Rwys 2, 14** turn left/ right. **Rwy 20,** turn left (except via FTI R-215). **Rwy 32,** turn right.

Departures via FTI VORTAC R-001 CW R-215 climb on course. Departures via FTI VORTAC R-216 CW R-360 proceed direct FTI VORTAC. Climb in FTI VORTAC holding pattern (hold north, left turn, 192° inbound) to cross FTI at airway MEA/MCA. (NOTE: climb in hold not authorized for turbojet aircraft).

LEADVILLE, CO
LAKE COUNTY (LXV)
AMDT 2 08101 (FAA)

DEPARTURE PROCEDURE: **Rwy 16,** use LOZUL (RNAV) DEPARTURE. **Rwy 34,** use DAVVY (RNAV) DEPARTURE.

LONGMONT, CO
VANCE BRAND (LMO)
AMDT 1 12040 (FAA)

DEPARTURE PROCEDURE: **Rwy 11,** climbing left turn to intercept GLL VOR/DME R-221 to 7000 . . . **Rwy 29,** climbing right turn to intercept GLL VOR/DME R-221 to 7000 ...

... All aircraft proceed on GLL R-221 to GLL VOR/DME. Cross GLL VOR/DME at or above MEA/MCA for route of flight.

NOTE: **Rwy 11,** trees beginning 130' from DER, 191' right of centerline, up to 80' AGL/5119' MSL. Vehicles on roadway, 449' from DER, 395' left and right of centerline, 17' AGL/5046' MSL. Trees beginning 1383' from DER, 434' left of centerline, up to 80' AGL/5109' MSL. **Rwy 29,** trees beginning 4105' from DER, 220' left of centerline, up to 80' AGL/5189' MSL.

LOS ALAMOS, NM
LOS ALAMOS (LAM)
AMDT 1 12152 (FAA)

TAKEOFF MINIMUMS: **Rwy 27,** NA-obstacles and airport restriction.

DEPARTURE PROCEDURE: **Rwy 9,** climb heading 092° to intercept SAF R-354. Northbound climbing to 11000 on V83. Southbound climbing to 9000 on V83.

NOTE: **Rwy 9,** terrain and trees beginning 101' from DER, 178' left and right of centerline, up to 60' AGL/7139' MSL.

LOVINGTON, NM
LEA COUNTY-ZIP FRANKLIN MEMORIAL (E06)
AMDT 1 99364 (FAA)

DEPARTURE PROCEDURE: **Rwy 3,** climb runway heading to 4700 before turning on course.

NOTE: **Rwy 12,** 35' AGL power line 1250' from DER 150' right of centerline. **Rwy 21,** 40' AGL tower 936' from DER 273' right of centerline. **Rwy 30,** 50' AGL windmill 1800' from DER 50' right of centerline.

MEEKER, CO
MEEKER (EEO)
AMDT 1 08157 (FAA)

TAKEOFF MINIMUMS: **Rwys 3, 21,** 4100-3 for climb in visual conditions.

DEPARTURE PROCEDURE: **Rwys 3, 21,** for climb in visual conditions: cross Meeker Airport at or above 10500 before proceeding on course.

NOTE: **Rwy 21,** multiple trees beginning 843' from DER, 20' left of centerline, up to 100' AGL/7190' MSL. Multiple trees beginning 227' from DER, 187' right of centerline, up to 100' AGL/6862' MSL.

MONTE VISTA, CO
MONTE VISTA MUNI (MVI)
AMDT 3 01025 (FAA)

DEPARTURE PROCEDURE: **Rwy 2,** climbing right turn. **Rwy 20,** climbing left turn. **All aircraft,** climb direct ALS VORTAC, continue climb in ALS holding pattern (SE, right turns, 301° inbound) to cross ALS VORTAC at or above 11000, except V210 westbound 11200 and J102 northeast bound 13700, before proceeding enroute.

13262

TAKEOFF MINIMUMS AND (OBSTACLE) DEPARTURE PROCEDURES

FIGURE 225.—Takeoff Minimums and (Obstacle) Departure Procedures.

LAMAR MUNI (LAA) 3 SW UTC–7(–6DT) N38°04.18´ W102°41.31´ **WICHITA**
3706 B S4 **FUEL** 100LL, JET A OX 1, 3 NOTAM FILE LAA **H–5A, L–10G**
RWY 18–36: H6304X100 (CONC–GRVD) S–45, D–55, 2D–100 MIRL **IAP**
0.4% up S
RWY 18: REIL. VASI(V4L)—GA 3.0° TCH 45´. Road.
RWY 36: REIL. PAPI(P4L)—GA 3.0° TCH 45´. Hill.
RWY 08–26: H5001X60 (ASPH–PFC) S–35, D–50, 2D–95 MIRL
RWY 08: PAPI(P2L)—GA 3.0° TCH 30´. Road.
RWY 26: REIL. PAPI(P2L)—GA 3.0° TCH 31´. Fence.
AIRPORT REMARKS: Attended 1500–0100Z‡. For svc after hrs phone 719–336–7701. Be alert, intensive USAF student training invof Colorado Springs and Pueblo Colorado. Rwy 18–36 now has distance remaining signs. Twr 500´ AGL 4.5 mile SE unlighted. ACTIVATE MIRL Rwy 08–26 and Rwy 18–36—CTAF. NOTE: See Special Notices—Aerobatic Operations in Colorado. USAF 306 FTG Flight Training Areas, Vicinity of Colorado Springs and Pueblo Colorado.
WEATHER DATA SOURCES: ASOS 135.625 (719) 336–3854.
COMMUNICATIONS: CTAF/UNICOM 122.8
DENVER CENTER APP/DEP CON 133.4
RADIO AIDS TO NAVIGATION: NOTAM FILE LAA.
(H) VORW/DME 116.9 LAA Chan 116 N38°11.83´ W102°41.25´ 168° 7.6 NM to fld. 3944/12E.

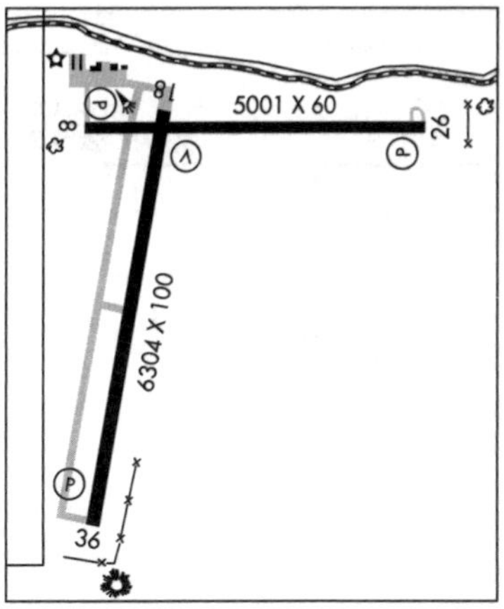

LAS ANIMAS

CITY OF LAS ANIMAS – BENT CO (7V9) 1 S UTC–7(–6DT) N38°03.24´ W103°14.31´ **WICHITA**
3915 S4 NOTAM FILE DEN **L–10F**
RWY 08–26: H3870X40 (ASPH) S–5 HIRL 0.4% up W
RWY 08: REIL. Fence.
RWY 26: REIL. Road.
AIRPORT REMARKS: Attended Mon–Sat 1500–0000Z‡. Be alert, intensive USAF student training invof Colorado Springs and Pueblo Colorado. Rwy 26 has +30´ poles 105´ from thld 210´ left of extd rwy centerline, +15´ tank 321´ from rwy end 270´ right of centerline. Thld lgts NSTD; three lgts each end. Thld lgts OTS indef. Rwy 08 thld lgts 23´ from thld. Rwy 26 thld lgts 12´ from thld. Rwy 08 numbers located 216´ from pavement end, Rwy 08–26 numbers smaller than standard, no centerline markings. ACTIVATE HIRL Rwy 08–26—CTAF. Med ints 5 clicks, high ints 7 clicks. See Special Notices—USAF 306 FTG Flight Training Areas, Vicinity of Colorado Springs and Pueblo Colorado.
COMMUNICATIONS: CTAF 122.9
RADIO AIDS TO NAVIGATION: NOTAM FILE LAA.
LAMAR (H) VORW/DME 116.9 LAA Chan 116 N38°11.83´ W102°41.25´ 240° 27.5 NM to fld. 3944/12E.

LEACH (See CENTER on page 220)

LEADVILLE

LAKE CO (LXV) 2 SW UTC–7(–6DT) N39°13.17´ W106°18.99´ **DENVER**
9934 B **FUEL** 100LL, JET A NOTAM FILE LXV **H–3F, 5A, L–9E**
RWY 16–34: H6400X75 (ASPH) S–20, D–20 MIRL **IAP**
RWY 16: PAPI(P2L)—GA 3.0° TCH 45´. Rgt tfc.
RWY 34: PAPI(P2L)—GA 3.0° TCH 45´.
AIRPORT REMARKS: Attended May–Oct 1430–2330Z‡, Nov–Apr 1500–2330Z‡. For svc after hrs call sheriff dispatch 719–486–1249. PPR for svc after hrs call 719–293–5110. Rwy 34 has +50´ power lines 750´ from right of thld. Twy C and old ramp have potholes and loose aggregate. All twys and new ramp area marked with blue and white reflectors. ACTIVATE MIRL Rwy 16–34 and PAPI Rwy 16 and Rwy 34—CTAF.
WEATHER DATA SOURCES: ASOS 118.375 (719) 486–2735.
COMMUNICATIONS: CTAF/UNICOM 122.8
DENVER CENTER APP/DEP CON 119.85
RADIO AIDS TO NAVIGATION: NOTAM FILE DEN.
RED TABLE (H) VORW/DME 113.0 DBL Chan 77 N39°26.36´ W106°53.68´ 104° 30.0 NM to fld. 11800/12E.

• • • • • • • • • • • •

HELIPAD H1: H150X100 (ASPH–CONC)
HELIPORT REMARKS: Rwy H1 has 6–8 inch lip all around edges, concrete has longitudinal and corner cracking. Rwy H1 has 20´ to 30´ trees 130´ east of pad.

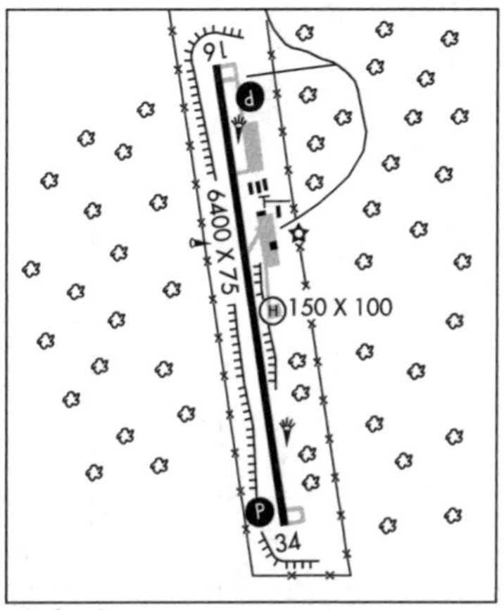

FIGURE 226.—Excerpt from Chart Supplement.

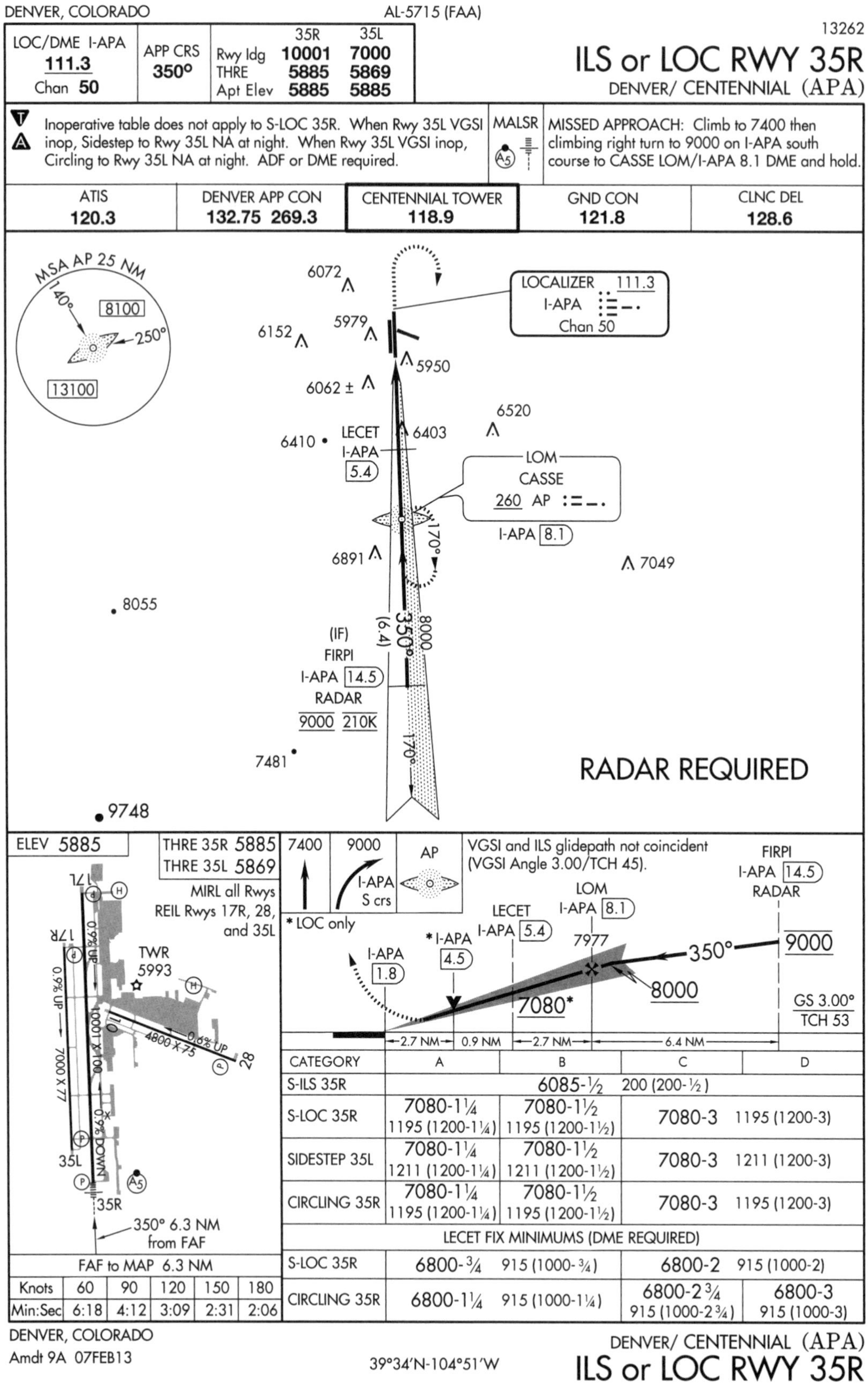

FIGURE 227.—ILS or LOC RWY 35R (APA).

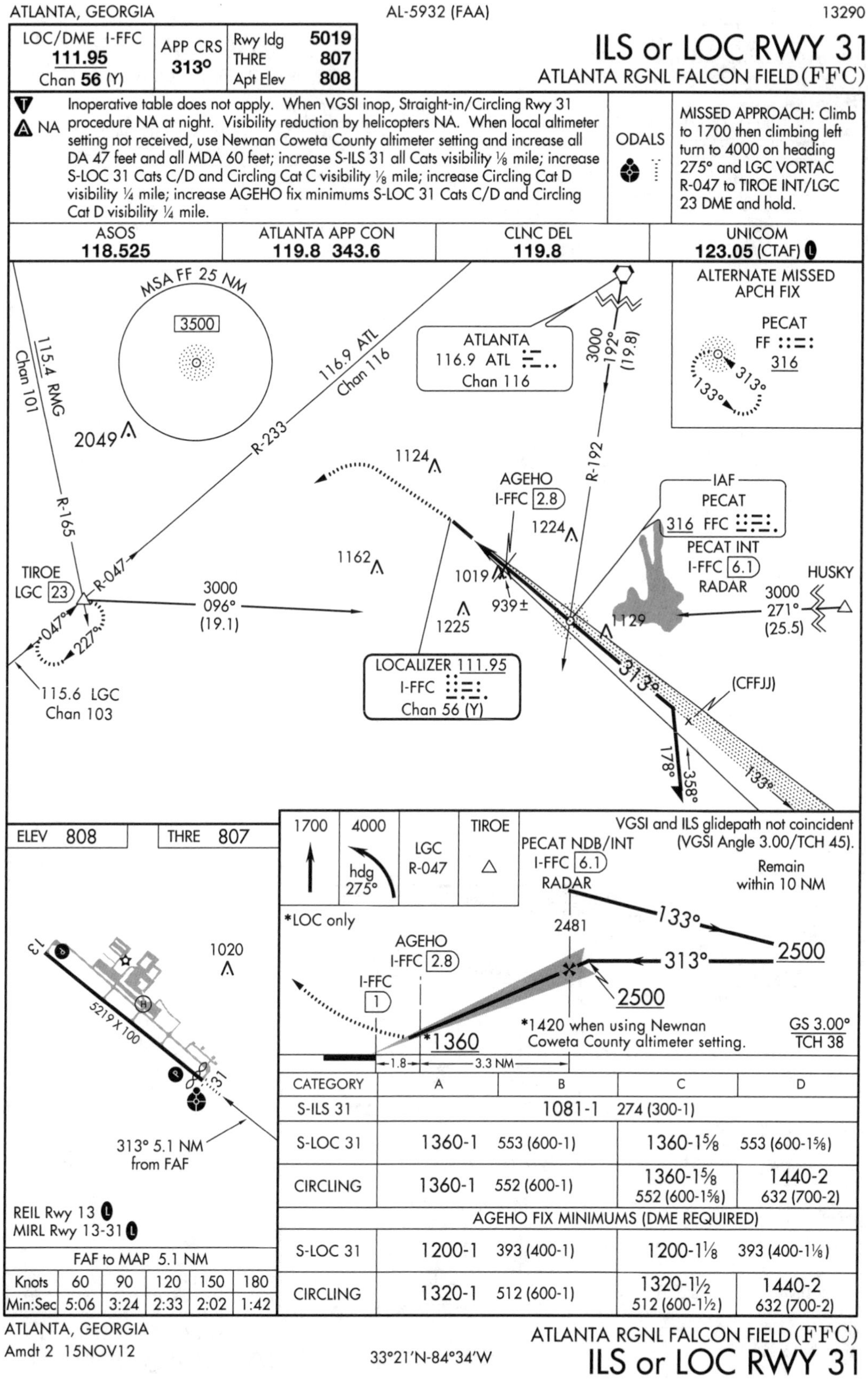

FIGURE 228.—ILS or LOC RWY 31 (FFC).

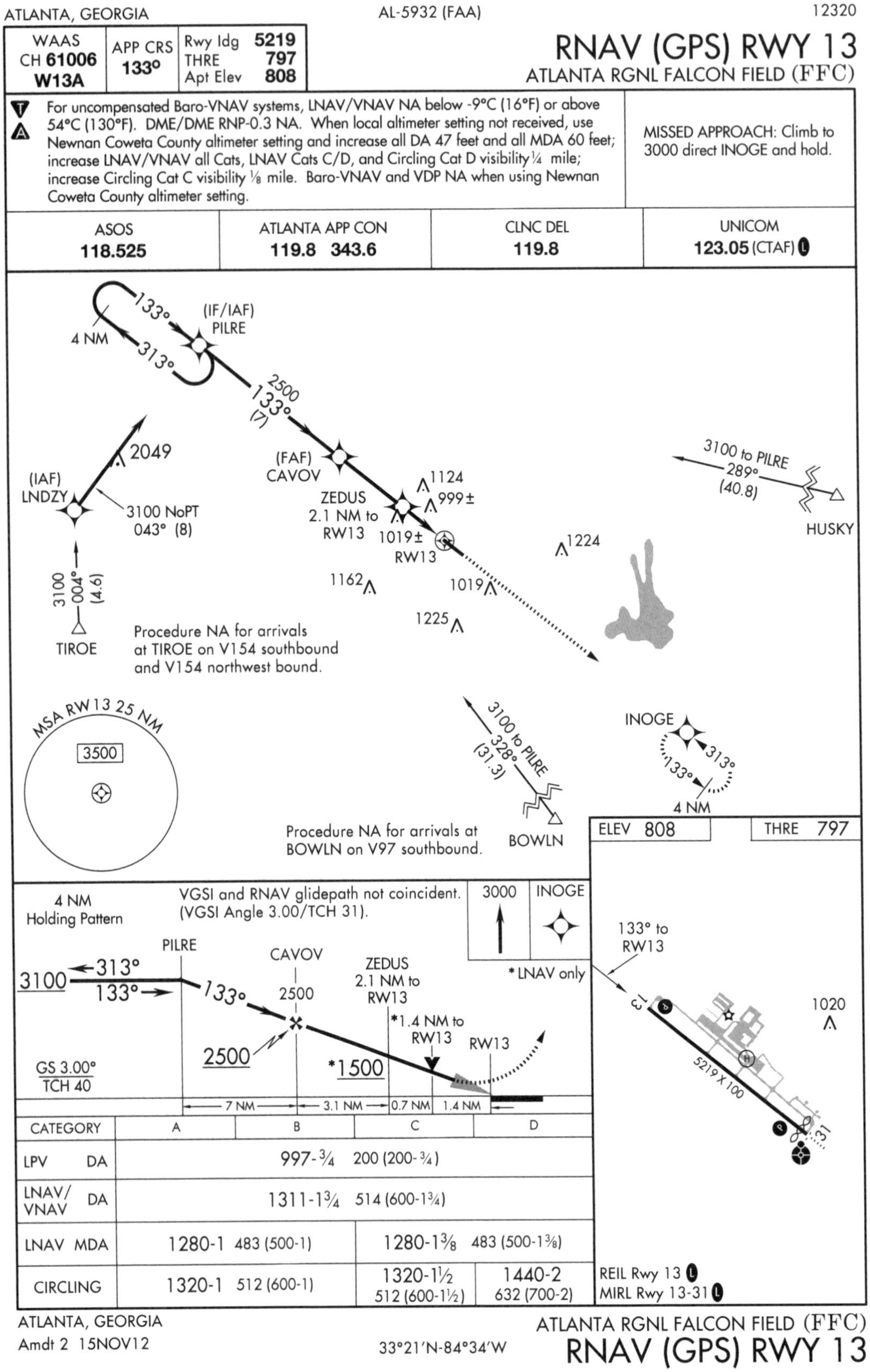

FIGURE 229.—RNAV (GPS) RWY 13 (FFC).

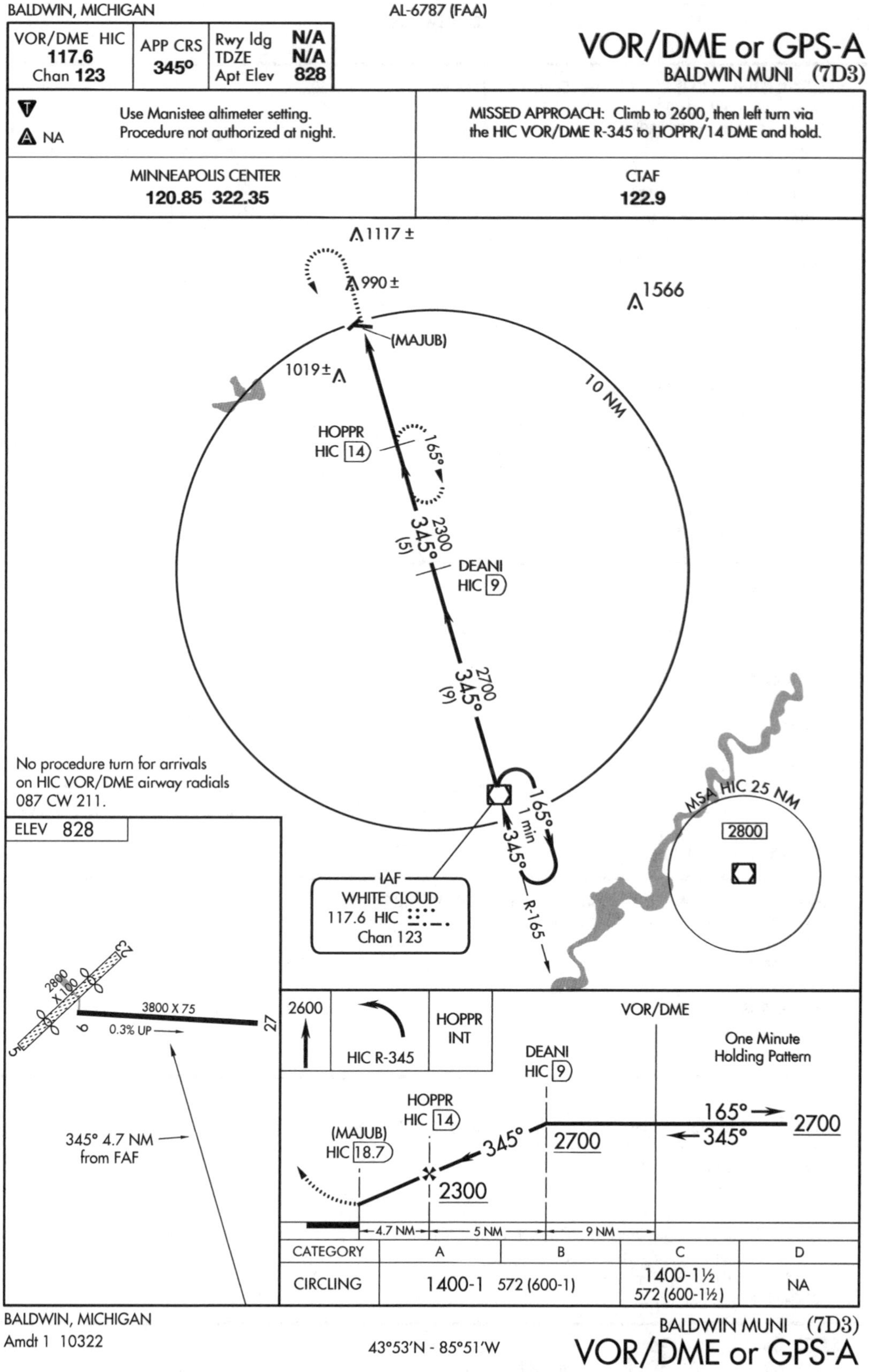

FIGURE 230.—VOR/DME or GPS-A (7D3).

130 **MICHIGAN**

BALDWIN MUNI (7D3) 2 S UTC–5(–4DT) N43°52.53´ W85°50.53´ **CHICAGO**
828 TPA—1828(1000) NOTAM FILE LAN **L–28I**
RWY 09–27: H3800X75 (ASPH) S–10 0.3% up E **IAP**
RWY 09: Trees.
RWY 27: Trees.
RWY 05–23: 2800X100 (TURF)
RWY 05: Thld dsplcd 800´. Trees.
RWY 23: Thld dsplcd 800´. Trees.
AIRPORT REMARKS: Unattended. Deer on and invof arpt. Arpt CLOSED Nov thru Apr; no snow removal. Arpt manager cell 231–250–2551. Rwy 09–27 sfc considerable pavement cracking with vegetation growing through cracks. Rwy 05–23 and dsplcd thlds marked with 3´ yellow cones.
COMMUNICATIONS: CTAF 122.9
Ⓡ**MINNEAPOLIS CENTER APP/DEP CON** 120.85
RADIO AIDS TO NAVIGATION: NOTAM FILE LAN.
WHITE CLOUD (L) VOR/DME 117.6 HIC Chan 123 N43°34.49´ W85°42.97´ 344° 18.9 NM to fld. 920/1W.
VOR/DME unusable:
020°–090° byd 30 NM blo 3,000´
DME portion unusable:
270°–290° byd 35 NM blo 3,000´

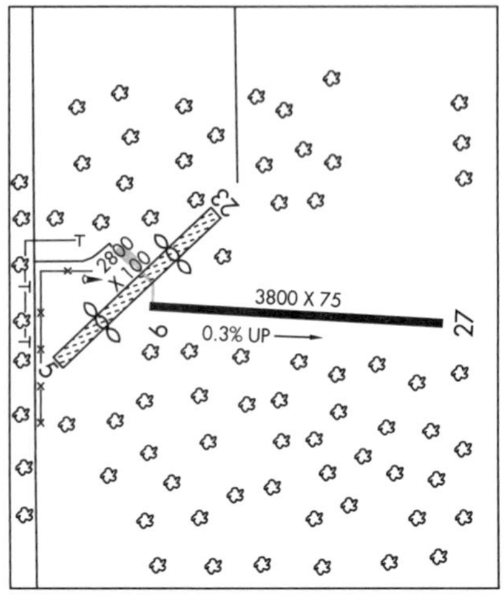

BANGU N45°00.88´ W84°48.49´ NOTAM FILE GLR. **LAKE HURON**
NDB (LOM) 375 GL 097° 4.5 NM to Gaylord Rgnl. Unmonitored.

BANNISTER

SHADY LAWN FLD (4M4) 2 E UTC–5(–4DT) N43°07.72´ W84°22.88´ **CHICAGO**
680 TPA—1680(1000) NOTAM FILE LAN
RWY 09–27: 1850X50 (TURF) LIRL
RWY 09: Bldg.
RWY 27: Trees.
AIRPORT REMARKS: Attended irregularly. Ultralight and AG activity on and invof arpt. Deer and birds on and invof arpt. Crops adjacent to rwy during summer months. NSTD LIRL color and configuration, by prior arrangement. Rwy 09 and Rwy 27 marked by 3´ yellow cones.
COMMUNICATIONS: CTAF 122.9

BARAGA (2P4) 4 W UTC–5(–4DT) N46°47.10´ W88°34.67´ **GREEN BAY**
845 TPA—1845(1000) NOTAM FILE GRB
RWY 09–27: 2200X100 (TURF)
RWY 09: Trees.
RWY 27: Trees.
AIRPORT REMARKS: Unattended. Arpt CLOSED Nov–Apr except to ski equipped acft. 25´ p–line 850´ from thld Rwy 27. Deer and birds on and invof arpt.
COMMUNICATIONS: CTAF 122.9

BATH

UNIVERSITY AIRPARK (41G) 2 NW UTC–5(–4DT) N42°50.42´ W84°28.75´ **DETROIT**
856 B S2 NOTAM FILE LAN
RWY 08–26: 1988X100 (TURF) LIRL
RWY 08: Trees.
RWY 26: Tree.
AIRPORT REMARKS: Attended irregularly. Rwy 08–26 occasionally soft/wet areas E end during spring thaw and after heavy rain. ACTIVATE LIRL Rwy 08–26 and NSTD rotating bcn—122.85. NSTD flashing strobe and alternating white/red bcn. Rwy 08–26 marked with 3´ yellow cones.
COMMUNICATIONS: CTAF 122.9

BATOL N42°21.72´ W85°11.07´ NOTAM FILE BTL. **CHICAGO**
NDB (MHW/LOM) 272 BT 225° 4.4 NM to W K Kellogg. **L–28I**

FIGURE 231.—Excerpt from Chart Supplement.

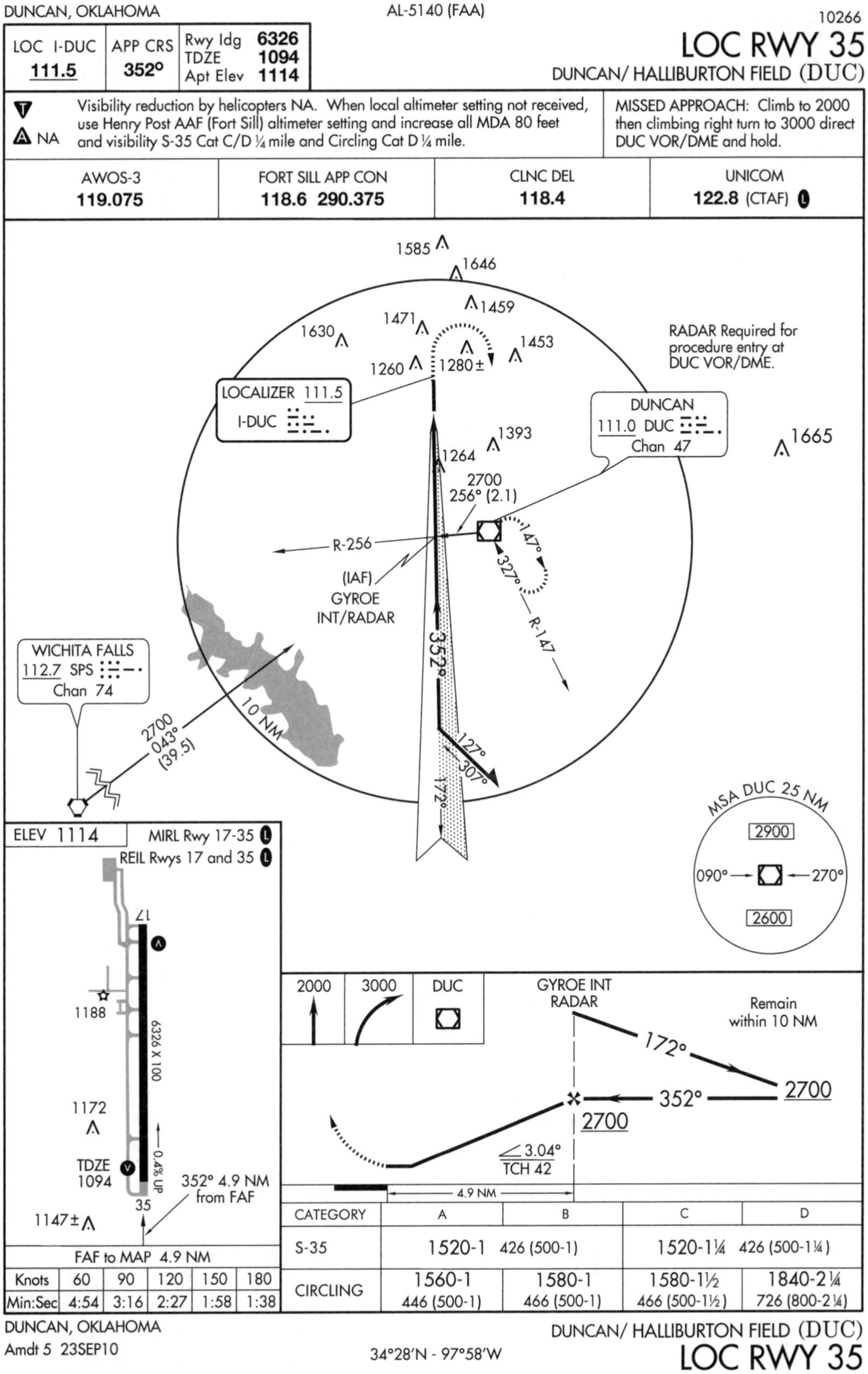

FIGURE 232.—LOC RWY 35 (DUC).

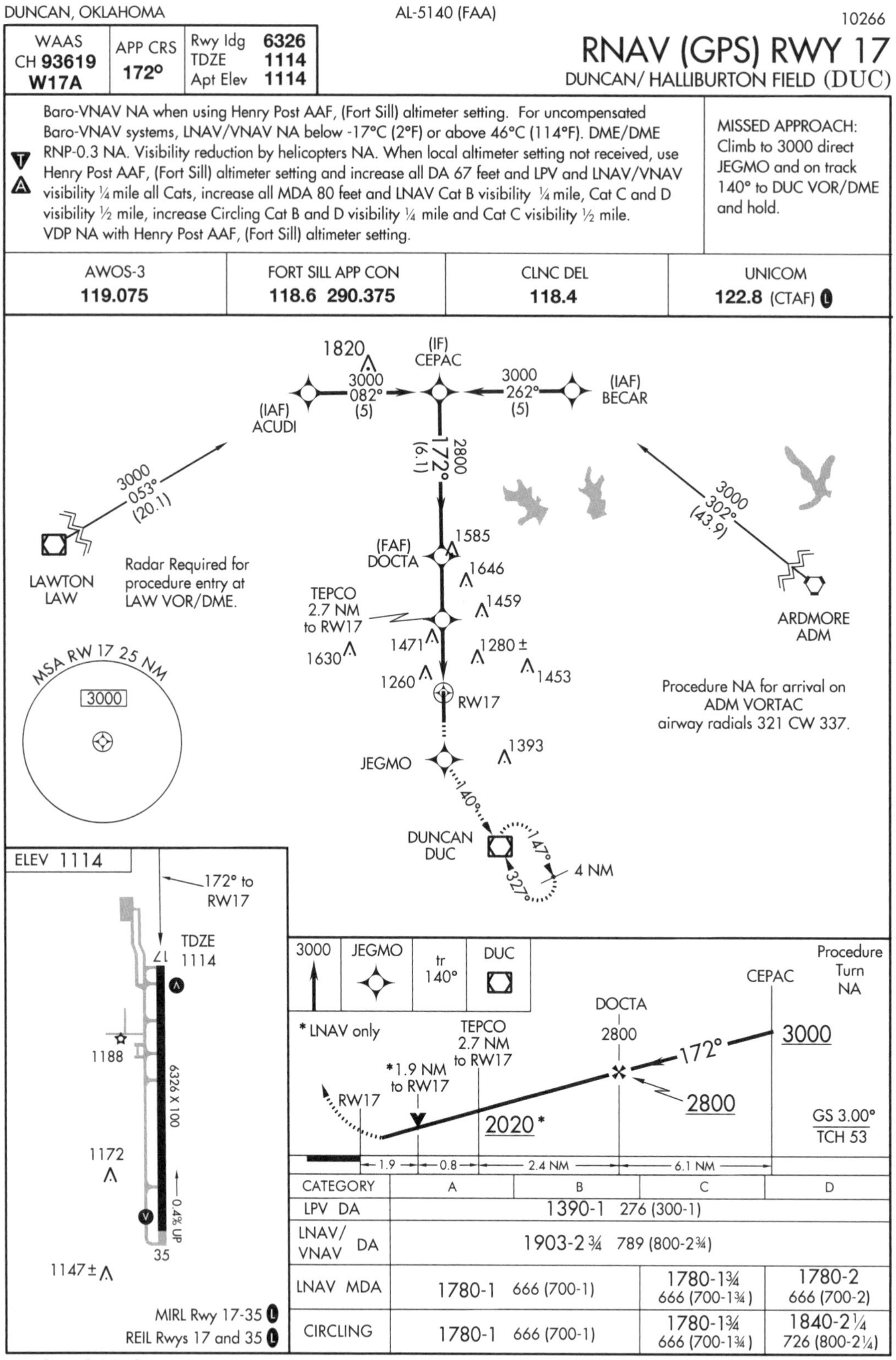

CATEGORY	A	B	C	D
LPV DA	1390-1 276 (300-1)			
LNAV/VNAV DA	1903-2¾ 789 (800-2¾)			
LNAV MDA	1780-1 666 (700-1)		1780-1¾ 666 (700-1¾)	1780-2 666 (700-2)
CIRCLING	1780-1 666 (700-1)		1780-1¾ 666 (700-1¾)	1840-2¼ 726 (800-2¼)

DUNCAN, OKLAHOMA
Amdt 1 23SEP10
34°28'N - 97°58'W
DUNCAN/ HALLIBURTON FIELD (DUC)
RNAV (GPS) RWY 17

FIGURE 233.—RNAV (GPS) RWY 17 (DUC).

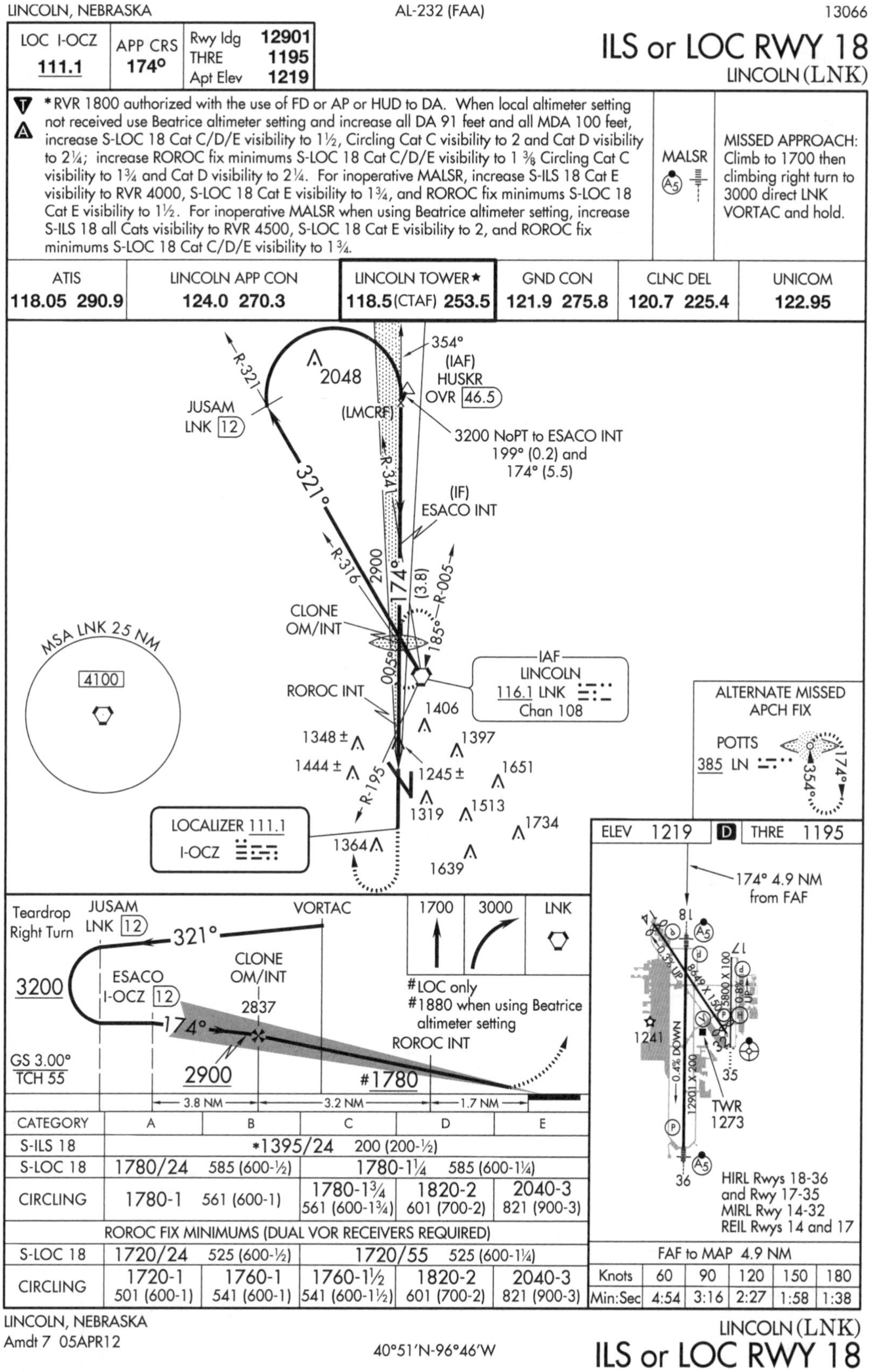

CATEGORY	A	B	C	D	E
S-ILS 18	*1395/24 200 (200-½)				
S-LOC 18	1780/24 585 (600-½)		1780-1¼ 585 (600-1¼)		
CIRCLING	1780-1 561 (600-1)		1780-1¾ 561 (600-1¾)	1820-2 601 (700-2)	2040-3 821 (900-3)
ROROC FIX MINIMUMS (DUAL VOR RECEIVERS REQUIRED)					
S-LOC 18	1720/24 525 (600-½)		1720/55 525 (600-1¼)		
CIRCLING	1720-1 501 (600-1)	1760-1 541 (600-1)	1760-1½ 541 (600-1½)	1820-2 601 (700-2)	2040-3 821 (900-3)

FAF to MAP 4.9 NM

Knots	60	90	120	150	180
Min:Sec	4:54	3:16	2:27	1:58	1:38

FIGURE 234.—ILS or LOC RWY 18 (LNK).

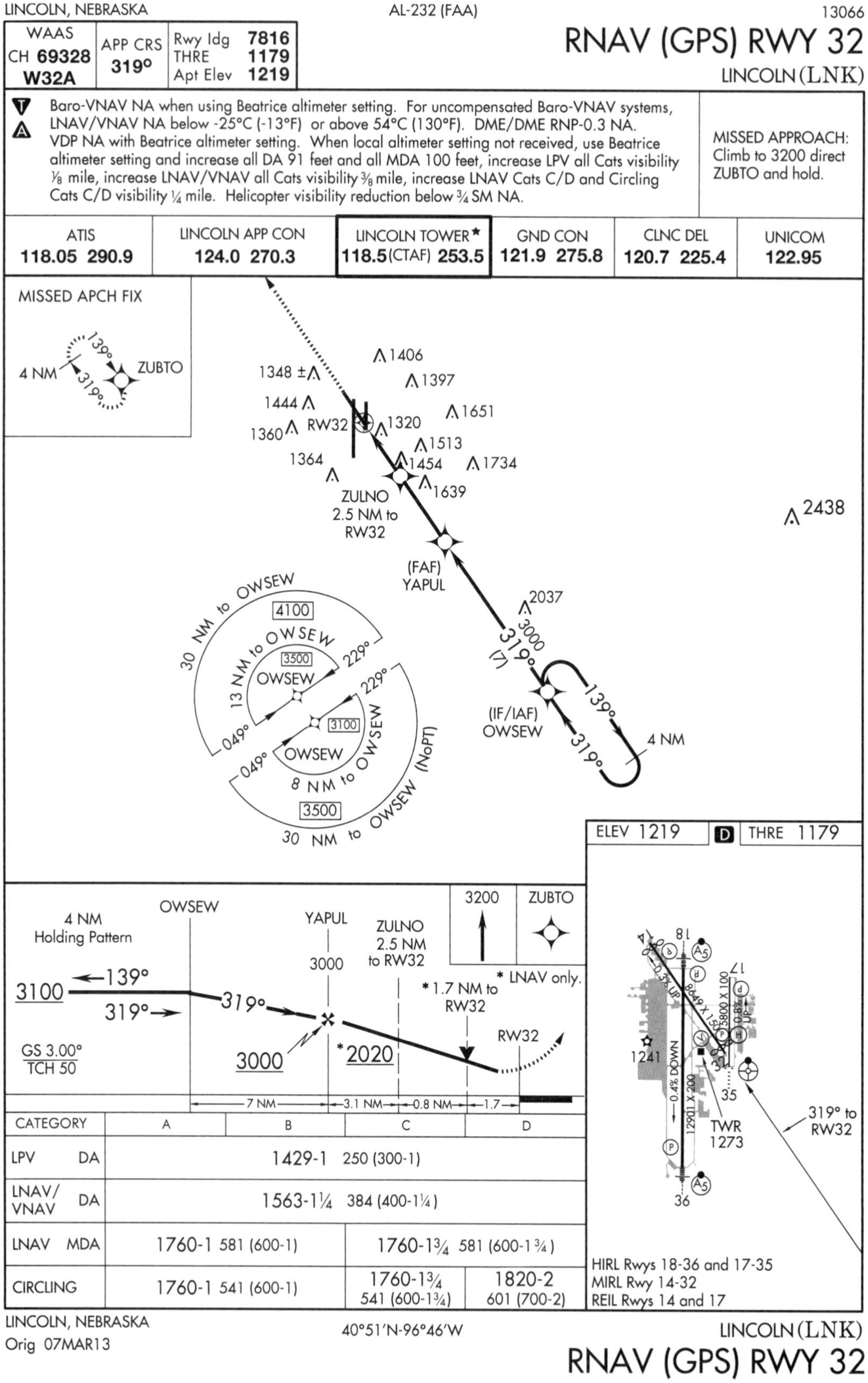

FIGURE 235.—RNAV (GPS) RWY 32 (LNK).

DOTHAN, ALABAMA — AL-123 (FAA) — 13178

ILS or LOC RWY 32
DOTHAN RGNL (DHN)

LOC I-DHN	APP CRS	Rwy ldg	8496
108.3	**318°**	THRE	382
		Apt Elev	401

**RVR 1800 authorized with use of FD or AP or HUD to DA. For inoperative MALSR, increase S-LOC 32 Cat C/D visibility to 2½ miles.

MALSR

MISSED APPROACH: Climb to 1000 then climbing right turn to 3000 on hdg 130° and RRS VORTAC R-089 to BLALY INT/RRS 19.8 DME and hold.

ATIS	CAIRNS APP CON★	DOTHAN TOWER ★	GND CON	UNICOM
135.72	125.4 327.125	118.4 (CTAF) 257.6	121.7 348.6	122.95

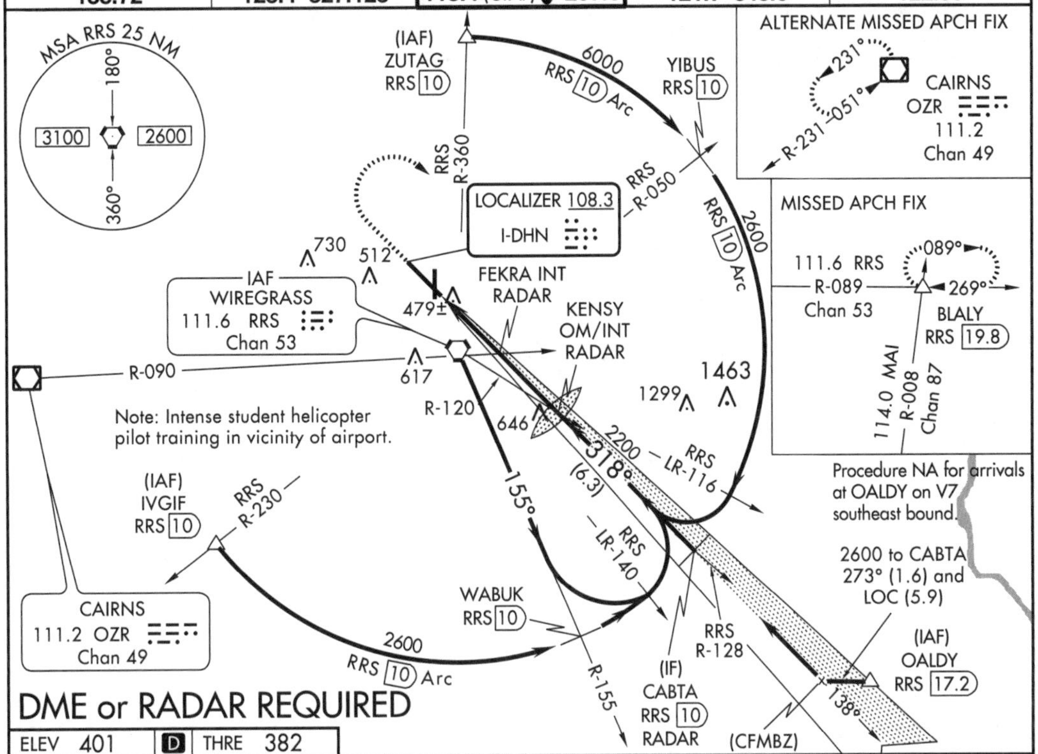

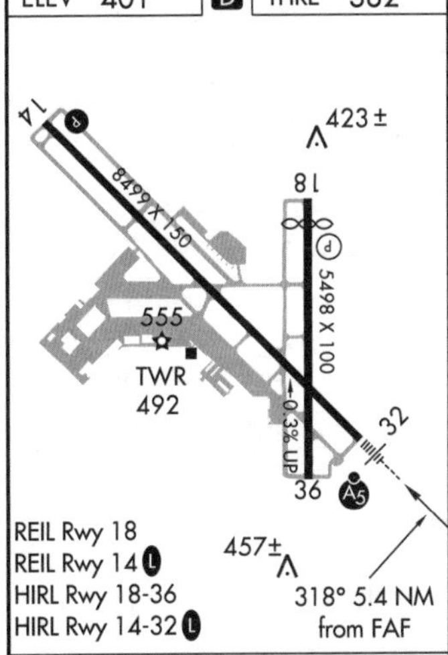

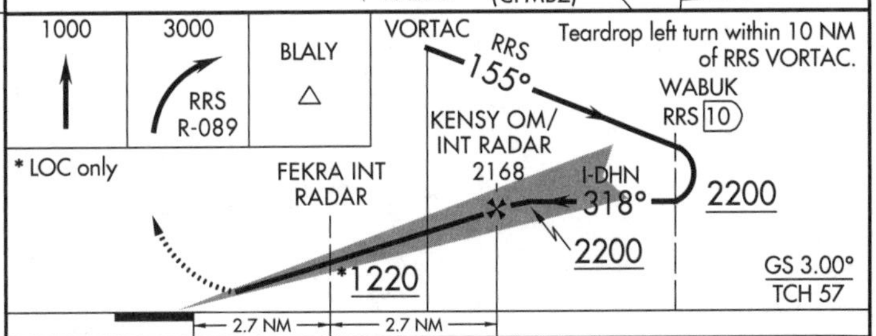

CATEGORY	A	B	C	D
S-ILS 32	**582/24 200 (200-½)			
S-LOC 32	1220/24 838 (900-½)	1220/40 838 (900-¾)	1220-1⅞ 838 (900-1⅞)	
CIRCLING	1220-1¼ 819 (900-1¼)		1220-2½ 819 (900-2½)	1220-2¾ 819 (900-2¾)
FEKRA FIX MINIMUMS (DUAL VOR RECEIVERS OR RADAR REQUIRED)				
S-LOC 32	820/24 438 (500-½)		820/40 438 (500-¾)	
CIRCLING	860-1 459 (500-1)		860-1½ 459 (500-1½)	960-2 559 (600-2)

FAF to MAP 5.4 NM

Knots	60	90	120	150	180
Min:Sec	5:24	3:36	2:42	2:10	1:48

DOTHAN, ALABAMA
Amdt 9 26JUL12 — 31°19'N-85°27'W

DOTHAN RGNL (DHN)
ILS or LOC RWY 32

FIGURE 236.—ILS or RWY 32 (DHN).

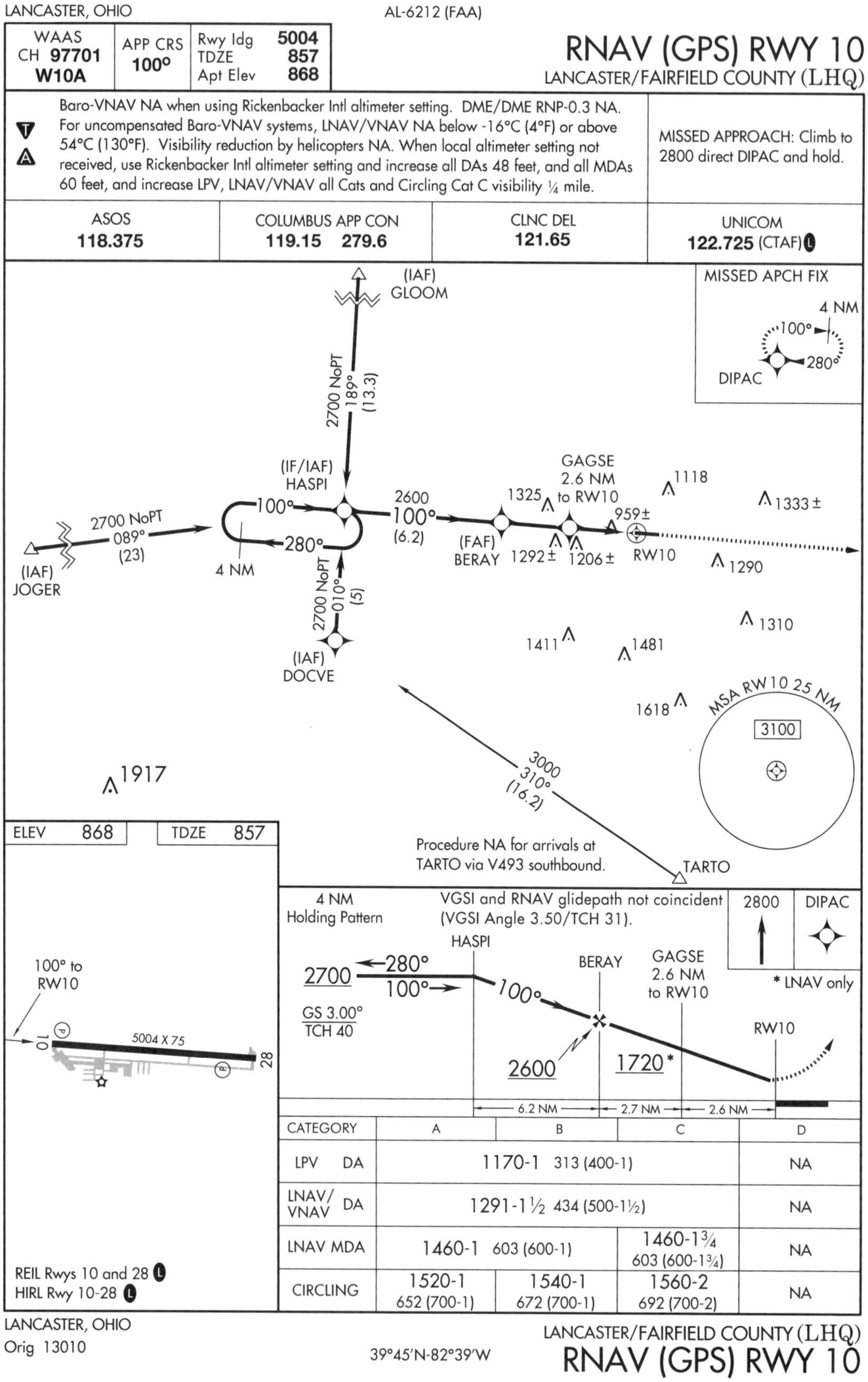

FIGURE 237.—RNAV (GPS) RWY 10 (LHQ).

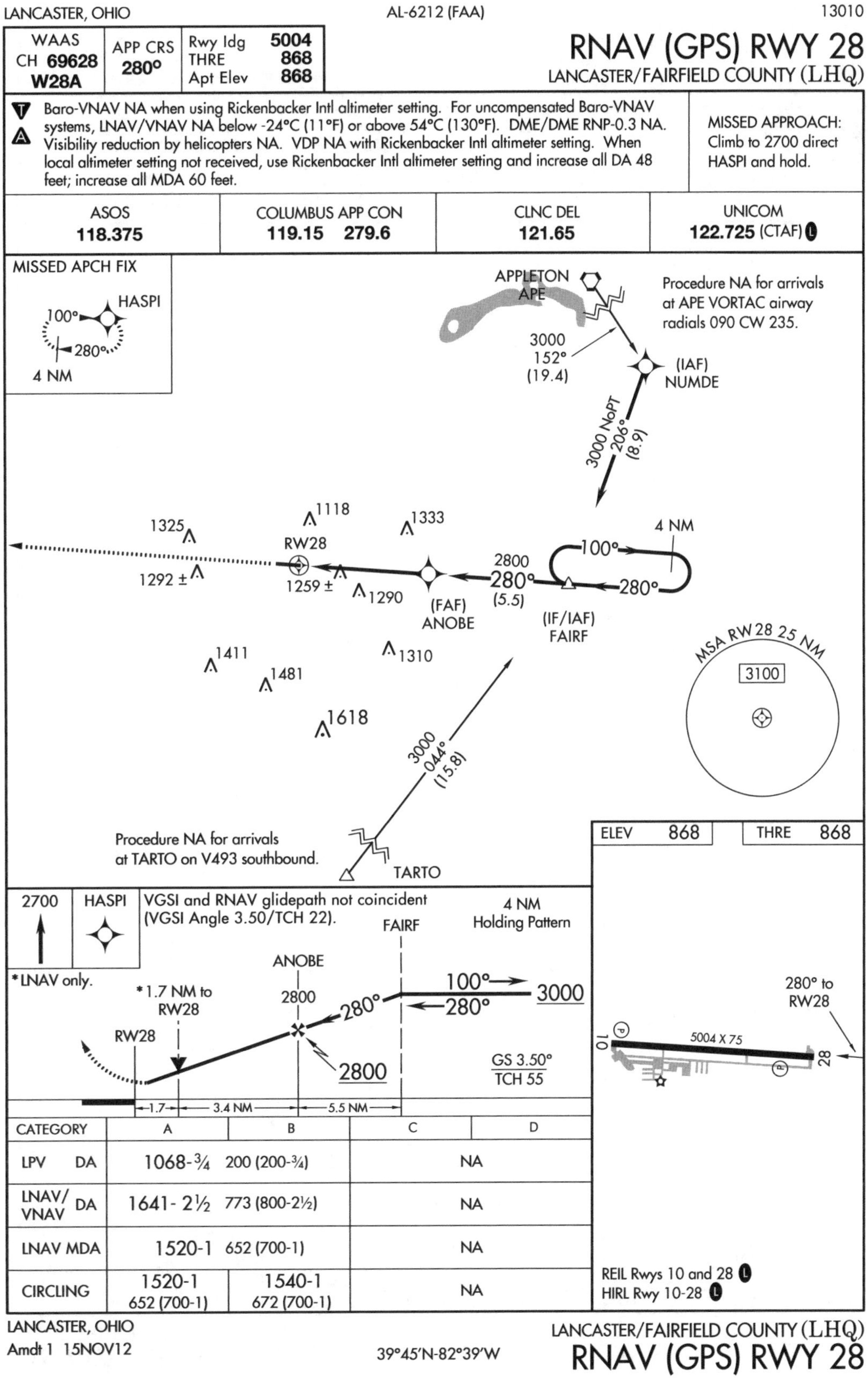

FIGURE 238.—RNAV (GPS) RWY 28 (LHQ).

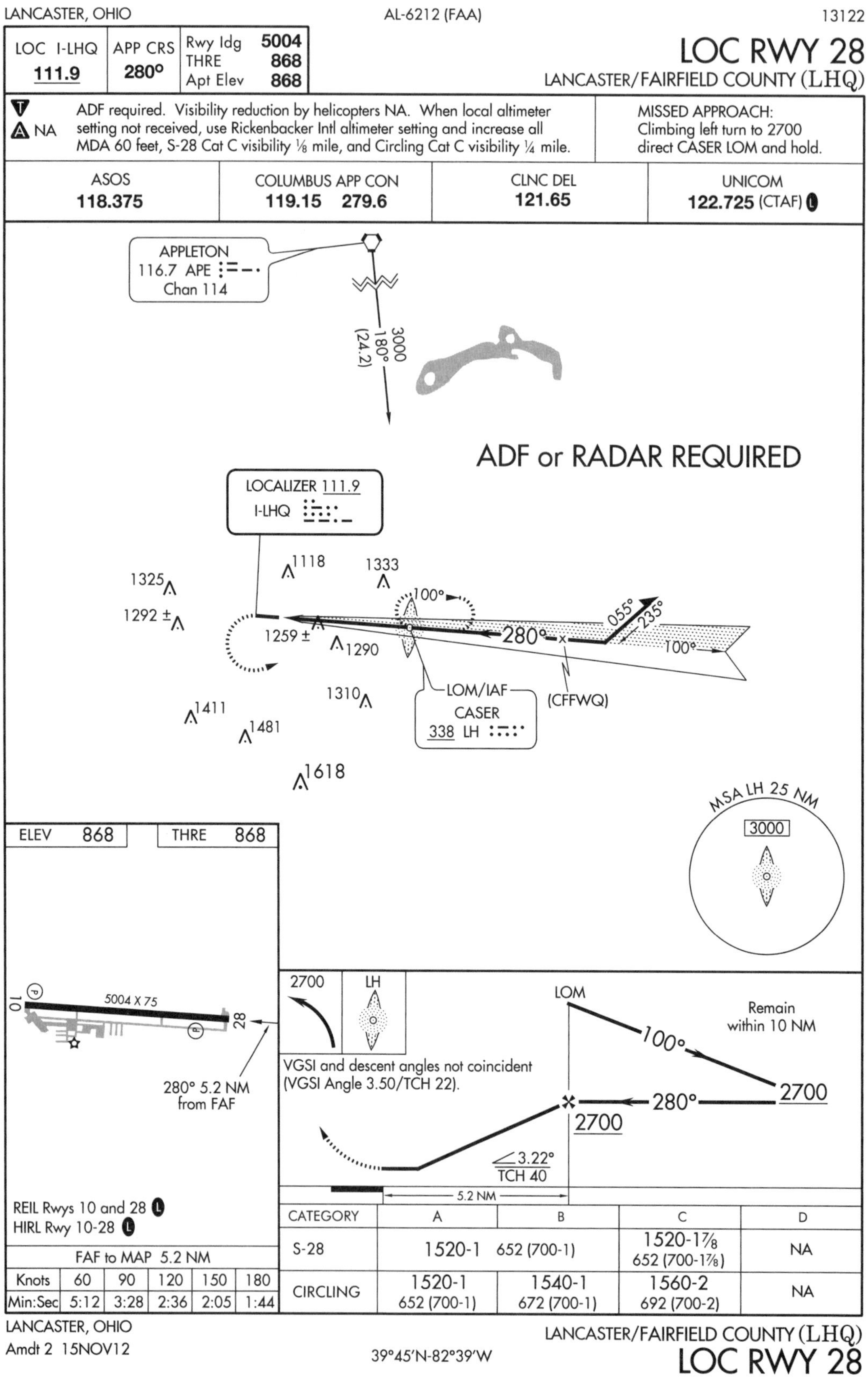

FIGURE 239.—LOC RWY 28 (LHQ).

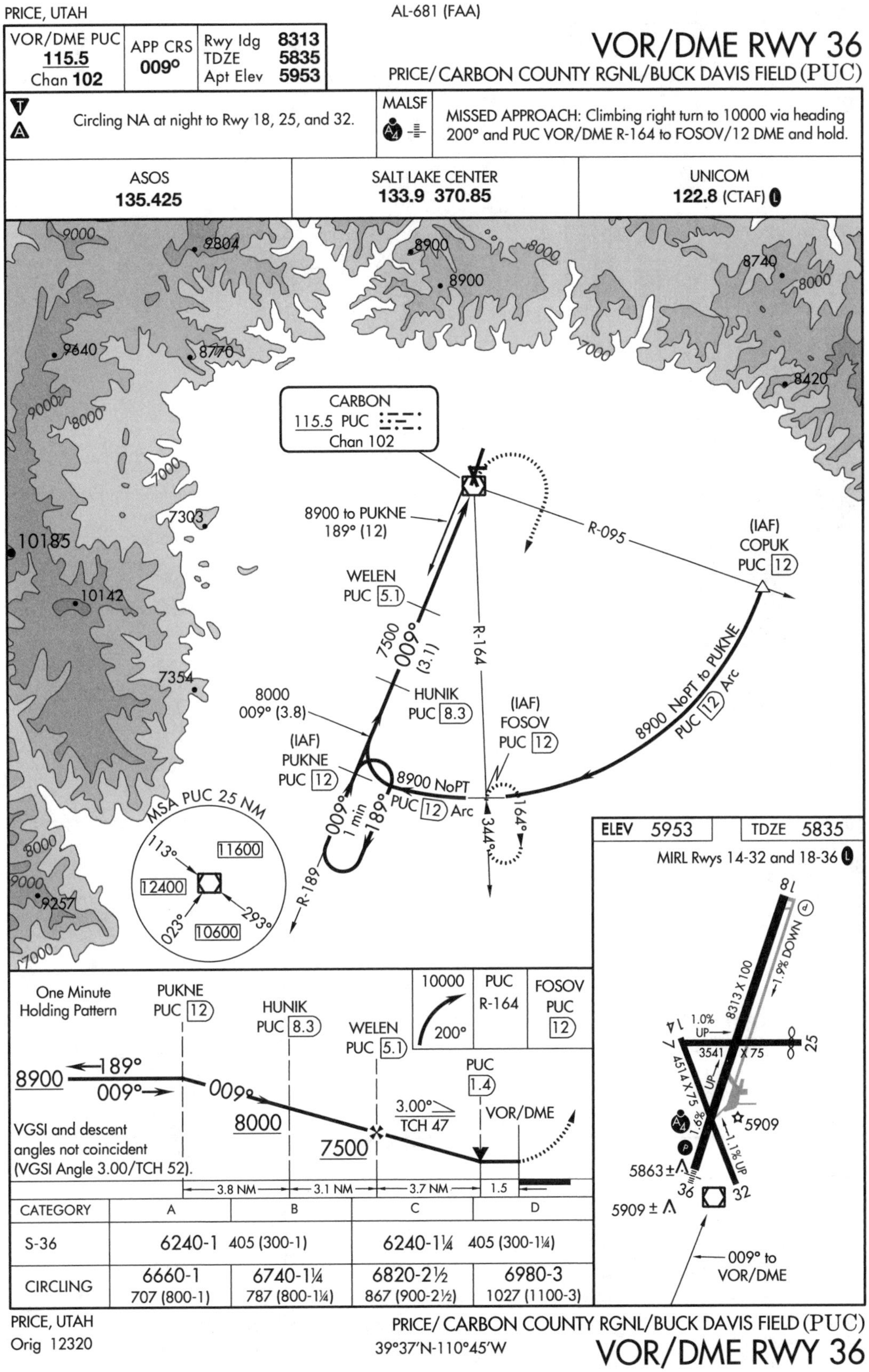

FIGURE 240.—VOR/DME RWY 36 (PUC).

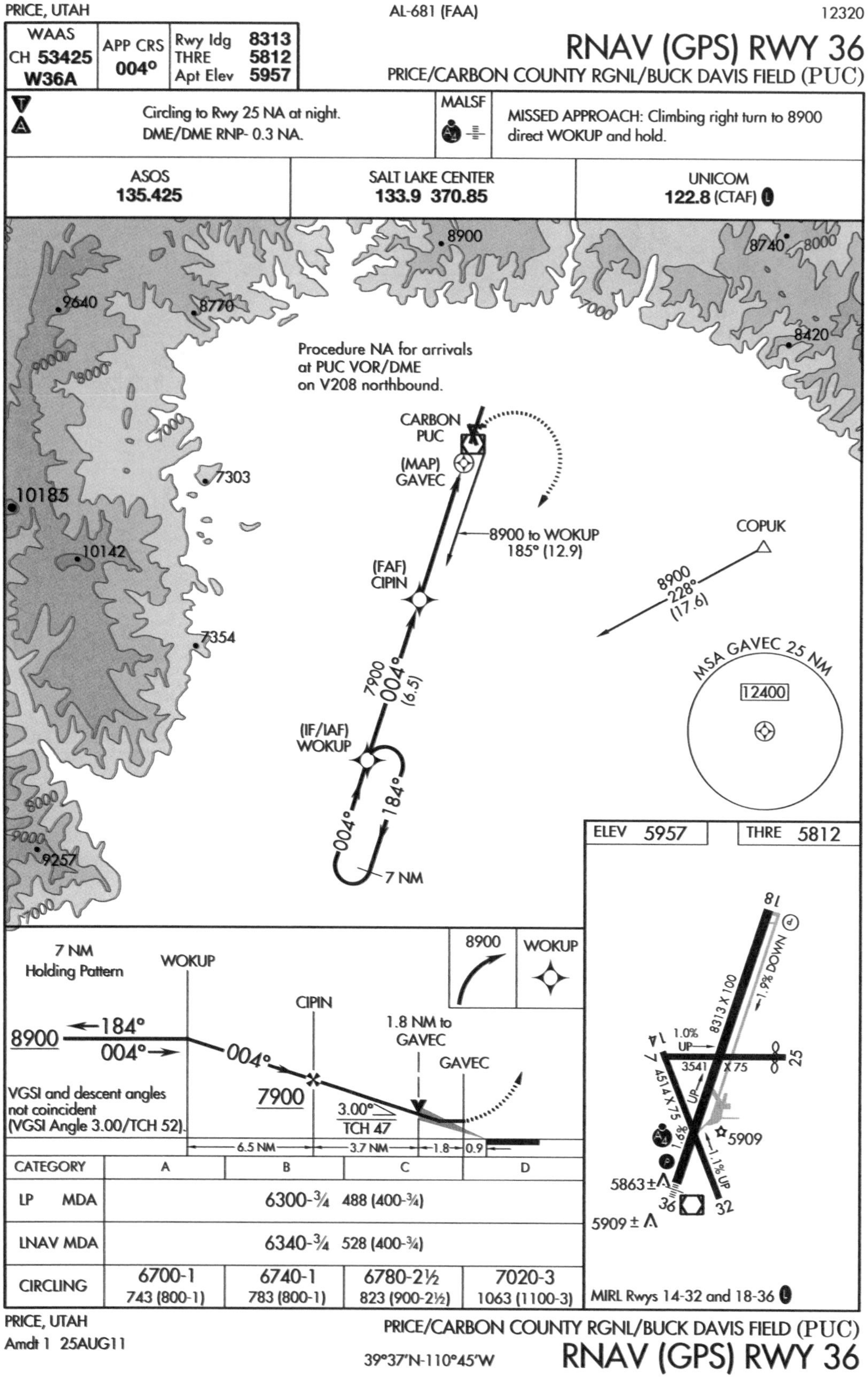

CATEGORY	A	B	C	D
LP MDA	6300-¾ 488 (400-¾)			
LNAV MDA	6340-¾ 528 (400-¾)			
CIRCLING	6700-1 743 (800-1)	6740-1 783 (800-1)	6780-2½ 823 (900-2½)	7020-3 1063 (1100-3)

FIGURE 241.—RNAV (GPS) RWY 36 (PUC).

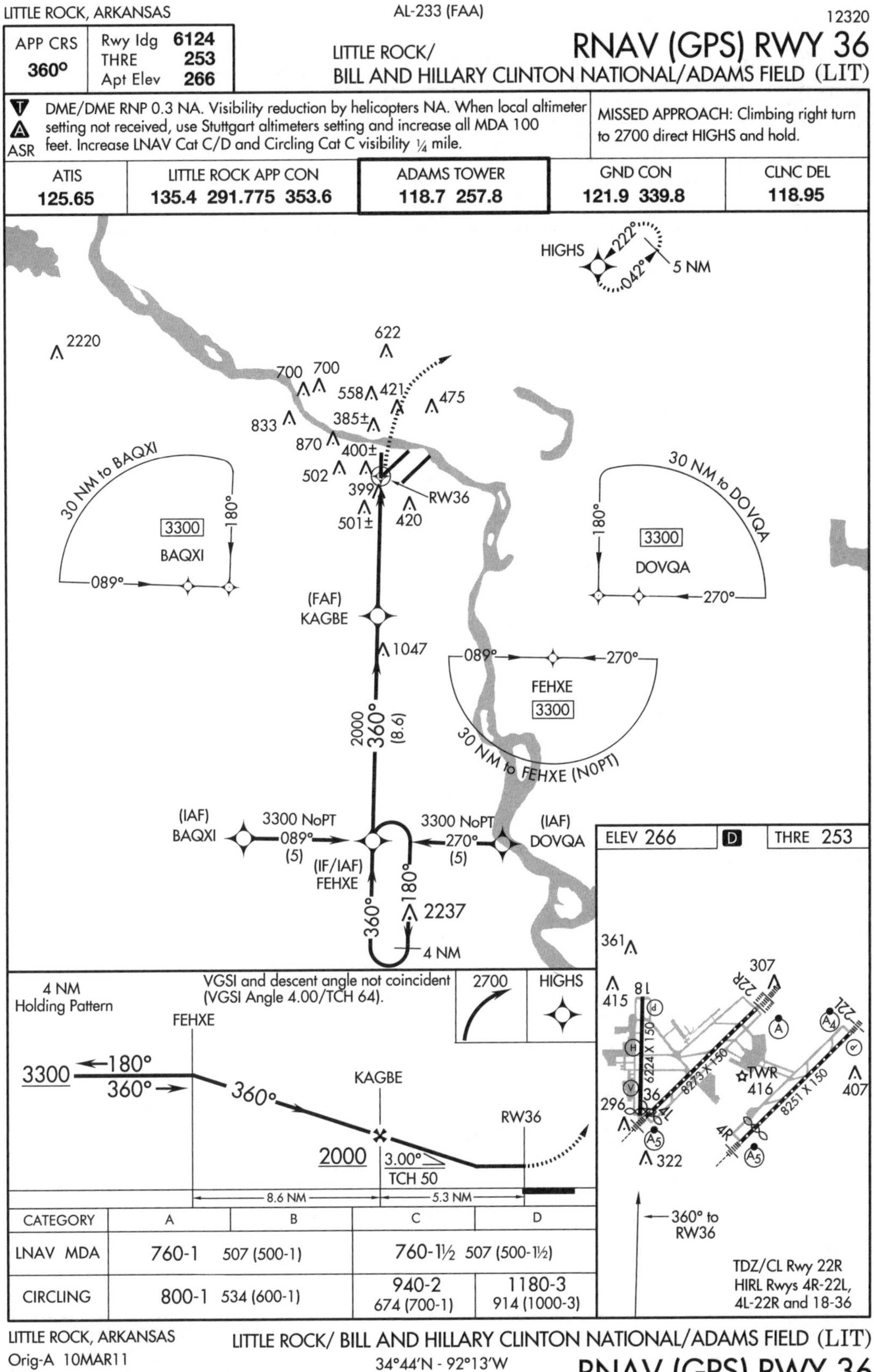

FIGURE 242.—RNAV RWY 36 (LIT).

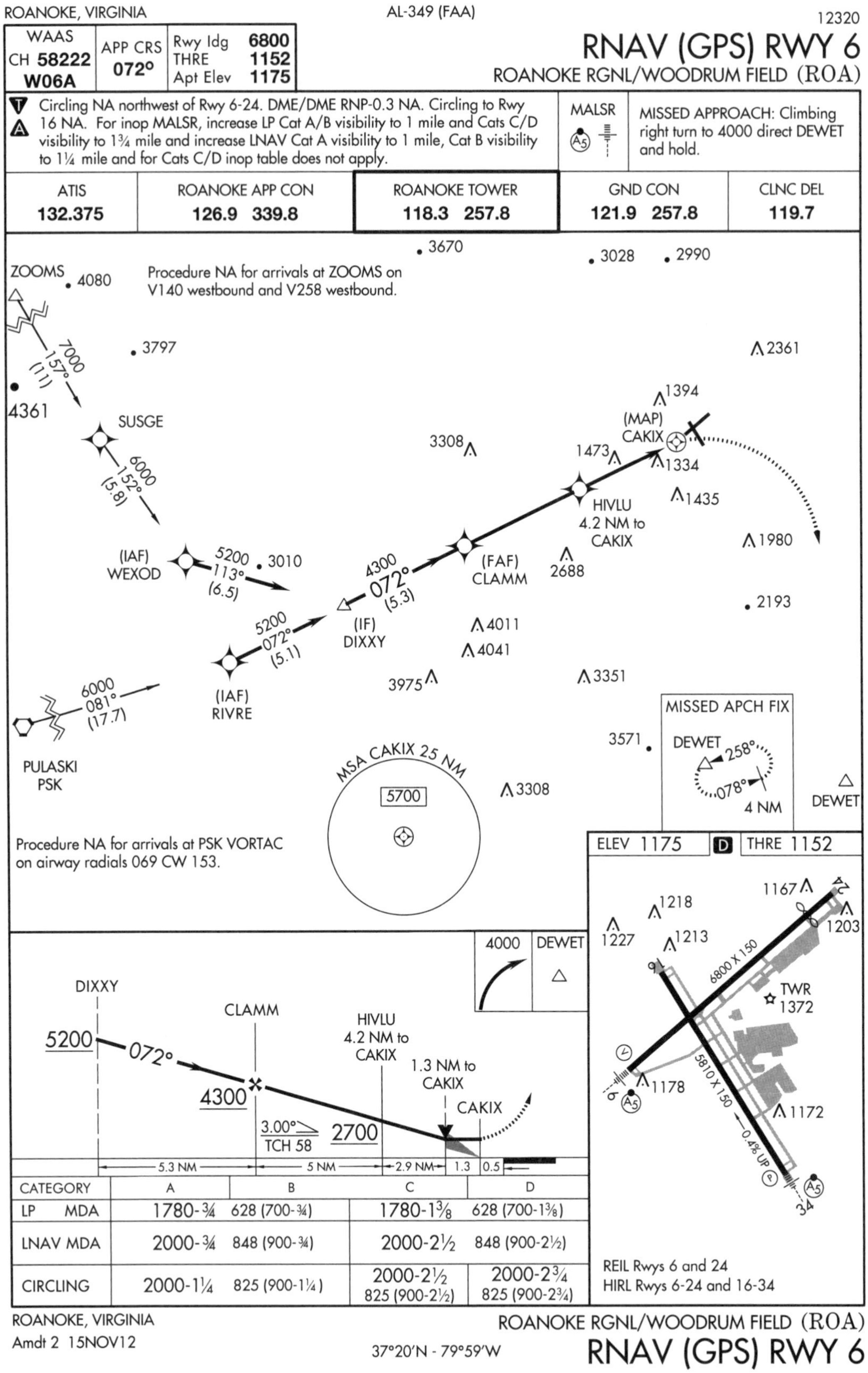

FIGURE 243.—RNAV (GPS) RWY 6 (ROA).

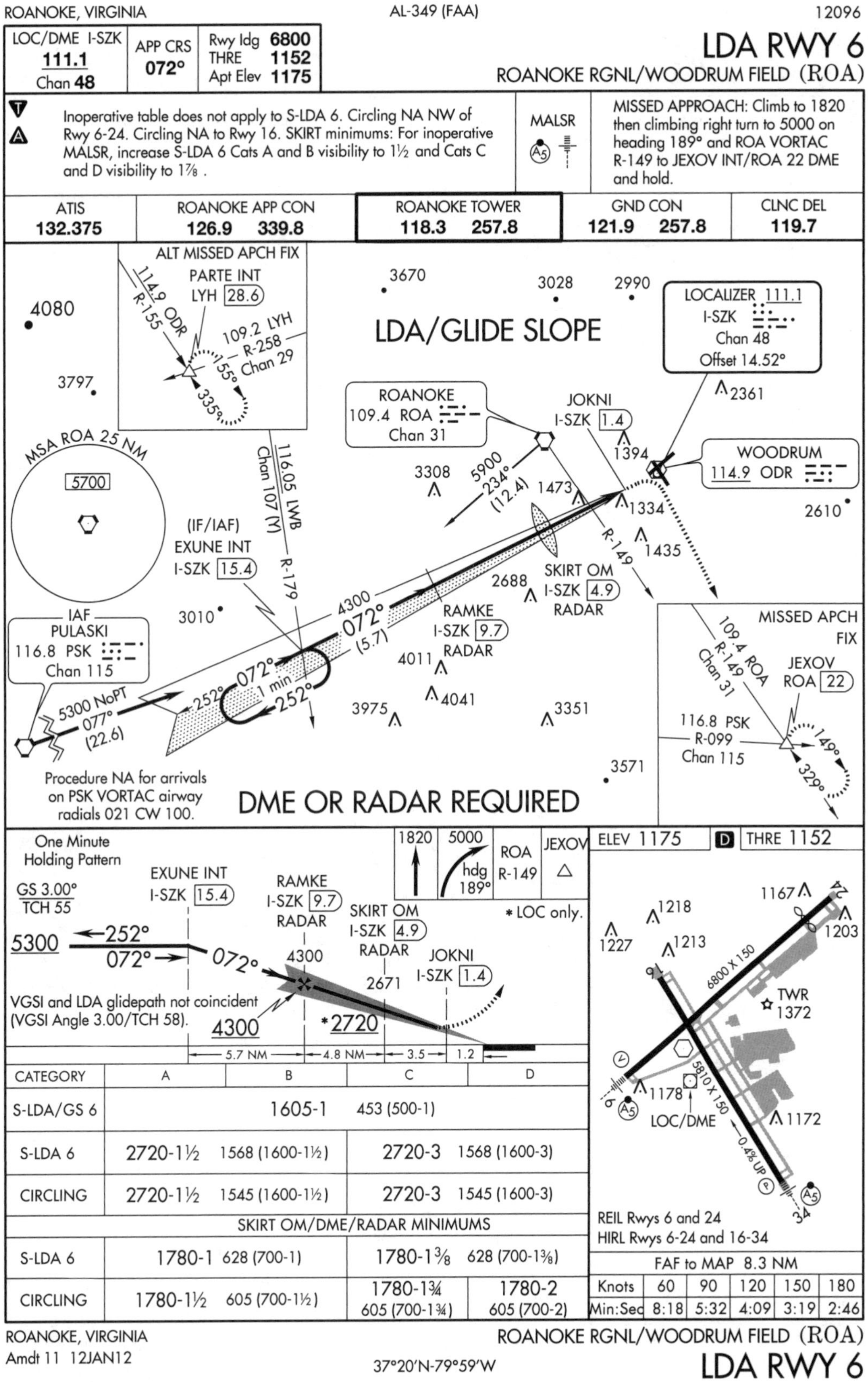

FIGURE 244.—LDA RWY 6 (ROA).

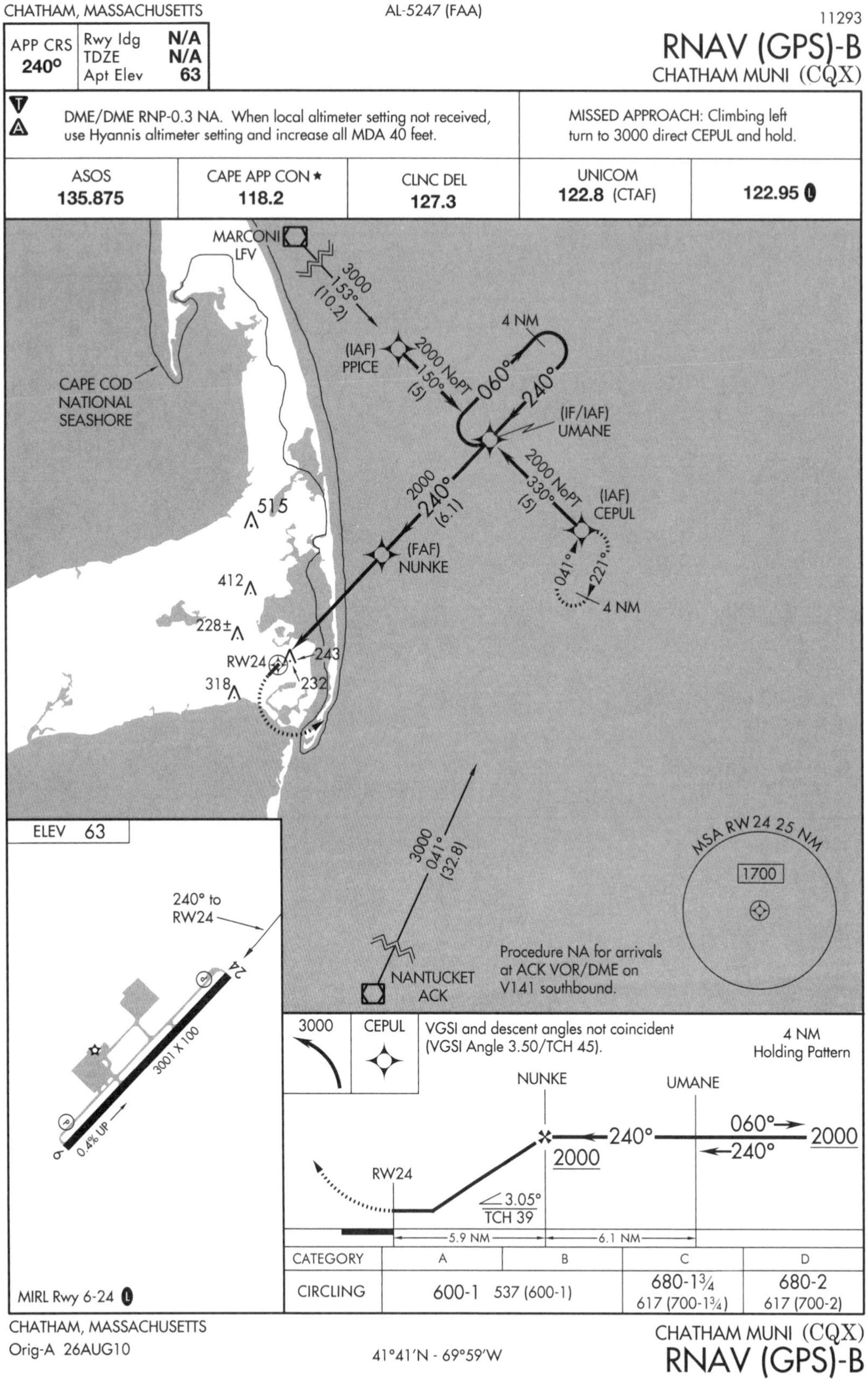

FIGURE 245.—RNAV (GPS)-B (CQX).

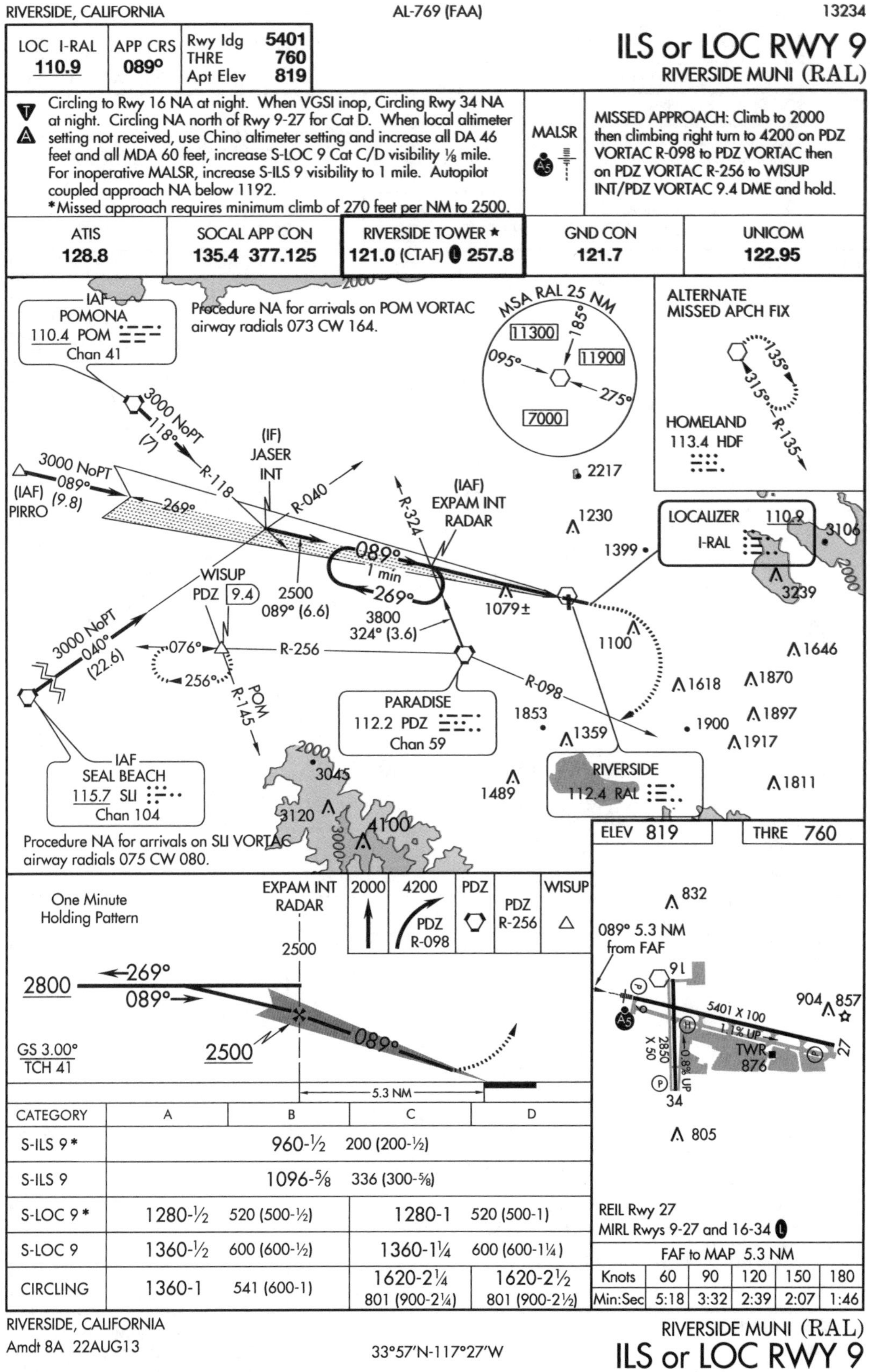

FIGURE 247.—ILS or RWY 9 (RAL).

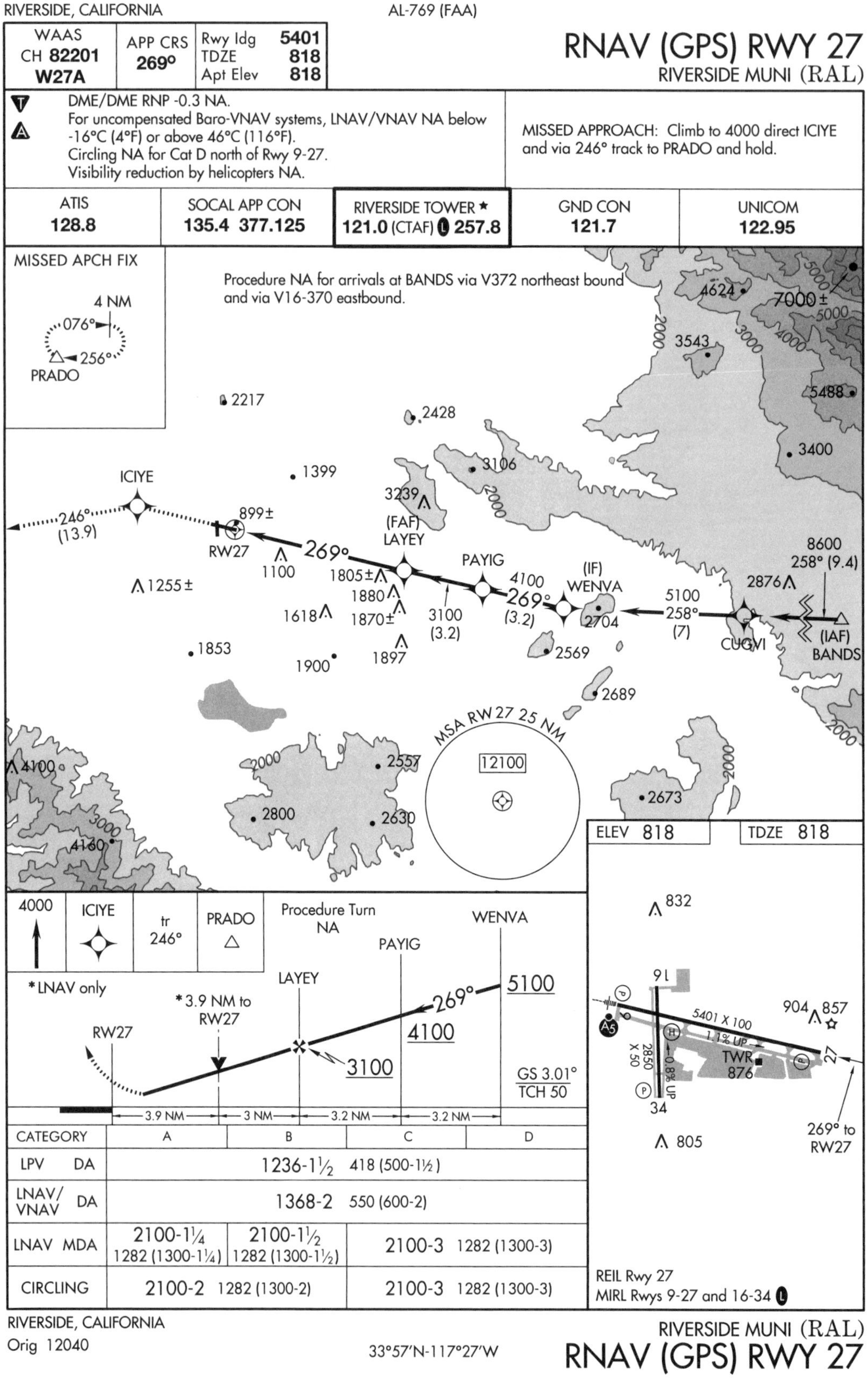

FIGURE 248.—RNAV (GPS) RWY 27 (RAL).

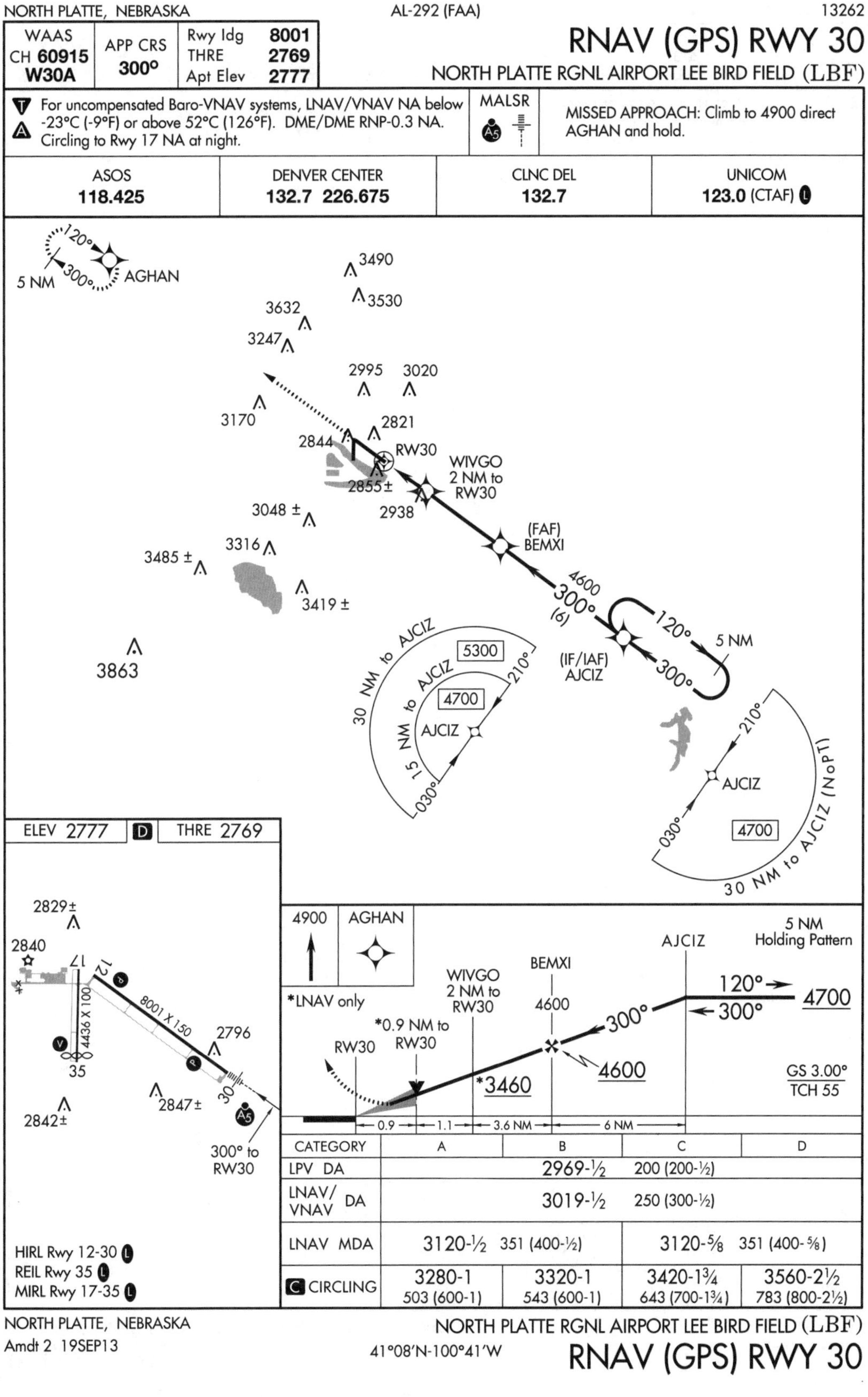

FIGURE 249.—RNAV (GPS) RWY 30 (LBF).

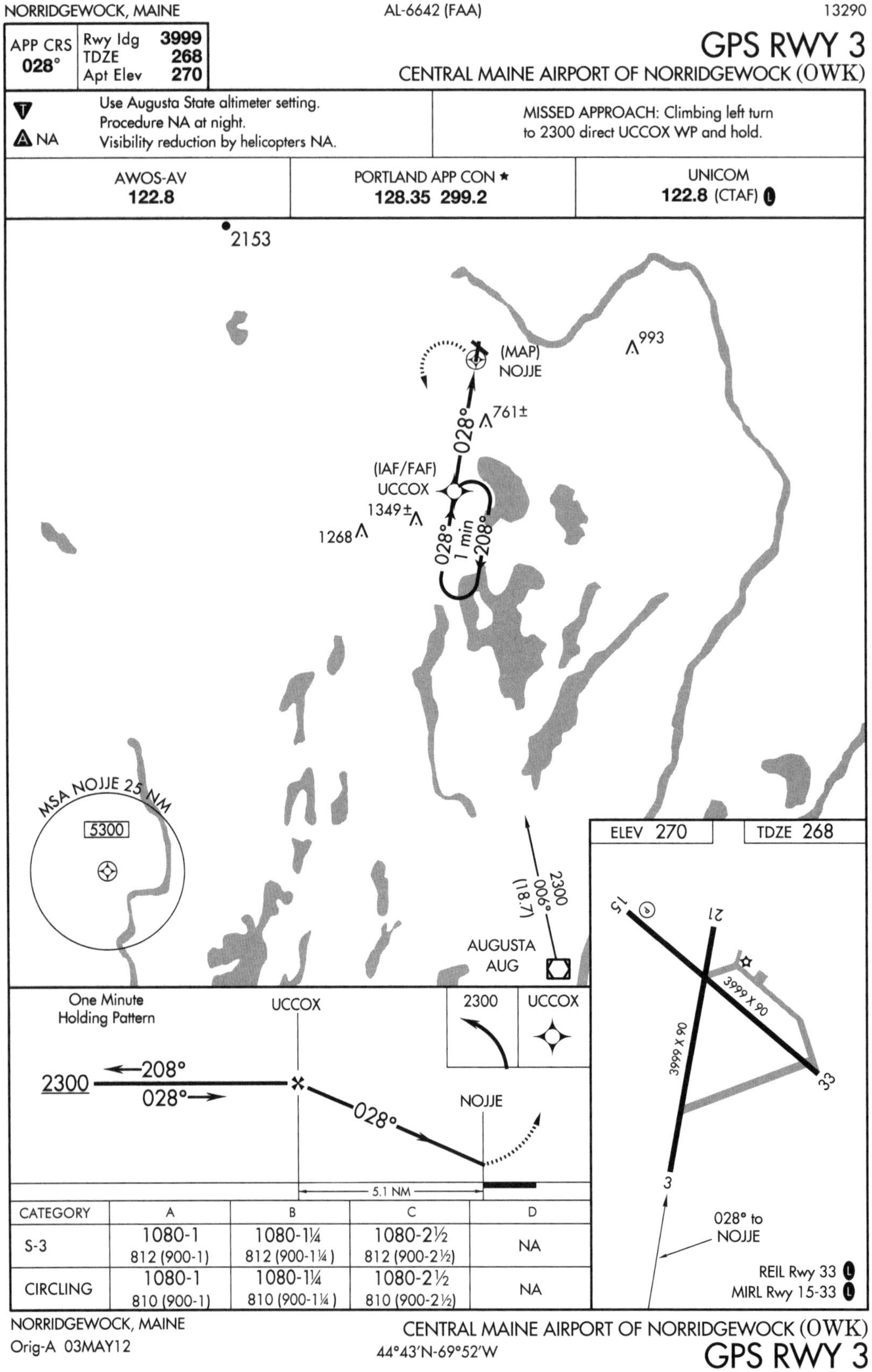

FIGURE 250.—GPS RWY 3 (OWK).

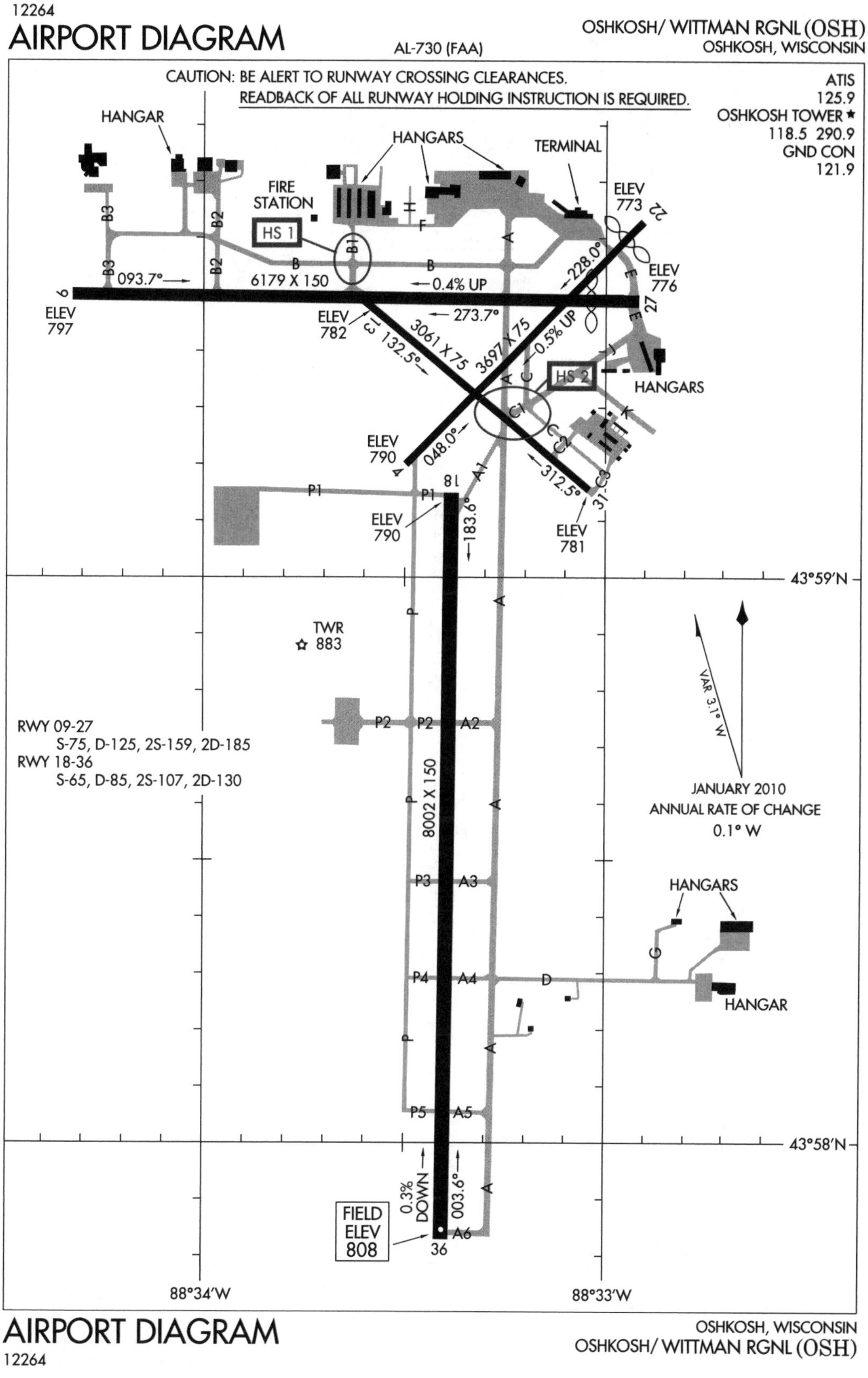

FIGURE 251.—Airport Diagram: Osh Kosh/Wittman Regional (OSH).

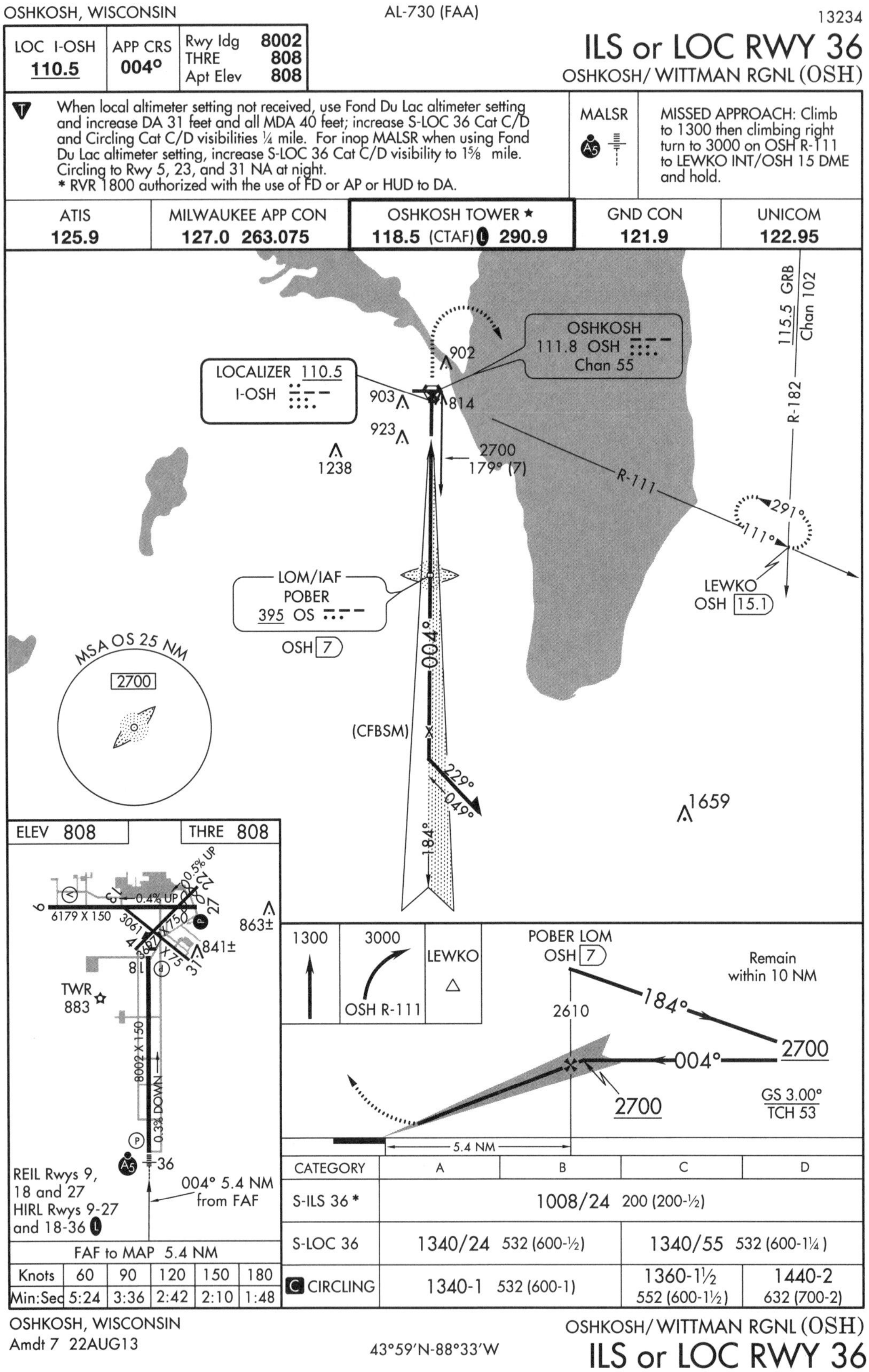

FIGURE 252.—ILS or LOC RWY 36 (OSH).

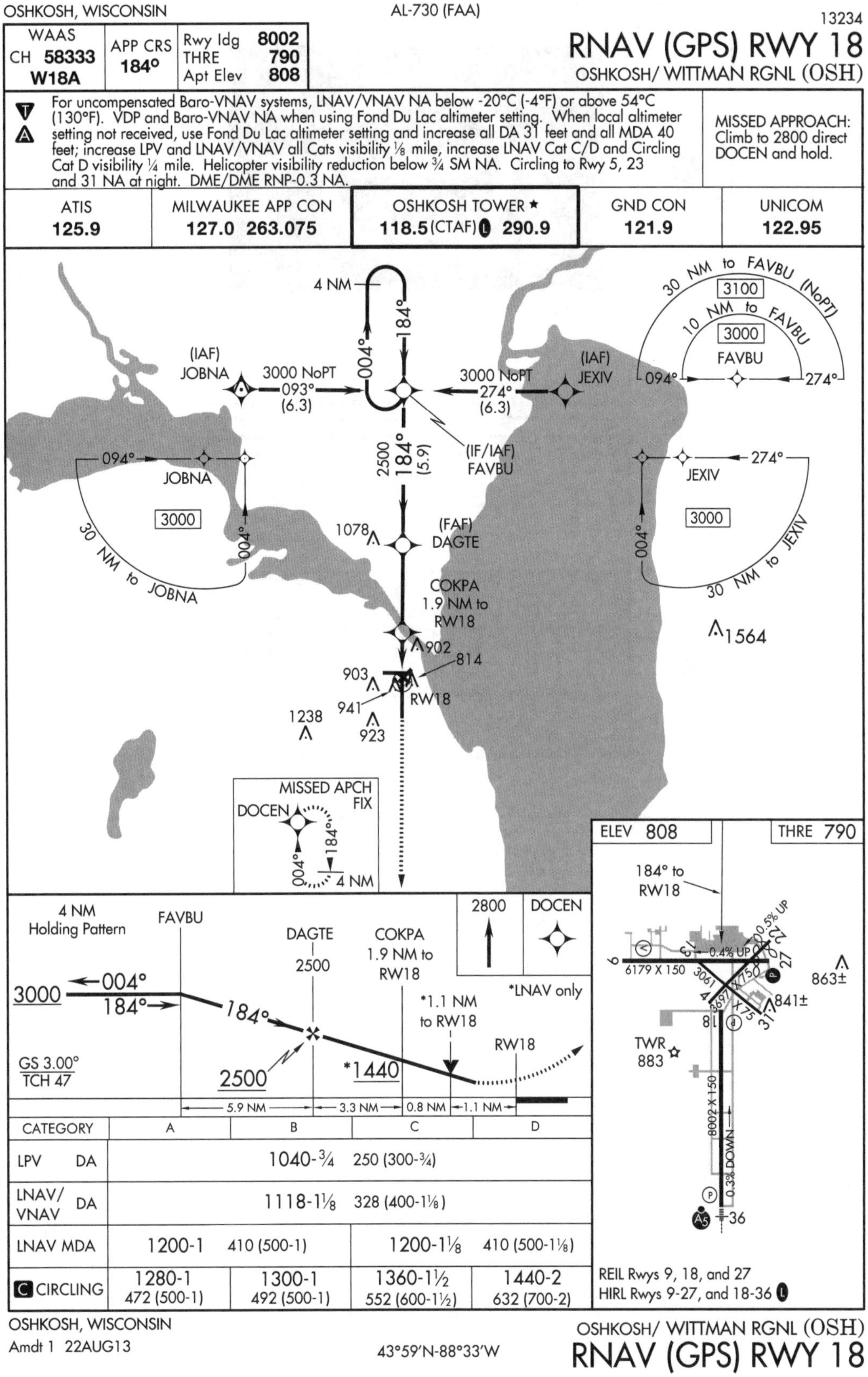

FIGURE 253.—RNAV (GPS) RWY 18 (OSH).

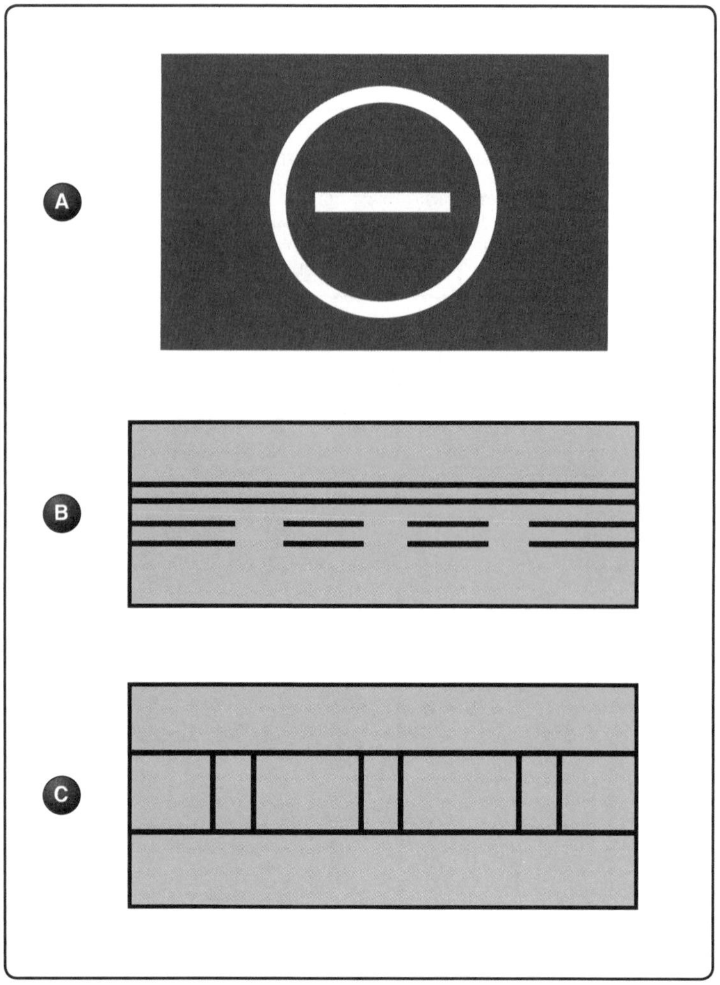

FIGURE 254.—Airport Sign.

FIGURE 255.—Two Signs.

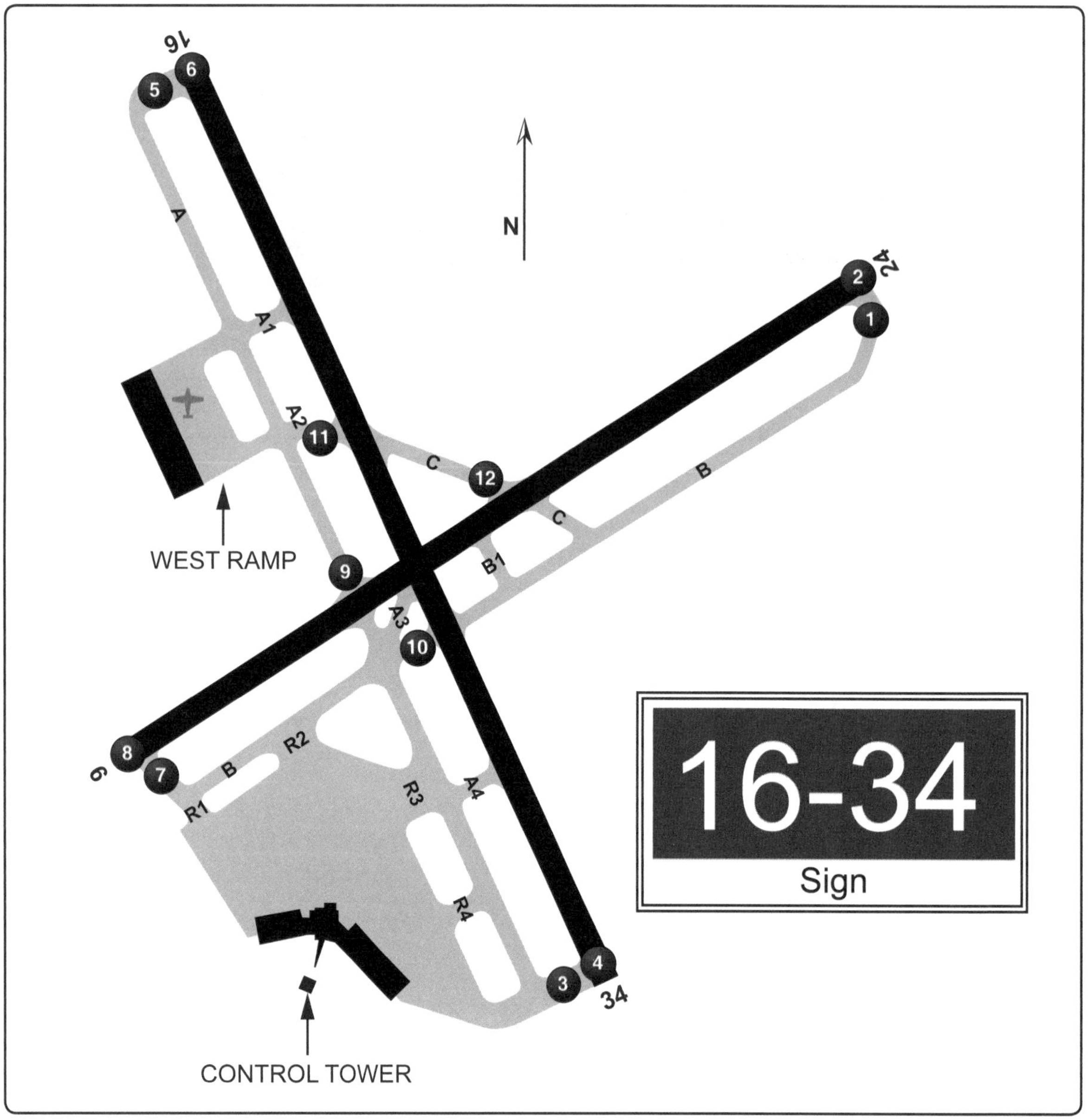

FIGURE 256.—Airport Diagram and Sign.

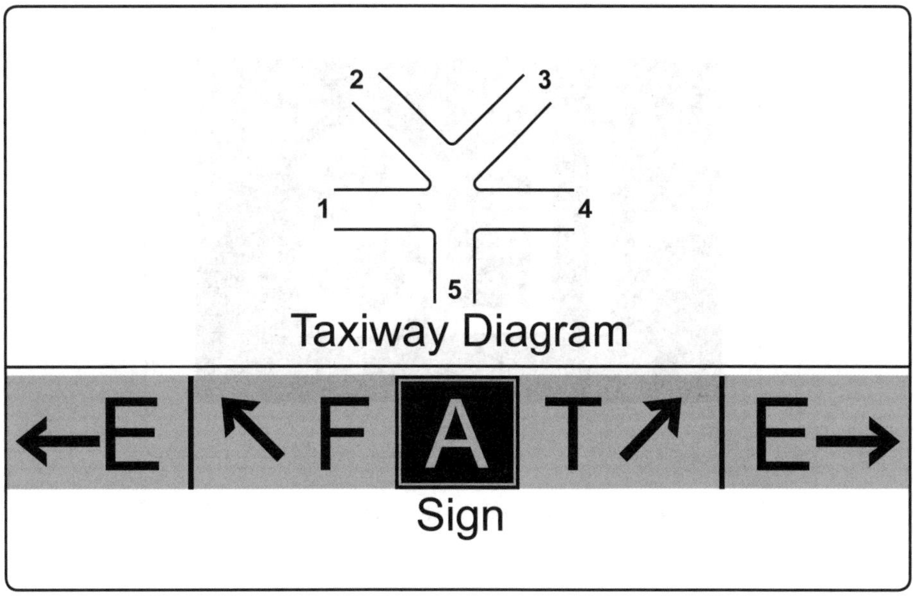

FIGURE 257.—Taxiway Diagram and Sign.

FIGURE 258.—Instrument Landing System (ILS) Critical Area Markings.

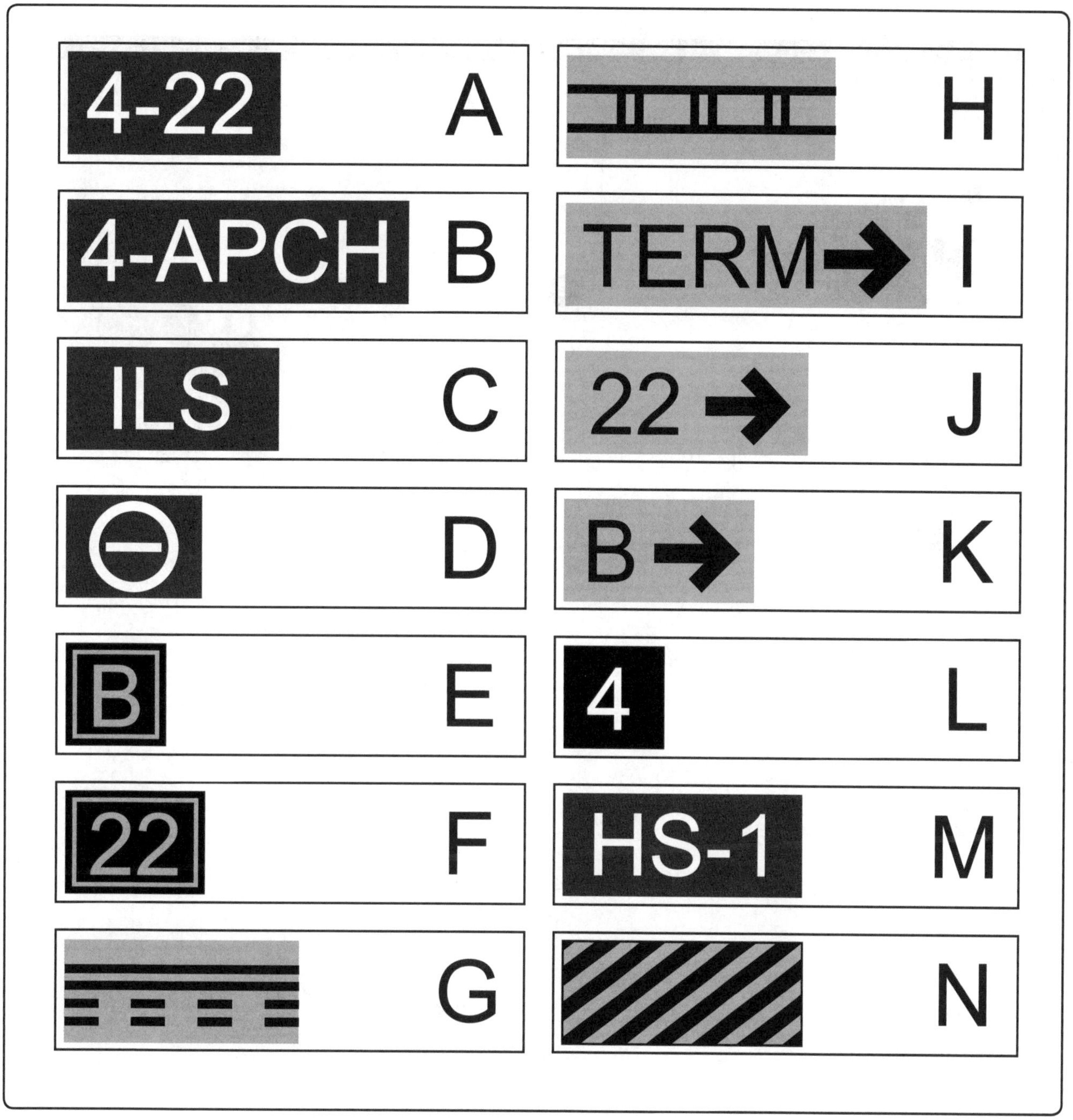

FIGURE 259.—Airport Signs.

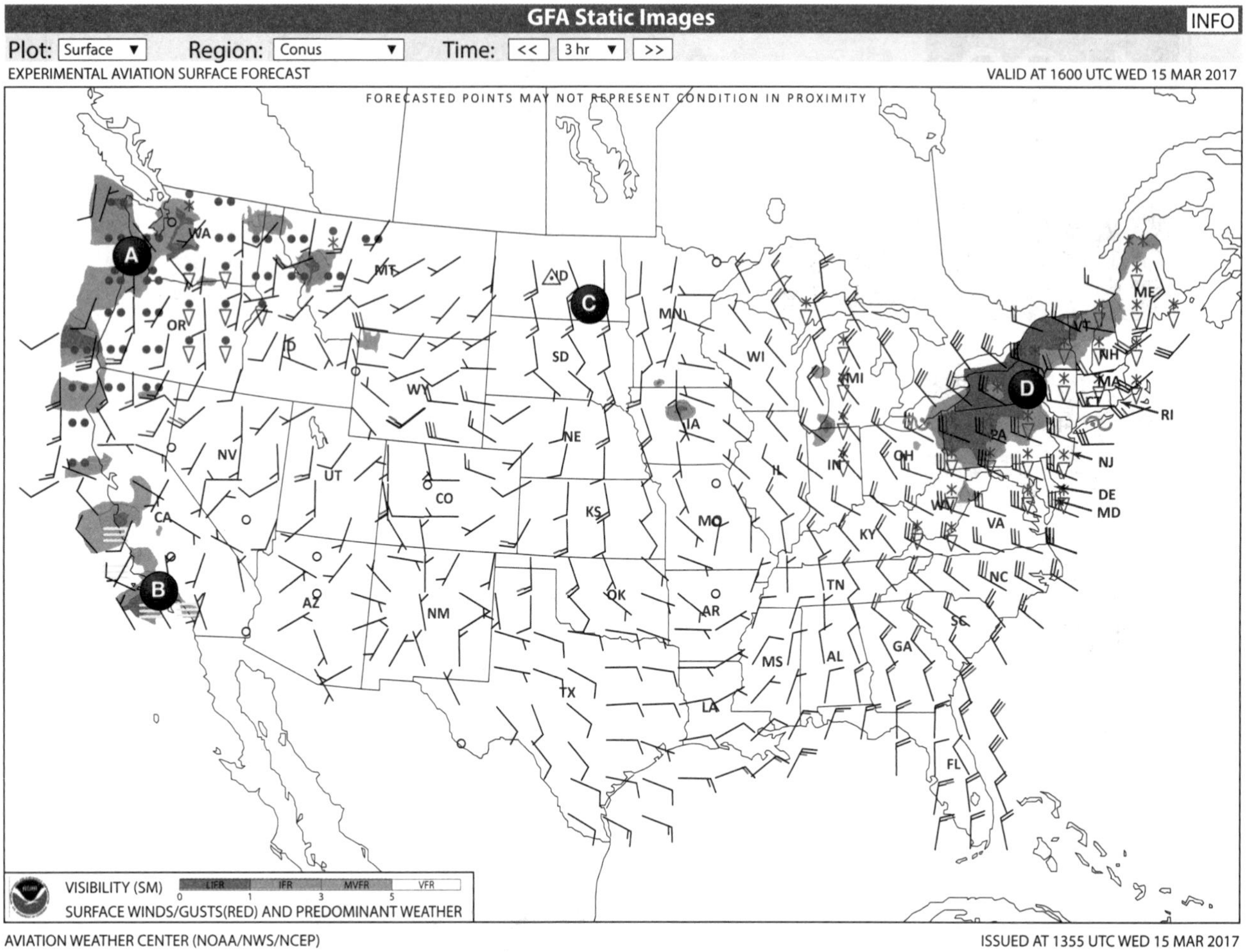

FIGURE 260.—Graphical Forecast for Aviation.

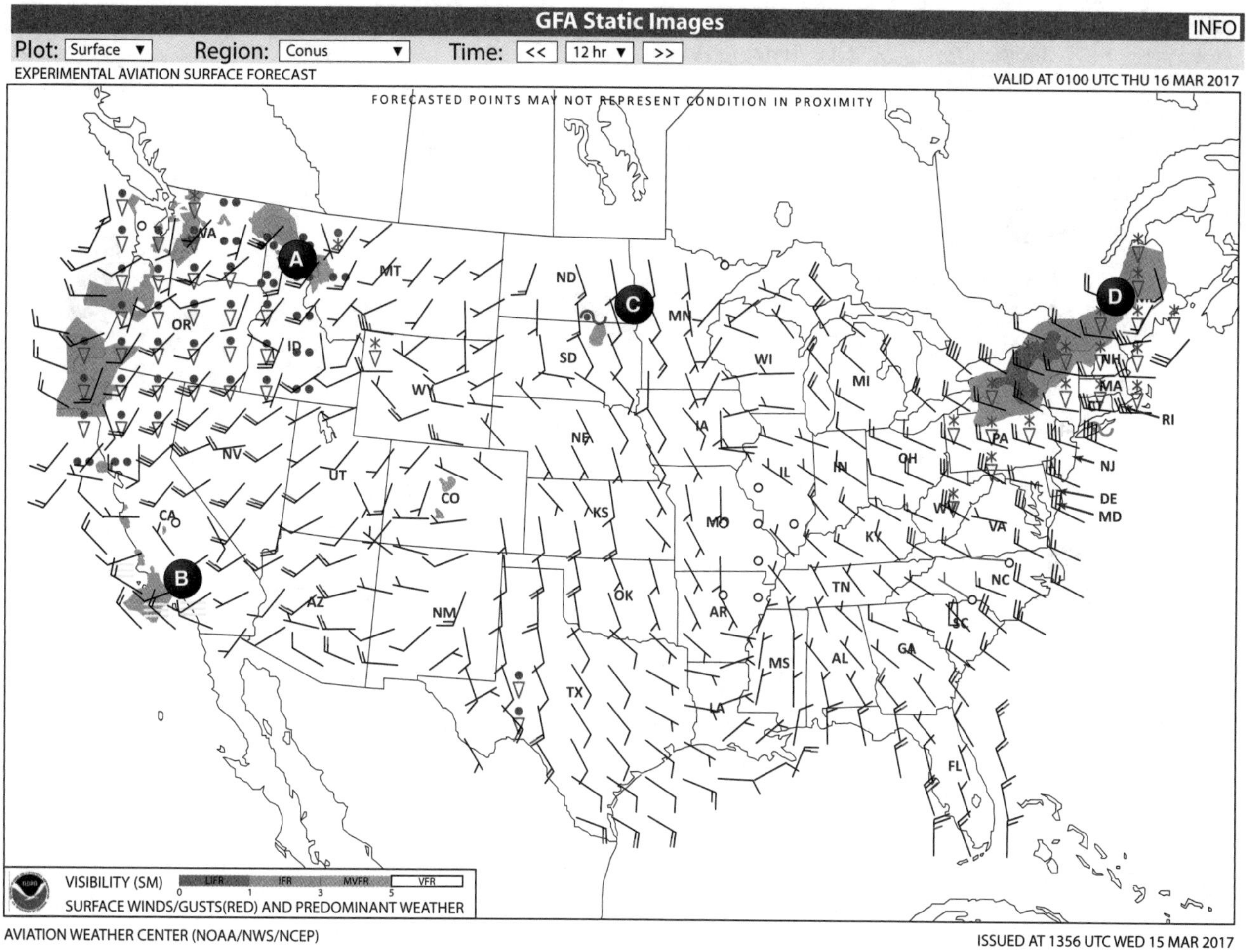

FIGURE 261.—Graphical Forecast for Aviation.

Appendix 2

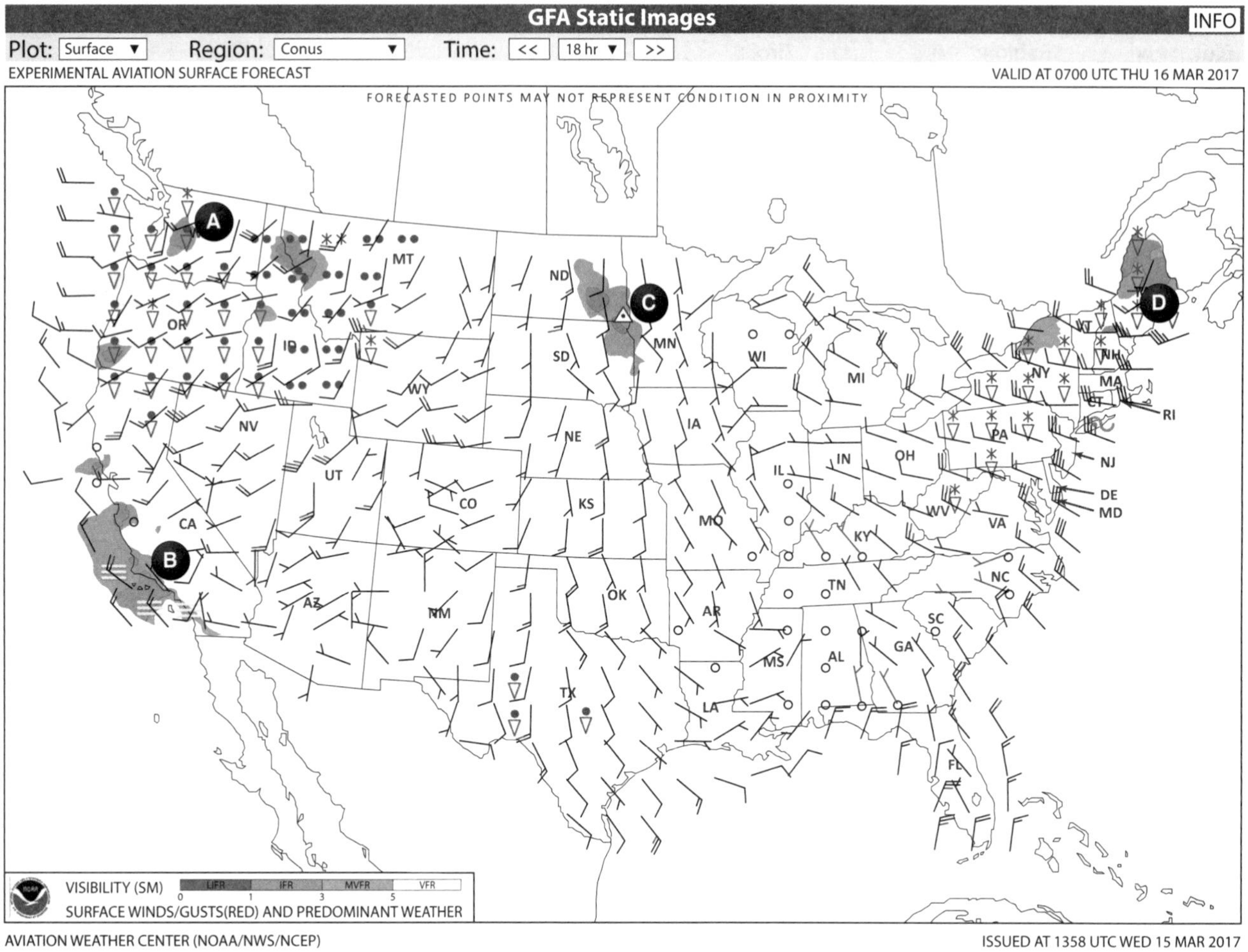

FIGURE 262.—Graphical Forecast for Aviation.

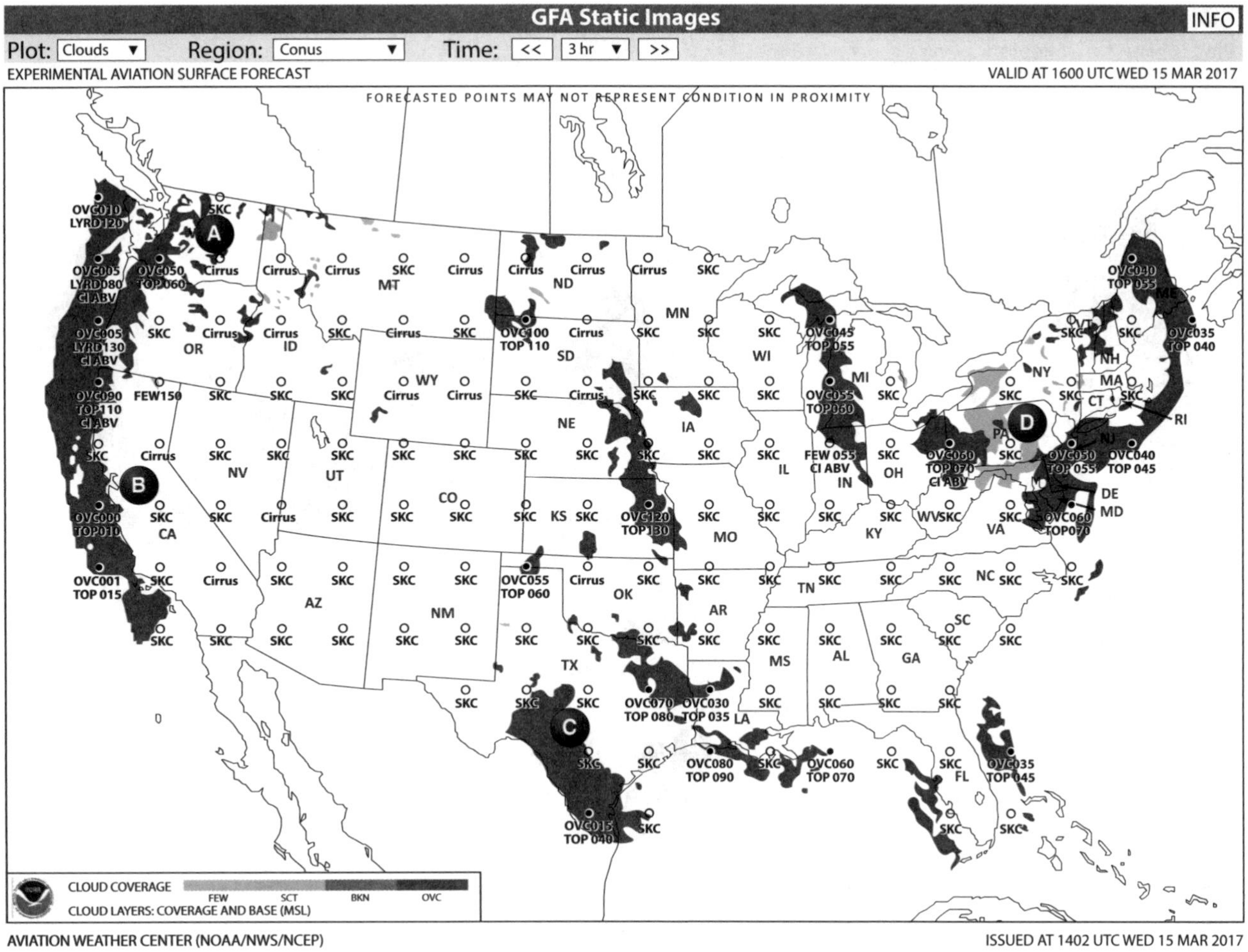

FIGURE 263.—Graphical Forecast for Aviation.

Appendix 2

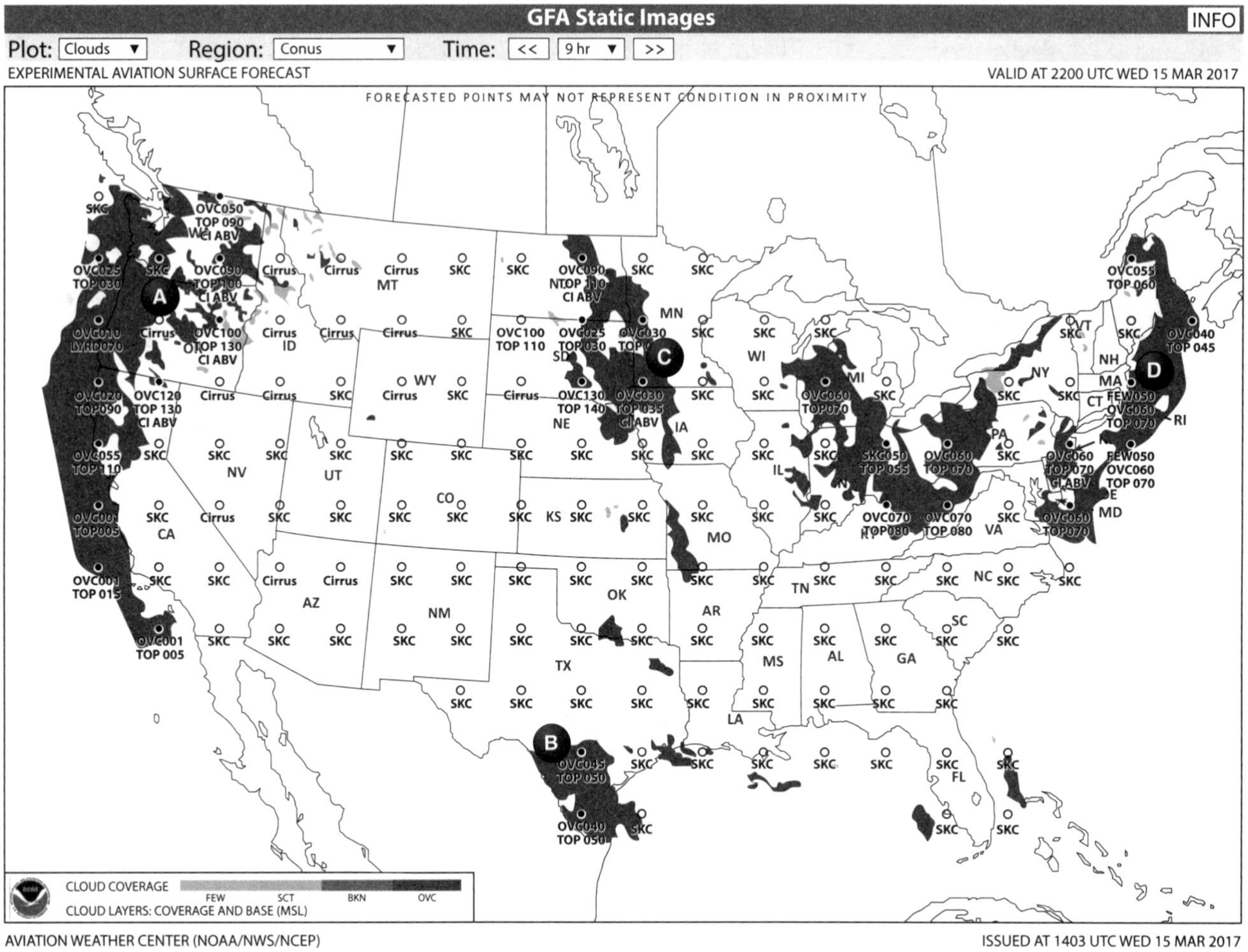

FIGURE 264.—Graphical Forecast for Aviation.

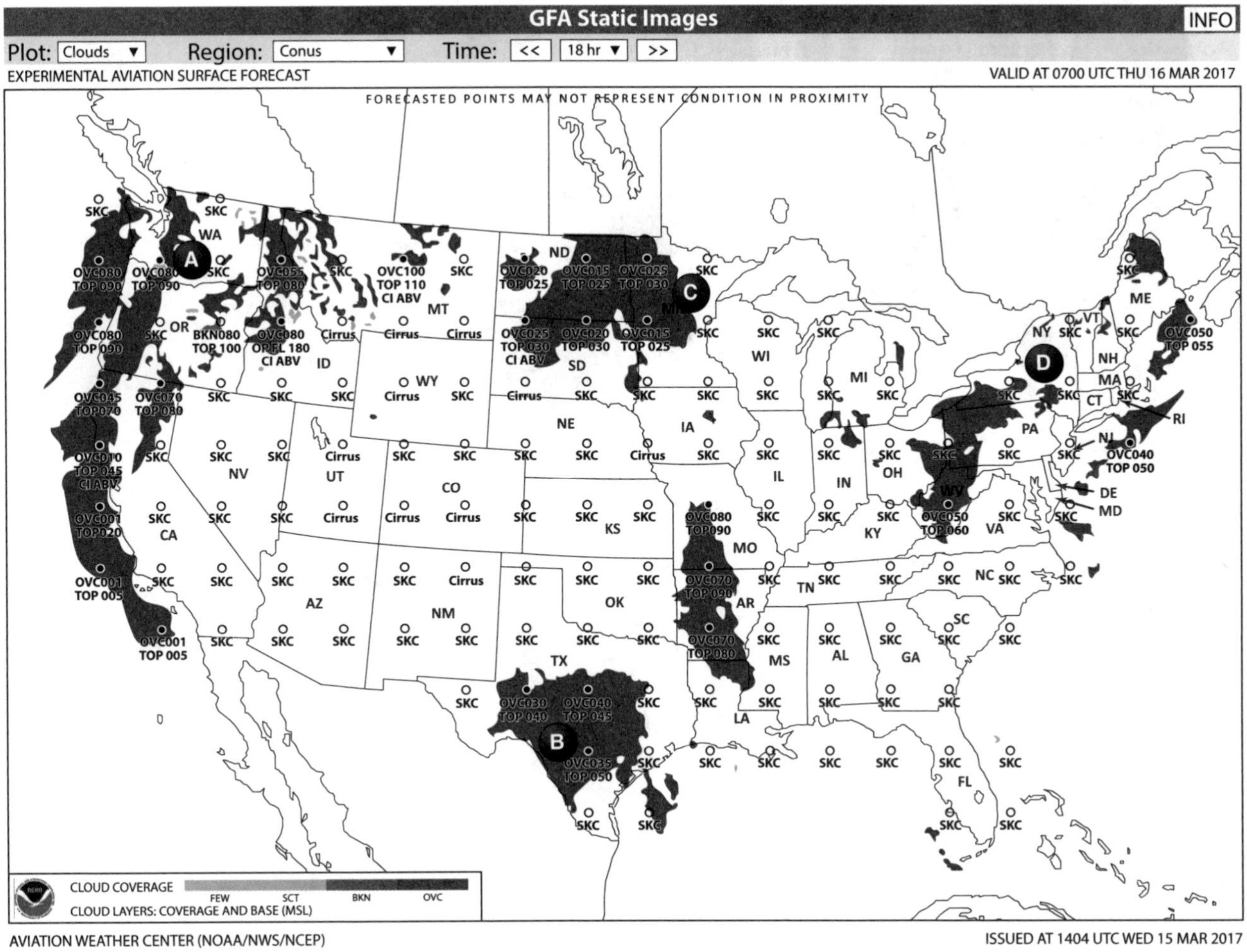

FIGURE 265.—Graphical Forecast for Aviation.

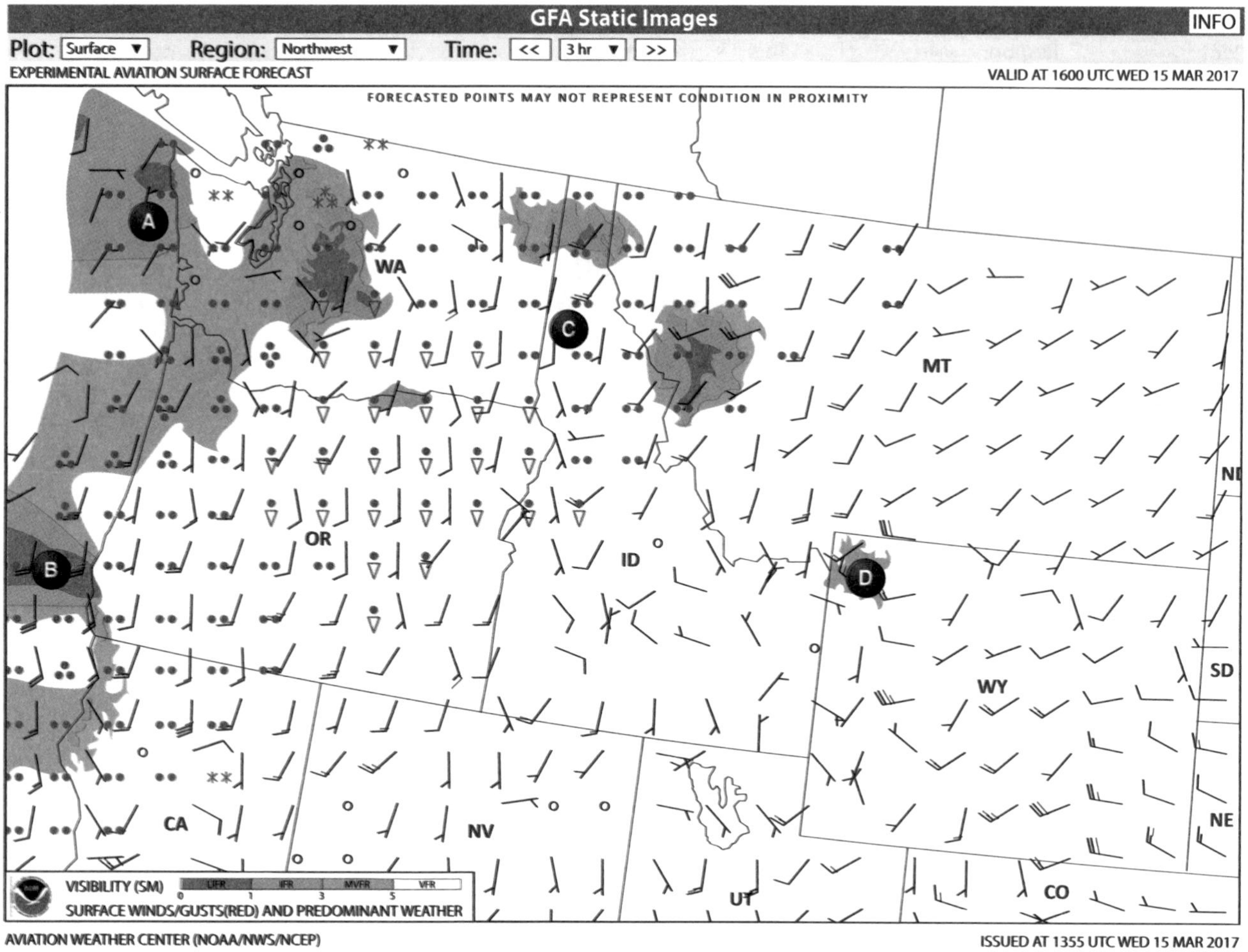

FIGURE 266.—Graphical Forecast for Aviation.

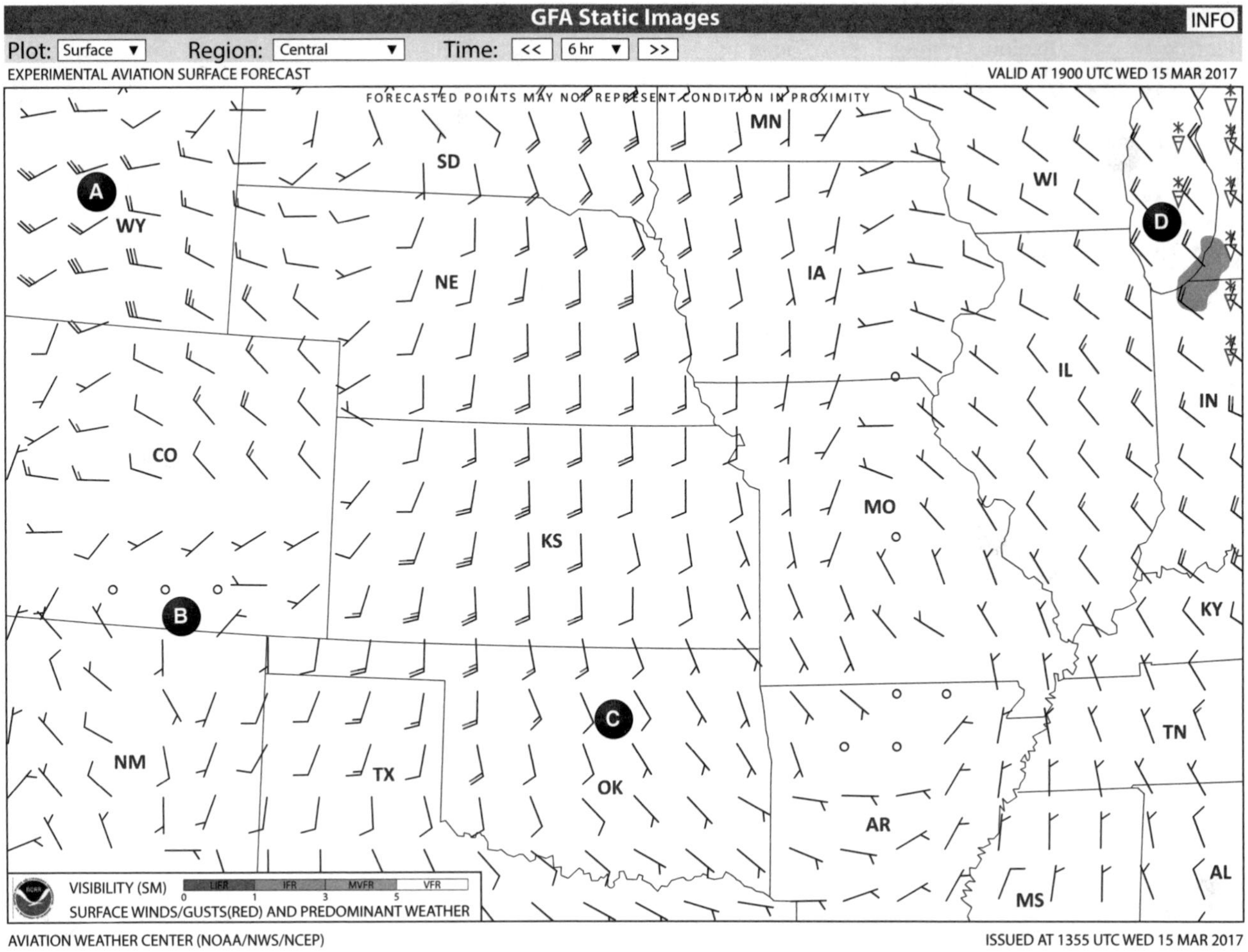

FIGURE 267.—Graphical Forecast for Aviation.

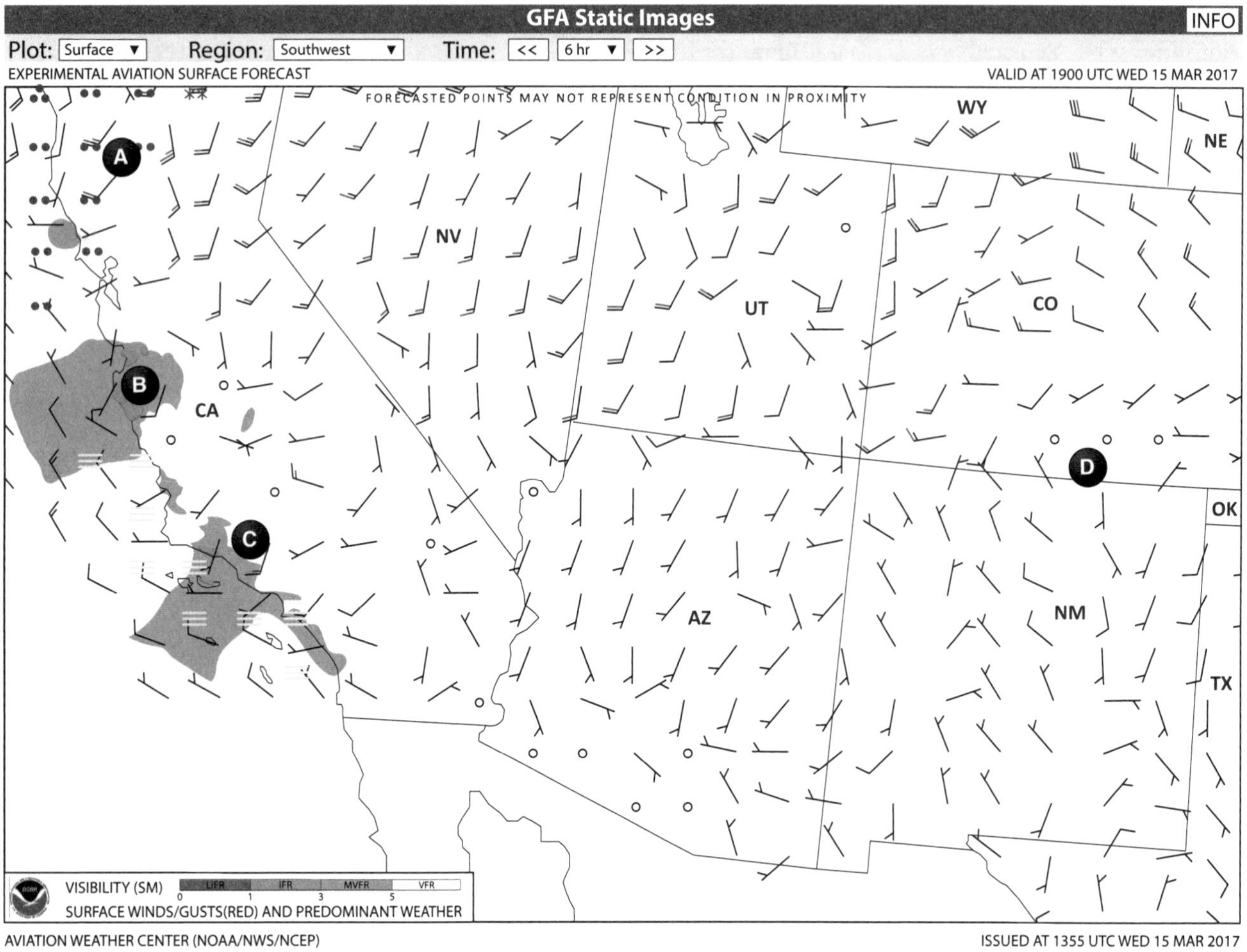

FIGURE 268.—Graphical Forecast for Aviation.

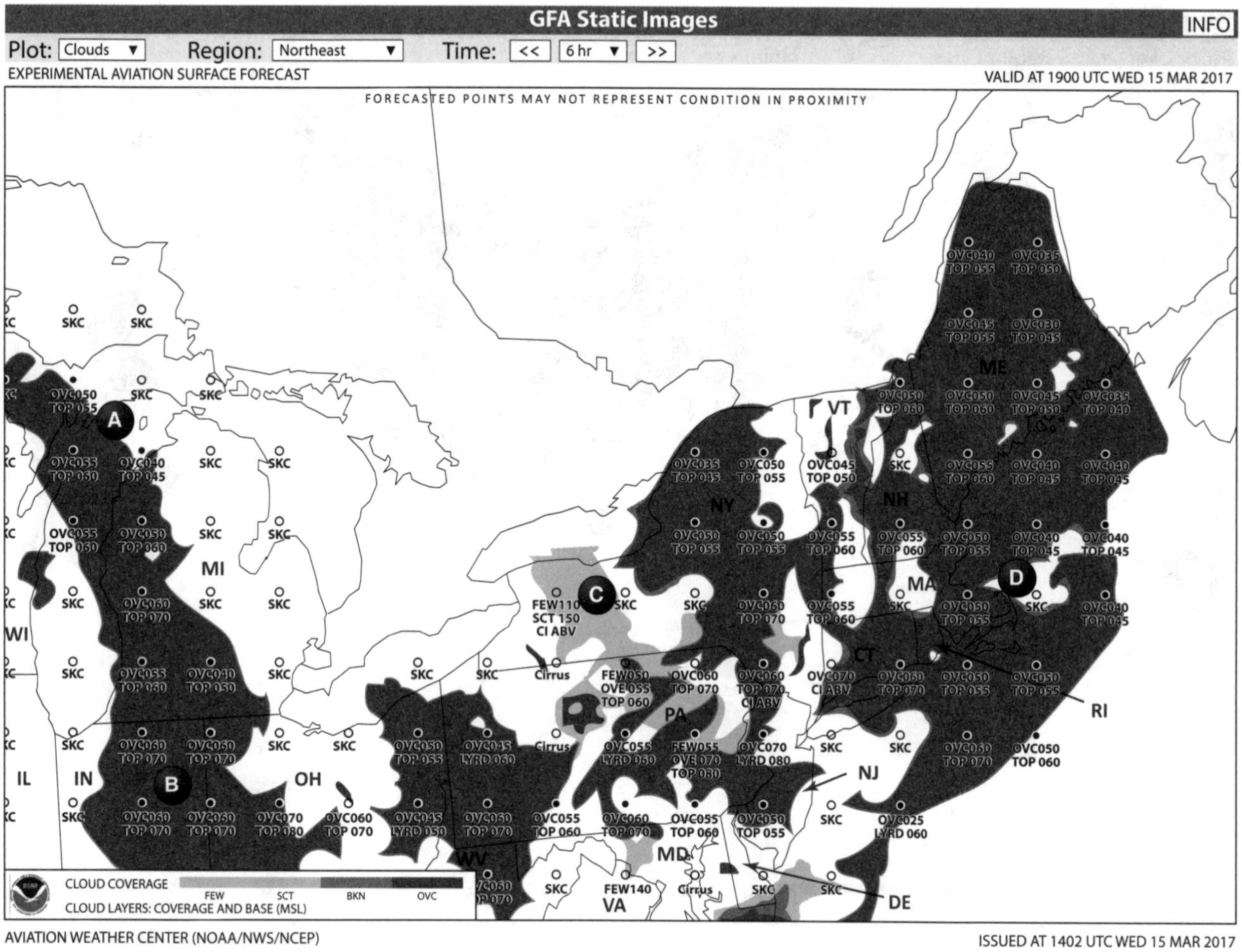

FIGURE 269.—Graphical Forecast for Aviation.

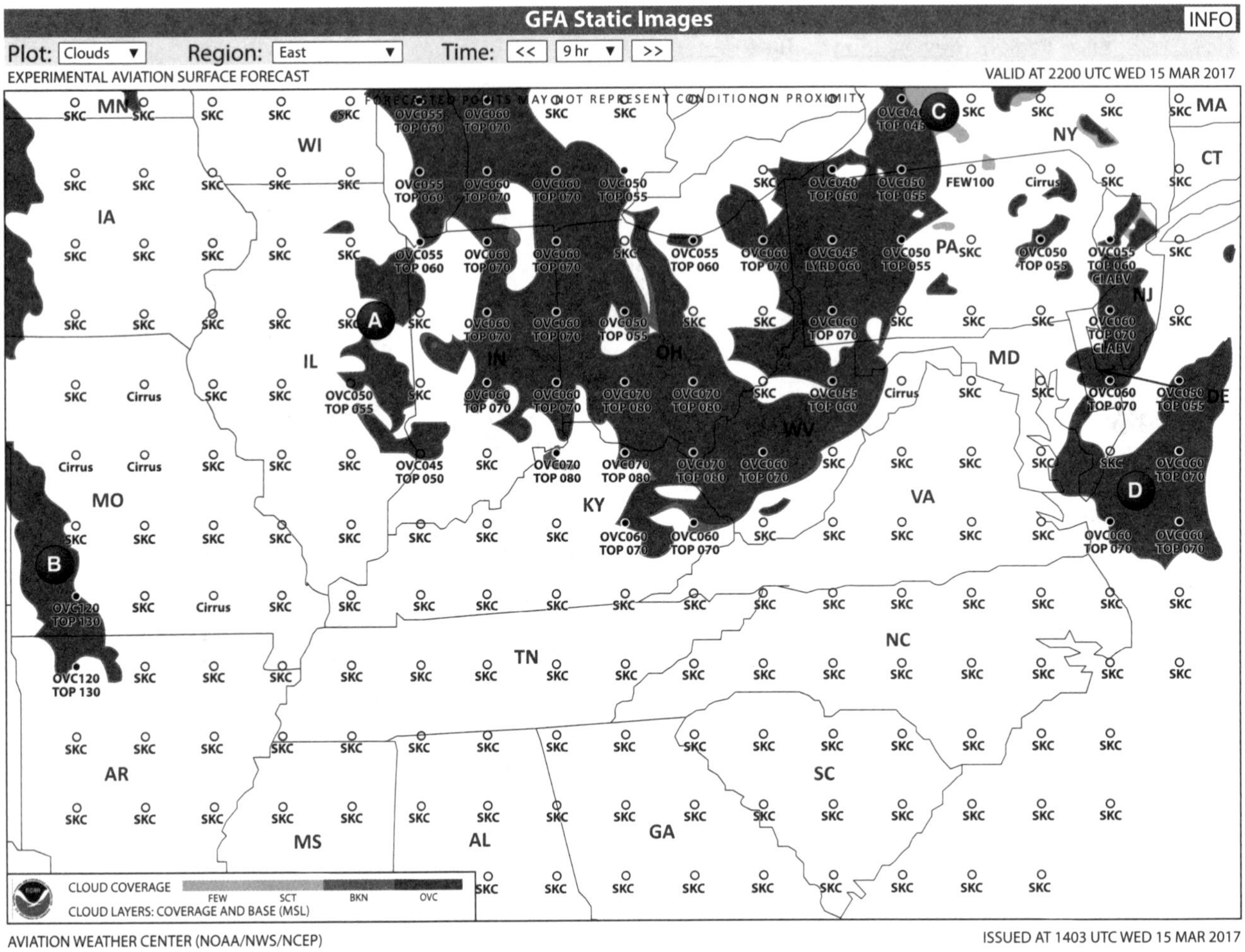

FIGURE 270.—Graphical Forecast for Aviation.

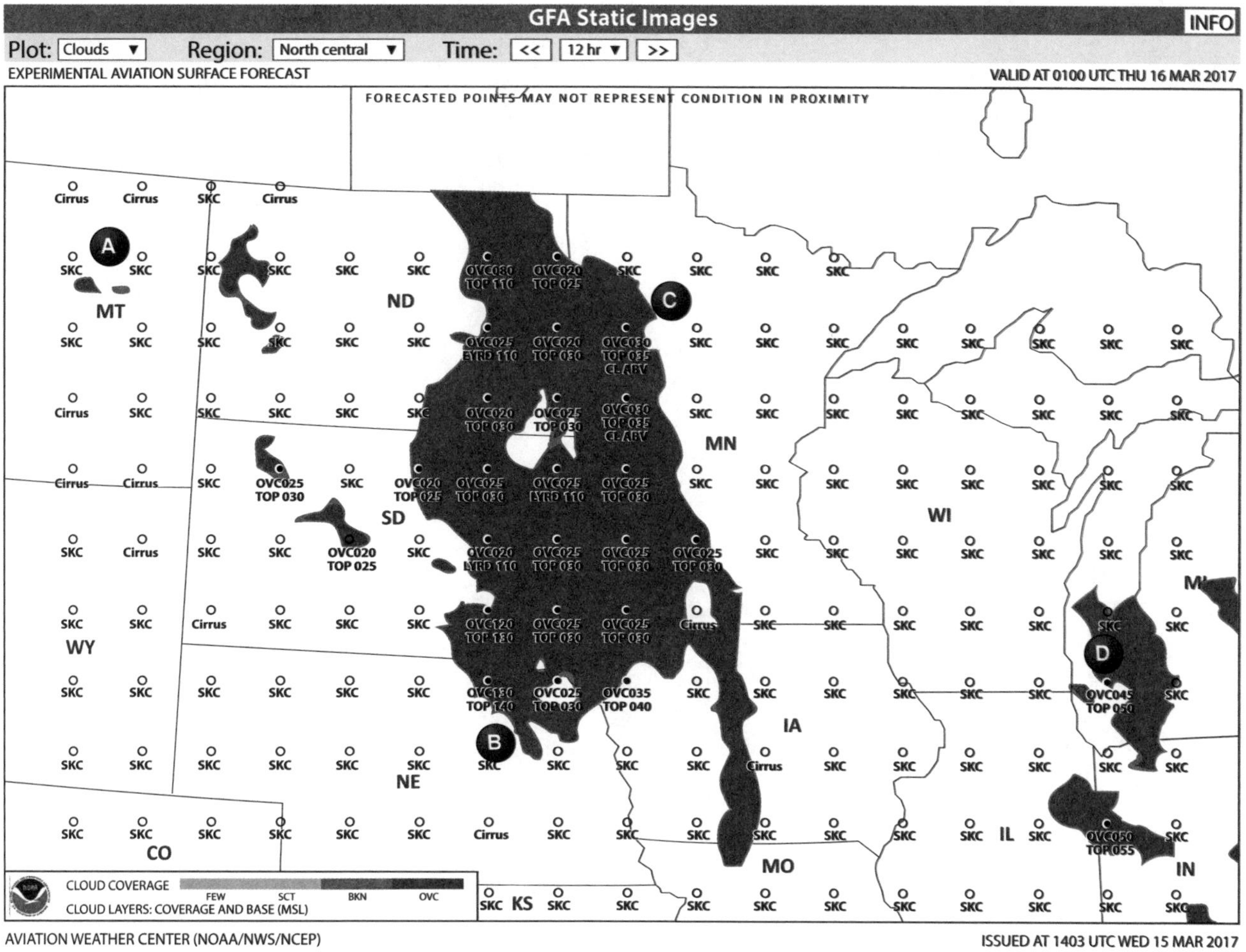

FIGURE 271.—Graphical Forecast for Aviation.